Sunday, Bloody 'Sunday

A Soldier's War in Northern Ireland, Rhodesia, Mozambique and Iraq'

The Story of Jake Harper Ronald
as told to Gregory Michael Budd

A SOLDIER'S WAR IN NORTHERN IRELAND, RHODESIA, MOZAMBIQUE AND IRAQ

THE STORY OF
JAKE HARPER-RONALD
AS TOLD TO
GREGORY MICHAEL BUDD

First published by Galago Publishing in July 2009 as

Sunday, Bloody Sunday:

A Soldier's War in Northern Ireland, Mozambique, Rhodesia and Iraq

By Gregory Michael Budd

Front cover pic: Jake Harper-Ronald operational in Mozambique wearing Rhodesian SAS beret, Chicom webbing, British DPM uniform and carrying an AKM rifle modified with a PKM stock.

I firmly believe that any man's finest hour,

his greatest fulfilment to all he holds dear,

is that moment when he's worked his heart out in a good cause

and lies exhausted on the field of battle – victorious.

Vincent Lombardi (1913-1970)

In loving memory of Richard

And

For Jake who won the war, but lost the final battle

And for those who were with him then.

TABLE OF CONTENTS

ACKNOWLEDGEMENTS

There are certain people I would like to thank without whom this book would not be possible. Firstly, I would like to thank Jake who gave me the opportunity to record his story. 'By the Light of the Moon' was a joint venture between author and subject that crossed the barrier of international boundaries. I must say it was a task completing the manuscript while we were worlds apart! Jake tirelessly assisted with the provision of information via email, phone and cell phone and with collections of photographs, video tapes, recordings and diaries despite the suffering he went through. Good one Jake and I am forever indebted to you! The world will know your plight.

I would also like to thank Maggie, Paul and Hugh who were encouraging throughout the course of putting the story on paper. There were many times I would have rather given up yet their encouragement, as well as Jakes, kept my nose the grindstone, hammering out the rough edges and providing succour in a sea of doubt.

There were many publications that assisted with some finer detail, another angle to the story or merely a date and time here and there. Amongst these were 'The Elite – the story of the Rhodesian SAS' by Barbara Cole, 'The Silent War' and 'Warfare by Other Means' by Peter Stiff and 'Selous Scouts Top Secret War' by Ron Reid Daly as told to Peter Stiff. On occasion the passage of time had eroded memory and it was by these books that minute technical detail and chronology of events became available.

Sue thanks for your meticulous copy checking and encouraging words despite the subject material not being your particular cup of tea.

Finally, to my own family I would like to extend my love and appreciation, for behind me I have what must be one of the most fortunate upbringings in the world, born as I was in that marvellous country that was Rhodesia.

AUTHOR'S NOTE

I would like to point out that certain chapters in this book may contain descriptions that some readers will find offensive. It must be understood that this book was written in the context of the time when the events described took place, therefore certain words have been used as they would have been used then and interchangeably. Particularly in the chapters about Rhodesia and Mozambique, the resistance movements are referred to as either the enemy, bandits, terrorists, terrs, rebels or guerrillas. These terms are not a reflection on any particular liberation movement or political party; they are merely descriptions, or terms, that were in common use at the time.

Furthermore, because of the confusion that existed in the then Mozambique, it could often not be determined to which particular faction an 'enemy' belonged. As will become apparent in the text, incidents occurred which remain a mystery to this day as the perpetrators were never found. In chapters 38 – 43, for the most part I have used the term 'rebel' when RENAMO was clearly involved. Otherwise, I have loosely used the terms 'bandits' and 'enemy' as in many cases those responsible for an incident could have been any one of the known Mozambique factions, or were possibly unattached to any of them.

Some factions are referred to by more than one name. For example, the MNR (Mozambique National Resistance) and RENAMO are two names for the same grouping; I have used these two names interchangeably to suit the text.

In addition, I have spelt certain Mozambique place names either phonetically, or as they appeared on hand-drawn maps. Chilembene, pronounced as it sounds - but spelt Xilembene - is a case in point.

I would also like to stress that this work is not an historical document. Some dates may not be entirely correct and some events may be slightly out of sequence. That the events took place there is no question. I have tried to be as accurate as possible in depicting the correct chronology; sometimes, however, even the diarised accounts appeared confusing.

Finally, in order to protect the identities of certain individuals, I have used pseudonyms in some cases.

PREFACE

As a military history enthusiast I enjoy studying the events of 20th century warfare, in particular the wars that came after World War II. My main interest, however, has been to focus on Special Forces/ Special Operations and the development of their raison d'être – a changing scenario in this day and age.

In conjunction with this, as a born Rhodesian of English descent and as an ex-serving member of the military, and other units – the events I have been most interested in, naturally, have occurred around those two countries. And so it was with monumental intrigue that I first met and then learned more about Jake Harper Ronald. His story most certainly deserves to be told.

I first ran into Jake in the mid-1990s as an associate of a friend who I occasionally assisted with checking written material, as well as technical information for a fledgling defence journal; a publication outlining current and past military events in Africa.

My introduction to Jake was the beginning of a fascinating view into the life of a man who had, I thought, a tale to tell that was far more compelling than those recounted in recently published military biographies.

I am honoured to be given the opportunity to tell Jake's tale. I hope I can convey it to you with the same humility, humour and pathos that he expressed so well over the years while I learnt his story, for it took much to convince him that it should be told.

For 35 years Jake was involved in military and para-military events, on three continents; from his early years as a young national serviceman in post-Federation Rhodesia, through the formative and brutal years on the ground with the 1st Battalion of the British Parachute Regiment (1 Para) in Northern Ireland.

Through the bush war in what was then Rhodesia, from the early seventies in units such as the Rhodesian Special Air Service (SAS), the Selous Scouts, Special Branch (SB) and the Central Intelligence Organisation (CIO), to the cessation of hostilities there, and then on to Mozambique where he trained and formed in its infancy a unit which was to be inaugurated into the Mozambique Special Forces, Jake faced his trials with the professionalism often associated with career soldiers, particularly those who have spent most of their time at the sharp end.

At one point in his life Jake was conducting work for four different intelligence agencies: the Zimbabwean CIO, the American CIA, the British MI6 and the South African National Intelligence Service (NIS)! Double agent? You will have to decide for yourself.

But apart from the adventure, the face-to-face combat, the intrigue, the loss and the heartache, his is also a story of hope. It is not merely a story intended for military enthusiasts and adventurers, or one for those soldiers who served then, there or now.

It was during the period that I worked with Jake that he was diagnosed with cancer, underwent major surgery along with radiation treatment and chemotherapy – and all this in the midst of family breakdown and trauma.

He had also lost his son Richard in a car accident. Richard was likewise a former member of Her Majesty's forces and a Gulf War veteran.

Despite all these unfortunate events, Jake went on to conduct security and close protection work in post-Saddam Iraq.

Many of the operations that Jake took part in were highly sensitive at the time and remain so today. It is neither Jake's nor my desire to make enemies as a result of what is written here. Neither of us set out with any intent to defame any person, institute, organization or government that may still exist today.

This story has been told as it actually happened and as close to the truth as memory allows, sometimes going back more than three decades, but often there were Jake's diarised accounts to support the narrative.

Of course, it would seem foolish to even begin writing this book if much of what is written remained unsubstantiated. I have therefore interviewed many of Jake's contemporaries. Some desired to remain anonymous and I have respected their wishes.

Sunday, Bloody Sunday – a Soldier's War in Northern Ireland, Rhodesia and Mozambique is not a political document, neither is it intended to glorify any person, regiment or country. It merely tells the tale of a man who found himself in the middle of the turmoil of some of the most important events in post-World War II history.

It does not set out to apologize for anything that happened. The men featured here were professional soldiers doing what professional soldiers do.

Some of the events that happened to Jake within only one or two weeks entail more thrilling adventure, more heartfelt sorrow and more shady intrigue than other entire texts have been written about.

In his story telling Jake often used the phrase 'By the Light of The Moon' when glossing over his experiences. The phrase itself was loosely coined among SAS soldiers for that period of the full moon when night operations would meet their peak, ambushes would be laid and people would die.

More appropriately, I think the phrase would make a fitting epitaph for his life – for by the light of the moon… and the sun, Jake lived.

This is his story.

PROLOGUE

Harare, Zimbabwe, October 2003

If you have been there you will know how true it is. The heat in Harare at this time of the year is sweltering and unrelenting, made tolerable only when the rains set in around mid-November. By then, if the precipitous banks of cumulus clouds from the international tropical convergence zone have not burst their seams, it is said that the country will be in for a drought.

Until then, for the month before, humidity hangs like a wet blanket cast across a grey sky. To those who live there, October is known as 'suicide month' and this morning matched the description admirably.

It was 9 am on a Tuesday and as we usually did, Jake Harper Ronald and I sat at a coffee table amid the cacophony of dying morning trade as those who had jobs drained their cups, paid their bills and hurried off to their places of work.

Our daily meetings at Trax Coffee Shop in Newlands, Harare, had become something of a habit for Jake and me. Neither of us held regular jobs as we were self-employed. As a result, the mornings were our own and most of the hours between 7 a.m. and 9 a.m. were spent at this popular spot.

On most mornings we would be joined by a host of other friends and acquaintances, some regularly, others less frequently, but Jake and I were always there and as is always with mates, we were there to catch up on news, enjoy the view of the passing ladies and generally chew the cud.

This morning was a little more sobering than usual. After weeks of testing, Jake had just been diagnosed with cancer. As usual, he gave this news to me as though it was the dullest titbit of information. There was never any drama in his manner, whether he talked about taking a Sunday stroll or, as on this occasion, when he just been given the news that 'his ticket was punched'. Jake always faced everything in a professional manner without a feeling of self-pity or self-importance. I felt for him as I admired him.

Over countless hundreds of coffees, over several years, one subject that regularly came up were the stories of Jake's and my experience in the military or para-military units. I must say I always felt a little sheepish in the company of men like Jake, not for fear of them, but for their wealth of experience which made mine pale into insignificance.

With the information I had just so casually received from him, I felt compelled to record his story because – as life often shows – if we put off for tomorrow what can be done today, the right time will never come.

My concern lay not only in the fact that Jake's story would not be remembered, but I was also reflecting on how many other great, tragic or sad tales must have had been told over coffee tables, remembered last as their dying whispers faded into those of others.

The silence that hung over the table this morning, almost palatable, was disturbed by the buzz of Jake's cellphone. I don't normally engage in eavesdropping, but the overriding tone in which Jake spoke made this call seem important – at least, to me that is. As he soon told me it was 'old hat'. After a pause, Jake explained.

A representative of the British High Commission had on this and several other occasions requested an audience with him so as to discuss events that occurred more than 30 years before on Sunday, 30 January 1972.

That day, to some, would live in infamy as 'Bloody Sunday'.

The representative, at the behest of the British government, requested Jake's attendance in the United Kingdom to stand as a witness at a hearing for events that unfolded on that day so long ago, a hearing that had not been finalised at the time of writing.

Why did they want Jake there?

On that day, in Londonderry, Northern Ireland, Jake Harper Ronald served on the ground with 1 Para. Besides carrying a weapon, he also carried a 35mm camera, as he was the official 1 Para Intelligence Section photographer.

Many of the images that exist of that fateful day are there because Jake took them.

In the event, the High Commission was provided with a medical certificate, from his physician, stating he was too ill to travel.

Jake looked at me, his eyes turned inward. He was experienced and wise. I was younger and wanted to understand.

The only real journey of discovery is not in seeking new landscapes it's in having new eyes

Marcel Proust (1871-1922)

CHAPTER 1:
THE FORMATIVE YEARS

I suppose you could say I came into this world in much the same way as I plan to leave it -- kicking and screaming. It's just not in me to go down without a fight. And aside from the doctor giving me a fair whack to jump-start my internals, I'm told that he also hit my mother -- in disgust of me being so ugly.

On the 9 April 1948 I blessed my parents with my company, after a tumultuous birth which my mother endured for many painful hours. I was not a large baby as far as things go, but I always remember being told, in my early days, that I was quite a package to handle, whether I was clawing my way out of the womb or raging against society in a bid to find my place. My mom, I think, must have been a tremendous woman and one graced with infinite patience.

I was born in Potchefstroom, South Africa, as Earl Harper Ronald, the youngest of three sons evenly spaced at four-year intervals. My brothers, David and Ian, saw their first light of day in 1940 and 1944 respectively; and when I came along, there was finally someone to bully.

My father, George David, was born in Durban in 1916 to my grandparents who had emigrated from Scotland in the early 1900s. Before World War I my grandfather ran a photography shop on King Street in Durban, but when the war broke out he volunteered for service in the South Africa Scottish Regiment. He went to Europe, where he was killed in action shortly after arriving.

I never did hear anything of my grandmother, who remains a mystery to me, but my Dad was adopted by a kindly gentleman going by the surname Ronald. My father kept the name Harper and tagged them together as Harper Ronald.

At the age of 14, in 1928, my father flew the coop and enlisted in the Grenadier Guards as a drummer boy. In 1940 he married my mother, Mabel, in a union that was to last a lifetime.

During World War II, while my mother endured the blitz in London with my older brother David, my father was retraining after taking part in the Dunkirk evacuation with the British Expeditionary Force. He was later posted to the Guards Armoured Division, as a tank instructor for the D-Day landings. After the war he returned to South Africa to enlist in the Tank Corp; but sometime later was sent back to Bovington in the UK, for a course to learn about the new Centurion Tank which had been adopted by the South African Army as its main battle tank. He became the first instructor based at the Bloemfontein tank school to train South African crews.

In the early 1950s my father joined the new Rhodesian Army. He was sent to Llewellyn Barracks in Bulawayo where he became an instructor on the Stag Hound armoured car. Shortly thereafter he was transferred to the Rhodesian Staff Corps and permanently based at Llewellyn, with Bulawayo becoming our home. These were my stomping grounds as a young lad and in hindsight I feel I had little, or no other choice of a career, as the military way of life coursed firmly through my veins. I always dreamed of adventure and couldn't wait for the day I would join the army.

There is no doubt that my father was a military man through and through. Later, well into my own career, he was transferred to Cranborne barracks in Salisbury to help in the Service Corps' Quartermaster stores. He never held a commissioned rank and preferred the anonymity of being a non-commissioned officer.

After his regular stint in the Rhodesian Army, he was offered a job in the Special Air Service (SAS) QM stores as a civilian attached. This duty he carried out with a high degree of professionalism and with the enthusiasm born of his passion for the military.

When the bush war was over, he moved back to Durban and was offered the same position at the Bluff, as a civilian attached to the quartermaster stores for 1 Reconnaissance Regiment, South African Special Forces. Unfortunately, he never made the post and after 53 years in the military, he succumbed to cancer of the throat. His battle was finally lost – but a great man was my dad!

When I was in my early teens my eldest brother David did national service. David, although we got on, was a different sort of animal to Ian and me. He somehow managed to reach adulthood uninfluenced by our army upbringing. He carried out his duty with aplomb, but slipped back into civilian life with great appreciation, preferring the normality of civvy street to the military. It was the 1960s and what was to become the Rhodesian bush war was then only the ranting of African nationalism, interspersed with civil strife and a few petrol bombings.

In 1961 Ian served in the newly formed Rhodesian Light Infantry (RLI) at Brady Barracks in Bulawayo, where it was originally based. He was only 17 when he volunteered. The RLI in those days was far from what it became later and had many undesirable characters in its ranks. When it was first put together as a regular all-white infantry battalion, adverts were posted in the South African newspapers to recruit prospective soldiers – unfortunately many of those who applied were the down-and-out types. Compounding this, it was no secret that young men facing legal imprisonment in Rhodesia were often given two choices – go to jail or join the RLI. Not all, but many of those who served with the RLI, were the pus of society; they were often unemployed or were trying to avoid the long arm of the law. As a result, there were numerous run-ins with the police, as fights ensued publicly between civilians and soldiers – usually over women – which tarnished the RLI's image.

Unfortunately for Ian, he became entwined in a few illegal dealings, which did little to enhance his reputation, or for that matter, that of the RLI. I was told later that he was quite a good soldier until he got involved with some South Africans in the unit. After that he was always in trouble, AWOL or in detention barracks.

After about a year, the RLI moved to Cranborne Barracks in Salisbury. Ian went with his unit and was deployed to the Congo border of Northern Rhodesia to help quell the troubles there. Returning to Salisbury after active service, he again clashed with the law for crimes ranging from grand theft auto and assault, to grievous bodily harm. He was the proverbial rebel without a cause. The RLI couldn't get a handle on Ian's behavior, so they discharged him and he was sent to a reformatory school in the Matopos Hills for a year.

At 21, in 1965, on the promise of adventure and riches, Ian joined the ranks of Mike Hoare's mercenaries in the Congo. I was 16 'going on 20' at the time and was keen on following in his footsteps; but my Dad refused to sign the forms that would have released me as a minor. Although I was unimpressed, with little understanding of his reasons at the time, in retrospect I think I was utterly mad and that my father did the best thing for me.

Ian returned home sometime later, with stories of battle and high adventure, as well as 'high' adventure of the cannabis kind. Although he was still in one piece, his future was uncertain. Ian's tales only served to increase my fervour for all things military, but I was a good lad and promised to finish school before throwing myself into an army career. Suffice; I was army-barmy to say the least bought up as I was as a military brat.

Rhodesia was then in her heyday and it must have been one of the best places in the world to have grown up. Like most teenagers I didn't really appreciate this particular Eden with its vast landscapes, beautiful vistas and bountiful wildlife.

For the most part I endured my schooling at Milton School in Bulawayo, as a junior and at Guinea Fowl School, 16 kilometers south of Gwelo, where I was a senior boarding pupil from January 1961 to the end of 1965. It was there that I obtained the nickname Jake, bestowed upon me by a mate called Chris Viljoen. It stuck with me pretty much for the rest of my life. Despite my family's military lineage and having grown up in a city environment, it was at Guinea Fowl that I got to know and love the bush; albeit if only for the hours of fun it provided us for our antics and games.

I clearly remember the enthusiasm with which my mates and I 'warred'. Dividing ourselves into teams as 'skins' versus 'shirts': Sterling House versus Lincoln House, we had great fun belting one another with pieces of clay. I can vouch for the fact that a lump of sticky clay hurled from the end of a bendable stick at 90 kilometers per hour is most unpleasant when it hits a bare back. I was always a 'skin'. Maybe it had something to do with the suntan I acquired running around half naked all the time.

My good friend Hugh Mackay, Hugo for short, organized these clay 'latjie' (from Afrikaans, the dimininutive form of 'lat', a bendable stick) wars and I must say we got it down to a fine art over the years. Hugh, unlike me, came from a very conservative farming background and was most adept in the bush, as were most pupils at Guinea Fowl School. When I arrived I had 'stove pipe' trousers, leather jackets, a slicked-back Elvis Presley hairstyle and other fashionable accessories of the time. I was like a fish out of water for the first few months until I managed to accustom the others to my trendy ways.

For our clay 'latjie' wars we used dustbin lids both as shields and to carry our ammunition. We also had several short bendable sticks for fast use at short range and one long stick (the 'lat') for shots that required a little more distance. If you were smart, you would reload all the sticks with a lump of sticky clay at every opportunity.

The key to success was not to get cornered. It happened to me on several occasions. The entire opposing team would pelt the trapped warrior and this would result in grotesque welts all over the body. On one occasion I was so severely 'winded' by a lump of clay that I lay prostrate, unable to breathe for several minutes. The opposing side, the guys responsible for the injury, thought I was dead and were thrown into a panic until I recovered. However, my popularity as a good sport rocketed when I got up, brushed off the clay and allowed the game to resume.

With this kind of exercise going on, it's small wonder that I never really took to sports. I did play rugby often, but being a small chap I was far too light for the game. Anyway, my rugby aspirations were dashed when I injured my shoulder one day and was unable to play.

I was good at cross-country running and I even managed to come third in the school one year. Being the short shit that I was, I surprised even myself when my legs carried me over the finish line yards ahead of most of the others. I like to think that I ran fast that day only because I didn't want to miss out on the clay latjie finals being fought down at the dam at the same time!

I was also a keen school cadet. Cadets were something entirely different. While most young aspirants fumbled through the fundamentals of 'boy soldiering', I got stuck into it like a fly sticks to the windscreen of a fast-moving car. Of course, the reason had to do with my deeply rooted aim of becoming a good soldier (something I never confided to my mates) and I thoroughly enjoyed the afternoons being 'beasted' around the sports fields in army fashion.

Another game we played was 'raids', whiling away the time as wannabe soldiers. This was at the time when the school was divided into an upper and a lower part and looked like a small town with streets and avenues.

Late at night, in true commando fashion, we would creep out of our beds, escape from the dormitories and with the stealth of jackals in a chicken run, cross the fields and fences and enter the lower school. The object of the exercise would be to get as close to the opposition's dormitories as we could, remain undetected and then carve our initials into trees, benches and whatever else would yield to our blades. Our enemies would then get up in the morning and realise how close to 'death' they'd been.

When we felt more confident and enterprising, we would enter our adversaries' dormitories and pelt them with paint-powder bombs, the contents of which were stolen from the art room during art class. Our bombs consisted of paper packets containing brightly coloured powder paint in its pre-mixed form, into which was inserted a penny flash bomb with the fuse sticking out of a small hole. Like miniature sticks of dynamite, our penny flash bombs were so-named because each one cost a penny. On detonation the packet would erupt, sending clouds of blue, red, green and orange dust into the air, saturating the dormitories with a powdery Technicolor brilliance. Of course, we couldn't just leave it at that and once the mess was made our reserve forces, patiently waiting in the rear, would open up with the fire hoses that belonged to the dormitories, creating a slurry of wet color that stained everything.

I'm certain that if I went back now there would still be powder paint in the crevices between the floor boards and underneath the skirting boards of Blenheim and Lincoln dormitories. Thinking back, it surprises me that we never got caught. These were the manifestations of the exuberance of youth and I have no regrets for our skullduggery!

I understand that now, the lower school has once again become a military barracks – as was the entire school during World War II, when it constituted one of numerous Royal Air Force bases in the country. In fact, the Rhodesian Air Force became part of Britain's strategic air arm from the end of World War II right up to the Unilateral Declaration of Independence in 1965.

On excursion weekends our wars spilled over into the bush outside my father's house behind Llewellyn Barracks. No longer satisfied with clay 'latjies', we used pellet guns as our main armament inserting real lead slugs into them as ammo. This continued for quite a while until some guys were seriously hurt and common sense prevailed. It was okay explaining on one occasion why pellets had to be removed from skinny white buttocks, but thereafter our excuses became far too lame and we decided it was best to quit while the going was still good.

Below the sports fields at Guinea Fowl was the sewerage pit. This was really a small, foul-smelling dam into which we believed the sewerage from the school was pumped. It was here that some of our clay lykie battles were fought, as the muddy banks of the dam provided an endless source of lykie ammunition. It was here too that new pupils underwent their initiation. They had to endure a slimy swim across the dam's evil-smelling surface. To really gain respect, if one so desired, you could swim the dam's length under water – but this was a feat of which legends were made. My own initiation ended seconds after it had started with my feet barely getting wet. I was either stupid or brave while growing up, but not brave enough to do the dam under water.

I remember once being punished for allegedly smoking. This episode is relevant for what will become apparent later in this story.

On a Wednesday afternoon a few mates and I were walking to the Guinea Fowl railway siding to buy cold drinks from a small kiosk. The tuck shop at the school was closed and the siding was the only place where we could also get sweets and crisps. We were walking along when a Volkswagen Beetle pulled up alongside and screeched to a halt, cutting us off. Mr. Berkinstein, the headmaster, alighted with a gleeful grin across his mug.

'That's it,' he said, with the glow of victory a bright red on his aged face. 'I've finally caught you smoking. You're in for it now.'

Had we all been smoking it might not have been such a bitter pill to swallow. The fact was that I wasn't smoking, but nevertheless we all had to report to his office for a caning the next day. Despite my pleas of innocence we were lined up and given six of the best. It was the only caning that I clearly remember because all the others were well deserved!

I have always been the kind of person to accept responsibility for my actions, but it has irked me when I've been innocent of a crime and 'done the time' anyway. I began to strongly resent false accusations and I held grudges against people who wronged me. It was not the last time I'd have to answer for crimes of which I was completely innocent. But more about that later.

During my final school years the nature of our games had more sinister consequences. The theme of good versus evil, 'skins' versus 'shirts', remained much the same but our toys got bigger and our weapons far more dangerous. Utilizing cherry bombs (enlarged penny flash bombs) as propellant and .303 cartridge cases as projectiles, we fashioned cannons from crude bits of steel pipe fixed to wooden butts with conduit fasteners. The idea was to block the one end of the pipe by hammering it flat, thus creating a breech and then light the cherry bomb, or two in tandem and drop them down the barrel, closely followed by the cartridge case. We would then point the thing in the desired direction and wait for it to go pop.

Invariably, the resulting explosion was worse than expected. Sometimes the entire pipe would split like a banana, peppering our bodies with shrapnel, but more often than not the cartridge case would go off like a rocket, with a resounding boom, at our foe.

Our accuracy left much to be desired, so fortunately the damage was minimal. I knew little of contained explosions or of the fundamentals of explosive ordnance then and we were quite happy with the excitement of being able to hurl projectiles hundreds of meters at 150 kilometers an hour. Regardless of the harm that could have been caused, I remember the way we pranced about like cocks in a hen house after every successful launch.

I was always fascinated by explosives. Heaven knows why I never suffered serious injury, considering the way I experimented with pool acids, drain cleaner and other chemical compounds in my quest for a bigger and better bang. With these and other shenanigans we used to get up to, it's no wonder that I progressed to the army, which in essence I saw as the big boys' version of our 'games'.

My family travelled around Rhodesia a lot, but my interest in tourism did not last. I remember camping trips and safaris, but in my formative years I also discovered the comforting effects of alcohol and music, along with girls and frivolity. I always abhorred smoking and was lucky in not getting hooked, apart from a few puffs now and again.

I spent many a long night carousing with friends, chatting up the chicks at bars, houses, schools, drive-ins and anywhere else that afforded the opportunity. The Rolling Stones were the new kids on the block back then and I have fond memories of hammering out the beats to *Paint it Black* and the like, while enjoying some 'bonding' time with the mates – not to mention a girl from time to time.

Life never treated me badly, but I wonder sometimes where I would be had my upbringing been different.

I honored my promise to complete my education and I left the school in Gwelo midway through my seventeenth year. My grades were nothing to be really proud of, but I finished with acceptable marks – and the world was my oyster. I really looked forward to my national service and relished the thought of becoming a real soldier. The winds of change were sweeping across Africa and

Rhodesia declared itself independent of Britain on 11 November 1965.

Ian Smith, a World War II Royal Air Force hero, had taken over the reins of the country the year before and in a shrewd move, on the eleventh hour of the eleventh day of the eleventh month – Armistice Day, to remind the British of Rhodesia's war record – he shrugged off the machinations of British rule and took responsibility for the country's future. No-one knew how it would end.

The only other country to have done a similar thing was the United States of America, whose independence declaration led to an invasion by King George's soldiers and the War of Independence. Rumors abounded that Britain would invade Rhodesia and years later it came to light that British soldiers had in fact practiced on Malta, parachuting onto the airport in preparation for taking Salisbury.

I heard much later that Britain's SAS had got to the planning stages of conducting military operations against the Rhodesians, but in an unprecedented move they refused, virtually to the man, to carry out the task. Such were the ties between Britain and Rhodesia that most Rhodesians had kith and kin in the United Kingdom. In addition, C Squadron, the Rhodesian SAS had also operated with 22 SAS in Malaya as part of the Malayan Scouts and more recently in Aden, the result of which were strong ties between individuals and the units themselves. In fact, it was only in June 1978, long into the start of the bush war, that 'C' Squadron became 1-Special Air Service Regiment (Rhodesia), casting aside her sister regiment's affiliation, although her place in the 22 SAS order of battle remains vacant to this day.

Nothing really came of it, but independence fuelled African nationalism and the war soon started in earnest. Within a few months of UDI, 21 ZANLA guerrillas of Ndabaningi Sithole's party had infiltrated Rhodesia's border area from Zambia. They split into three groups, each heading for predetermined targets, but were quickly neutralized. It was a sign of things to come.

On 28 April 1966, seven ZANLA insurgents were killed by security forces in a battle at Sinoia, barely 120 kilometres outside Salisbury. The nationalists were to mark this as the beginning of their armed struggle, or Chimurenga.

In this incident although the guerrillas were outnumbered, their Siminov and Kalashnikov automatic rifles were more than a match for the .303 Lee-Enfields of the security forces. At that stage any militant aggression against the country was considered an action for the police to handle and although the army had adopted the SLR (Self Loading Rifle) the police's weapons were antiquated. The incident caught the Rhodesians napping. From then on the country began to fine tune its war machine.

I never really thought about moral issues, or about what was right and wrong. I suppose no young patriot answering the call of his country stops for a moment to reflect on the moral standing of its cause. To me the chance of serving in the Rhodesian forces was a just and noble vocation. Terrorism in any form was barbaric and archaic and besides, I thought it was a natural progression to leave school and join the army. The enemy I would be fighting would surely be like the nefarious image of the Germans that were portrayed on Allied posters during World War II. It would be 'skins' versus 'shirts' reincarnated – a battle of good against evil.

I wasn't far wrong but I did need to learn a thing or two.

CHAPTER 2:
INTO SERVICE

While I was still at Guinea Fowl School my call-up papers arrived. I was requested to attend Intake 78 at Llewellyn Barracks. I barely had time to breathe, after completing my studies, before I had to report to A Company, the Royal Rhodesia Regiment in January 1966 as Rifleman 46422. Although the country had divested itself of its status as a colony in the previous year, the regiment retained the 'Royal' in its name for a while longer.

On my arrival at Llewellyn I was greeted by familiar faces. Before I knew it, I was marking time at the double with a broomstick held at chest height. When I checked in at the barracks, the regimental policemen standing at the boom happened to be a couple of mates of mine and they enjoyed throwing their weight around at my expense. Payback is a bitch and I marked them out for future retribution.

I thoroughly enjoyed my national service and got stuck into the army way of life with relish. After basic training we were involved in numerous classical warfare exercises, but did little in the way of counter-insurgency (COIN) training. We spent many miserable nights on the freezing plains outside Gwelo, wallowing in foxholes that we had dug in the frozen earth. I felt at the time that we really should have been training for unconventional military situations. COIN was left to the professionals in the regular army.

I celebrated my eighteenth birthday while I was serving in the Royal Rhodesia Regiment. I well remember that evening in the canteen as we plied ourselves with alcohol. My mates decided that I had to get drunk. They lined up 18 beer dumpies (small bottles) in front of me, one to celebrate each year that I had lived. I only managed ten before I was a stumbling, slurring wreck and my buddies poured the remaining eight bottles of beer over me in disgust at my drinking ineptitude.

We certainly painted the barracks red that night and I remember clearly the hangover I had the next day. Standing on parade the following morning I was the image of self-pity as I fought a losing battle to control my stomach spasms and hurled up all over the cleanly swept bitumen. The company sergeant major (CSM) on parade was a picture with his face turned purple and his chest puffed out like a mating cock. I think he saw the lighter side of the incident and I got off lightly. But having to stand rigid to attention for a few hours in the blazing sun, after all the others had left, was not what the doctor ordered considering the hangover I had.

However, I look back on that year with great fondness and I smile to myself when I think that the other lads and I actually thought we were soldiers. We were the very best canteen cowboys and the army taught us to drink well.

After the first stirrings of armed struggle, terrorist sightings were reported on the Botswana border and we were put on high alert. The RLI and British South Africa Police (BSAP) bore the brunt of most terrorist contacts back then, so we never really did anything.

In 1967 I applied for selection in the Rhodesian SAS and travelled to Cranborne Barracks in Salisbury to undergo the recruit course. Shortly after arriving, my girlfriend back in Bulawayo, the love of my life, called me in panic, sure she was pregnant. Her parents were fuming and wanted to see me.

We had taken the precaution of putting her on the pill – which I had surreptitiously stolen from my sister-in-law – so I couldn't understand how it had happened. I took leave of training, with a promise to be on the next course in six months and returned to Bulawayo.

My girlfriend's parents were infuriated and thought we had made a mistake. They blew things out of all proportion. They insisted on terminating the pregnancy and forbade me to see her again. They even got the law involved and had a few strings pulled which culminated in a restraining order against me prohibiting any further contact with her.

My girlfriend was only 17 at the time, far too young to mother a child; but the legal age of sexual consent in Rhodesia was16. I was young and I never really understood their attitude. I was prepared to do the manly and righteous thing, but my dad saw the situation for what it was and encouraged me to seek my fortune in the United Kingdom. He never really liked her anyway and used to goad me by telling me she was the army groundsheet. Apparently everyone, including my army buddies, was after her and while I was away, she would mess around. He was certain that the baby had sprung from loins other than my own!

In retrospect, I suppose my dad had already endured the embarrassment of one prodigal son and he felt the dust should settle first before I returned home. I couldn't help but think that in his opinion, the apple had fallen far from the tree – right next to Ian's.

I left for England dour hearted, leaving behind my aspirations of a military career and arrived in Middlesbrough in May 1967. With the enthusiasm of youth I took to my new life like a duck takes to water, working as a labourer for a year, among other things. For a short period I did come unstuck and lived on a park bench in Hyde Park. A couple of people from the Salvation Army befriended me and helped out by providing me with food and some warm clothing. I've had the utmost respect for the Salvation Army ever since!

Being the sort of chap I was, there was never any shortage of carousing and its associated benefits of women. While I was in Middlesbrough I met a beautiful blonde by the name of Sheila. It was love at first sight and it didn't take long before we were inseparable. The result, a few months later, was that she vomited every morning as I left for work.

In view of the pregnancy we decided to get married, so at the tender ages of 21 and 17 respectively, we tied the knot with a small church ceremony. It was nothing grand but it suited our needs perfectly.

I had filled Sheila's head with stories of home and I was planning to take her to Rhodesia one day. I was convinced that she would eventually come around to seeing my point of view. At the back of my mind the dream of becoming a member of the Rhodesian SAS never really left me and I yearned for the day I could return home. I didn't know it then, but it would be another long six years before I would finally realize that dream.

In January 1969, while walking through Middlesbrough, I was struck by an image on a poster adorning the window of a small army recruiting office. The photograph showed a Parachute Regiment patrol in Aden. I was immediately taken in by the image. The Paras were attired in World War II disruptive-pattern smocks and armed with SLRs. The selling point on the poster was typical of the period and in bold print it declared: 'Join the army and travel the world'. I wondered how many other young men were attracted by these appealing promises. Looking back, it seems to me that the youth of today would not be as gullible as I was then. But then again, they also seem to lack the adventurous spirit that was so common in most young men at that time.

Instantly I knew that this was what I wanted. Suddenly my dreams changed and my life was ready for a completely new course. I entered the office and was met by a rather rotund soldier with spectacles. He seemed a bit out of place in uniform and I remember thinking that he would be more suited as a professor behind a lectern at some university. I can't remember the soldier's rank, but when I enquired about the Paras he tried to change my mind. 'Why the Paras, young man?' he asked. 'Do yourself a favour and join the real army. The Corps of Transport is looking for good men right now.'

I didn't care much about what he had to say. My mind was made up.

With a one-way ticket to Aldershot, I signed on the dotted line and set off home to Middlesbrough full of the joys of spring. Only problem was it was winter and really cold.

While I waited for the bus in a blustering gale I experienced a strange sensation. Somewhere between my balls and my stomach a small muscle tweaked at my bowels like a guitar string. It felt as if a large winged insect was ricocheting off my stomach lining, like popcorn bursting in a pot. The manifestation of excitement and of stepping into the unknown was a feeling I was unfamiliar with, but strangely comfortable. It was one that I would get to know well in the years to come.

On 15 April 1969 I started a new chapter in my life. Leaving Sheila, seven months pregnant, at her mother's house where we lived in Middlesbrough, I caught the train to Aldershot and took a taxi to Browning Barracks, Depot Para, with £15 in my pocket, nervous and uncertain. I was among numerous army wannabes undergoing physical and medical evaluations. I remember considering dropping out before I even entered the gates. It would have been far easier to return home in the taxi and take a pint or six down at the pub.

As we entered the camp the provost corporal, who was our administrator, pointed out places of interest. The first thing I noticed was a Dakota DC-3 aircraft of World War II fame as it stood like a sentinel by the gates. I suppose I would have been more interested in it at as a historical artefact, but these types of aircraft were still in use by the Rhodesian Air Force. I had seen them many times before back home while doing national service.

Right from the beginning prospective paratroopers were expected to be a cut above the rest. The brainwashing was immense from the start. We were told that the only real kind of human being in the world was a paratrooper. The second thing we were told – and I think it was in that order – was that 'God is airborne – repent all craphats'.

We were warned against conferring with craphats. The only other acceptable human beings were the SAS and everyone else was inferior. The Royal Marine commandos (or cabbage heads, as they were called) were borderline and might rate the odd mention.

When we saw a craphat we were told the saying was: 'Why do the Russians laugh in their sleep?'

The arrogant answer that was brainwashed into us: 'Why shouldn't they when Britain has craphats defending her?'

It was drummed into us that we were the be-all and end-all. No one else mattered. Beyond the gate's recruits jostled, queued and ran everywhere. The recruits were easy to make out from the experienced Parachute Regiment recruit staff. Apart from the obvious dress differences, all you really had to do was to look for differences in complexion. Most of the instructor's faces were on the verge of exploding; red as they were with the flush of futile expectation.

I knew it was too late to back out when we were issued with our force numbers – instantly Jake Harper Ronald, a young man with feelings and personality became Private Harper Ronald, 24161731, a numbered cog in a very big machine – and a small cog at that!

I was very worried that my fitness levels were not what they should be because for the past year I had lived quite a casual existence, never taking exercise and drinking far too much. I was very undernourished at the time as my diet consisted mainly of greasy take-away foods bought whenever I had change from beer money. I must have been about ten kilograms underweight for my size – and my size was not very big to start with.

I soon learnt that my worries were justified. On the first day it was impressed on us that Paras do not walk anywhere. Everywhere we went, whether we were doing a medical, being issued with kit or sorting through a pile of administrative tasks, we had to double time, or trot at a fast jog. Most recruits didn't know how to march, so it was quite difficult to keep in step. As with most aspiring Paras, new to Aldershot, we looked more akin to a gaggle of goslings, chasing their mother as we stuck to the Recruit Staff's backsides like bubblegum to a shoe. It was an unnerving experience and I remember thinking that I must do as I was told, remain the grey man and then I would get through it.

I don't know how many shades of grey there are, but after our first run I shot right through the colour spectrum and well off the chart, as I paid dearly for my previous social vices in a display of technicolor puking. When I recovered I was far from grey, more of a milky green in fact, as the recruit staff and other recruits leered at me in my predicament. I consoled myself with the knowledge that at least I had completed the runs but from that day on I knew I was a black mark in every one of the recruit staff's notebooks.

I continued to vomit after every run and assault course for the first few days. The assault course had to be completed within a time limit and was one of many exercises in the Para initial selection tests. This and the other physical training we went through was to prepare us for 'P' Company, the Para selection proper. It was an endless hive of activity with no chance to rest. When we weren't being beasted around the depot, we were mercilessly drilled into the ground, or constantly revising weapons drills. Even in our own time, back in our rooms, there was the unending task of polishing and cleaning kit and weapons, chores we could never quite do to the satisfaction of the staff as there was always a criticism here and there.

Those early days were a new experience for me entirely. Until then I never thought it was possible that the human voice box was capable of keeping every tone above ten decibels. I'm sure I was showered with more spit in my first few weeks at Depot Para, being yelled at, than in my entire military career. It literally drizzled spit and it very nearly became hard to distinguish between that and the crappy weather outside. We were the lowest of the low back then and certainly, in the recruit staff's eyes, we were no higher on the scale than a single-cell amoeba. Deep down I knew they loved us really and it kept me going.

I managed to pass the initial selection, scraping through on tenacity alone. By this point, of the 30 applicants who had started, many had already dropped out and I congratulated myself that I wasn't one of those.

The attitude of the recruit staff towards us began to soften, but it never really let up. I think we had managed to climb a rung of the ladder to the stage of a two-cell amoeba – but we weren't quite Paras yet. 'P' Company was yet to come and until then we remained a low form of life.

The next months fused into a blur of repetitive physical training, learning the bread-and-butter of infantry tactics, parachuting and confidence building. The confidence part of training came in the form of the aerial assault course which every recruit had to negotiate to remain in the game. An intimidating structure of scaffolding and boardwalks, the assault course, or rather, the inability to negotiate it, spelt the end of many recruits' service. A particularly foreboding part of it came in the form of a leap from one platform to another at a height of 40 feet (12 metres). When my time came I only took the plunge because others had done so before me. At this stage I couldn't bear the ridicule of failure. The shame would be tantamount to cowardice in combat and besides that, I was the token recruit representing Rhodesia. What would my buddies back home have said if I had dropped out?

My parachute training was conducted at Western on the Green, the RAF base in Abingdon, where my first jump was out of a balloon rigged on a cable at 400 feet (122 metres). Again I think it was only peer group pressure that made most of us jump. After the first leap of faith it was actually quite exciting. I couldn't wait to get back to the balloon for another go.

Para training was a highly physical aspect of the course. We were constantly doing push-ups to strengthen our arms and upper bodies. When working the risers of a parachute the arms are always presented above the head; a very difficult pose to maintain for long periods of time. To this end we also did 'pokey drill'. Swinging our rifles around at shoulder height, from one arm to the other, was a sure way of gaining extra muscle and stamina in the shoulders, chest and arms. I turn green with envy when I think of today's soldiers who have the good fortune of bearing much lighter assault weapons, quite unlike the 9.9lb (4.5 kg) SLRs we had to lug around.

By the end of it I had regained the ten kilograms I had previously lost, but this time in the form of lean, hard muscle.

One Sunday morning, while on parade, one of the recruit staff, a sergeant I was familiar with, noticed me as I stood to attention, trying to avoid being noticed. I had received a telephone call from Sheila the night before, informing me that her contractions had started and that she thought she was going into labour. I was highly pissed off that I would miss the birth of my first child but being part of the maroon machine, I naively thought that it would not have the compassion to grant leave for such a worldly event. I made my apologies to my wife and told her I would ask for compassionate leave at the earliest opportunity. Unbeknown to me, Sheila's mother had already informed the duty officer at

Para HQ of the situation. The duty officer informed the recruit staff and they assumed I had already left to be with my wife.

As I stood there an enormous voice reverberated through my ears:

'P-R-I-VATE HAR-P-E-R R-O-N-A-L-D'! the sergeant bellowed so close to my nose that his spittle blended with the drizzle that was coming down. 'What the FUCK do you think you're doing here?'

I was a little taken aback and immediately my perpetually guilty nature began to flash warning signs to my brain as I wondered what I had done. It hadn't crossed my mind that if I wasn't on parade, then where else was I supposed to be?

'I'm on parade, sergeant,' I stuttered, stating the obvious, uncertain of his point.

'Do you think the Paras are heartless bastards?' he asked, the question seeming more rhetorical than anything else.

Now I was really stumped. How to answer that question? It seemed to me I was being led into a trap: damned-if-I-do, damned-if-I-don't type of thing. A 'yes' might be taken offensively, but a 'no' might very well imply that I thought we were a bunch of soft cocks.

'Err-umm–err,' I replied, without getting far with my attempted rebuttal.

'Private, your wife is having a baby and you had better be on the platform for the next train out of here,' he said. 'If you are not gone in twenty minutes, I am going to put you on a charge.' This was the sergeant's way of being kind.

I didn't need any further coaxing. Excusing myself, I doubled to the barracks to collect some kit and then headed for the station. On the way out I collected a two-day leave pass.

Richard was born a few hours before I arrived at the Middlesbrough Hospital. I was mortified that I had narrowly missed the birth, but I was overjoyed at having a son. Looking back over the whole affair it seemed it was such a rush – almost a dream – but I was intoxicated with fatherhood. Sadly, the two days leave went by quickly and I soon had other issues on my mind. The day was looming near when I would have to prove myself worthy as a paratrooper.

'P' Company came and went and I passed with above-average marks. I wasn't the best recruit physically, but the Para's build-up training stood me in good stead for the pole-carrying tabs and other tests. The log race was a packaged killer and young and fit as I had become, I really thought I was going to die. I got through it though and managed to drag myself over the finish line, hanging onto the cumbersome pole with my feet barely touching the ground. Being short does have its advantages! Jokes aside, it really was a ball breaker.

Milling was something I was averse to, as are most recruits. We dreaded the day when we were each squared off against another recruit of similar size for a minute of madness in the boxing ring. In my case there was no-one who was actually my size – so my opponent would be a chap who had at least ten kilograms on me.

It struck me that one of the very fellows with whom I'd bonded, the same chap I'd helped through the rigours of training, as he'd helped me, I was now supposed to beat the crap out of.

There was nothing for it, so I got into the ring and set to with the tenacity of a bulldog. Unfortunately for me, my opponent had the same idea and the ensuing fight, if you can call it that, was a mêlée of flailing arms punctuated by soft moans and guttural grunts as we knocked the wind out of each other. When the bell finally tolled, neither of us had gained the advantage, but I do distinctly recall feeling that I might have won had the fight continued. Awarding myself brownie points is one way I've always managed to get through things.

In the end, fifteen of us passed 'P' company. It had been a close call for me in the beginning but by the time I passed out I could even add the award for best rifle shot of the platoon as a feather in my cap. I almost got the award for GPMG, but the machine gun I was using malfunctioned on test day and I constantly had to put into practise the immediate action drills we'd learnt for stoppages. If there had been an award for that I would most certainly have got it but as it was, I came second for GPMG.

My passing-out parade was attended by my wife and by my brother Ian, who was then living in the UK. It was a grand affair indeed, complete with the Gurkha band playing, among other compositions, *The Flight of the Valkyries*, the regimental song.

The feeling of accomplishment among all the recruits that day was tremendous and was evident by the huge grins that sat on faces under maroon berets. I for one had a sense of achievement, unparalleled in my life until then. I finally knew that I belonged to something special – a brotherhood with no equal.

After the parade we gathered with the recruit staff for postings. These were remarkable men and had warmed up to us considerably. It is funny how bonds can form between men whom we had previously thought of as the enemy. Before my passing-out parade I would have been quite happy to hand out the fire department's number to each member of the recruit staff, as I wouldn't so much as piss on them if they were on fire. Overnight their attitudes changed to congratulatory backslaps and heartfelt 'well dones'. We were now officially Paras and with that honour came their immediate respect and friendship. We'd all gone through the same ordeal, albeit at different times and we were now accepted almost as equals.

I didn't have a choice as to which battalion I would be posted. The recruit staff rattled off our names followed by our postings and I learned that I would go to 1 Para.

We squared away our kit and prepared ourselves for nine days of well-deserved leave before reporting to Battalion HQ. I left Aldershot in a jovial mood, looking forward to being reunited with my wife and rewarding my efforts with a few cold ones. I hadn't spent time with Sheila for a while, not since Richard's birth, despite the close distance between us. I revelled in the knowledge of having nine days of uninterrupted rest and recuperation or, as I saw it, intercourse and intoxication. I caught a taxi from the depot gate and headed for Middlesbrough. The sun was shining that day to increase the warm glowing sensation I felt all over my being.

Turning into the road where we lived, the sight of a police panda car outside my mother-in- law's house was a little startling. As the taxi pulled up alongside the front entrance I got out with trepidation, expecting the worst. I thought at first that some fate had befallen the household, but this was quickly replaced by my own feelings of guilt. I knew I was a rebellious type but once again, I couldn't for the life of me think what crime I'd committed that was so heinous that the police would be waiting to pick me up as soon as I left the depot.

I approached the bobby cautiously as he leaned against the car, a quizzical expression on my face.

'Mr. Harper Ronald?' he enquired, his businesslike manner making me even more suspicious.

'Yes'

'I've orders for you to report back to your battalion immediately. I'm here to put you on the train.'

I hadn't yet walked into my front door and already I was being ushered back to Aldershot! I couldn't believe it.

'What's the problem, sir?' If I had made the same inference back at depot to an NCO, I might have been shot.

'Big trouble in Northern Ireland, son. Your battalion has been put on an emergency footing. You're to report back there immediately.'

If I wasn't startled before, I was now. Surely, I asked myself, there are others in the battalion with more experience than I had for this sort of thing. Fuck. I had only just finished training!

Why would they be sending the likes of me to Northern fucking Ireland, I thought?

The policeman seemed sympathetic when I aired my views. He couldn't exactly bend the rules, but he told me to go inside, have a cup of tea and explain the situation to my family.

I was unimpressed to say the least and it was as if the bottom had just fallen out of my world. I didn't join the army for this! Couldn't they just give a man some peace?

Sheila was even less pleased with the policeman's orders. After calming her I explained that I was in the army now and I had to follow orders, not fully convincing myself with the lame excuse.

I phoned the depot just to make sure that it wasn't a fix and my buddies were having me on, half hoping, while the phone rang, that this would be the case.

My buddies wouldn't be that nice to me and from the enquiry I heard it was genuine. The warm glowing feeling of earlier was replaced with a cold, hollow foreboding. It had less to do with the deployment than not being able to spend time with Sheila and Richard and knocking back a pint or two.

The only good news I heard on the phone was that I could report back on my own, unaided by a police escort. I stepped outside and told the policeman. He hesitated to leave, but said that he would return to his station to confer with the member-in-charge. I didn't hear from him after that, so I assumed they had phoned the depot themselves.

The harsh reality of my imminent departure left a glum air about the house while we sipped tea. I took advantage of the small respite and bonded as best as I could with my newborn son.

CHAPTER 3:
TEMPERED BY FIRE

I arrived back at Depot Para on a blistering autumn day, frustrated and disillusioned. Blistering for the UK, that is. They said it was one of the hottest autumns in twenty years; but they always say that, don't they?

After drawing my kit, which included strange items I'd never seen before, I was put into C Company. Among the new additions that had to be hauled along with our rifles, webbing and personal kit, we now had to lug batons, shields and gas masks. We spent an entire morning practising archaic drills such as the Paras had used in the Middle East for riot control.

Marching in platoon formation, carrying a big sign which read 'Disperse or we will open fire' wasn't exactly the type of training I thought relevant to what we might come up against. I'd heard a little about the 'Troubles' in Northern Ireland and even my pea-sized brain could put two and two together. There was no way that those glassfibre shields would stop a burst from a .22, let alone a Tommy gun.

Concluding our morning's activity, we were rounded up into a company cluster and told that we would be leaving for Northern Ireland that afternoon. Now I was really stumped. I must say that it was an immense shock to the system to leave training in a peacetime environment and learn that one would be actively deployed the next day.

I really didn't know anything about Northern Ireland and my interest in politics was non-existent. It was only much later that I learned a little of the background story that resulted in our deployment.

Ireland had long since suffered for various reasons, which included the potato famine of the 1800s and internal squabbles over self-rule. Home rule for Ireland was about to be granted in 1914 when World War-I broke out, effectively putting self-government on the backburner. A group of Irish nationalists, impatient at the delay, rebelled in 1916, but the revolt failed. The Protestants of Northern Ireland wanted no part of the independence movement.

Much later a guerrilla war broke out in southern Ireland between a volunteer force called the Irish Republican Army (IRA) and British troops. The war ended after a treaty was signed which gave self-government to the 26 southern counties, but left the six northern counties under British rule, as they had wished.

Sinn Fein, the leading political party in Ireland, was founded in 1905 and had authorised the IRA to campaign for independence, resulting in the southern counties becoming the Irish Free State on 6 December 1922. On 1 April 1949 it became the Republic of Ireland. The Republic formally laid claim to the northern counties (Northern Ireland), but the claim was not pressed.

Things were quite okay for some time and might have remained so if the Protestant parliament of Northern Ireland had not discriminated against the Catholic minority in jobs, housing and local government. Catholic protests led to riots in 1969 when Protestant mobs attacked them with sticks, stones and petrol bombs.

The IRA at this point had been quiet for some years, but when the riots broke out they split; a militant splinter faction forming the Provisional IRA (PIRA), seeking retribution from the Protestants and launching themselves on a crusade of violence to secure the union of Ireland. The riots and terrorism in Northern Ireland got so bad that the Provincial government appealed for help. 1-Para, commanded by Lieutenant Colonel Michael Gray, came to the rescue in October 1969 and that's where we came into the picture.

We left for Southampton to catch the ferry to Belfast. The journey in the back of the military transport was quiet, the occasional nervous chatter rising above the drone of the engine. Off Southampton the sea was rough. I had never been on the ocean before and I dreaded the possibility of becoming seasick. We boarded the Royal Fleet auxiliary ship *Sir Galahad*, a troopship and were told to focus on the horizon and never to look into the boat if we didn't want to fall ill.

The sight of 300 Paras ogling the shore as we departed was one I remember well. There we were, tough paratroopers emblazoned in riot and combat gear, eyes fixed on a gradually receding coastline, looking more like school kids out on a day's excursion. Among us were men who had combat experience behind them and one or two who had just returned from Northern Ireland. That did little to comfort me at the time, but my nervousness was replaced by that unfamiliar feeling again and I began to get excited about the darkness that waited ahead.

I've always had a deep sense of nostalgia which has remained with me all my life. As we sailed, I wondered how many other young men had left the shores of Great Britain on the *Sir Galahad*, never to return. Sadly, many years later, on 9 June 1982, during the Falklands campaign, the *Sir Galahad* was sunk by Argentinean bombs as she sat exposed in Port Fitzroy. The 1st Battalion Welsh Guards suffered heavy casualties during the daylight attack.

We were in Belfast for only one night before we experienced the hell that was Northern Ireland. I don't profess to claim that Ireland was the be-all and end-all of soldiering, but it certainly had the ability to sort out the men from the boys.

The Protestants were burning the Catholics out at the time and we were dropped at the bottom of Shankill Road in the early hours of the morning to restore order. We organized ourselves into our platoon formations as we had been taught the day before and marched out towards a barrier where another unit was getting the shit knocked out of it with bottles, bricks and paving stones.

My heart was in my mouth and I recall feeling very insignificant in the grand scheme of things.

The Protestants behind the barrier were using catapults with ball bearings as ammo. They had obviously learnt from experience and were firing the ball bearings a few metres in front of our shields so that they bounced under them and into our shins. A few men went down with cries of pain and before long we were all cowering in doorways, the only sanctuary out of harm's way, venturing out only when one of us fired gas in a protective formation.

The tear gas didn't seem to work as I thought it might. Everyone was so high on adrenalin that the canisters seemed to have no effect at all. The protestors, I noticed, were just covering their faces with shirts and handkerchiefs and throwing the gas containers right back at us. More enterprising individuals among them, those with experience, just shoved them down manholes, into sewer drains or dunked them into buckets of water and ran with them from the fracas to where they could do no harm.

Later, I would learn to use the canisters the same way that the rioters used their catapults and ball bearings: by firing them so that they skipped across the tarmac at knee level. That way, on impact, at least they would have the desired effect – and maybe even break a bone if fired at close enough range.

We hadn‘t quite yet adjusted to the terror of the non-lethal weaponry levelled against us when machine-gun rounds ricocheted off the tarmac at our front. It didn't last long, no longer than a minute, before it petered out; but it was enough to let us know that we could die out here. It was the first time I had ever been under fire and the incident remains a milestone in my life, although being shot at was a bit different from how I had imagined it. It was over so rapidly that the fear that I thought might take hold never came. It just fused into my overall concern of possibly being injured at any point in the riot. We were told later that the machine gun was an old .303 Vickers, being fired from the top of a building somewhere. Other troops assaulted the position and managed to capture it.

Cowering in a corner, trying to make myself as small as possible, I questioned the reasoning that had brought me here. I only joined up because I wanted to go to the jungles in Malaya or Borneo. Even Aden would have been better than this shit! I had led a nice life back in Bulawayo; quite unlike this. I didn't even know why the Protestants and Catholics hated each other. That day was the first time I questioned my sanity.

We got fucked up for that first 20 minutes. When there weren't enough doorways for us to hide in, we ended up huddling in a cluster using our shields as walls. When the protestors ran out of ball bearings, they began hurling paving stones at knee level, hoping to find a flaw in our defensive perimeter. They were real pros!

I knew how organised they really were when I witnessed milk floats being used to bring new ordnance to the front in the form of petrol bombs. A few non-combatants, so to speak, milled about the rioters dispensing bombs from the trolleys to those at the sharp end, as if they were milkmen going about their daily deliveries. I can almost swear I heard one of them cry ‘Petrol bomb delivery, petrol bomb delivery, one or two pints?’ But that was the workings of a terrified imagination and I dismissed the idea as soon as it came.

One of the boys in my company was set alight when a bomb burst in front of him, but he was soon extinguished as his mates belted him to the ground. I think it must be one of the most ghastly things to be set on fire.

My first impression of the battle, one that remains with me, was of the terrifying noise. The protesters, once they had regrouped after every scuffle, would march back to the barrier, bashing bricks together in unison. It reminded me of the movie *Zulu*, one of Michael Caine's first films, where the Zulu warriors beat their assegais on their shields before attacking the garrison at Rorke's Drift. The terror that beset those brave defenders in Natal that day must have been complete.

Once we had truly seen our arses, things began to cool down. The OC of our company called in the Saracen armoured cars and then the rioters were no longer so keen to joust. I think they had learnt from experience that when the Saracens came in, it was a step before all-out war began – when real bullets began to fly and people got hurt. I was more than relieved to see the ugly silhouette of the armoured cars as they rumbled down the Shankill Road.

I escaped from my first encounter no worse for wear. I was beginning to think that I was learning a thing or two about soldiering but I hardly was, given that this was my first day out and I have no shame in saying that my survival had nothing to do with my soldiering ability, bravery or prowess.

The remainder of that three-month tour was pretty peaceful when compared to my introductory package to Northern Ireland. After the Shankill, for the first few days in Belfast, we just patrolled, our task being to keep the warring Protestants and Catholics apart. I was quite happy with such duties as we were all still reeling from our first day's mauling, but after a few weeks it became boring and we couldn't wait to get back into the thick of things. With hindsight, it seems we too easily forget the nasty things in life!

Maybe it was because we administered as good as we got, or maybe it wasn't, but the likes of Shankill were not repeated on that tour and we spent most of it on patrol or freezing our balls off with relentless guard duties.

It was early years then and we were very naive. The regiment had not yet earned the reputation for toughness, sometimes bordering on brutality, that it would gain in the future. Looking back, it was that first encounter and the stories that grew from it that instilled a deep-rooted pride in 1-Para and in C Company particularly. Sure, the home team may have got the better of us on that day, but it was for that very reason that it would not happen again. The visitors would be back with a vengeance.

Speaking for myself, I resolved to be tougher from then on, but I think my feelings were shared among the entire battalion. I suppose this was largely because of the camaraderie that the Parachute Regiment fosters. We were all eager to back up our buddies when they were in a fix and prove to ourselves what we were made of. When I look back on it, as serious a business as Northern Ireland was, it probably wasn't prepared for the fire it had kindled under 1 Para's arse that day. In my time in Northern Ireland that fire grew out of all proportion to the small spark that ignited it. As far as we saw it, we were no longer going to be fucked with, whichever side it came from.

Despite this, before we discovered that brutality was the answer to our problems, we did attempt to resolve things by more congenial means. We formed the Green Line between the Falls Road (Catholic) and the Shankill Road (Protestant) and built a club on neutral ground. The Paradise Club, as it was called, was an attempt to get youths of the two factions to mingle. Being artistic I was given the job of painting murals on the inside walls instead of having to do guard duties. With great enthusiasm I painted images of young men and women dancing and highlighted them with a few well-aimed lights and a mirror ball. When it was finished, a picture of me appeared in the *Daily Mirror*. It was a full-page colour photo showing me holding up a beer in front of one of the murals. I got all the praise for the Paradise Club. I was also given a keg of beer that we polished off one night at the club's bar. The carpenters and the builders got nothing and were green with envy at my good fortune.

Another task was to organise discos in order to encourage the kids to frequent the place. We were not much older than they were and it was right up our street. Unfortunately, despite the huge amount of effort we put into the place, it never took off as expected. With hindsight, I suppose we were pissing against the wind. Who were we trying to kid? If we couldn't quell all that hatred with our tear gas, batons and boots, how could Mick Jagger succeed with only his voice?

When 2 Para took over after our tour, the Paradise Club was burnt to the ground by the Catholics. As far as I know, no further attempts were made to engage the youth of both sides in social interaction.

CHAPTER 4:
SNIPPETS AND SNIPING

On returning to Aldershot I was fortunate to get a place on secondment to 3 Para in Malta, after I put my name down for a sniper cadre with personnel from the brigade. I would be leaving in a month's time to join them as they stood by as the reaction force for any trouble while the Brits pulled out of Libya. We used Malta because of its fantastic weather and superb long ranges. In all, 23 of us from the different battalions would make the journey as the Paras needed new blood in the shooting teams at Bisley the following year.

Content with the posting, I caught up with Sheila in Middlesbrough and we spent some quality time together. Sheila had struggled with my being away all the time, but she looked flush and fresh after the birth of our child. My mother-in-law was a great help during those days and assisted with the baby tremendously.

Our marriage was still young and we were very much in love, but I could sense in Sheila a small degree of annoyance with my going away again. I was overjoyed with the prospect of spending three months in sunny Malta but looking at it retrospectively, I should have shown more compassion towards her, although I couldn't have done anything about it anyway. I still had a little time to spend with her and that was enough for me.

Having said that, young men will be young men and I'm not proud to admit that I did mess around on occasion. Aldershot, and to some degree Depot Para in those days was not far removed from a Wild West town, complete with bars and maidens. The local women hated us for reasons that should become apparent, but there was plenty of talent at the WRAC base in Aldershot who were willing to test our waters. If sex wasn't a willing addition to a young Para's life, then it was paid for in the brothels of West End London. To be honest, I never did visit a brothel, but that was largely because it wasn't necessary. There was never a shortage of young women aspiring to meet tough Paras off duty. Not far down the road the nurses from the Queen Alexandra's Nursing Home were bountiful and beautiful.

The town itself was pretty much off limits to craphats and those from other regiments, who hardly dared to venture there, so we had all the women to ourselves. It was almost like dipping your hand into a box of Quality Street and taking your pick. The quality mightn't have been there, but the sugar always was.

While I was in Depot I really got to enjoy our Sunday routine. When we weren't training, the holy Sabbath was all ours to catch up on chores like cleaning and polishing. First thing on a Sunday morning my mates and I would usually pack our army issue Bergen rucksacks with dirty washing and head off to the launderette, which in army parlance left over from Indian Army days, we called the Dhobi. Once there we would feed the washing machines with the weeks dirty clothing, insert our 2s and 6d and then move on to the pub next door.

The Havalot bar was a thriving congregation of needy, hard-sprung young groins that serviced paratroopers, girls who wanted to be with paratroopers and a few other regular types. After the customary two pints we would wonder back to the dhobi, move our washing to the driers and then return to the Havalot for another customary two or three pints. This was followed with a casual amble to the barracks and the inevitable ironing while we relaxed and watched TV.

On one occasion at the Havalot, after taking care of our laundry, my mates and I were confronted by four females lurking at the bar, all of whom looked like hookers on a bad day out. Their appearance was so startling that conversation was only initiated when a mate went up and enquired as to who they were and why they were dressed so funny.

'We read the *News of the World* and we've come down from London to see if its true.' came the reply. Obviously Aldershot was a little behind the times when it came to fashion sense!

When my mate asked what they were talking about, we learnt that an article had appeared on the front page of the newspaper the day before, heralding Aldershot as the centre for UK gang bangs! The body of the article told of huge orgies in which women were being used by Paras to satisfy their sexual cravings. Our intrepid foursome had travelled some way to verify the matter and to see if they could get a little piece of the action.

To say my mates entertained the idea is a bit of an understatement. I would love to take some credit, in the spirit of being a young, sexually active, time-bomb waiting to explode, but at that point the guilt of cheating on my wife was too much too bear and I just ogled the proceedings as a bystander.

After smuggling the sex kittens into the barracks, an impromptu party blossomed, as the ladies began to dance on tables to the melancholy sound of Jimmy Morrison. Within minutes other Paras were queuing at doors and hanging in windows, while articles of clothing gradually disappeared from our lively entertainers writhing to the hypnotic beat. Soon they were as naked as the day they were born and Paras were cupping breasts and pinching bottoms. One guy, it seemed, almost wished he had another hand, as eight bouncing bosoms became too much for his biological limitations. With a breast firmly grasped at each extremity he writhed in unison, with his tongue dangling out, trying to capture another in his mouth before anyone else could get there.

I've never taken hard drugs, but from what I saw, with our mood that day, we might as well have all been on some hallucinogenic. Young men and women, zombie-like in trance, undulated around the place in a sexual frenzy.

Needless to say the women got what they came for and for the next few hours our room was a hive of bobbing bottoms and flailing legs. One of the adventurous travellers squealed out the window as a Para backed up behind her and pounded away his pent-up frustration.

It was really quite something, although I'm not sure that I'm proud to have been a part of it. I excuse myself from these little excesses with the sexual fervour of youth prevalent in most at that age. It was the 1960s after all and the era of free love, although I can guarantee that we were the furthest thing from hippies you could find.

These sorts of shenanigans happened all the time in the barracks. When a Para picked up a chick, he would normally be given one of the corporal's bunks, allowing for a bit more comfort and the boys would line up outside for their turn.

I took two females back one night, in a totally inebriated state, hoping for a bit of slap and tickle myself. I was far too gone, however, and ended up at the NAAFI drinking hot chocolate with my erstwhile conquests. I can't remember much after that, but when I woke up in the morning it was to the cheers and congratulations of all my buddies.

I returned to the NAAFI for a morning brew, puzzled why everyone was slapping me on the back as I passed, huge grins on their faces. When I got there, some of the guys who were on guard duty the night before came up to me and thanked me for the wonderful evening. They had carried me to my bunk after I had passed out and with a true sense of camaraderie and displaying the finest traditions of Parachute Regiment's *esprit de corps*, they had taken over my shagging duties. The guardroom was the most popular it had ever been, apparently. Thanks, Jake!

Another evening, as I returned to barracks, I saw a whole lot of Paras attired in their birthday suits chasing a prospective and equally naked night fighter down the road just outside the gates. Incidents like this were not without their disciplinary action if and when the offenders were caught.

One morning, during my service at Mons Barracks, the battalion CO, the adjutant and the company commanders were walking through the barracks conducting an inspection for needed maintenance work, when they stumbled across a few ladies of the night in the NAAFI. This didn't go down at all well and there was hell to pay. When it was enquired of the ladies as to their reasons for being present, they replied that they lived there – as they had done for the past two weeks! One of them even went on to show off the watch and other trinkets that she'd been paid by the guys in return for her affections.

A parade was called and all the companies got into formation with the RSM, the CSMs and the adjutant marching their scantily clad captives around the troops to point out all the guys they had been shagging with. Many a Para was awarded extra duties that day and some even went to the stockade.

On another occasion, a young lass arrived at the barracks HQ to complain about money missing from her purse. She explained to the CO that she had been used as the army mattress the previous night and that while she was on the job, the guys, having paid her minutes before, were stealing the money back out of her bag! There was enormous trouble in the land thereafter and sentries were posted to deny unauthorised female access to the barracks. In retrospect, it did little to hinder the passions of male youth and a neat little racket developed when the posted guards secretly organised their own lucrative business of importing female company. You just can't tame a wild animal, I guess.

In January 1970 I left for Malta. I had been on countless flights in Argosy aircraft and in C130s, although never of such a long duration. I had left most flights I was on by parachute, before the aircraft's wheels touched terra firma again, but this was the first time I was airsick. So much for my worries about our ferry ride to Belfast that had concluded without incident!

Being airsick, I imagine, is much like being seasick. Therefore the remedy would be the same. The big difference is that in a military aircraft you haven't really got a horizon to focus on. When there aren't clouds to obstruct the view of the ground, the aircraft is either travelling too high, too fast or there aren't available windows to peer out of in the first place.

I learnt this lesson well during the flight and arrived in Malta looking much as I had during my first few runs at Depot Para. With no chance to recover I squared myself away in my accommodation and paid a visit to the CO of 3 Para to check on my standing orders. Despite my rather green complexion, I didn't fail to notice the laid-back attitude among the soldiers at the barracks. I was impressed with the casualness about the place that was totally unlike Aldershot.

I learnt that a company of United States Marines were in location and that the sniper cadre were to cross-train with them for a few days. Thus began a fulfilling period of training that did much for my marksmanship as we rehearsed theoretical and practical shooting and tactics.

Although it wasn't recognised at the time, with the only recognised sniper course being conducted by the Royal Marines, we covered all the ground necessary to become fully qualified snipers.

The British military sniper weapon at the time was the old faithful L4A1, essentially a reconfigured Lee Enfield Envoy .303 rebarrelled to the NATO cartridge. This was fitted with a modified version of the No. 32 telescopic sight that was used in World War II.

The Americans made do with an upgraded, scoped version of their standard service M14 and although it was a semi–automatic weapon, not usually suited to these applications, it served their purpose well and was a superb sniper platform. Essentially it was the same weapon with which a Marine, Carlos Hancock, achieved a record distance kill of over 2 000 metres during the Vietnam War. The record would remain until it was beaten by Canadian Special Forces in Afghanistan using .50 calibre, anti-materiel sniper rifles.

A few days into our cross-training venture we paired off and shot against the Americans, on a number of different ranges, using our service weapons. With the

7.62 calibre NATO SLRs we shot poorly that day, the Marines beating us with their M14s of the same calibre and we ended up having to buy the beers after the shoot. I had always thought that the SLR was an incredible weapon, sturdy, accurate and robust, but the next day we swapped weapons and using their M14s, the Paras whitewashed the Marines. I was very impressed with the M14 thereafter and took every opportunity to fire one.

Our sniper course culminated with a day of leisure on the USS *Forrestal,* an aircraft carrier that formed part of the American fleet based in Malta at the time. The *Forrestal* had just undergone refurbishment after returning from Vietnam, where it had been involved in a serious accident. Loading napalm bombs onto an aircraft before a sortie, one of the bombs fell off, exploding and setting fire to the upper deck. Sadly, many American servicemen were killed while others were horribly disfigured.

But our day was more than satisfactory. We were given a tour of the ship and treated like foreign dignitaries. One thing I will say is that even though it was only 1970, the Americans seemed to live in the lap of luxury. Their fresh rations exceeded ours by far and their quarters, although cramped, were comfortable and clean. Much later in my life I would see how this had progressed to the verge of encouraging a soft edge among many American troops, provided as they were with all the conveniences of a modern home while on operational deployment.

The course behind me, I spent the remainder of my three-month swan in Malta, revising what I'd learnt with endless hours on the range. 3-Para, was never deployed to Libya and we enjoyed one of the most laid-back deployments ever. Of course, there were guard duties and piquets, but for the duration of the trip, I took advantage of the weather, the after-hours socials and most of all, doing what I loved best – getting in the shooting practice.

It was a far cry from my initiation in Northern Ireland and I loved every moment of it.

CHAPTER 5:
A CALL TO ARMS

On my return to Aldershot I was immediately selected for the 1 Para shooting team at Bisley, but before I could take part in any events, my aspirations were put on ice. The battalion received orders for a two-year posting in Northern Ireland, where we would be the reserve battalion for the whole operational area.

The good news was, as it was such a long posting, those of us who were married were permitted to be accompanied by our wives, who would be put up with us at Palace Barracks, Hollywood, just outside Belfast.

Sheila was overjoyed with the news and I delighted in seeing her and our son. Given short notice, she was ecstatic that she could come along this time, but was a little concerned as to the nature of the accommodation we would be provided with, particularly as we now had an addition to the family. Despite her reservations she was soon well into the swing of things and was raring to go.

For the next few months the battalion prepared for its deployment, this time allowing a greater build-up period of training for the troubles ahead. New patrol formations were designed for confrontations of the kind that we had experienced in the past. Snatch patrols were practised time in and time out, with civvy-clothed Paras acting as subversive rioters. The box formation came into being where a group of Paras forming a box with a hollow centre, shields facing outwards, would press themselves forward into the mélée to snatch identified ringleaders. As the formation neared the target individual, the box would open at the closest end and from its midst would run extra Paras to grab and drag the miscreant back into the mobile fort. The formation would then retreat into its own lines where the unfortunates could be severely dealt with.

The whole idea was to rid groups of protesters of their leaders, as it was believed that without guidance, the organisation of riots would collapse. Cut off the snake's head and the body will die.

We also trained for other eventualities. The terror campaign in Ireland continued to escalate and by mid-1970, Provisional IRA gunman were freely firing on and throwing grenades at soldiers who were trying to keep the peace. The IRA wrongly thought that the army had sided with the Protestants and brought a terror campaign to the doors of the battalions who, by this stage, took turns conducting four-month tours of duty.

With this added threat we honed our standard infantry skills in preparation to send out search patrols to engage IRA gunman in the type of battle we were trained for.

On deployment to Northern Ireland I was posted to the machine-gun (MG) platoon in Support Company. The shooting team officer, Lieutenant Tom Simpson, another Rhodesian who happened to be in 1 Para, insisted on the move as he had great visions of me climbing the ladder of rank, as well as attaining champion levels in shooting.

The MG platoon, in a way, was known as a cushy number in Northern Ireland, adversely so because they did so much work! Aside from the standard duties assigned to the infantry platoons, which they also had to do, theirs was a specialty skill requiring additional training. Thus, individuals within were more likely to be promoted. I appreciated the lieutenant's concern, but I didn't want the other guys to think that there was any favouritism. As soon as I started, I let it be known that I wanted out.

About two months later I approached the battalion Intelligence Officer, Captain Milton, as I heard there was a vacancy in the Intelligence Section. Most of all, I was tired of standing on street corners freezing my bollocks off, conducting tiring duties and having to do the MG platoon training in between. The shifts never let up and I might as well have left Sheila and Richard in Middlesbrough as I hardly ever saw them.

My application was successful and within a few short weeks I was posted to the Intelligence Section. Tom Simpson was furious and he felt that I was not only letting him down, but myself as well. I tried to explain my way out of it, but I don't think he ever came around to seeing my side.

The Intelligence Section offered me the acquisition of new skills and within a few days I was posted to Northern Ireland HQ to take part in a photography course. There I was outfitted with a 35mm SLR camera and taught a variety of methods for taking photographs.

The course was quite thorough and I would never have thought that there was so much to this photography lark. We learned to use a variety of different cameras as well as how to build hides for covert photography, blending in to our surrounds, processing film in dark rooms and a myriad of other intricacies to do with the skill. It was the first time I saw another side to soldiering and I liked what I saw.

Captain Milton even managed to get me into the office of the *Belfast Telegraph*, the local paper, to learn even more about photography and darkroom techniques. I had landed with my bum in the butter and spent two weeks working regular office hours in civvy clothes. This served not only my purpose but the family's as well and we spent many nights together as husband and wife should, enjoying home-cooked meals and whiling away the hours talking. For the first time I really began to feel like a father and part of the bigger picture. Unfortunately, it was short lived, but the nights were our own and a part of me wished it could always be like this.

At the *Telegraph* I was supplied with film and told that if I ever got any newsworthy photos, I should pass them over to them and I would receive a financial reward if the pictures made the front page. I would thus be receiving money, on the side, for any picture printed but that, in effect, was pocket money and nothing to write home about.

Again I felt a sense of achievement, having qualified as a photographer. Back at Battalion I wasted no time building a darkroom at Palace Barracks. I then put my name on the duty board of the company that was on standby. Whenever they were called out, I would deploy with them. Over the next few months I travelled to the scene of the most troublesome hot-spots in Northern Ireland.

Sometime later, having settled comfortably into my new task, I realised I would have to train one of the other guys in the Intelligence Section in the art of photography. The demands on me were coming in thick and fast and I couldn't keep up with the pace. I had somehow lapsed into ignoring Sheila again, not by choice and hardly went home as I was either on call-out, or developing the day's photos in the darkroom at night. Richard was more than a year old and I needed a break to bond with him. I took my mate Chris from the section and taught him what I knew. This helped me considerably and he would often go out in my stead, leaving his film on my desk for processing.

Work became unbearable during the lead-up to internment (imprisonment without trial) in 1971, even with the two of us, as we were required to attend and photograph every rally, gathering, funeral ceremony and parade in the province of both Catholics and Protestants. Under the internment regulations, law enforcement agents, backed up by the army, would swoop on certain known trouble-spots and arrest miscreants for prior misdemeanours and crimes and then put them in jail without trial.

The number of photos taken at each event could amount to six rolls of film, as close-ups had to be taken surreptitiously of every individual. That was only part of the task and the hard work really came in when I had to enlarge each facial picture, many of which needed enhancing and reproduce them dozens of times in the darkroom. The task was tiring and I wonder now how I ever got through it.

When internment came, the police and army used little black books filled with my photos to identify people. It was midway through 1971 and a company from 1 Para assisted 2 Para in the search-and-arrest operation.

After rounding up troublesome individuals, the police had at their disposal a means of identifying every gathering the alleged offender had attended, though often to their dismay, as they invariably denied everything. I shudder to think of the sleepless nights and hundreds of hours that Chris and I put into that little exercise, but it paid off in the long run. Years later the ID books were still being used to identify troublemakers who at the time had not yet come into prominence.

While deploying into the Ardoyne early one morning at 04:00, the platoon I was accompanying came under heavy fire. It was the second time in my life that I had been shot at and it was probably rated as the most disgusting. It happened as we crossed the Crumlin Road and we all hit the tarmac for cover, crawling off to the verges of the road. When we reached the verges, having inched forward under accurate sniper fire, we ran straight into piles of refuse and shit that had been stacked up over months! As a result of the violence in the area, the council refuse collectors hadn't ventured near the site for some time and the inhabitants of Crumlin Road had emptied their garbage, and their toilets, out of the way of their homes.

We were pinned down in a bog for hours while a sniper potted away merrily at us. As the fire drew nearer we had to crawl through more and more shit until we were covered in the stuff. The smell alone was enough to make us hurl, but we had to sit it out.

Eventually we decided to draw the sniper's fire so we could see his muzzle flashes. In fire-and-movement drills we took turns and darted across the road from house to house with the tarmac being ripped up at our feet. It was really terrifying! When my turn to draw fire came I popped my head out of the garbage and dashed to the opposite side of the road. A round ploughed into the ground behind me stinging my legs with debris.

By daybreak we had managed to take the Ardoyne with no casualties on our side. The sniper was captured, along with other Provisional IRA activists who had aided him and we dealt out our personal retribution. One of the lads found a particularly large pile of shit and buried the terrorist's face in it. So wanting for breath was he by the end of the ordeal that he inhaled, swallowing a whole lot of crap in the process.

After internment, the Catholics staged a huge uprising on the Falls Road, attended by the entire IRA. On lining up to march we were deployed to cover them, Paras six abreast, accompanied by a couple of other battalions from all over Ireland. I was with Captain Milton at the time who ordered me to approach the IRA, all attired in uniforms and berets and snap away in the hope of identifying known subversives. We approached to within 30 metres of them and I began to take pictures of their faces.

Suddenly, the guy in charge of the parade gave the order for 'eyes left' and all the terrorists turned and faced the opposite direction. They knew what I was up to and weren't going to allow me to photograph them. At the same time they were shuffling in unison towards me until the gap between us closed to about three metres. It's unnerving coming up against your enemy knowing full well that given the opportunity, they would mete out on you the most agonizing death. I could feel the hate among them and I knew they despised me more than I despised them. I didn't like what they did, but I was a professional soldier and it wasn't a personal thing with me.

I must admit that I was terrified and I expected at any moment to be taken out with a concealed handgun or by a sniper in the arrears. But my worries were needless and the incident passed as little more than a playground standoff between two schoolyard bullies.

After that, whenever we met the military wing of the IRA in tentative peaceful situations, they would wear sunglasses and cowboy-type masks tied around the back of their heads. They made no secret that in future army photographers would be a priority target for their shooters. From then on, whenever I was taking photos, I preferred to go covert.

CHAPTER 6:
SOMETHING MORE SINISTER

One night in July 1971, IRA terrorists detonated 20 bombs in Belfast alone, causing widespread carnage and mayhem. The total amount of British soldiers lost by that stage in Northern Ireland exceeded forty, most of them taken out by Provo action.

We were often called in to quell the disturbances caused by IRA bombs, many of which led to wholesale looting and general mayhem. I must say it was one of the most nerve-racking tasks, as experience had shown us that the terrorists would often set off a small explosive device, knowing full well the army would respond, followed by a larger bomb when we got there. It was the cruellest of traps and was aimed, I suppose thankfully, at military targets.

It was not always that way, however. Most bombers were indiscriminate in whom they maimed or killed and the grief they caused was ongoing. One of the worst bombings I saw occurred in the centre of Belfast in August 1971. Terrorists had phoned the local police station warning of an explosive device in one of the main streets, leaving enough time for the cops to evacuate the area. The cops arrived in force and managed to remove everyone from that street into an adjacent street, where they were told to stay and remain calm. While civilians milled around waiting for the inevitable explosion, the bombers detonated a device, a 300 kilogram car bomb, with nuts and bolts as shrapnel, right where the civilians were waiting – where the bomb had been all along. It was a clever and diabolical ploy to concentrate civilian and police targets in a preplanned killing ground; the carnage it caused was terrible.

When I arrived on the scene with the Intelligence Officer, the entire street was a mess. Around me were hundreds of casualties; some, the walking wounded, groaned and screamed helplessly and in shock. The Para battalion medics helped out where they could and came around scrounging all our field dressings to assist the ambulance crews. The car in which the bomb had been hidden, was just a twisted scrapheap, unrecognisable as to its former shape.

Everywhere I looked people lay writhing in pain.

We secured the shop windows against looters and let the medical orderlies get on with the enormous task at hand. It was evil in its cruellest form. Young men and women would have to live the rest of their lives without limbs, blinded and disfigured. The devastation was as senseless as it was complete.

After some time the police began to cordon off that area of town and started searching for other devices. I took the opportunity to record the carnage on film, but ran out after my fourth roll before the task was finished.

Countless policeman and civilians died that day while many more were injured. The images I took appear in my nightmares to this day.

Another incident, the aftermath of which I also recorded on film, occurred at a popular café in Belfast. This device, smaller but just as cruel, was left in a shopping bag under one of the coffee tables. I remember it well because of the nature of injuries it caused. When the bomb exploded underneath the tables, the table tops all but shielded the victims from the powerful shrapnel-filled blast, creating, in effect, a pattern of injury from the waist down. Many people, young and old, male and female, lost their legs that day or had to have them amputated later.

It's hard to describe the presence of evil at a scene like that. It was as if Hades had surfaced from the earth's depths for a day. Horror was the intrusive ploy on the Devil's playground.

I often felt much the same as I imagine police crime photographers do; only the incidents I captured on film were more frequent and brutal. I was forever attending scenes to photograph the evidence of IRA crimes. The worst, I suppose, was when I was called out to take pictures of dead and injured civilians and squaddies. It doesn't make for good morale to see your comrades broken, dismembered and lifeless, spread out like mincemeat across the tarmac.

The bombers back then may have employed crude technology, but it appeared to me that they made up for it in cruel intention and devilish savvy. On more than one occasion I was surprised by the depth of planning that went into their murderous actions.

In the Ardoyne area of Belfast a bomb was once floated down the sewerage drains, on a large boat-like platform, towards a military sangar (lookout post).

The idea was that when it passed under the army post it would detonate, causing damage inside. Fortunately for us, the device was rigged with a timed fuse and had been set to explode at a precise moment when the platform reached the end of a pre-measured length of string.

The sewerage flow that day was not as it had been when the terrorists practised their dummy runs and although the bomb exploded on time, it happened before it reached its target. It probably got snagged up owing to the shallow run. Just outside the sangar a huge explosion ripped a five-by-five-metre hole in the road, but casualties were avoided. Thank goodness for the bowel movements of the locals that day. I hate to think what might have happened if more toilets had been flushed!

Other devices the terrorists used indiscriminately were pipe bombs, nail bombs and home-made Claymores, all in effect the same thing when observing the damage they caused. Virtually every night the windows in our quarters at Palace Barracks would rattle as another bomb erupted in the distance.

Returning to Palace Barracks with C Company one day, we were lucky to escape a car bomb that detonated 30 seconds behind our motor transport. The whole road behind us disappeared in an enormous thump and cloud of smoke as we rounded a corner. The bomb, we discovered later, had not been set for us, but we were unlucky enough to have been there at the time. The target was a pub down the road that known Protestant officials frequented.

The terrorists even managed to get into Palace Barracks one night and lay a device in one of the armoured Saracens in the Motor Transport section. The bomb blew the vehicle to bits, but there were no casualties as it detonated during the early hours of the morning. It did give us a wakeup call. Rumours abounded that the IRA had moles in 1 Para Battalion.

CHAPTER 7:
OF PEEPING TOMS AND PIRATES

I was often used on sneaky jobs with the Military Reaction Force (MRF) guys from D (Patrol) Company. These men were affectionately known as the 'Secret Squirrels'.

D Company were allowed to grow their hair and wear civilian clothing, running around like 007s most of the time, catching rides on buses, hoping to get hijacked. These tasks required a higher security clearance level than the standard soldier, so I should have been checked out by Special Branch. Whether I was or not, I don't know, but they needed a photographer anyway.

One such job was at Roger Casement Park, a sporting facility that served Belfast. The facility was complete with a club frequented by known IRA terrorists.

In the dark of a winter night, three of us snuck into the grounds dressed like Ninjas and we hid out in the score box for three days. The idea was to look like IRA terrorists, if we were spotted, as they themselves were so brazen in the area that our presence would hardly raise an eyebrow. The job was a dangerous one as the areas surrounding the park were sympathetic towards the IRA.

Aside from our black kit we also donned black balaclavas and carried 9mm Browning pistols in shoulder holsters. I had a black gas mask bag in which I carried my camera kit and spare mags for the Browning. We each took along a Stirling 9mm SMG – with two magazines taped together in case we got into the shit – and individual rations for up to four days. The third man on our team was a radio operator who carried a transmission set. Water was available on site from a tap outside the hut, which had been identified on a previous reconnaissance.

I managed to photograph through a telephoto lens every individual who came and went from the club, over a three-day period. I had taken the precaution of upgrading the film for night use and the photos were good. With just a little enhancement back at the lab, they could be used for ID purposes.

Our jolly little jaunt was compromised on the third night when one of the other lads took a leak outside the hut. A group of kids playing football in the grounds below saw him and we decided that discretion was the better part of valour, despite our disguises, as the real IRA might be on to us within the hour. I was quite pleased with having to abandon our position, as for three nights in the dead of winter we had almost frozen to death with little in the way of warm clothing. Had the untimely piss not compromised us, I have no doubt that our chattering teeth would have done so sooner or later.

On our withdrawal we had a small problem. We couldn't raise the call-sign that controlled our area of exit. The radio was malfunctioning and in our haste we didn't have time to assess the problem. Leaving the grounds, we ran a few blocks, rounded a corner and ran smack into the patrol. It was dark and I had visions of us being misidentified and shot as IRA terrorists, as the whole patrol dived for cover. Fortunately one of my team mates, obviously thinking the same thing, threw his arms in the air and managed to convince them of our real identity. It was a very close shave and could well have ended in tears.

While I was in the Intelligence Section, C Company, we were put on standby to react to an incident at Magilligan Internment Camp, near Londonderry, on the shores of one of the lochs. I deployed with them early one morning to photograph the scene but, as always, I carried my riot gear and a weapon as well. The Royal Green Jackets were the on-site battalion at the time but had in the past received a pasting at the hands of protesters. The Paras were called in, as insurance that it didn't happen again.

Intelligence was received that a large group of IRA sympathisers were going to cross the loch in boats and would arrive at the shore to confront the military and protest the 'illegal' internment of certain IRA characters.

When we arrived, the loch was dead quiet and a thick fog hung over the still water, restricting visibility to about ten metres. Green Jackets were pacing up and down the beach nervously, their boots crunching against the loose pebbles. Nothing much was going on and we mingled for a few hours, Paras puffing at smokes and sharing a joke or two with the RGJ guys.

Two-and-a-quarter hours later, just when we were thinking it was a false alarm, a murmur of distant voices was heard over our casual banter. An instant hush settled across the beach as soldiers stopped pacing, cigarettes were extinguished and eyes peered across the bay into the dense fog. Soon the slop of paddles could be heard and above that, the sounds of incantation as the voices grew in pitch and penetrated the blanket mist. It seemed like hours, but was in fact a few minutes, before we recognised the sad melancholy of an Irish dirge. It ascended in pitch again as the sound drew nearer and the first wooden bow loomed through the milky daylight toward the pebbly shore, pushing a frosty wave before it. The Jackets shifted nervously, Paras among them, as webbing belts were fastened and batons and rifles changed hands.

Soon there were two boats, then three and suddenly 20 and they just kept pouring through the fog across a wide front.

When it arrived, the armada was laden with wheelbarrows full to the brim with rocks and other missiles that they planned to hurl at the Royal Green Jackets. It was a fantastic sight and reminiscent of days gone by, when the British or Spanish fleets squared off against each other's shore-based garrisons. The protesters were completely unaware of the Paras' presence and expected to find a soft target on the beach where they were to land. Even before they reached shore, many were already standing up and hurling rocks and other objects into our midst.

The dirge faded over the next thirty seconds and it was replaced with vulgar proclamations directed at the troops. Above the cacophony of near-battle I heard rude references towards our mothers and others that were dear to us.

For a moment time was frozen, neither side sure of the others' reaction, but they kept on coming until the first bow scraped sand. Suddenly, as if given an order, the Paras surged forward among them, wading waist-deep into the icy water to close with their foe. The Jackets remained where they stood, only involving themselves when stragglers broke through into their ranks in a desperate flight for sanctuary.

The protestors never knew what hit them. Individuals were pulled by the scruff of their necks right out of the boats and dunked unceremoniously into the water, followed through with butts and boots to their ribs and heads. The brave cries we had heard only minutes ago, changed into pleas for mercy, but C Company were unrelenting as they continued to pour their anger into a now pitiful adversary.

Other photographers representing newspapers and magazines had gathered on shore before the battle and snapped away with their cameras. I saw one photographer take a close-up of a Para as he booted a cardigan-clad, prostrate figure floundering in the shallow wash. The picture made the front page the next day with the bold caption 'Paras put the boot in!' It served only to solidify the reputation we had begun to cultivate.

In other quarters, after the incident, utterances were made of brutality and excessive force. Even a Green Jackets officer, who was on the scene, a man I think we had saved, castigated us. He was appalled by our tactics and behaviour, he said in an interview later.

The attitude among us at the time was one of nonchalance. Most of us had seen how the Catholics and Protestants operated and we felt our hands were tied. If they could use dirty tactics, why shouldn't we? Was it necessary to compensate for their dangerous and brutal behaviour; to make allowances for the fact that they were civilians, some of the time at least, while we were soldiers? Most of us didn't see why we had to treat known terrorists with kid gloves after we had seen our mates blown apart by IRA bombs. You don't pull a knife at a gunfight. That's when you see your arse.

Many Paras carried banned weapons when on riot duty in the form of coshes and knuckledusters. I heard stories of some men going as far as carrying pellet pistols and silenced .22s, although I never saw any myself.

A dirty tactic we did enjoy was dropping troublemakers in their respective adversary's strongholds. For instance, when we found a particularly troublesome Protestant, whom we knew would walk once he was given his civil rights, we would take him for a drive to the Catholic area and drop him slap-bang in the middle of it. This did little to satisfy our sense of retribution unless, of course, we then heralded his presence to the local Catholics, or vise versa.

We thought little of the individual's wellbeing considering the verbal abuse we so often got. Much of the time they believed we would never actually go through with our threats and they told us so. It was grim satisfaction seeing the look of worry on their faces as we pulled away and their foe descended on them.

I also heard stories of other Paras provoking hot-headed mobs of Catholic youths in an effort to provoke retaliation which they could then match with further violence.

It must be understood that the policies in Ireland at the time favoured the sectarian groups, much as political correctness, or bleeding-heart liberalism, seeps in to undermine modern society at times. The people we were dealing with knew just how far to go, which was a pretty long way, before the gloves came off. With our hands firmly bound behind our backs, we thought that the Irish should solve their own problems, even if it meant us contributing in a small way.

CHAPTER 8:
SUNDAY, BLOODY SUNDAY

The following week we turned our berets inside out so that the black inner hid the maroon outer. We also hid the Para badge, as well as the disruptive pattern smocks that distinguished us as paratroopers and headed north once again to Londonderry.

I travelled with TAC HQ to a car park just outside Londonderry, predominantly a Catholic area, armed with a Sterling SMG. Here the battalion was assembling in dribs and drabs. I was pretty used to being out in the cold at that time of morning, but another kind of chill crept down my spine as we arrived in the deserted car park. A dark sense of foreboding was at the back of my mind and did little to comfort the hollow pit that was my empty stomach.

I had taken my camera kit and additional film, as I had an inkling that something big was going to happen that day. It's hard to describe the feeling that was inherent in all of us at the time. Word was that the Provisional IRA (or Provos) were planning to exact retribution for having their arses kicked at Magilligan and we expected some blood would be spilt. At the time we thought it would be ours.

Security was very tight as it was thought that gunman may be hiding somewhere, lying in wait for the security forces, or that a bomb might have been planted along one of the routes we would take. For this reason, trucks full of Paras arrived from different directions over the next hour, having taken alternative roads to Londonderry.

Before leaving, we had taken the Paras Pegasus stickers off our vehicles as another precaution to disguise our identity. With unmarked vehicles, black turned-out berets and hidden Denison smocks, we felt confident we would not attract undue publicity. The fallout from Magilligan the week before had not subsided and the Paras were public enemy number one.

In the car park we milled about for some time waiting to be deployed. It was in the early hours of Sunday, 30 January 1972. We didn't know it yet but that day would live in infamy as Bloody Sunday.

A Catholic civil rights group was about to embark on a march to protest against army brutality as well as against the other things they usually protested about.

1-Para, now commanded by Lieutenant Colonel Derek Wilford, was trying to keep the peace during the march which had already been declared illegal, but the organisers decided to go ahead with it anyway, declaring that neither the army, or anybody else for that matter, was going to stop them.

I was posted to A Company on one of the flanks and told that we probably wouldn't see any action. I gave my spare camera to one of my pals, who would be on another corner and asked him to take photos just in case I didn't get into the scrap.

We lurked discreetly in the background for a few hours, before the marchers could be seen and heard approaching towards one of the military barricades. From where I was I could see that it included a large number of young men of about military age, who were soon throwing bricks and paving stones at the waiting soldiers.

I took a few pictures from where I stood and then went with the Intelligence Section officer to a barricade at the end of the road. Through the bitter smoke of tear gas it wasn't easy for me to find my way without running headlong into trouble.

The barricade was manned by craphats from an infantry battalion, who jostled nervously as the crowd drew near. Once they arrived, a few individuals shouted hateful abuse at the soldiers and hurled missiles in their direction. It looked as if things were getting out of hand fast.

A craphat officer took up a loudspeaker and warned the protestors to disperse. He had been given orders that no-one should pass the barrier, but it was obvious that the protesters thought differently. I slung my weapon and took up position with my camera, taking cover by a wall a short distance back, as the crowd erupted into a full-blown riot. Soon gas and bricks were being thrown all over the place.

It stands to reason that, as an Intelligence Section photographer, I would be scanning the entire area, looking for interesting shots (perhaps more than the average

Para on the ground could have seen), so I think I had a decent view of what went on. Of course, I couldn't be everywhere at once, but at least I didn't have to think of my mates' welfare, only of my own and I wasn't laden with the responsibility of being a member of one of the sections.

Despite that, from my perspective, I was as confused as the rest of them.

It wasn't long before a shot rang out but I could not say from which direction it came. I heard later that the shot was fired by Provos who were mingling among the civilian demonstrators and it was aimed in the direction of the Paras. All hell was breaking loose and there was a feeling among us that we were being set up and that vengeance was at the fore of Provo action as retribution for Magilligan.

When things got out of hand and the police and army could no longer cope, the Paras were called forward from the flanks to engage the protestors in a pincer movement and to make as many arrests as possible. The Paras always did boast that they were good at that sort of thing with the slogan 'one para, one arrest'; cocky little bastards that we were!

Within minutes the Paras displayed their army-issue Denison smocks, turned their berets the correct way around and overran the barricades as Support Company and C Company laid into the rioters. Mayhem ensued when the rioters realised they were dealing with the Paras and a human stampede developed. They panicked, many of them dropping whatever weapons they had and ran for the Bogside.

I wasn't at the front when the shooting started in earnest, but according to the incident reports I saw later, it began when a couple of Paras shot a young lad as he tried to ignite a nail bomb. Crude though it was, this explosive device was capable of causing severe injury and even death as it contained six-inch (15 centimetre) nails as shrapnel, wrapped around a core of plastic explosive. In effect, it was a home-made fragmentation grenade, only more lethal.

Other mates of mine told me that it started when some clown opened up on the Paras with a .45 Thompson submachine gun. For his trouble he was shot dead in the process.

The sound of gunfire intensified at the front and I ran forward for a better shot. I could hear that the reports were not emanating from the rubber-dick guns (affectionate term the Paras used for rubber baton charge guns as the projectile resembled a big rubber penis) which some of the Paras had. The baton guns made a hollow thump compared to the SLRs' resonant boom. In the distance I could see Paras leaning into their rifles as they took aim at targets that I could not see. It seemed to me they were moving forward as if in a fire-and-movement drill.

A policeman, ducking into a doorway, yelled for me to take cover. He warned me that the Provos had placed snipers in the buildings, but I wasn't sure of that. I joined him where he was and I remember him telling me that in the fifteen years he had been on the force he had never seen anything as chaotic as this. That was pretty strong coming from a Northern Ireland cop!

The amount of gunfire, I must say, seemed unlike a one-sided battle. On active service in the regiment, every shot has to be accounted for and an incident report has to be filled out if a weapon is discharged. From the reports later it certainly appeared that more gunfire was heard than rounds accounted for.

A few other policemen joined us and I moved forward with them, heeding the previous warning, as we took cover door to door.

On reaching the corner of the road I could see Paras running forward, rifles still into their shoulders, but I still couldn't see what they were shooting at. The crowd was thick at that point and it obstructed my view.

I made sure I was out of the firing line and ducked behind a wall with the cops. A Para joined us, offering little in the way of explanation. He did tell me that Provos had fired shots at the barricades. My heart raced and as seasoned as I was, I recognised a feeling of sheer disbelief inside me, not because I knew that people were probably dying at the hands of my mates, but at the absolute audacity of the situation. Above the noise I heard Paras screaming the 'all clear' as a single shot echoed off into the distance. I yearned to know what had transpired, but I couldn't just dash into the fracas as it was far too dangerous.

I don't know how much time passed, but I would say it was about fifteen minutes since the shooting began. Confusion reigned across the street as I moved towards a bunch of C Company guys who had gathered together groups of civilians and wounded.

About me other civilians wandered about aimlessly, shock apparent on their pallid faces. I remember seeing one man searching the ground, walking in circles, as if he was looking for something.

On the road, spread over a large area, lifeless bodies lay where they had fallen. I half expected them to get up, but then I saw large pools of blood around them. Some of the wounds were grotesque. A 7.62mm projectile - travelling at 823 metres per second - causes severe damage when its path is impeded by skull and bones. I took some pictures of the carnage, but my pace slowed when the enormity of it hit me. It had all happened so fast that I was in a daze, unsure if I was in the place I was supposed to be at the time.

Moments later I was called back to the Intelligence officer. A whole heap of suspects had been rounded up and their pictures needed to be taken. One thing that struck me was how soon the ambulances arrived, waving white handkerchiefs out their windows, as if they'd been prepped for the occasion. It seemed to me that someone knew that people were going to die that day and had pre-orchestrated the event for propaganda purposes. I think they might have expected the Paras to get brutal with a few strategic shots.

The official count of dead was thirteen. Guys, who had been at the front, told me later that they thought there were more. We had learnt in the past that the IRA would remove weapons from the bodies of their gunmen to make it appear that the deceased person had been an innocent participant. The actual terrorists didn't have to do this as they had sympathetic civilians who were involved in the battles to do it for them. A search of the area, including stormwater drains, revealed no firearms although we had found them in such places in the past after similar incidents.

The IRA masterminded this propaganda tactic in order to get maximum publicity in the press. Of course, there were many press people who sympathised with them and it didn't bode well for our cause. The pen is mightier than the sword!

Although there had been many women and children among the marchers that day, all of the dead were young men of fighting age. Although no weapons were found at the scene, individual incident reports later revealed that they had been there.

I was privy to the reports, filed through the Intelligence Section, which told of further casualties that just didn't add up. Perhaps several Paras were claiming the same kill, something one wouldn't normally do because of the red tape involved and possible legal action taken against the shooter. In terms of all these reports there should have been more than 20 bodies on the streets that day. Furthermore, every soldier in Northern Ireland had to carry a Yellow Card in his left breast pocket. Ostensibly this entailed his orders for when to open fire. If you were caught without it, you could be charged with an offence. If you happened to fire your weapon without it, you would be in big shit! In other words, military bureaucracy would have you consult your card before any incident – you would have to read through it and decide under which authority you were going to fire your weapon. Unless you had military law down pat, a man could die in the time it took to look it up. One authority permitting a soldier to open fire at that time was if a person was seen carrying a petrol bomb. There were no petrol bombs on Bloody Sunday, but the Para who opened fire on the pipe-bomb-wielding rioter was justified in taking the action he took. The petrol-bomb clause was later deleted from the Yellow Card, resulting in a lot of horrific burns on British soldiers serving in Northern Ireland.

Back with the Intelligence officer, I took photos of more than 40 arrested individuals. When I was finished, they were packed like mules into the back of trucks and driven, under guard, to the local police station.

Behind me the shooting had died some minutes before. The Paras, order restored, advanced towards the Bogside but were ordered back. We were told that IRA terrorists had set up an ambush and were waiting for us with automatic weapons if we followed the fleeing demonstrators. It was said that this had been part of their strategy all the time.

C Company was ordered back to the car park and I joined my mates on the way. The conversation was slow and it was hard to get any sense out of them. I think we all knew that something had gone terribly wrong. A bridge had been crossed that day. Not one of the guys I spoke to was ashamed of his actions, as they all thought they had done their duty and followed orders; but there was bitterness among them for being drawn into the quagmire in the first place.

That night we stayed at the local military barracks in Derry with TAC HQ and drove back to Belfast the next day. On the way we passed through Shankill Road, the Protestant area and received a heroes' welcome. I remembered my initiation to Northern Ireland on that very road years before at the hands of these people – and I said a silent 'fuck you' as we rumbled by. Hundreds of them lined the streets clapping their hands and cheering as if their local football club was returning from a won game. On the walls behind them, slapped on with whitewash in big, bold print, was written 'Paras 13, Londonderry 0.'

The covert work continued in the Intelligence Section after Bloody Sunday. There was an unending demand for evidence to support police cases and I had scarcely a moment to breathe. I was involved in lots of jobs, sneaking around the place with an escort at my back in case of trouble. In the aftermath of Bloody Sunday the army had a case to prove and I was tasked to track many of the subversives and organisers responsible for the carnage that resulted that day.

In many of these tasks I would have to conduct a prior reconnaissance, to ascertain positions from where I could shoot. This would require dry runs past a certain area on foot, in civilian clothes, to check which buildings were occupied and which were not. Once I'd found a building that offered a loft, or the like, from which I could observe a target area, I could then plan to infiltrate it, most often during the hours of darkness.

I was forever climbing into attics and rooms in grubby, dusty buildings – many condemned as uninhabitable and due for destruction – in my search for the perfect hide. I must say I became quite good at it.

Often, once satisfied I was secure in my hide, I would set up my camera a distance back from a dusty window and shoot pictures through the tiny breaks and cracks in the glass.

On one occasion I was joined in a loft by an officer from the Coldstream Guards. His patrol was downstairs covering an IRA funeral march with some of the guys from 1 Para. The crowd was giving the Paras the usual Nazi salute which, unbeknown to them, our guys loved. It was quite a sight.

I had snapped a few images for the photo album, when a lieutenant came up to me. He stood next to me and was peering through a small hole in the roof tiles above the window where I was perched – and then suddenly – he was gone. All that was left of him, on either side of the hole he had fallen through, were two pattern-58 webbing pouches, neatly lying where they had ripped off his belt. He had stood on a rotten patch of weatherboard and disappeared in a cloud of dust, falling a couple of floors to the basement below. It was quite comical and I couldn't stop myself laughing. Some of the guys on the floor where he landed were in stitches and were rolling about the place uncontrollably. Luckily for us he also saw the funny side of it, otherwise we might have been put on a charge.

It reminded me of the Looney Tunes cartoon where Wiley Coyote, forever at the receiving end, disappears through a perfectly coyote-shaped hole. Luckily for him, the officer's webbing pouches had given way, otherwise he might have been stuck in the ceiling at waist level for quite some time. I think even some of the Catholics found it amusing. However, the incident put an end to my undercover photography.

Another task was photographing all the arrested people, who allegedly had been involved in the riots. The photos were needed for court cases later, when the guys would pitch up in suits with closely-cropped haircuts, each one claiming he was someone else. It was important to get facial profiles, as at the time of their arrest they were often scroungy-looking individuals with long hair and flaring bell bottoms, which were the fashion at the time. With my close-ups they rarely got away with their assertions and my photos helped incarcerate innumerable troublemakers.

CHAPTER 9:
PRIVATES, PLANES AND PARIAHS

There was small reprieve from the deluge of work, but even life in the Paras had a lighter side to it and not everything I witnessed revolved around killing and death. Quite a few characters I became acquainted with went on to win fame and notoriety at later stages of their lives. When I knew them they hadn't quite got there yet, but were well on their way to making an impression. Some of them provided us with interesting entertainment as a result of their foolhardy antics, others with their quest for prominence, fame and riches.

Private Seedy was one such guy. He had been in the army for 18 years without promotion and at his age he was used more as a runner, often seen about the place as he sped between buildings on his bicycle, delivering messages. Whenever we saw him we exchanged pleasantries in a good-natured, but humorous manner which, unbeknown to us, he resented. 'Hey Seedy, better stay on that bike for as long as you can 'cause it's the only ride you gonna get' sort of thing.

Feeling sorry for him, given that he had not progressed in life for such a long period, the Battalion CO decided one morning to give him a stripe and promote him to lance corporal. With his new status, by that afternoon, he had put more people on charge than all the NCOs combined could have done in a week!

'Hey Seedy, what's with that stripe on your arm? Did a crow shit on you?' was the most common utterance. 'That's it Private, you're addressing a senior rank. You're on a charge, son.' he would retort.

Needless to say, by the afternoon of the day he was promoted, he had incited so much red tape and paperwork that he was demoted to his former rank. He had managed to stay a lance corporal for an admirable six-and-a-half hours.

While I was at Mons Barracks, at another time, an incident occurred which nearly landed us in more trouble than we could handle. A certain corporal and I, sharing guard duty, had taken a fascination to the aerial sorties of the model aircraft club, that used a strip adjacent to the barracks to land their radio-controlled planes.

On Sundays, when they got together, we were entertained to impressive displays of air rallies that filled the sky, with expensive model aircraft whining overhead.

We always kept on hand four pellet guns back in the barracks, which we would use (to relieve the boredom) by engaging in small wars – much as I had done as a teenager in Rhodesia. The guns were relegated to the guardroom after someone inadvertently shot another Para through the cheek.

Bored to tears one Sunday, we decided to take pot shots at the aircraft as they flew above the depot, thinking that we could never do any damage to such fast-flying machines. Before long, four of us were banging away at a solitary aircraft as it gracefully dipped to turn over the entrance. We had created an effective four-barrelled anti-aircraft battery!

As the plane levelled after a turn, it gave a bit of a jig, pitched right and then left and headed away from the strip towards Basingstoke canal. We all gulped as we realised we had managed to sever one of its control cables with a pellet. We watched, panic-stricken, as the plane continued on its course and disappeared from sight.

On the strip a man ran after it, turning knobs and twiddling with joysticks. From where we stood we heard him swearing and cursing at his misfortune.

The airguns were hidden away immediately and we resumed our duties. As every minute passed we waited for the cops to arrive, wondering all the time if we'd been seen. Later that night, while sitting in the guardroom, the military police phoned to ask if we knew anything about the expensive missing aircraft. I took the call and naturally denied everything, although I thought I sensed a bit of disbelief in the policeman's tone.

The next day the same cop got hold of me and asked me to organise a search party to look over the Basingstoke canal area. Gleefully I learnt that a reward had been posted for the aircraft's safe return. A company of us went in search of the downed plane, but as luck would have it, the search was in vain. Unfortunately, the plane had vanished without trace. Naturally, the reward was not forthcoming. We hoped we would have better luck searching for real downed pilots – another eventuality we trained for in wartime situations.

Another delinquent I served with was Nick 'Nobby' Hall, although his shenanigans resulted in more dire consequences.

Nick, a bit of a 'Jack the lad' with strong political convictions, served as the Intelligence officers' bodyguard and later progressed to the Intelligence Section serving alongside myself, in an intelligence-gathering capacity. His appointment to the section opened up new contacts for him and he was soon big chums with many officials from the Protestant sector. He made no secret of the fact that his sympathies lay with the Protestants and he was often very vocal about how the war should be run against the IRA, as he saw it, without any restrictions. He resented the political constraints placed on the army and he thought we would all be far better off if we took the war to the terrorists. This eventually led to a two-year prison sentence after he was caught selling arms to his Protestant pals.

I suppose you could say that, in a way I was an accessory to his crimes. I didn't take part in the deal but I did know about it before it happened, as he had asked me if I wanted to be involved. At the time I thought that it would never take place and that the idea would eventually die. Nick was forever the idealist and came up with all sorts of scatterbrained schemes that never materialised. The arms deal was just another such scheme as far as I was concerned.

As it transpired, Nick managed to steal the key to the TAC HQ armoury one evening and he absconded with six SLR rifles and a few Sterling submachine guns, which he passed on to the Protestant Ulster Volunteer Force in a premeditated deal. It didn't take the army long to figure out what had happened. Within a few days of him going AWOL, he was arrested and incarcerated.

It wasn't until 1975 that I heard of Nick again. I had left the Paras by then and returned to Rhodesia. While I was waging war against African nationalists, Nick was gaining a reputation for himself among the ladies in another part of Africa and specifically in the nightclubs of Kinshasa, Zaire, where he was serving as Holden Roberto's personal bodyguard.

Holden Roberto was a suave African leader who had a dream of a non-Marxist, independent Angola. The brother-in-law of Mobuto Sese Seko, president of Zaire, Roberto had formed the FNLA in 1960, to oppose the then Portuguese rulers of Angola. In 1961 the FNLA initiated a guerrilla war that was to last for 13 years, until Portugal's leader Marcello Caetano was ousted in a coup led by the socialist idealist António de Spinola. Shortly thereafter, in 1974, the Portuguese fled Angola, leaving its governance in the hands of the Marxist MPLA, the strongest of the three nationalist factions at the time. Roberto's FNLA and UNITA, led by Jonas Savimbi, continued to fight against the new rulers and were backed by covert American and later, South African, assistance.

Nick, true to his idealistic nature, had managed to involve himself with Holden's organisation as part of a mercenary force recruited by John Banks for Angola. Whether he actually did any fighting remains to be substantiated. Accounts of the campaign, that have subsequently come to light, reveal that other than a few trips across the border into Angola, he preferred the social side of things, swaggering about in crisp military uniform, chatting up the local ladies at bars and nightclubs. It certainly sounded like the Nick that I knew.

Other acquaintances of mine also travelled to Angola, as mercenaries for John Banks' private army. One of the more ambitious characters was Costas Georgiou. I met Georgiou in 1 Para when I first started my service. A Greek Cypriot by birth, he was a fiercely competitive and aggressive individual who, surprisingly, took to army life in a casual transition from his Greek Orthodox Christian upbringing. The difference between Nick and Costas was that the latter didn't really care who he fought for, as long as he got himself into a good war, with the prospect of financial gain.

Likewise, hamstrung by the political restraints in Northern Ireland, Costas felt robbed of his rights as a soldier. Why should he fire rubber bullets and tear gas when he could be firing the real thing?

Costas and a few disillusioned mates of mine, one day decided to rob a post office in Bangor, using military weapons. The huge haul of £93 was hardly worth the effort.

It wasn't hard for the police to nab the culprits when the post office staff told them that the robbers all carried Sterling submachine guns, spoke with British accents and had short hair. The fact that they wore masks did little to hide these obvious military traits – and when the battalion minibus was seen in Bangor that day, the police jumped to natural conclusions. The robbers were all arrested within twenty-four hours and sent to prison for five years.

When Georgiou arrived in Angola in 1975, it was initially in his capacity as a medical orderly to assist Donald Belford, a FNLA sympathiser and close personal friend of Holden Roberto. For reasons not entirely apparent he had changed his name to Tony Callan.

Georgiou, eager for action, had circumvented Nick Hall's plans and contacted Belford behind his back. Nick was the first to offer his services to the

FNLA, through Belford, and it was he who originally phoned Georgiou about the lucrative contract. Georgiou didn't care much about money, so he said, and was keen to get into a war zone to assist the underdogs with his military prowess. Belford admired these traits and together they flew to Kinshasa with Colin Taylor, Belford's personal bodyguard, for an introduction to Holden.

I heard much later that Georgiou's initial attraction might have been in the form of a vast treasure of FNLA diamonds which, Taylor had told him, were being stored in a vault at the FNLA's HQ in Carmona, a small town in northern Angola. These claims are unsubstantiated as the diamonds were either removed or never found at all.

For the first part of his stay in Africa it is believed that Callan actually did some good, travelling across the Zaire/Angola border with Belford, to field hospitals to treat the wounded. On one of these trips he ran into some Portuguese mercenaries, who told him of the intense fighting between the MPLA and FNLA. The FNLA could not hold their own against the military might of its adversary and were retreating in disarray towards the border.

The stories stirred Callan's enthusiasm for the fight, but he continued with his task, remaining in Carmona while Belford and Taylor returned to Kinshasa.

On 18 December 1975 Callan woke up late, wondering why the guard had allowed him to oversleep. Peering through the window he was confronted with the sight of a T34 tank belonging to the MPLA and he correctly concluded that, overnight, the FNLA had retreated, deserting him in Carmona.

Grabbing a weapon he managed to find his way out of town and caught up with the FNLA at Negage, twenty-five kilometres distant.

With Belford and Taylor now out of the way, Callan felt it was about time to exert his authority and go back to being a soldier.

Organising a rearguard action, he enlisted the help of two Portuguese mercenaries for a counter-attack on Carmona. By this stage, word was received that a large MPLA column, complete with tanks, armoured fighting vehicles and 'Stalin Organ' multiple rocket launchers, was advancing on Negage.

Together, with the two mercenaries, Callan retraced his steps to engage the MPLA in combat.

There is no accurate picture of what transpired next, but from most accounts it is believed that the small force, led by Callan, attacked the vastly numerically superior MPLA column and routed it. One account paints a picture of Callan running about the place like a demented demon, firing LAW 66 rockets at tanks and vehicles, causing utter confusion and mayhem among the enemy. The same report claims that the three mercenaries, but particularly Callan, destroyed four 'Stalin Organs' and numerous tanks, and killed more than sixty enemy personnel. If that is at all accurate, it is no wonder that Callan showed such a huge ego later, when he gloated over the guerrilla war that everyone made such a fuss about!

Whatever transpired, when reports of the attack reached Holden Roberto, he was so impressed that he immediately promoted Callan to the rank of colonel and made him overall commander of the FNLA army. It was a rags-to-potential-riches opportunity that gave Callan the autonomy to do as he pleased.

The rest is history, but certain facts of the campaign deserve further mention. With the notorious 'Colonel Callan', the FNLA temporarily looked as though they might have a hope of successfully closing with the MPLA in combat. What actually happened over the next few months, however, was a series of desperate rearguard actions conducted by Callan's mercenaries, as the MPLA's war machine gained momentum, dropping FNLA-held towns in its wake, like skittles in a bowling alley.

There is no doubting Callan's bravery as he fought an impossible battle against superior odds. However, he went overboard with his ruthlessness and the campaign was pockmarked with murders and atrocities.

In the short time that Callan commanded the FNLA army, he was personally responsible for murdering hundreds of people, military and civilian, both black and white.

Further testimony came to light when Scotland Yard investigated reports of the deaths of fourteen British nationals at Maquela. The mercenaries, having recently arrived in Angola – mostly to fill non-combatant roles – were executed by automatic-weapon fire after a comedy of errors which resulted in a blue-on-blue attack on friendly forces.

Callan was infuriated by the incident and sent some of his men, ex-Paras whom I knew among them, to gun down the offenders in a grisly massacre. Callan himself shot the first man, 22-year-old Philip Davies, on the parade square when he admitted to having been part of the fiasco. Casually walking up to him with an apologetic grin on his face, he drew his 9mm Browning pistol and declared 'This is the only law here'. With that he fired three rounds into the man's head. Philip Davies had been in Angola for all of three days.

On other occasions Callan, Charlie Christodoulou ('Shotgun Charlie' – so-called because of the shotgun he carried and couldn't wait to test on human flesh) and Mick Wainhouse – other Paras I knew from our Northern Ireland stomping grounds – ruthlessly tortured men to death merely because they didn't like the look of them, or because they seemed out of place.

At a bridge outside a small town, they used to line up locals on the road, accuse them of petty crimes or of being in the wrong place at the wrong time and dispatch them with shots to the back of the head, watching their bodies fall into the river below. It really was a display of the most abysmal human temperament, as they laughed at the terror they could wield through the barrel of a gun. Often their first shots were not successful and they would fire at their victims maniacally as they thrashed about in the water, terrified or maimed.

I even heard of a report where Callan called over one of his own troops who doubled over to him and snapped his heels to attention. As he stood there Callan raised the .44 magnum revolver he'd wanted to test and blew the man's brains out.

These stories appalled me and did little for the Paras' reputation. Yes, we were aggressive, sometimes ruthless soldiers, but Callan, a psychotic murderer, was a bad apple in the barrel. He became highly unpopular when these stories were aired. And to think I used to socialise with him over a few pints at the pub.

Callan eventually got his just deserts and was captured by the MPLA on the run after an ambush. He and another thirteen captured mercenaries were incarcerated, or executed by firing squad after a highly publicised trial. The execution was a fiasco in itself and Callan was, unfortunately, one of two men to die relatively quickly and with some dignity. Having been scheduled for three o'clock in the afternoon on Saturday 21 July 1976, after months of incarceration, four men were marched out onto a field in the blazing sun. There they remained for two-and-a-half hours while the firing squad and assembled viewers awaited the late arrival of the Angolan minister of justice.

When the execution actually took place, Callan stood to attention as if on parade. Defiant to the end it was almost as if he wished that the bullets would strike him effectively and accurately. When the order to fire was finally given Callan fell – shot through the gut and with two rounds through the chest, ending it relatively quickly for him. Andy McKenzie, a Briton, also died almost instantly.

The other two who were shot, Daniel Gearheart, an American who had not fired a single round in the war and Brummie Barker, another Briton, were dispatched in a messy display of incompetence attended by MPLA officials and foreign dignitaries.

Gearheart, wounded in the collar bone, lay screaming on the ground as the officer in charge of the firing squad ran up to him firing his pistol in an attempt to finish him off. Most rounds actually missed but the officer did succeed in wounding the man further. Gearheart's cries only grew shriller and eventually the officer emptied his pistol, at close range, into the mercenary's head before dropping it in panic and running from the field.

Barker, captured separately from Callan, as he tried to save others at San Antonia when it was taken by the MPLA, was missed entirely by the five riflemen assigned to each condemned man. He was shot in the head when he woke up on a stretcher as his body was carried to an ambulance by the side of the field. A doctor had already declared him dead.

Such are the wages of war.

When I joined the Paras, 85 percent of the recruits on my course were either juvenile offenders or jailbirds, having been arrested for petty crimes like assault and grievous bodily harm. Most had only joined the army to escape incarceration. Their lawyers, in court, had negotiated deals for their clients to join the army for the minimum period, in lieu of going to prison, in order to save taxpayers' money.

The other recruits I served with were adventurers, or had delusions of being 'born killers'. All they thrived on was the opportunity to get involved in a real war with the hope of killing legally. They just wanted action and directed all their attentions toward that goal. Callan was one of those, except he thrived on power alone, as depicted by his slaughter, in Angola, of many unarmed men. He was the worst of the worst that I ever had the misfortune to meet, but there were others of similar – if not quite such psychotic – ilk.

Bob Pyke was another individual I befriended during my service in the Paras. He later followed me to Rhodesia where I was to have many regrets for having recruited him in the first place – but that will be dealt with in a later chapter.

The Paras nurtured the spirit of adventure, even to the point of accepting into its ranks some guys who were borderline psychotic. War is a nasty thing and the ends sometimes justify the means. You can't go about recruiting choirboys when you're about to stage a hard rock band.

Jim Young, whom I met many years later and who appears in the chapter about my Mozambique service, told me that he had once done a two-year attachment to the Paras from the Royal Marines. He said that he used to send reports back to his parent unit containing information about the types of person who joined the Paras.

Whereas the Marines were dedicated soldiers, carefully honed and trained (the same can be said of the Paras), we were in favour of all-out aggression. Many in our ranks were rebellious types with previous criminal records. In Jim's words: 'If I knew I was going up against the Paras I would run a mile'.

CHAPTER 10:
CAVORTING WITH CRAPHATS

Toward the end of 1972 my services were required, as a sniper, to assist a craphat artillery unit in Northern Ireland. The unit, stationed in one of the IRA areas, was very inexperienced and mostly manned by youngsters fresh into the army. Why they were there in the first place, I don't know, as they tried to act out an infantry role to which they were not entirely suited, thereby opening themselves up to all sorts of trouble.

The IRA just loved soft targets like these and took advantage of their lack of aggression. This particular unit was coming under fire in their sangar every night from different positions and the young lads were terrified. They had tried to send out clearance patrols after the shootings but by the time they had reacted, the gunmen were gone.

Even their street patrols were messy. Lacking the *esprit de corps* and aggression that the Paras thrived on, they would often be cowed by mere children, who hurled rocks at them as they went about their duties. As a result, it was decided that they should be bolstered by experienced blood.

When I arrived at the post it was with the hope of setting up a fixed hide from which I could possibly take out the gunmen who were terrorising the poor lads. I was to get myself into position where I could react, when rounds started coming in on the building as, so far, no-one had even fired back.

Unfortunately, because of the craphats' stupidity, I was spotted when I arrived. They were all so chuffed to have a Para there that they swarmed outside to meet me as I debussed my vehicle, beret removed, with my L4A1 bagged on my shoulder. It was as if Santa had just arrived for Christmas and I'm sure the artillery chaps wanted the locals to know about it. I suppose they hoped that the mere presence of a Para was deterrent enough to stop the nightly shootings, but they should have realised that I wasn't always going to be around and when I was gone, the terror would resume.

I got on with the task anyway. That night I set up a position behind one of the corrugated sangar walls, peering through a long slit that offered a commanding view of the area. If the shooting started I was sure that a muzzle flash would give away the gunmen's position.

Needless to say, after enough coffee to kill a small-sized animal, the night passed uneventfully and for the first time in many moons nary a shot was fired.

I'm sure word had got out that the Paras were in town and no-one came out to play. The next day

I returned to Palace Barracks and put in a report. The following evening the sangar was hit again when a 3.5-inch rocket tore through the very slit from which I had peered the night before. The rocket was fired from a drain culvert outside and unfortunately, a few of the chaps inside were injured. I think that had I been there, it might have torn me a new arsehole.

The craphats in the British Army at that time were mostly pretty useless. Whenever they patrolled, they were often beaten up and the Paras had to be called in to rescue them.

Wherever we went, the IRA mostly were not. As soon as we arrived at a scene in late 1972, our reputation had gone before us and the area went quiet. The perpetrators of injustice then knew that the gloves were off and that we were the new bullies at the party.

The guys on the shooting team were often sent out as sniper support on these types of missions. Bloody Sunday had taught us that it was the command element at the rear of most riots that incited violence. Every so often it was from the rear of the fracas that shots were fired into our midst, in an effort to goad a bloody reaction from the soldiers, which could then be capitalised on for their sectarian group propaganda. If and when we witnessed this, it was our task to take out the shooters.

On another occasion, while I patrolled with Support Company on Springfield Road, the lead elements of the patrol came under sniper fire from a high-powered rifle. I was among them and we all took cover. Fortunately nobody was hit, but the sniper fired several shots into our midst before he fled. We frantically searched for him from house to house and eventually found his firing position in the loft of a building. Scattered around were numerous .303 cartridge cases. We discovered he had been lifting the tiles and firing through them. A very smart idea and one for which I give him credit. No wonder we couldn't find him when we looked at the rooftops.

The dream shot I always waited for never came. I think most snipers feel that their bodies are a tool, honed and prepared for that one shot that might arise from the chaos. I spent hundreds of hours training, being pelted with all sorts of missiles, being shot at on occasion and having the dignity ripped out of my family virtues with vocal abuse, only to get my own back physically in the lawless turmoil that was Northern Ireland.

Before we knew it, our two-year stint across the water was up.

Even before I returned home to Rhodesia I had heard via family members and had read in the press that the war had intensified and that the army had a neat little scrap on its hands.

On the 21 December 1972, ZANLA terrorists attacked Altenna Farm in the north-east of the country, in the Centenary farming district. On that fateful evening ten guerrillas had closed in on the humble farmstead and opened fire with AK-47 assault rifles and RPG7 rocket-propelled grenades. Inside, a young white girl was injured as she lay sleeping in bed.

The incident, of no particular strategic value for the guerrillas, marked the beginning of the decisive stage of the war. In the UK, I began to get hot under the collar and pined to have a piece of it.

Sheila, not entirely sympathetic to my needs, came around to my view and agreed that when my time in the Paras was up, I should travel to Rhodesia and set up home. Whether or not she would join me remained to be decided.

Two months after returning to Aldershot, we were sent back to Northern Ireland for Operation Motorman. This time it was a three-month tour and it was designed to take down all the barricades that had been erected across the province by both the Catholics and the Protestants. It was believed that force would be necessary to remove them, as both parties had refused to do so, even in the face of threatening them with Para action.

The build-up to the operation intensified when the IRA, the Protestants and the Catholics – in fact, everybody who was anybody – threatened to take on the army if they came.

Psyched up for the fight, we arrived fit, angry and ready for anything. On our first deployment, when the protestors saw us, they took down their barricades with barely a question asked. That was to be the norm except for a few occasions when 1-Para became overzealous in dealing with the odd subversive and laid into the protestors anyway. The way we felt was that we'd been egged on into a fight and we were very disappointed when no-one was prepared to join us in the sandbox.

The hatred for the army in Northern Ireland grew in all quarters. Little old women used to come up to us in the streets and start beating us with their brollies, only to be beaten back on occasion by a young Para who felt wrongly done by. We all thought we were doing some good and we couldn't understand the behaviour of some of the people we tried to help. Regardless, little old ladies with black eyes in the news did not make for good publicity and the army reined in our conduct with swift disciplinary action. The granny-beaters were often awarded time in the box as the penalty for what they had done.

While I was in Belfast I visited my old mates at the *Belfast Telegraph,* where I had done my photography attachment. The reception I received was far from welcoming and I was run out of the place, closely followed by books, chairs and lever-arch files that were hurled at me in anger. 1-Para, I was told, had been far too brutal.

The papers were accusing the Paras of bringing into the fray contraband weapons in the form of knives, air pistols and coshes. This was true – but what did they expect with the type of loathsome adversaries we were facing?

Thanks to all the publicity we were sent home from Operation Motorman two weeks early. The GOC Northern Ireland was furious. He said later that 1 Para had managed to damage two years of carefully built public relations in two minutes flat.

CHAPTER 11:
WHETTING THE APPETITE

After being in Northern Ireland for almost three years I decided I didn't want to go back there. The pining to return home began to gnaw at me and I think that, in my last months, I was a less effective soldier, although thankfully not deployed on active service. The Battalion was deployed for six months on a UN tour to Cyprus but luckily, I was engaged on exercises with D (Patrol) Company and the shooting team, so I only spent a month there. It was a crappy deployment spent mostly patrolling and I really didn't feel up to it.

While with D Company, a few of the lads and I did a freefall parachute course. We weren't supposed to and did it in our free time at one of the civilian clubs not far from Mons Barracks. The Red Devils were on site and I jumped with them often, lapping up the freedom that freefall parachuting instilled in me.

On return to Aldershot, D Company were deployed for a six-week jungle warfare course in Malaya. I really wanted to attend, but I was granted compassionate leave for the second time in my service. Sheila and I were having problems over our future and we couldn't agree on a path that was mutually beneficial. Besides, I had a few administrative tasks to conduct for the Battalion, as well as my duties as a shooting team member and so I remained behind to sort out my personal life.

When D Company returned from Malaya I was really pissed off and all my mates were gloating over what a swan it had been. I was told that although the course had been tremendously hard work, they were rewarded with a few days on the beach afterwards. My suntanned buddies revelled in waving photographs in front of my nose of tropical beaches and clear warm water. I regretted having stayed behind.

In January 1974 the Battalion was sent to Kenya for a six-week deployment with three years' supply of surplus ammunition. It had been kept in reserve for years and was approaching its effective use-by date. Kenya offered the British Army a diverse range of training scenarios with its arid bush, thick jungle and semi-desert terrain.

We flew to Kenya in the back of an Argosy, which was another uncomfortable flight taking ages to get there. For the deployment I was posted to A Company as a number two mortar man. I really got stuck into things and gained back my enthusiasm for soldiering.

In addition to the thousands of rounds of ammunition we expended on range practice and in live-fire exercises, I also became a proficient mortar operator and was fortunate to have had a never-ending supply of bombs. Over the three months we spent there I must have personally fired off hundreds of bombs.

The mortar in general is not a precise instrument of warfare, despite the fact that it is terrifying to face and is used mainly as a weapon to soften up targets, keeping the enemies' heads down and covering infantry advances. Despite this, the opportunity I was given enabled me to drop bombs with surprising accuracy on given targets. Another task I performed was dropping smoke bombs from the mortar tube, as a target indication for the patrol commander to give artillery-fire control orders. If I could place the bomb on target, then the artillery could follow up within seconds and bloody the enemy's nose.

We also trained for speed and devised scenarios where the mortar team would race to a predesignated spot, fire off ten bombs in quick succession and then move to repeat the performance elsewhere. All our rounds were expected to land in a chosen area that represented an enemy base. I became so good at it that invariably, at the end of an exercise, had there been an enemy, the infantry advance would not have been necessary, as the bad guys would probably have been decimated by mortar fire alone. At least, that's what I like to think.

Another weapon I used for the first time was the Carl Gustav 84 mm anti-tank weapon. This is a recoilless shoulder-fired weapon with a lot of clout. I was assigned the number two position in 2 Platoon which meant that I was mostly reloading. The number two has to be aware of his environment the whole time and acknowledge who is in the area at the moment of firing.

The Carl Gustav has a fearsome back blast of about 40 metres. Anything within that area behind you could be incinerated. It was my task to load the ammunition, check the 'back blast danger area' (BBDA) and clear the gunner for firing. This was done with a pat on the head after screaming — at the top of my lungs — 'BBDA CLEAR'.

We culminated our practice with a Battalion advance to contact, a live-fire exercise that was fantastic fun. Our most likely enemy at the time was still the Soviets, so we trained for that scenario firing machine guns, mortars and rockets in a huge display of firepower. The exercise continued into the night and we were entertained by a pyrotechnic display of British military might. The noise and the light were incredible and the memory still sticks with me.

Once again, while in Kenya, I developed a bronzed tan and fell in love with warm-weather soldiering. The entire deployment was enjoyable and quite casual when compared to standard Parachute Regiment procedure. Under the blazing African sun we were allowed to remove our shirts once in a while and go topless. As long as we kept some sense of formality, it seemed as if anything went.

In Kenya I jumped out of a new type of aircraft for the first time. The Battalion was conducting cross training and familiarising itself with foreign weapons and airplanes. We did several jumps from De Havilland Canada's DHC-5 Buffalo, which was a derivative of the Caribou. It was a great pleasure jumping from these transports, although in essence they were very similar to the larger C130s that had just come into service.

It was then and there that I finally made up my mind to return to Rhodesia and try out selection in the SAS. I had had enough of the cold drizzle and snow in the United Kingdom, where the most I could look forward to was a warm shower, some of the time and possibly a room-temperature pint at the pub when off duty. I resolved to leave the Paras and return home, with or without Sheila, if necessary.

The battalion exercise ended and we spent ten days on the white beaches of Mombasa, drinking copious amounts of local beer. It was a brilliant finale to an enjoyable deployment.

Back in the UK I received very good reports from the platoon I was with in Kenya. I was approached by the A Company CSM and told that I was wasting my time in the Intelligence Section and would be of better use to the A company Support Platoon. There was an open place for me whenever I wanted it. As chuffed as I was with the unexpected attention, I declined the offer and told the CSM of my plans. I think he thought I was a little bit mad, but he understood my patriotism.

Within a few weeks I had bought my discharge for the tidy sum of £200 and an interview with Lieutenant Colonel Wilford. The CO 1 Para tried to change my mind by dangling the promotion carrot in front of me, but I was confident I had made the right choice. The only thing left to do was to convince Sheila.

I left Aldershot for Middlesbrough in May 1974 and took up a temporary job on a building site as part of my preparation to become fighting fit for selection. Every morning, before work, I packed my Bergen with 18 kilograms of bricks and left for a five-mile (eight kilometre) run around town. The Paras had hardened me for this sort of physical training, as tabbing with a heavy weight was a byword of regiment philosophy.

A month after leaving the army I wrote a letter to the Officer Commanding C Squadron, Rhodesian SAS, applying for the next course. I explained that although my previous promise to return in six months had turned into more than six years, I was still very enthusiastic and that I now had some hard years of soldiering experience behind me. I added some information about what skills I had learnt and boasted about my rank of lance corporal, enquiring what would be expected of me in Rhodesia.

The reply, prompt and satisfying, informed me that I was immediately acceptable to commence SAS selection and should I so wish, I could return to Rhodesia before three months were up and take part in the next course, scheduled for January 1975. The cream on the cake was the snippet at the end of the letter that said I would retain my rank of lance corporal.

I was even more excited when four of my buddies from 1 Para, including Jock Patterson and Bob Pyke, who I had constantly kept informed of my plans, decided to apply for selection as well and were accepted. Jock would try out on the same selection as me and Bob would follow in a few months, taking part in the next course. Instantly I felt accompanied in my quest for adventure although it must have been a lot harder for my mates who were travelling to a totally foreign and distant land.

Unfortunately Sheila would have no part in it and was reluctant to leave behind her family and all that she knew. I can't really blame her and it's only now that I realise what an enormous move I was proposing. She had never left home and didn't really understand the situation in Rhodesia. In hindsight I might as well have asked her to join me for a frolic in the battle of the Somme during World War I. She couldn't have known, despite my best efforts, that the war in Rhodesia rarely intruded on the casual social life people enjoyed in the cities.

A month before I departed the UK, we discovered that Sheila was pregnant again. Her mother, I think, always saw the better in me and had thought that I was a good prospect for her daughter. She persuaded Sheila that, in view of a further addition to the family, she needed support to raise the children and should therefore follow me back to my home country. Rather grudgingly, Sheila saw the sense in her mom's argument and agreed to join me in three months' time.

At the beginning of November 1974, I flew back to Rhodesia to take up a new life. Behind me I left the experience of Northern Ireland and my transition from innocence that I had hardly noticed passing. When I joined the British Army I was a 21-year-old, know-it-all, with defiant eyes, pimply skin and a huge ego. The pimples had gone and the ego had taken a bruising here and there, but my eyes had hardly changed. If anything, they were harder now, only occasionally glazed by the images they'd seen in that grey and dull place across the water, images that resurged, on introspection, with splashes of red and gore.

CHAPTER 12:
COMING HOME

You would never have thought that Rhodesia was at war had you landed there in November 1974. Even more absurd would have been the notion that international sanctions had taken hold and were propelling the country toward economic collapse.

Even at Salisbury International Airport, after I exited the plane and kissed the ground at my feet, there was prosperity in the air and people went about their daily lives, unconcerned by what were then trivial issues.

In fact, the only effect sanctions had was to motivate the economic sector into self-reliance. Rhodesia, although not quite the awakened giant, gained enormously from international attempts to bring her to her knees, as Harold Wilson had forecast, within a matter of weeks.

The Unilateral Declaration of Independence (UDI) was nine years old and Britain was struggling to rein in her distant cousin by keeping in place the commodity control and the denial of war materiel that she had imposed instantly after independence. The Rhodesians were ingenious people who improvised solutions whenever they lost the usual providers. They were people who forged their own path irrespective of what the world had to say.

If I think of one aspect, in which Rhodesians stood out from the rest, at that time, it would be that they knew they were fighting their war alone. When you back any animal into a corner, it will come out frothing at the mouth, ferocious enough to win its survival.

Of course, behind the scenes, there was a constant worry about an uncertain future. But ask anyone who was there and they will tell you that Rhodesians, like most people in similar circumstances, hid their worries behind a thick veneer of bravado – and an even larger tumbler of cognac. At least, that is, the privileged upper class whose young boys were fighting a war against terror for the less privileged people in the country – and for their parents. Young men always fight their daddy's wars. And that's one point I will stand by. Anything else beyond that is open to interpretation.

The guys who were actually doing the fighting, both black and white, were mostly real patriots, although many of them never really appreciated this. Some, of course, did it as a job because there was nothing else in life for them. Their lot was not the crystal cognac tumbler, or the façade of bravery; it was simply trying to survive. It was trying to keep yourself, your mates and your country alive when the rest of the world did nothing. It was a matter of appreciating another day with a bottle of ice-cold beer in the mess after a contact. Or relaxing, after responding to another landmine incident where soldiers and civilians were killed. Or maybe sitting back, after reacting to an incident at a kraal, where the village headman and his wives – and possibly even his cattle and dogs – were needlessly slaughtered for the greater good of African nationalism. It was their lot to appreciate a simple existence after having witnessed atrocious acts perpetrated in the name of supposed freedom.

I was not one of them. I came for the adventure, above anything else and I felt a little resentful that my school buddies might be having more fun than I was. I was a patriot and I loved Rhodesia, but at the time I did not feel the stirrings of a national cause. Soldiering, to me, was like a gene and had grown in me much like the genes that determined my hair colour, the colour of my eyes and my sex.

I was a willing participant in man's oldest profession and without wanting to sound lame, I felt like a sentinel standing guard over the virtues of genuine freedom. Having said that, there is no way I would have fought for the opposing side, or for a cause that I did not agree with. The enemy I came to face was brutal and cruel. I had faced that kind of enemy once in Northern Ireland and I would face him again.

Settling into life in Salisbury was a pleasure after living in Middlesbrough. The city was resplendent with large tree-lined avenues that bordered sprawling properties. It really was a beautiful place back then; at certain times of the year it resembled an artist's palette of pastel hues when the jacarandas and flamboyants burst upon society, paving the streets with gentle mauves and flaming scarlet.

I found a neat little place in Hatfield, a suburb in the south of the city and was confident that Sheila would take to it comfortably, settling in to her new life.

The first week I arrived back I reported to Cranborne Barracks and enlisted as serviceman 4577869 in C Squadron SAS. My previous service number had changed, due to an administrative error at army HQ and I think I became one of the few Rhodesian soldiers with dual identities. Later, when the war ended, I became the proud recipient of two general service medals.

In an interview with the Squadron OC, Major Brian Robinson and the Adjutant, Captain Curtain, I was told that it was unfortunate that guys like me had to do full selection. The OC explained that it was necessary because others had arrived from the UK with documents, attesting to their service in 22-SAS, that were nothing more than forgeries. These might have been bought at newsagents or carefully doctored with homemade stamps. A lot of such guys were complete wankers, who had never done a day's service in their lives. It floors me to think what they might have done had they got into a real scrap with terrorists.

I was also warned that the Rhodesian Army did things its own way. It was frowned on for foreigners to say things like 'back in so-and-so we did it like this or like that'. I was encouraged to utilise my experience, but also to learn about tactics and techniques, developed by the Rhodesians, which had been forged in combat. I was told that slight differences in protocol were there for a reason and had been revised after the lessons learnt in bush warfare.

The OC then informed me that he didn't expect a problem with me as he knew I was Rhodesian by birth. His only concern was for me to conform to the ways of the squadron and leave behind me a few habits that might have been instilled in me as a paratrooper. I was told they wanted a 'fresh piece of clay' to mould into their own form.

As it happened, the selection course would not run until mid-January 1975, so I had to wait around for two months, helping the squadron with odd jobs, while the festive season got into full swing. It was no walk in the park by any means, as there was much to keep me busy.

Around Cranborne, a couple of other aspiring SAS wannabes dribbled in from other units like the Rhodesian Light Infantry. One of the lads was a medic who wanted to test his mettle in the likes of the SAS. Others, like my Para mates, came from distant lands, seeking the ultimate adventure, but there weren't many of us.

During those final months of 1974 I had my first inkling into the differences between foreign and Rhodesian soldiers. Around the barracks it seemed that the two groups stuck together in separate cliques. A few guys managed to get along with everyone, but mostly the Rhodesians were in one group and the foreigners in another. Because of my service in the UK I was accepted into both.

The Rhodesians always felt that they were alone in their war on terror. While they were fighting for the very existence of their homes, they thought the foreigners had come along for the ride; their help was appreciated but, at the end of the day, they could always return to their roots if the war didn't work out as planned.

Unfortunately the foreigners interpreted this indifference as snobbishness. They felt that the Rhodesians thought they were better than they were and placed themselves in a higher class. There were a couple of instances when individuals adopted that attitude and unfortunately the cultural indifference was to remain and socially the bridges were never crossed.

I never forgot about training and acclimatised myself to the heat, with regular runs, carrying absurd weights. I was assigned an instructor for pre-selection training who was a complete prick. I began to feel like a recruit at Aldershot again, although my instructor was an exception to the rule. He was far, far worse than anything I experienced in the Paras and came across as an egotistical jerk who thought the sun shone out of his arse. I think his attitude towards me developed because he was a Rhodesian and he thought I was a Pommie. I had not picked up an accent while in the UK, but he was aware of my service in the Paras and in his ignorance he misinterpreted that fact.

Most of the badged SAS soldiers treated us newbies with some respect. Unlike most selection courses, the one we were to take part in was made up entirely of ex-serving soldiers. The Rhodesian SAS, owing to operational pressure and lack of manpower, was unique, in that it took young men directly from school and trained them from scratch. When I arrived it was a relatively new concept and the idea was only beginning to get off the ground.

After four months of pre-selection, recruit and weapons training, the new recruits were put through the selection course proper and the cream of them passed. It may seem like a waste of time, given the large proportion of recruits who failed, but those individuals then went on to other units where, with the training they had received, they became valuable assets. Fortunately for our course there were no inexperienced soldiers, or national servicemen, among us. As a result, all of us were afforded a modicum of respect.

In addition to the physical training, while we awaited selection, courses were run on familiarisation of Warsaw Pact weapons and infantry tactics revision. We were certainly kept busy most of the time in-between preparing ourselves physically and attending the various classes. I began to feel confident that my fitness was at its peak and that my preparation was adequate for the rigours ahead. Jock Patterson and a few of the other lads accompanied me on many of the tabs around the Cranborne area. I'm sure we were a familiar sight to passers-by who lived in the surrounding suburbs.

In early December I began to regret the fact that I was allowed to retain my lance jack status. The few among us who had previous rank were allotted positions like 'guardroom commander' and 'cleaning detail lackey'. Mine was the unfortunate task of running the guard shifts on most days and every weekend.

On one such evening the squadron returned from operational deployment and after cleaning their kit and weapons, they had a few well-earned drinks.

As guard room commander I was approached by the duty officer, who shall remain nameless and ordered to make sure the troopies' mess and the corporals' mess were closed by 22:30 and cleared by 23:00. Approaching that time, I wandered over to the Winged Stagger – the Corporals' mess – and noticed that the party was raging in full swing. It seemed to me that there was no way that this little shindig would be over by the required time.

At 22:15 I peeped through the window and saw that the revelry was gaining momentum. Around the bar a bunch of NCOs were throwing back the drinks, partying away six weeks of operational fatigue.

Avoiding the certain unpopularity that would come with raining on their parade, I decided to ignore the order, leaving them to their own devices, while I returned to the guard post.

At 23:15 an enraged duty officer stormed into the guardroom to enquire why the mess was not closed. I lied with a straight face, telling him that I had tried my best but the NCOs had all told me to piss off.

The duty officer wasn't having any of it and he stormed off to sort out the insubordinates. I followed at a safe distance and watched as he entered the mess, his face flushed with anger and frothing at the mouth. After a few heated words a tussle developed which resulted in a full-blown punch-up. Corporal James Hayden, whom I would later get to know well, was obviously not in an agreeable mood and challenged the order to close down.

The fight was soon broken up and the SAS NCOs returned to their quarters.

The next day I expected the worst when I noticed a rather sheepish duty officer going about his business with a black eye. I honestly thought that he would have found out about my lie – which would have resulted in a charge at the very least. Not a good thing, considering I hadn't even done selection!

Thankfully, the incident was soon forgotten. There was some trouble for Hayden with the squadron sergeant major, but it wasn't taken as far as it could have been.

At the end of the day, I think, it saved certain people a lot of embarrassment and was viewed as spillover from the pressures of active service.

Without warning, selection was upon us and we were given the customary revving by Captain Johnson, the squadron training officer and by 'Snake' Allan, the squadron sergeant major. Selection had been brought forward by a week because of operational commitments and a lack of personnel in the SAS troops. Severely undermanned, their numbers required bolstering and it was hoped that enough of us would pass to achieve that aim.

As it was, the selection course I was on was one of the smallest in the unit's history, with only eight individuals taking part. It was pretty much just thrown together to allow the foreign soldiers a chance of getting into the squadron. If the average pass rate of 10 percent was anything to go by, then one of the troops could look forward to a new addition – or at least a fraction of one! Being small, our selection did have one advantage to it: the directing staff (DS) who were running the course could pay special attention to each individual. On our course there was one DS per man and hardly any room for error.

The Rhodesian SAS was structured very much along the same lines as 22 SAS, with a squadron broken down into specialty troops. In the UK however, the different troops have the time to focus on their areas of expertise, whereas in Rhodesia, particularly as the war intensified, all the troops became much of a muchness as they got stuck into the day-to-day fighting of the war.

On a warm and wet summer's night we were rudely woken up by the DS, banging on trunks and lockers. With five minutes to assemble our kit, we were told to gather outside in the car park for a four-hour drive.

We drove to Inyanga in the eastern highlands, arriving during the early twilight hours of the following morning. As we gained in altitude the temperature increasingly dropped, exacerbated by the perpetual drizzle outside. While we were debussing the Mercedes 2.5 Unimog truck, the sun's rays fought their way through the haze and were peeking over the distant hills as the fiery orb rose across a vast Mozambique landscape.

Even though it was summer, the air was crisp as the rains had been ongoing for the past few months. With the thick cloud cover came an uncomfortable chill that would last until around mid-morning, when enough warmth was trapped in the earth's atmosphere to heat our tired bodies.

Inyanga is made up of the same kind of terrain you would expect to find in the Welsh countryside. It is a harsh and unforgiving landscape of rolling, rocky hills covered with green shrubbery, dense bush and thick forests. Given its altitude, it is also blessed with a cooler climate than most areas in the country. Many holidaymakers migrated there during the summer to escape the sweltering heat in the cities.

We had hardly arrived when the DS began issuing instructions and shouting out grid references. Even at this stage, if you weren't on your toes, vital information could be lost – which could spell disaster. You couldn't exactly walk up to the DS and ask him to repeat his orders, as that would be an immediate black mark against you. In the confusion of combat, second chances are rarely given.

The first leg of selection was a team march, carrying a telegraph pole. In addition, we each carried our Bergen, loaded to 60 pounds (27 kgs), an FN FAL rifle, pattern 58 webbing with full complement of ammunition and water, as well as our maps and compass.

We were given a route of about ten kilometres, that traversed the thick bush behind the Troutbeck Hotel, crossed the swollen Inyangombe River and culminated at the Inyangombe Falls. It was hard-going right from the start. I had managed to pick up a few blisters during build-up training that immediately began to rub raw in my sodden boots.

A kilometre or so into the march we discovered that it was far easier taking turns to carry the pole individually. The thick vegetation and tight spaces made it impossible for us to carry the pole as a team. No matter what we did, our lack of co-ordination got the better of us, so we took 15 minute turns hauling the thing on our shoulders, the tail end ripping up the dirt behind us.

Crossing the flooded river was an exceptionally difficult task. We came together as a team again, spreading the weight of the pole across the length of our formation, as we fought the rushing water in single file. With every step we took one of us would lose his footing and would drag the whole group into the chest-deep water. Once the pole was submerged, it would create additional drag and we would all thrash around like spastics in a bathtub, until we gained purchase on the slippery bottom. We managed to get through the river and sorting the chaff from the wheat, we recognised each other's strong and weak points.

At the falls the DS were waiting. They were quite surprised that we had made it in good time – so they threw in an additional leg just to annoy us: this time without the pole.

The weather was really coming down around us and we all shivered in our soaked uniforms. Without a care in the world, an instructor rattled off a grid reference, telling us to be there by 06:00 the next morning. They then jumped into the dry warmth of the Land-Rover and disappeared, jovial and smiling.

Along the route, the eight of us separated as we all got into our own rhythm. Jock Patterson and Clive Mason were in and out of sight for most of the march, but the others I hardly saw.

I arrived at the rendezvous late that night only to meet a couple of the lads who had got in before me. Over the next few hours everyone trickled in except Cisco Guerreiro, a Portuguese volunteer who was on his second selection course.

Cisco had already served in the Squadron years before, but had left to join the army in Mozambique where he fought against FRELIMO guerrillas, who were fighting for independence from Portugal. In 1975, when the Portuguese left Mozambique, he returned to join the unit. He was made to do selection again and I could tell, when I first met him, that he was not too enamoured with the prospect.

My Para buddies and I were more acclimatised to this sort of soldiering and had benefitted a great deal from our Para Regiment days, when we were used as virtual pack mules. It was certainly hard, but I was thankful to have had that previous experience under my belt.

The few hours gained were put to good use, cleaning our gear and catching up with a bit of shuteye. Early the next morning, as we waited with the DS, Cisco strolled into the camp, fresh and dry. We were all a little suspicious at his appearance, but the DS left him to his own devices and didn't say a word.

Before departing on the next leg, the instructors called for an inspection. Carefully perusing our equipment and weapons, they gleefully awarded black marks for any discrepancies. Each black mark meant an additional white-numbered brick that we would have to cram into our packs and haul along for the duration. I was lucky and only had one mark awarded -- for dust on the cocking handle of my FN. Some of the guys were given as many as three black marks. The whole process was designed to exhaust us to the point of not caring. With the fatigue that was rapidly growing it was expected that we would become casual about our gear and thus gain additional bricks along the way.

After the inspection we were ordered onto the vehicles and driven a few kilometres down a winding dirt road. At one kilometre intervals we were each dropped off and handed a piece of paper on which was written a six-figure grid reference. A slap on the back later we were told to get to the new rendezvous, 25 kilometres distant, by 06:00 the next morning. As an afterthought, the DS warned us to stay off the roads.

Covering 25 kilometres on foot, tired, wet and with 90 pounds (41 kg) of weight, is a hard task in itself. Add to that the nature of the terrain and the undulating landscape and the distance virtually doubles. Throw in the type of impassable, dense vegetation that was prevalent during the rainy season and you have a recipe for utter exhaustion.

Alone on the road, I settled down with my map, working out the best route to take. In Inyanga a compass bearing doesn't always work as you're constantly coming up against thick, impenetrable walls of vegetation. You've then got to take another bearing on your rendezvous and walk some kilometres around to get back on track.

Taking heed of the warning, I headed south toward the meeting point. There were numerous roads in the area that I avoided entirely. I had been told that the DS often checked the roads for tracks and would then hunt down the offender by identifying the sole marks on his boots. If caught using the roads, it would spell immediate disqualification.

Nothing had been said about the firebreaks, so I chose a relatively safe route that meandered in the direction of the rendezvous. I think some of the others had the same idea as I came across military boot tracks that had covered the ground before me.

For the most part, selection was a test of initiative and endurance. Once we reached a certain checkpoint, we were given further references and told to make the next rendezvous in a given time. The pressure didn't let up and with each new route march, the timeframes were narrowed while the distances became greater. Sleep deprivation became a problem and all the time we had limited rations. The third day into selection we were given a second ration pack which was to last until the end of the course. Water was never a problem because of the abundance of crystal-clear streams in the area.

I noticed that some of the Rhodesians on my course battled with the endurance tests. One of them was on his second attempt and he seemed to have reached his limit. Along the way, as I passed some by, the strain was evident on their faces as they stumbled under the heavy weights they were carrying.

After walking all day through pissing rain, I managed to reach the rendezvous in the late evening, 10 hours before schedule! I caught myself thinking that SAS selection was becoming a walk in the park. The blisters on my heels, though, were really becoming grotesque, festering sores and I appreciated the respite from being constantly on my toes. Digging in my Bergen I extracted a small med kit I had bought along and unwrapped a few plasters. Cleaning the blisters with water, I covered them and relaxed, stretching my legs out in front of me for a moment. Once rested, I set up my bivvy to afford some shelter from the drizzle and made a quick brew. I managed to get some food into me, but my eyelids were heavy so I changed out of my wet clothes and settled down to sleep.

As the sun came up the following morning I woke up and cleaned my kit and weapon, wary of being caught the second time around and dished out another brick. I put on my wet gear, which took some getting used to in the cold, as I shivered uncontrollably while my body adapted to the icy garments. Across the clearing I noticed Cisco wandering into the camp, fresh and dry once again.

The DS rallied us for inspection and I approached one of the instructors, confident that I was squeaky clean. My boots, although wet, had received due attention with the mud scraped off them and thick polish hiding any dirt. The polish also served to waterproof them, to a degree, although I think at that stage it was only keeping the water inside. With every step my feet squelched inside the wet leather confines.

Lining up, the DS went over us, carefully criticising an incorrectly fastened bootlace here and a rattling object hanging off webbing, there. The instructor who inspected me was quite satisfied with my appearance and with the state of my weapon. He then motioned me over to the area I had slept in and began to go over it with a fine-tooth comb. It wasn't long before he found a piece of used Elastoplast from my previous night's medical effort. I was instructed to go over to one of the Land-Rovers and retrieve another brick. This one I had to name after one of my former girlfriends, so I called it Sheila. Sheila, I was told, had to be well looked after and should appear in immaculate condition at the end of the next leg.

The day's order of events would commence with a speed march over a distance of 15 kilometres. I was very worried that my blisters would play up and my pack was already digging deep furrows into my shoulders. It was to be a chaperoned march, with the DS following in Land-Rovers, encouraging us to throw in the towel.

Half way through the march I had to dig deep into my reserves of stamina. It felt like my feet were on fire, as grit rubbed into the open wounds on my heels. One of the Land-Rovers passed me with an instructor perched spread-eagled on the spare tyre on the bonnet, casually sipping a cold fizzy drink. I suppose he didn't want to be rude and he offered me one so I told him to fuck off.

My little experience of personal hell continued and I was constantly hampered by my decaying feet. Slowing, I arrived at the rendezvous 15 minutes behind Jock Patterson and Clive Mason. The feelings of bliss I felt when I finally sat down were enormous. I refrained from taking my boots off, knowing that my feet would probably swell and it would be difficult to get the footwear back on again.

The respite was short lived. As the others trickled into the rendezvous, with Cisco always bringing up the rear, the DS informed us that we didn't look tired enough and the march would continue. We were each given different tasks that had to be completed within certain time-frames. My task was the unenviable opportunity of climbing to the top of Inyangani Mountain, where an instructor was awaiting my arrival. I was told that Captain McLean, the selection supervisor, had something for me and I was to retrieve it and bring it back to the DS at the foot of the enormous rock.

Not wanting to gratify the instructors by showing my disappointment I smiled at them, donned the nemesis that was my pack, picked up my rifle and set off on my way.

Three hours later, after fighting a constant battle with loose gravel, slippery mud and large boulders, I found myself on a moonscape of desolate rock. The fact that I knew it was rock at all was surprising, as I could hardly see a thing when I walked through the lower cloud base that had descended on the mountain. Just when I was about to throw my toys out of the cot I looked up and saw the captain perched on an ominous boulder. I waddled over to him, nursing my feet and reached up to grab the object he was offering. I'm sure he was thoroughly enjoying every moment of my displeasure as he just sat there in silence, beaming a huge smile at me.

I was not thrilled when I discovered what the object was that had caused me so much pain. Loosening my brittle fingers, I peered into my palm and saw a bottle top with my initials crudely engraved on it. The officer told me to hurry down the mountain and give the bottle top to the instructors below. This sort of torture was designed to test a man's temperament. Many a man, once he realised that a mere trinket was the reward for all his superhuman exertions, would lose his temper, throw in the towel and give up. It was the same with the bricks. The key was to keep smiling.

The climb down the mountain was twice as bad as the climb up. My knees jolted with the forward momentum of my uncontrolled amble as gravity took effect. My feet became lumps of numb putty as they broke the fall of every step. Trudging on, I broke through the cloud base and could see the camp below me. The problem was that they could also see me and thinking I was on a Sunday stroll, one of the DS shouted for me to double back to the vehicles. I was absolutely stuffed but I ignored the pain and arrived with the same smile on my face as when I left.

I was running short of rations and that night I had a growling stomach, interrupting the precious little sleep we were given. I was happy to get a warm brew of tea into me and set to polishing and cleaning my gear. Sheila and her twin provided me with endless hours of entertainment as I did my best to ensure that they remained in the same benign state as when I had first won their affections. I could not afford to let my guard slip as I had heard it said that the DS could steal the bricks back, just so they could have something on us; doubling the quota for every brick we had 'lost'.

The sun threatened to break through the clouds once again the following morning, but I think that was just a ploy engineered by the DS. With their godly status it wouldn't surprise me if they were in cahoots with the heavenly powers.

After breakfast, which consisted of greasy bacon and eggs on toast (in our dreams), we were unceremoniously stacked onto a Land-Rover and driven some distance from the previous night's camp. Again we were dropped off, this time at intervals and told to make the next rendezvous within a given time.

This was one of the hardest legs as the DS had made sure that there were no firebreaks to use in the area and the terrain was the densest I had experienced so far. To make things worse, we had to make the rendezvous by 16:30 that day, effectively narrowing the margin for success.

Studying my map, I planned my route and was delighted to discover that the march culminated at World's View! As the name implies, this is a very high feature in the Eastern Highlands and one that affords a grand view of the entire area. From World's View one can peer across the border into the depths of Mozambique.

It struck me that not far away, possibly within 50 kilometres, the very enemy I was preparing to fight against was probably in training too. I know one thing for sure – his training could not compare to the hell I was experiencing.

After the sun's initial attempt to show itself, the day had turned into one where thick fog hung over a damp landscape. Worse still, as I ascended toward my objective, the cloud base merged with the fog to shut down visibility entirely. I marched that whole day on my compass, all the time telling myself that this must be the final stage of selection. It was a mindless slog of placing one foot in front of the other and counting out the paces.

Fortunately, my compass took me directly into the DS camp. As I crested the steep face of World's View I could see the instructors relaxing and sipping tea. Jock and Clive, as usual, were ahead of me but the others were nowhere in sight. I had no idea what happened to Cisco, but our suspicions were that he had probably caught a bus and was waiting out of sight to appear at the last moment. As we suspected, he did just that, strolling into camp with minutes to spare!

Somehow that night, I managed to convince myself that selection must be over and I lapsed into a dreary state. It was a stupid thing to do and I would pay for it the next day. I had expected selection to be hard, but not a continual slog like this. My blisters had bought my overall performance down and I knew that I was under close scrutiny by the DS.

The following morning dawned exactly as the last and the DS began to inspect our equipment. I scraped through the inspection and was overjoyed that Sheila and her friend would not be gaining a companion. My joy was replaced with unbelief when we were told that another leg was in store and that this time we had a smaller margin in which to complete it.

The route was an individual effort from the top of World's View, down its steepest face and finishing up at the Inyangombe campsite. I can't remember the exact distance, but it was enough to put a real damper on things. I remembered clearly my downhill slog from two days before and I dreaded the thought of what lay in store for me. I learned then that to overcome adversity, you must not constantly think about it. You need to replace those thoughts with others of a gentler nature and just rely on your body and energy reserves to do the rest.

I began to think of Sheila (the wife, not the brick) and got stuck into the march as best I could. The day passed in a blur of stumbling and falling, but I got through it. That day I can remember less than any of the others. I think selection had done what it was designed to do: to whittle down my reserves until I had only my will to rely on.

When I arrived at the campsite it was with little time to spare. I was in an enormous amount of pain, but too proud to show it. I think my limping gave it away as I stumbled to the final mark. Jock and some of the others had apparently cruised into camp way before me. One of the DS called me over and asked what had taken so long. I eventually told him about my feet, wrestling with my boots to expose a pulpy mess. I told him that despite the pain I was ready for the next leg. Casually, he directed me to bivvy up under a tree and go for a hot shower in the campsite ablutions. As I left he said I should report, after the shower, for a hot meal at the DS tent.

I didn't know what to think of this unexpected kindness and for a moment, I thought it was a trap, or that I was being withdrawn from the course for medical reasons. I remained confused for some time while the tail-enders lurched into camp, way behind schedule.

It was only when the DS interviewed them that I realised I had passed. It seemed unkind at the time, but they were given another ration pack each and told to settle in a far corner of the campsite, out of sight. On failure they were already ostracised from the unit.

The elation of having passed left little pity for those who had failed and I got stuck into a slap-up meal with the DS and the other successful candidates. Just as I had experienced in the Paras, the DS softened towards us and got rid of their superior pretensions.

The meal over, we were told officially that we had passed – for the time being at least. We would still have to prove ourselves in the bush and that was yet to come. At the time, I suppose with my elation, I told myself that it hadn't been as hard as I expected. I was just euphoric that I had got through selection unscathed. Then again, I was at the fittest level I had ever been. I had managed to get through seven different arduous marches over countless kilometres, two thrown in just to piss us off and had come through it all only a little worse for wear.

After selection, with hundreds of kilometres behind us, we all began to wonder why Cisco had arrived at each rendezvous smelling like a cheap French whore, while the rest of us were utterly exhausted and on the brink of collapse. It didn't escape our attention that every time we crossed paths he was clean and dry, while our rain and sweat-soaked bodies shivered under a grey overcast sky. We all knew he had been on selection before, but surely even badged SAS soldiers suffered the effects of harsh physical abuse? It eluded our dazed imaginations that there could be any skulduggery behind his immaculate conception.

Fortunately Cisco escaped the attention of the DS, who were running the course. Maybe because of his previous service, he was shown some leniency and they realised that his second attempt was just a formality. Whatever the story, Cisco passed endurance as one of six successful applicants. Although it was a small course it held the record for the highest percentage pass rate. From my point of view, as previously stated, we were all already exceptionally fit soldiers coming from exceptional units. Despite that, Rhodesian SAS selection was one of the hardest physical tests I have ever gone through.

Much later we found out that Cisco had friends who lived in Inyanga. Once each leg of endurance started, he would lag behind and await a pre-arranged lift, so that he could return with his mates to their villa for a relaxing night in front of the fire. In the morning, his mates would drive him to a point, a few kilometres from the scheduled rendezvous and he would then take up the pace as if he'd been marching all night.

Apart from the pole-carrying exercise and the speed march, on which he came last, Cisco had managed to cheat the instructors on every leg of selection. He even told me later (which we had suspected) that he had caught an African bus, on the

World's View leg, which dropped him off a few kilometres short of his objective. Good on Cisco! In the years I knew him he was an utterly professional soldier and one with whom I would have been happy to storm the gates of hell.

Later, Cisco joined the Selous Scouts and managed to pass their rigorous selection. I don't know if he used the same crafty techniques to get through that course, but I think it was improbable, as their selection was conducted in a more remote part of the country.

On one operation, while he was still in the SAS attached to the Selous Scouts, 72 of them attacked the guerrilla base at Pungwe Nyadzona in Mozambique. Cisco was left behind with another operative, also a good friend of mine, by the name of Paul Holt. Together they had to perform an incredible escape-and-evasion exercise, walking more than 80 kilometres back to Umtali in Rhodesia.

I bet Cisco wished he had paid more attention to SAS selection then!

CHAPTER 13:
DÉTENTE

On passing selection, we returned to Salisbury and were immediately sent to New Sarum Air Force base for a parachuting conversion course. To obtain SAS wings, as all of us were qualified paratroopers, the course consisted of six jumps with full equipment, two to be conducted at night. It was a cinch, jumping out of Dakotas, compared with the Buffalo, the Argosy and the C130s. I really loved it and it gave me a sense of nostalgia to jump out of the historic aircraft. Standing in the door I could almost envisage the scenery below, changing to that of the French countryside in a different era – to World War II, when airborne troops descended on France in the D-Day invasion.

After the parachuting course, came an intensive period of learning the intricacies of Special Forces soldiering, which was to take up the next few months. Primarily, we all had to do a signals course, basic medics, more foreign weapons handling and a small-boat and canoe course. Some leniency was granted when our instructors realised that many of us had previous experience from our former units in some of the skills.

The year 1975 started off as a relatively quiet period for the Rhodesian SAS. Détente was in progress and all around the country, the war lost momentum. During March, while I was busy with courses, Herbert Chitepo, the mastermind of ZANLA's 1972 offensive, was assassinated, reportedly by Rhodesian agents in Zambia. The resultant witch-hunt saw many ZANLA leaders being incarcerated by the Zambian government, including Josiah Tongogara, the military man behind ZANLA's war effort. This effectively slowed the pace of the guerrilla war.

Robert Mugabe, the future leader of Zimbabwe, was appointed head of ZANU, the political wing of the party and under his leadership they moved to Mozambique, opening up a new, unfriendly frontier, along hundreds of kilometres of Rhodesia's eastern border. ZIPRA, led by Joshua Nkomo, remained in Zambia, from where they continued to infiltrate terrorist gangs into the country's northern regions.

Suddenly Rhodesia found herself surrounded by unfriendly neighbours, actively assisting the terrorist war effort, on three of her four borders. South Africa, whose leaders had supplied the Rhodesians with ammunition and fuel, as well as with manpower in the form of police units, pulled out that year due to international pressure. Behind the scenes, however, they continued to assist their friendly neighbour.

With all the courses out of the way, I was really looking forward to active deployment though I was a little flustered with the way things were going in the country. I had come a long way to find adventure and it seemed that I had arrived too late. Of course, there were always operational commitments and the Rhodesian Army, particularly the SAS, could never let its guard down. When we were not fighting, we were preparing to fight, or gathering intelligence and conducting reconnaissance operations in our voyeuristic capacity. It's in times of peace that the smart man prepares for war.

In the early days of Rhodesian SAS history, like 22 SAS, before members were badged, they had to undergo continuation training in the form of a bush, or jungle warfare course, as well as an 'escape-and-evasion' exercise, which in Rhodesia was called the 'All In' phase.

Due to the war, escape-and-evasion had not been carried out for quite some time and freshly selected troops had been badged right after their paratrooper course and sent on operational deployment.

As luck would have it, because of détente, the military decided to run the first escape-and-evasion course in many years. Combining my course and the one before it, comprising ten successful candidates, we were to return to Inyanga and run amok in the countryside, evading search parties. For the exercise, the CO had the bright idea of deploying the remainder of the Squadron – only just back from a bush trip – as our opposition force. They were told that, before their R&R could begin, they would have to deploy to Inyanga and hunt all of us down. It was a devious little plan on the CO's part and naturally it made us very unpopular!

The exercise began with a very irate Squadron close on our tails. We left Salisbury early one morning by Dakota, heading for a predesignated landing zone (LZ) and were parachuted into the Inyanga hills with a one-hour head start. Before we jumped, the pilot faked a technical problem and the dispatchers panicked, trying to deploy all sixteen of us through the door. Behind us, the Squadron followed in three other aircraft, only too eager to get the job done.

A forward party had been sent ahead – in Sabre Land-Rovers – to establish a base and prep the Inyanga community of our imminent arrival. Those who lived, farmed or worked in the area were warned against providing us with any assistance whatsoever. Further, they were told to report our presence if they came across us.

The group of escapees had been divided into four callsigns, of four men each. We were to separate into these callsigns and rendezvous at an 'enemy' camp, to conduct a reconnaissance. Along the way we were given a few tasks to complete and had to send in two situation reports (sitreps) per day, advising the Squadron of our future intentions. We were told that this was because of the possible threat of running into real terrorists, so close to the Mozambique border. I don't know if they thought that we were all stupid, but it immediately became transparent to me that the sitreps were a ploy to give away our positions. Early into the exercise I resolved to be careful when communicating with the DS.

Supplied with rifles, maps, compasses and a radio per callsign, we would cover a large area teaming with search parties. The onus was on us to use what we'd learned in survival training, to catch, scrounge, beg, borrow or steal whatever sustenance was necessary to achieve our objective.

The whole concept was designed for us to get captured, leading in to the second phase of the exercise: resistance to interrogation, albeit in African form, which really consisted of a beating at the hands of our captors. Special Branch was brought in to assist in that area and we knew that they were real professionals when it came to that sort of thing.

Upon landing, somewhat ungainly, I found the other members of my callsign and we hurriedly hid our parachutes in a rocky crevice, covering them with branches and grass. We had been told to note down where they were hidden, for retrieval at a later date, as parachutes were hard to come by because of the sanction's boycotts.

On the run, we formulated a tentative plan, realising it was in our best interest to get as far away from the drop zone as possible. Among ourselves we designated a navigator and agreed to take turns at hourly intervals. The going was tough for the first few hours, until we had to give our first sitrep.

Settled into an area of thick cover, I left the rest of the group, taking with me the radio and headed up an escarpment towards a dirt road we had seen on the map. Just off the road I found a concealable area on the high ground and crammed my body between two granite boulders which afforded a grand view of the surrounding bush.

Making contact with the forward base, I informed them that we were on the run, giving our current locstat as a position 100 metres up the road ahead. Waiting for 15 minutes I was not surprised when two Sabres screamed up, debussing troops into a search pattern. From my vantage point I could hear the disappointment, when the opposition force realised they had been duped. So soon into the exercise, I am sure they would have been overjoyed with an early capture.

Leaving my hiding place I crept back to the others, making as little noise as possible. So far we had managed to escape detection, although we knew a mistake this early would result in ridicule and possible bodily harm.

When we reached our next resting point, we had managed to cover only a few kilometres in as many hours. It was a painfully slow process, tactically creeping through the bush with as much stealth as possible, but we were making headway and we congratulated ourselves on our fortune.

Hunger was becoming a problem toward sunset, so we ate the few dog biscuits we had managed to smuggle under the prying eyes of the DS. It wasn't much and we knew that by the next day our energy levels would be sapped and would require a top-up.

Our rendezvous for the night was about a quarter of the way to our destination, a kilometre or so from a marked village on the map. We realised that it was best to circumnavigate the village, but decided to mount a reconnaissance as it might be possible to find food. I remember that night well, as my stomach groaned in anticipation of the morning's feast.

The following morning we weren't disappointed and didn't have to go far before we found a field of maize. We tucked cobs into every available space, ate our full and were soon on our way. Cooking was out of the question as we feared the smoke could be seen for miles around. I was certain that an observation post had been positioned in one of the many surrounding hills. It wouldn't need a rocket scientist to figure out that smoke coming from a bushy area could not be ascribed to the local people and an investigation would be carried out. The maize cobs were edible and filling, but I relished the idea of salt and butter as I guzzled down my portion.

Every sitrep for the next few days was conducted in the same manner as the first. One of us always left the others behind and walked some distance before establishing communication. If he was unfortunate enough to get captured, then at least his demise would not precipitate our own.

Four days into the venture we arrived at the outskirts of the Squadron camp. It had been a relatively easy approach and I was surprised that we didn't run into clearance patrols. I suppose they thought that no one could possibly make it this far, so had dropped their guard altogether. I learnt later that the entire Squadron was searching another area closer to our original insertion point. It wasn't considered that a bunch of newbies might outwit their masters!

Two of the other callsigns had been captured on the run within the first three days. Carrying out a close target reconnaissance, I noticed them locked behind barbed wire, tied up and blindfolded, as naked as the day they were born. Many of them looked the worse for wear and I could see caked blood on a few faces. Most of them sat cross-legged, with their heads hanging forlornly on their chests.

Other than the small internment of captives, there was no-one else around, so I even managed to enter the camp and steal a map of the national parks area, complete with the campsite. I thought it might come in handy later, to prove how far we had actually gone.

As I quietly sneaked out of the camp and met up with my callsign we ran into Cisco, who was wondering around aimlessly like a child looking for his mother. My first thought was that he had been planted by the Special Branch guys to infiltrate our gang and give us up for capture. Cisco explained that although his entire callsign had been compromised, he had managed to evade his pursuers, escaping by legging it through the bush. Unfortunately, this was not before he was administered some cruel punishment in his brief, but painful, interrogation. His tales of abuse only increased our determination to remain undetected.

Cisco had been alone for the past day and was on the verge of giving up. Bolstered by our acquaintance, he joined us as we planned our next move.

Inside the camp the opposition force had left behind a Land-Rover which, much to our delight, was adorned with a bunch of keys hanging from the ignition. With that sort of temptation before us we did the natural thing and absconded with the vehicle down the road. Before we left, the five of us had been careful to select only the finest food items available in the camp. Refreshed, we mounted our 'pack horse' and drove away into the sunset. I would have loved to have seen their faces when the Squadron blokes returned from trying to find us – but hanging around would just be inviting trouble!

A few hours later we met up with the remaining callsign. They had recognised us as we passed by their hiding place on the side of the road. I am not sure whether I would have done the same thing, but a couple of them ran out in the road behind us, screaming and flagging us down. They too had managed to acquire a civilian Land-Rover by devious means. It struck me that we might soon have the police on our tails as well as our SAS brethren.

Sharing our food with our new comrades and after some humorous chat, we sped toward an agreed area that would conceal the vehicles. Once there, we made comms and reported into base. I was not on the receiving end of the conversation which followed, but it quickly became apparent that we had made a lot of enemies.

I felt sorry for the guys who had already been captured, as I thought they would be paying dearly for our sins. At the end of the conversation our radio operator was given instructions for our exfiltration route from the area into friendly lines. The point we were to head for lay about 20 kilometres away, south of a river, towards Umtali, an idyllic Rhodesian town in the south-eastern border area of the country. On arrival we would be met by a vehicle and taken to safety. It was made apparent that under no circumstances were we allowed to deviate from the given instructions.

It was approaching nightfall when we left to make our rendezvous. We were not the sharpest tools in the shed and decided to stick with the vehicles, which offered greater mobility and afforded some respite from the relentless leg-bashing. Using the roads, it wasn't long before we came up against a road-block which had been strategically placed to ensnare the stolen Land-Rover. What the DS didn't know was that there were now two vehicles in our entourage. I was lucky enough to be in the rear vehicle, when all hell broke loose and the enraged Squadron members swooped on the lead Land-Rover and dragged its occupants out onto the road, climbing into them with fists and boots. Discretion being the better part of valour, I leapt from where I sat and began legging it into the confines of darkness. The dirt slipped beneath my boots, as the rain pelted down around me. Behind me I heard the screams of my accomplices and looking back my heart raced when I saw three of the DS chasing me. I picked up my pace and darted from shrub to shrub in an effort to break free. I had only run about a hundred metres when the earth disappeared beneath my feet. The shock of the fall left my mind in a daze of stars as I landed flat on my face, knocking the sense and the wind out of me.

The small cliff I had run over loomed behind me as I scrambled underneath a bush, gasping for air that wouldn't come and covered from head to toe in mud and gunk. Above me, as blood trickled from my nose to merge with the rainwater, I heard the DS as they tore at vegetation, cursing as they searched for me. I lay as still as I could and hardly dared breathe. My breath, when it came back, was raspy from exertion and caught the phlegm in my throat, emitting faint wheezing sounds. I tensed for the beating which would surely come at any moment.

The next thing – I heard one of the DS calling a vehicle over to put on its headlights. I mulled with the idea of making another break for it, but decided that I was better off lying still. At a lower level I was confident that the vehicle's headlight beams would pass straight over me.

It was the rain that saved the day. With my face pressed into the dirt I felt little stings against my cheeks as the droplets got bigger and came down faster, splashing into the puddles around me. I knew that if the elements were uncomfortable for me, they were uncomfortable for my adversaries also; although I had been on the run for a few days without much food and my tolerances were lower. The food we did have was still in the Land-Rover.

Fifteen minutes passed before the DS succumbed to the comforts of warmth. I heard them as they walked away cursing their bad luck. It was another 10 minutes before I heard ignitions starting up and the vehicles rumbling away into the distance.

I still couldn't be sure if I was safe and I suspected they might have left someone in hiding. Their driving away might have been a ploy to get me to come out so I stayed still for another half hour, before my shivering body had to move.

When I eventually did move I got the fright of my life. Only two metres away, obscured by the rain, a lone figure was peering my way. The figure, whoever it was, seemed to be in as much shock when he saw me. We both remained motionless for a few seconds, before I recognised the apparition in front of me. There was no doubting Cisco's unique Portuguese features.

Our reunion was a joyous occasion and we hugged and danced like long lost friends, before he explained that he had also leapt off the vehicle and taken refuge underneath a bush only metres away from mine. He'd also believed that he was the only one who had managed to escape. Considering he had come this far and escaped twice, I began to admire his resilience, which I had previously doubted.

Cisco and I started walking along the side of the main road heading south for Umtali. We walked all night and a few hours into the morning until we were well into friendly territory. We had almost walked the whole way when we were picked up by a couple of hippies in a VW Combi. On reaching the drill hall in town, we said our thanks, jumped out and entered an office, looking for all the world as if we had slept in the bush for a week. We had.

Approaching a desk I asked a kindly gentleman, who stared at me wide–eyed, to inform the local police of our whereabouts. It seemed obvious they would know something about us and would get hold of the relevant people.

Our kit had been left on the Land-Rovers after our hurried departure, so we only had our rifles, but we had managed to clean up at one of Cisco's friends' houses. It was there that I learnt of his antics during selection.

The following day we hiked back to Inyanga, to find only two Squadron members waiting at the camp with a vehicle. Their surly attitude upon our arrival left us in no doubt as to the fate that awaited us. In a river next to the camp we were told to collect our kit which had been dumped from our Bergens by 'Snake' Allan, the Squadron sergeant major. It appeared that we hadn't won any respect in the popularity stakes.

After driving back to Salisbury in silence, we were debriefed at Cranborne by the CO and training officer. We were told that they were not happy with the way that the exercise had turned out. It had been designed to ensure that everyone got captured and our little escapade had apparently spilled egg on a few faces, although they weren't going to tell us that.

There were also many complaints about the brutality with which the captives were treated. I think some of the Squadron members went overboard and a few of the guys sported black eyes, fat lips, bruises and lacerations. One unfortunate captive even had his front teeth knocked out.

After that escape-and-evasion exercise it was decided that all new members had to prove themselves on active deployment before receiving their colours.

There was simply no time available for repeat escape-and-evasion exercises. Though the idea had been toyed with it became clear that the only way to test a man properly was through the rigours of actual combat. The Rhodesian SAS became unique in that, from then on, members were only badged after their first deployment. In later years many aspirants, some fresh from school, saw their first action before they were allowed to wear the sand-coloured beret.

My first bush trip came shortly afterwards and was one of many deep penetration patrols carried out to gather intelligence on ZANLA bases. The Rhodesian SAS had operated in Mozambique extensively at a place called Macombe back in 1973 and 1974. During those years they assisted a predominantly national service Portuguese army, who preferred to sit it out in their bases rather than actively engage the enemy. The SAS were there to stem the flow of terrorists who, on leaving Zambia, travelled down the Mozambique border to enter Rhodesia. The terrorists were actively assisted by FRELIMO whom the Portuguese were fighting at the time.

While the SAS had extensive knowledge of some regions in the country, there remained a lot of ground to be covered and many areas were previously untouched by Rhodesian boots. We were deployed 20 kilometres inside Mozambique beyond the Kanyemba border post by helicopter. ZANLA had recently moved into the country and we were sent to identify possible infiltration routes south of the Zambezi River.

Summer was over by then and it was the early days of autumn. The mornings were cool but, by midday, the heat was oppressive and unbearable.

We boarded Alouette 316B helicopters, four fully equipped men per aircraft, during the early hours of the morning. We left Kanyemba behind us and were across the border by first light.

The feelings that overcame me that day are indescribable. Behind the tension and uncertainty that arose from possibly running into the enemy was a deep, still excitement borne of the professionalism that had been instilled during training. I knew that the skills I had acquired, after more than six years in the military, would stand me in good stead when I faced those who would want to kill me. It was early days for me then but around me I knew I had professionals on whom I could rely. The faces I gazed upon, as we flew over a thick green landscape, were hard faces, expressionless and unforgiving. Underneath the black camouflage cream, they gave no hint of any uncertainty they might have felt inside.

The country we were flying over – barely feet above the trees – was new to us. The reason we flew so low was to give no opportunity for any possible ground fire as we sped fleetingly overhead. If there was anyone below us, they would have had only moments to ascertain our direction and prepare their weapons for firing – while we were gone as quickly as we had come.

It wasn't long before we were at our destination. The four aircraft hovered in a dizzy haze, before settling above the LZ, as we leapt the remaining feet to the ground and sprinted for cover in a defensive perimeter. Dust and leaves flicked up in the turbulence of the rotor wash, stinging our eyes as they strained through sweat – stung slits. Overhead, one of the choppers remained, circling low with its twin .303-calibre Browning machine guns, defiant for any threat. Then it too settled to drop its cargo, as another chopper took up watch.

The whole infiltration had taken minutes and before long the whine of engines and thumping of blades had faded into silence and the bush began to awaken from the intrusion. We knew we were accepted into our environment when the birds began to sing and normality resumed. In our four-man callsigns we blended into the foliage and became just another part of nature, making headway to our destined lying-up position (LUP). We extended ourselves in single file and followed hand signals on a plotted route. The marching was slow and hot as we strained to see and hear anything out of the ordinary.

After the chilly weather in Inyanga, I had to acclimatise fast to the heat and humidity. There were also new factors, in the form of teeming tsetse flies that added to our discomfort. They ambushed our naked skin and bit deep into it for sustenance. If it weren't the tsetse flies that were bugging the hell out of us, it was the mopani bees, another enemy we had to contend with. They hovered in thick swarms around our eyes and noses, drawn there by our sweat. So dense were they that a wave in front of the face would hardly perturb them and they continued to hover like ghostly spots that blurred our vision.

I learnt from that trip to carry a camouflage– netted scarf with me, to drape in front of my eyes when I wasn't scanning the ground for telltale signs. It also helped to wipe away the sweat and the camouflage cream that trickled down my brow to sting my eyes and obscure my vision.

At night, when the flies and the bees were no longer a hazard, we had a constant battle against mosquitoes. We had to be very careful, as most of the areas we operated in were within the malaria belt and we all took preventative medication while on ops. Despite this, I was to contract malaria on several occasions while serving in Rhodesia and elsewhere.

We spent nearly two weeks patrolling that area to no avail. It was sparsely inhabited by local villagers, who hunted, fished and grew crops for a living. We had to remain unseen as we knew the villagers would report to the FRELIMO authorities if they came across us. Most of the time was spent patrolling and setting up observation posts to observe the villages and the paths that crossed the area.

On patrol we would move slowly and tactically during the daylight hours, stopping late in the afternoon to do a dog leg and observe our own trail in case we were being followed. At last light we would move into position for the night, being careful to make as little sound as possible. It was crucial to not move around and disturb the grass and shrubbery. In the mornings, when the sun came up, any obvious sign of ours, or of the enemy's, would be accentuated by long shadows cast across the ground. It became harder in the middle of the day to pick up ground spoor, or aerial spoor among the leaves and branches.

When brewing up, which was avoided entirely at night, except for a few occasions, we would take it in turns with two guys on piquet, alert the whole time. We looked forward to these breaks which offered nourishment as well as respite from the boredom. Whenever we came across water we would drink all we had on us and replenish our bottles, again with two men remaining vigilant while the others filled up. We never knew when the next opportunity would present itself as many of the streams and rivers on our maps would be seasonally dry.

In an observation post (OP), the way we would run a four-man callsign was for two of us to be on observation while the other two rested. At night, during the light of the moon, one of us was on stag at all times during hourly shifts. If there was no moon, we would get into close formation to enjoy as much sleep as possible. We always ensured that a good supply of small rocks was on hand to wake up those who snored.

We were doing just that when, right at the end of that patrol, we had a run-in with terrorists (terrs) that still, when I think of it, leaves me with shivers running down my spine.

Rich (Heavy) Swan and I were on piquet in an OP one day, when we thought we were compromised by a local walking down a path. The man, who we observed staring in our direction, made no move or gave any sign of panic and we decided not to bomb out there and then. Sitting dead still, we remained in position until he moved off. That night there was no moon, so we all settled down within less than a metre of each other and tried to get some sleep.

Some hours afterwards, as I lay awake, I heard the soft murmur of voices and the crunch of leaves underfoot. I tensed and lay as still as possible, slowly reaching for my rifle. I thought about alerting the others with my small stash of rocks, but decided against it as whatever was making the sound drew nearer. Craning my head I looked to my right, straining my eyes to accustom them to the darkness. Within moments I identified the silhouettes of armed men as they loomed up from the low ground, advancing steadily in an extended line. I couldn't tell if the others were aware of the enemy's presence and I prayed that no-one would emit an untimely snore or a cough, or that they would not suddenly roll or shift in their sleep.

As I watched, the enemy walked straight on to our position. Fortunately we were all sprawled out under some bushes and they had to get around these: but every moment seemed like a lifetime and I was sure we had been seen. Only about a metre away from me, a ZANLA guerrilla paused, more to adjust his webbing than anything else, but I was certain he would look down and see us through the leaves. If I reached out I would have been able to touch the toe of his boot. He shifted a couple of times and then moved off slowly into the darkness, fading like the ghostly fallacy I wished he had been. Time stood still for the longest minute I have ever lived and relief came soon after I exhaled.

The moon was in our favour that night and we remained undetected. With the passing of the last enemy soldier I dared not move until I was certain they were far enough away. It seemed to take forever until the last crack of twig underfoot was heard.

When the small rock hit me from Rich's direction, it could just as well have been a round from an AK-47. Short of leaping for cover, it startled the living daylights out of me and I nearly cursed out loud. As it transpired, Rich and another member of the callsign had been awake and they had also lain frozen, wondering what would happen next. We couldn't understand how we had not been noticed.

It took a little more than a small rock to wake the final member of our group, who had slept soundly, oblivious to the passing danger. We spent the remainder of the night in stand-to positions, before finally bugging out before first light. It had been a harrowing experience and from then on we made sure that someone was always on stag, despite our standard operating procedure.

After Mozambique we were deployed to patrol the southern shoreline of Lake Kariba not far from Binga. It was suspected that gangs of terrorists were crossing the lake by boat or canoe to infiltrate under cover of darkness. We were to patrol for a couple of weeks, searching for tracks or for any sign that would prove the theory. It was quite a boring period really and we didn't come across anything to write home about. It was a lovely time to be at the lake and we indulged in viewing hundreds of wild animals of numerous species. We learned, from the more experienced bush men in the Squadron, how to deal with wild animals. It was thoroughly entertaining, watching young Squadron members, particularly those from overseas with no experience of dangerous game, finding their feet when it came to approaching, or retreating from, elephant and Cape buffalo.

The bush is a very neutral place and it can be your best friend if you understand it. If you don't, there is many a trap that can be walked into, resulting in injury or death.

The South African Police (SAP) units had not pulled out of Rhodesia entirely. Some of them were based on the lake-shore in our area of operation. It was an interesting study to note the differences between their bush camps and ours.

As most of them spoke only Afrikaans and only a little English, there was a communications gap which resulted in poor relations. It wasn't always that way, but when we saw how they lived in the lap of luxury, it certainly caused some mild resentment.

At their camps they were equipped with full-on cafeterias and gas freezers filled with ice-cold fizzy drinks and beers. All our bush camps were strictly dry at that time and apart from a brew of tea, or sometimes coffee, we rarely saw anything other than good old H2O.

The South Africans really thought they were on holiday, which is understandable since the police units hardly saw any action. I was surprised to discover that many of them had brought along their swimming trunks and sun beds, on which they lounged around a braaivleis during active deployment. It seemed they hadn't learned from experience.

At the beginning of détente in December 1974, shortly after the ceasefire, four South African policemen were gunned down when they lapsed into a state of false confidence. Believing the ceasefire to be observed by all sides, they were stopped by a ZANLA patrol as they drove down a road in the Kariba area and allowed themselves to be disarmed. Outside their vehicle they were murdered in cold blood, their corpses left to rot where they fell.

By the end of August 1975, the remaining SAP units had pulled out of Rhodesia, which coincided with my return to Salisbury. Henry Kissinger, the American envoy, had brought pressure to bear on the South Africans for supporting their naughty neighbour.

Back at Cranborne the new members of the unit were awarded their colours. In the two bush trips we had undertaken, since escape-and-evasion, it was decided that we had made the grade. Unfortunately, we hadn't encountered the enemy in a firefight, but Major Robinson was pleased with our progress. In a ceremony, unmarred by hype or pomp, he told us that there was much to learn and although we were now fully badged members, we could still be thrown out of the Squadron at any time if it became evident we were not suited.

I was overjoyed to have finally aspired to my dream, but the prospect of endless exercises and training did little for my enthusiasm.

To the south, the South Africans, forever caught up in our affairs, continued to put pressure on the Rhodesians to meet their enemies for negotiations. Kenneth Kaunda, the president of Zambia, was instrumental in proposing the peace talks, because of his country's economic losses due to the war. The border between the two countries had been closed and this reportedly resulted in the loss of over £112 million to Zambia in that year alone. With his status, as host to Rhodesia's warring factions, he united with the South African prime minister and bought pressure on the Rhodesians to end the conflict. It was a period that allowed the nationalists time to rethink their strategy, to recruit and abduct thousands more to their cause. It also allowed the terrorists to move around the country with impunity and subvert the locals into supporting them, mostly through intimidation. To the Rhodesians, it was a setback from all the progress they had already made.

The SAS meanwhile continued with internal operations and kept quiet when they went external. On my next trip I was deployed to Kariba again, with B Troop, this time to conduct maritime operations on the countless islands in the lake, by Klepper canoe and Zodiac inflatable craft.

It was a three-week deployment and I ended up manning a MAG (general-purpose machine gun) on one of the inflatables most of the time. It was thought that the terrorists were using the islands as temporary bases during the infiltration stage of their operations and were leaving arms caches buried close to the operational area for swift re-supply. We were to investigate the islands and make a sweep-through until we made contact with terrorists, or found any military hardware.

It was a frustrating period and most of us knew that our efforts were wasted. The operation ended with no contact made at all and not a single terrorist track was found on any of the islands.

During 1975 and détente, the Squadron started conducting refresher courses and retraining again. There were many instances of people leaving us to join the Selous Scouts, the new glamour unit in the army. Everyone thought the Scouts were getting all the action. Between boring bush trips there were endless exercises and a few deep penetration reconnaissance missions into Mozambique to seek out new ZANLA bases. All of these missions were of little real value and minimal contact was made with the enemy.

The Squadron lost many good operators to the Selous Scouts at that time. As a result, the powers that be thought it best to get us out of town where at least we would be out of the way of Selous Scout recruiters and where we wouldn't be bored out of our minds.

Sheila had arrived from the UK and was settling into life comfortably. She had made a few friends, which kept her occupied between nursing the kids, but I suspected she was resentful of my absence. Shortly after her arrival, I was sent on a tracking course in the Chirundu area of the lower Zambezi River. The course was to be part of a retraining exercise that would combine with minor infiltrations into Zambia to conduct follow-ups.

The tracking course was very good and we brushed up on methods of reading ground and aerial spoor, as well as learning a few new survival techniques. We were shown which plants were edible and which were not, and learnt how to make poisons to kill fish using the sap from certain trees. Contrary to the SAS hierarchy's earlier hopes, one of the instructors was a Selous Scout, who seemed to know everything about the bush. He taught us methods to trap small animals and how to make rope snares from different types of bark. I'm sure many operators admired his ingenuity and skill. I for one began to wonder what our brother Special Forces unit really got up to on operations. The course had certainly whetted my appetite.

It was an enjoyable time, but still we had made no contact with the enemy. Overall, as far as fighting the war went, 1975 was a distinctly slow period. Détente would soon end, as the peace talks crumbled and the war would intensify. As more and more terrorists filtered into the country, new means of stemming the flow had to be found.

The fireforce concept, a method by which security forces enveloped groups of terrorists using heliborne troops after being called in by OPs, was already being honed into a lethal instrument of warfare. Unfortunately, due to sanctions, Rhodesia was limited in the number of helicopters that could be mustered and therefore a means of delivering more troops to the scene of a fireforce action had to be found.

At the beginning of 1975, the SAS were the only parachute-qualified unit in the Rhodesian Army. We began to experiment with ways of delivering up to 18 fully equipped men, by parachute, to a scene, by conducting numerous jumps at Inkomo Barracks.

For weeks on end we jumped every morning into simulated fireforce actions, deploying stop groups that would work hand in hand with the heliborne troops and the K-car gunships. Over a period we refined how the fireforce commander, aloft in the command chopper, could best deploy his reserves and his main forces.

With practice it became a fine art. Each day we choreographed a ballet of death delivery and honed it to perfection. By the end of the year, it was decided to para-train the RLI, the Rhodesian African Rifles (RAR) and the Selous Scouts, so that they could, if necessary, be used in such a role.

I cannot claim to have had anything to do with the overall concept of fireforce, but it was the SAS who refined the finer points of parachuting in reserves and I am proud to have been a part of it.

With fireforce fully under wraps, the RLI and the RAR went on to huge successes in future contacts. When the manpower shortage became a problem, the SAS and Selous Scouts were used and when we were really scraping the bottom of the manpower barrel, even the territorial Rhodesia Regiment (RR) units did their fair share, quite successfully I must add, on fireforce call-outs.

That year we also trained in our maritime role, with extensive practice in Klepper canoes on Lake McLlwaine. I could not have known it at the time, but we were actually preparing for a live operation on the Zambezi River.

As part of a three-man Klepper canoe team, consisting of two oarsmen or coxswains and one diver, we did late-night infiltrations on the lake using police boats on which we attached our mines and police reserve personnel as the opposition force. With plenty of time on our hands we also got that down to a fine art.

CHAPTER 14:
REALISING THE DREAM

Later that year we were deployed back to Kanyemba, to put into practise the new skills we had acquired.

Previous reconnaissance had identified Zumba, a small Zambian town on the Zambezi, opposite Feira in Mozambique, as being the staging point for infiltrations of ZANLA terrorists into Rhodesia. My task was to take a callsign along the river, cross over into Zambia and approach Zumba where I would set up an OP overlooking the town. Once firmly in place I was to await the arrival of three Klepper canoes whose mission it was to lay charges on boats moored along the banks and infiltrate the town to blow up a fuel dump.

We were to witness the explosions, which had delayed fuses and then report back on what damage had occurred. I suppose, in current jargon, my mission was a classic bomb damage assessment.

When the operation came around I was over the moon. I had spent far too much time in training and the wheels needed some oiling before they fell off.

The infiltration was a simple task when it came to it and after entering the area on foot, we set up an OP in some dense scrub about 300 metres away from the outskirts of Zumba, making ourselves comfortable for the night ahead. We weren't going to be in the position long, so we wore light order with minimal rations, although we had brought along sufficient ammunition in case of compromise. I must say it was nice knowing that back-up was never far away, if we did get into a scrap.

As planned, at about 02:00, we watched as the Squadron guys in the canoes approached silently, downriver from the direction of Rhodesia. The moon was almost full that night and the Kleppers tucked close into the thick foliage that overhung the banks, eerily appearing in and out of the shadows.

The operation went like clockwork and before long the task was complete. Pulling alongside the three motorised transports, the operators laid their charges, finally creeping ashore to place a larger charge among a pile of 44-gallon fuel drums not far from the water's edge.

Back in the Kleppers they retreated out of sight, their mission complete. It wasn't a long wait – two and a half hours to be exact – before we reaped the fruits of our labours.

As we watched the fuel dump, what seemed like an enormous orange light bulb flickered on, as if a naughty child was playing with its switch. The bulb swelled to the point of bursting, taking milliseconds and then gave in to a resounding boom as a fireball momentarily created daylight, swathing the water around it with orange swabs of colour.

Almost synchronised, the smaller explosions erupted as boats became broken scrap. The bits and pieces of boat seemed to rain down forever as they splashed into the water, temporarily streaking the reflected highlights with dark, dancing spears.

Behind the explosions I could see the Zambians emerging from their corrugated iron huts and cabins, utter surprise on their faces; the view through my optics was an opera-mask of stark orange and black contrast.

Across the river in Feira, others appeared, FRELIMO troops among them, to see what the disturbance was about.

Then the firing started on both sides. Orange fire was joined by green, as tracer rounds ripped into every available space where an enemy could be hiding. For a moment the fire was directed at the heavens and not long afterwards at the water and then it came from both sides. All of it was a superfluous but an understandable reaction to fear.

It took 15 minutes before the enemy realised he was not under direct attack and the fire subsided. By then the place was a total mess. When they finally came to their senses, it was too late. The resulting fire had destroyed virtually everything, but they still attempted to beat back the flames.

When we returned to Kanyemba we joined the others for a well-earned drink. Someone had thought ahead and decided that to celebrate our resumption of the war, a bottle of whisky and a few beers were in order. Given our success, we could hardly be begrudged that simple comfort.

Personally, I was elated. It had taken almost a year, but I was back where I wanted to be. That sort of operation was the reason I had dreamed about the SAS for so long. It was the reason I had done everything, up until this point.

Although it was a great start, with the classic sort of operation that the SAS was designed for, B Troop were still used outside of their role, carrying out jobs that should have been assigned to the infantry battalions. There were numerous operations where our skills were under-utilised and where we were deployed on mundane tasks, like patrolling and reacting to terrorist sightings. But it must be remembered that the Rhodesian Army was always under strength, so this was understandable.

In hand with that, the government viewed many of the ideas that the SAS came up with as politically sensitive. It wouldn't be long before the gloves came off entirely and the country had to fight for its very survival.

The training courses didn't end either!

Not long after returning from Kanyemba I was put on an NCO cadre course at the drill hall in Salisbury. It really pissed me off after the thrills of active service. Maybe I shouldn't have applied myself as well as I did, but it ended up with Corporal Ken Roberts and me attaining the highest marks.

My achievement didn't pay off in the long run. Lieutenant Martin Pearse, who was our new B Troop commander, decided that I was to go on a drill-and-weapons course at the School of Infantry in Gwelo. Completion of the course meant I would become an instructor with the Squadron. The prospect didn't thrill me, so I approached the B Troop 2IC, Lieutenant Scotty McCormack and threatened that if I was posted I would leave the SAS and join the Selous Scouts. The Squadron had already lost too many personnel to the Scouts, so the 2IC was sympathetic and assured me it wouldn't happen.

A few weeks later I was told by the orderly room clerk that my name was indeed on the list to go to the School of Infantry. Things were not going my way. I preferred the prospect of having fun on ops instead of wasting precious time learning drill. I made plans to approach some of the guys I knew who were serving as parachute jump instructors (PJIs) with the air force at New Sarum. I hoped there would be an opening on a PJI course which I'd learnt about.

Fortunately, my efforts were rewarded and I got a posting to the Para School on the next available course. My application had been successful and I was one of three new PJIs to be trained. The others, whom I met shortly afterwards, were Paul Hogan, incredibly from Australia (but not the crocodile-hunting type) and

Pete, an ex-Squadron member who was joining up again.

I started the course well and was chuffed to have avoided the drill lark, but after a few weeks things were less rosy. For some reason or other it seemed that all of the currently serving PJIs were trying to leave their posts and transfer elsewhere. It seemed that we, the new guys, were taken on solely to speed up the process as they couldn't leave until we were fully trained.

Initially I was not too bothered and continued to absorb my training like a sponge, but I was always aware that the PJIs wanted out. I began to sense strongly that something was fishy in the state of Denmark.

I never did find out why everyone wanted to quit, but after a few more weeks of eating, sleeping and shitting parachutes (which was driving me mad), I too resolved to get out by applying for an RTU (Return to Unit) back to the Squadron.

It also annoyed me immensely that after all my years of service I was back to being treated like a squaddie. Even Paul, the civilian from Australia, was promoted to the rank of sergeant upon joining, while I remained a corporal.

When I contacted the orderly room at Cranborne, I was told that the cadre for the drill course had left and were happily ensconced in Gwelo. The news left me in a jovial mood and it looked as though I had avoided the farce altogether.

Content with the way things were panning out I next visited Flight Lieutenant Hales of the air force and told him I was not suited to the job. I requested that he keep my admission of incompetence confidential in the interest of my well-being and RTU me under the guise of me having flunked the course.

I was as happy as a pig in shit when Flight Lieutenant Hales called me a few days later, to reiterate my own belief that I was not, after all, suited to Para School and was therefore being transferred back to the Squadron. His compliance left me somewhat bewildered, although I think he may have felt it had been a cheek for me to have approached him in the first place, on top of which I had begged him to lie for me. Then again, maybe he was just helping me out.

CHAPTER 15:
MADMEN AND MAYHEM

Although I was only away for a month, during my absence the war had resumed in earnest. I joined my troop in Umtali where they were preparing for a cross-border operation with the rest of the Squadron and was utterly disappointed to learn that I had already missed out on one camp attack.

While in Umtali I ran into Bob Pyke, my ex-Para mate, who had passed selection and was posted to A Troop. In the few months he had served with the Squadron he had already gained a reputation as a thug and was utterly disliked by all the staff.

Shortly after having arrived in Rhodesia, Bob was in trouble. He started fights and on more than one occasion was reprimanded for the irresponsible use of firearms.

At his house in Braeside, a middle-class suburb of Salisbury, he regularly used to start gunfights, shooting up the entire neighbourhood while he was pissed! On several occasions the police had to arrest him for negligence.

Bob had bought along his wife, a redhead from the Falls Road in Northern Ireland, whom he had met while we served there. She was just as loony as he was and had the foulest mouth I've ever heard on a woman. They actually made a great couple and egged each other on to greater excesses as time went by.

One particular night in Cranborne, Bob had gone out on the piss and arrived back during the early morning. Along the way he had managed to run over a cat and brought the carcass back to the barracks. Upon entering the sleeping block, he went to the ablutions and gutted the dead animal in the basin, leaving a bloody mess of guts and skin lying on the floor.

He then lit up his gas burner in the middle of the barrack room and proceeded to boil the creature in a billycan of water. He thought this was hilarious, but it didn't pass unnoticed by the senior staff. When he finally began to eat the emaciated feline, I think he went too far. It wasn't exactly the sort of survival training practical experience that was expected of SAS troopers. Bob did most things just to piss people off.

I don't know if it was a specific experience which rattled his cage, but Bob appeared to have no respect for human life whatsoever, including his own. At the parachuting club where we freefalled, Bob coined a new expression to describe the packing of parachutes that he dubbed the 'miracle pack'. It was so-called because it would be a miracle if the damned thing opened at all.

After every jump, while we carefully folded our canopies to avoid friction burns on opening and took all the safety precautions necessary, he would just stuff his parachute back into the bag and get on with the next drink. Back then we used T10 parachutes which, unlike modern canopies that require less attention to detail, had to be packed with careful creases and folds. How he never came unstuck I don't know, but every time his canopy opened like a blooming flower. If you had dared me to exit an aircraft wearing Bob's parachute, I would have told you to fuck off!

The rumours of Bob's antics were rife in the Squadron and didn't escape my attention. I was totally embarrassed to have recruited him back in England and I felt that some of the others put the blame on my shoulders. Nobody ever said anything to me but I always felt that way.

While we waited for the cross-border operation, we did fitness training, running up and down steep hills around Umtali with heavy packs. The crunch came when the Troop embarked on a suicide run, with full weight, up Christmas Pass. This meandering route, on the main road from Salisbury to Umtali, is very picturesque – but only when travelling it in a car. Running up it in the heat of the day, you see little more than the tarmac pass under your boots, as you ascend a thousand feet in a few kilometres of road. It was absolute hell!

Revision of signals and medics were next and took care of the days that lapsed. We were all champing at the bit to go, but operational security was always tight and we weren't told a thing.

A week passed by and suddenly we were given the order to move. Arriving at Grand Reef Air Base we boarded Dakotas and were flown to Chiredzi in the lowveld. Climbing aboard Rhodef 45 (Rhodesian Defence Mercedes 1113) trucks, we drove for a couple of hours towards the border and through Gonarezhou Game Park, finally arriving at the confluence of the Sabi and Lundi Rivers, where they met before flowing into Mozambique.

At the temporary base camp, we were joined by some RLI troops and briefed on the mission ahead. We were to be one arm of a combined air and ground pincer-type thrust against terrorist bases in Gaza, while the other arm was to hit bases further north in Tete province. That night we walked across the border, heading for our objective, which lay 15 kilometres inside Mozambique. We arrived shortly before dawn.

The plan on reaching the terrorist camp was to split into four-man stop groups, which would effectively envelope the enemy and then await H hour. At dawn an RLI mortar team was to stonk the camp with 60mm bombs simultaneously, while Vampire strike aircraft unloaded their bombs and saturated the target with cannon fire.

We were to ward off any fleeing stragglers and then advance to contact towards the centre of the camp.

The walk-in was not too much of a problem except for a few occasions when we bunched up while our point detail found their bearings. After that it was plain sailing and we arrived before schedule.

When we got there we couldn't see many signs of habitation, except for a path or two that radiated outwards from a central location. My callsign headed in a southerly direction for about 500 metres, then circled around to block any escape to the north. The other stop groups in turn headed for their positions and settled in to conceal themselves.

Right on the mark, as an eerie light bought things into focus, we heard the RLI as they fired the mortars about 300 metres away from our position. The rounds landed on target and overhead the Vampires came screaming in from the west, unleashing their deadly bombs. Almost instantly the sky was filled with return fire from small arms and heavy machine guns. Tracer arced upwards toward the aircraft but was ineffective. I watched as one Vampire came in, spitting cannon shells, followed by blistering green 'hornets' as it accelerated to climb. The trail of fire was way behind it and within seconds it was out of range.

The Vampires came in on a few more runs and eventually silenced the heavy weapons with their cannon, while all around us small-arms fire erupted as the other stop groups engaged fleeting targets. I was listening to the battle when I heard the bush to our front crash open as three terrorists ran in our direction. We all fired at once and they went down, bowled over like skittles as they flopped into lifeless heaps, their AK-47 rifles clattering to the ground in front of them with the forward momentum. It was hard to tell who had hit who, but it struck me how fine the line was between life and instant death.

Just then, as if not aware of their comrade's fate, another two terrorists hurtled headlong through the leaves and the grass, dragging their weapons behind them. They were relentlessly followed by red tracer from four FNs which soon found their mark. I remember that incident well as I almost cheered for one of the terrs to get away. I was amazed as I watched a number of my own tracer narrowly missing him before someone's rounds punched into his side.

Suddenly, to our left, the bush opened up again and we all turned, instinctively putting down rounds in the direction of the noise. I couldn't see any targets but just then a duiker - a small antelope - bolted out of the undergrowth, darting left and right as it scurried for safety. It didn't say much for our marksmanship as the animal escaped unharmed.

Calm settled around us and we moved forward to the centre of the camp. It was slow going, as we searched under every bush and in every tree for hidden terrorists. The last thing we wanted at this stage was to get taken out by a lone, terrified terr. Worse still would be a friendly fire incident if we stumbled into another callsign.

The camp consisted of mud huts and thatched bashas. All the structures were ablaze and bodies littered the open ground, having been taken out in the aircraft strikes. We found scores of weapons and ammunition in open pits, covered with branches. Other pits contained medical stores and food items. One such cache contained brand-new Leica cameras with telephoto lenses, complete with rolls of 35mm film. I acquired one for myself, loaded it and began snapping away at scenes of burning huts and the effects of war, as did a few of the others.

In one of the pits we discovered two live terrorists, one of them badly injured. The injured man was given prompt medical treatment before Captain Murphy, an American in the Squadron, took charge, calling over Bob Pyke to look after them. Other callsigns were coming in and were redeployed to chase the odd terr running around. A small battle developed to the north and it was discovered that another part of the camp existed not far away.

Captain Murphy and Lieutenant Bob McKenzie organised a sweep line and we again prepared to advance to contact. Before leaving, Lieutenant McKenzie ordered Bob Pyke to stay in the arrears and look after our captives. They would be valuable sources of information in interrogation and he wasn't to take his eyes off them.

An hour later we had cleared the other sector and returned to the main camp, when Captain Murphy noticed Bob walking around dragging a dead terr behind him. Bob had found a sheet and tied the dead man's ankles together and attached the other end to his waist. Wherever he went, the dead man's head bumped along on the hard earth. When the captain asked what Bob was doing, he was told that the prisoner had tried to escape and he had shot him. He was dragging the man behind him because Lieutenant McKenzie had told him not to take his eyes off him! Bob's attempt at humour was not well received. Captain Murphy was enraged and rightfully so. We all knew that Bob had killed the man in cold blood, but it couldn't be proved.

The other prisoner, Bob told us, had died of his wounds. It was only much later that it was intimated, by Bob himself, that he had killed the man by injecting syringes of oxygen into his blood stream. He said that he wanted to see what effect it would have. Again there was no irrevocable proof and the man could have died of his wounds anyway. Captain Murphy swore he would take disciplinary action, but not much came of it given the lack of evidence.

Poor Captain Murphy was to die a few years later in a parachute accident after he joined the South African Special Forces.

After the operation the trucks were called in from Rhodesia and the bodies of the terrorists were loaded into them for identification. The weapons that we couldn't carry with us were destroyed on location.

Overall the operation had been a major success, but we learnt that two Rhodesians had died in Tete. Although we accounted for innumerable terrorists, the sad loss of the two put a damper on any celebrations that were to take place.

When we got back to Cranborne, I removed the film from my camera and gave it to Darrel Dickinson, the orderly room clerk. Darrel said he would develop it for me and deliver the photos. He also took a few rolls from the other guys who, with their liberated cameras, had suddenly become professional photographers.

A few days later Darrel, true to his word, came through with the prints. As there were a number of incredible shots on the film, he had multiples of many of the photos developed, selling them on as mementos to members who were on the operation. It wasn't long before the prints found their way to the B troop commander, Lieutenant Martin Pearse, who stormed into the orderly room and demanded to know who had taken them.

I owned up and took the blame for everyone. I didn't see why all of us should suffer his rage. Lieutenant Pearse was furious and reprimanded me saying that he would deal with the situation after he had conferred with the other officers. As he saw it, operational security had been broken and I should receive a court martial.

I was much indebted to the troop 2IC, Scotty McCormack and to Major John Murphy, who stuck by me and saw the situation for what it was. They argued that operational security had not been broken because I had acquired the camera at the camp and had not smuggled it in with me. They believed that no damage would come of the incident, as the film really depicted the aftermath of the operation and could hardly give away any secrets. As a result of the meeting, it was established that a need existed to have a Squadron photographer on hand during ops, to record such things for intelligence purposes and for posterity.

The incident, which began as a major thorn in my side, resulted in me becoming the unofficial Squadron photographer. Many of the images that exist today of that era, are there because I took them.

Amazingly, Bob Pyke stayed around for quite some time after that operation, although he eventually left the Squadron under a dark cloud. The authorities tired of his antics and finally snapped after he was caught driving around Salisbury shooting up passing cars.

Before he departed the Squadron, his crazy wife left him and returned to Ireland on her own. She too had tired of his lawless ways and constant womanising. Bob was on a mortar course in Gwelo at the time and went AWOL when he heard his wife was leaving. Convincing two RLI troopies that the journey would be a blast, he absconded with them and raced back to Salisbury to meet the plane before it left. Never one to lead a boring life, on the way he shot up a removal van, firing out of the window as one of the others drove. Even the RLI troopies couldn't believe his behaviour and they ducked out at the earliest opportunity.

Bob missed his wife's plane but talked his way out of an AWOL charge by claiming compassionate grounds for absence. The RLI guys were not so lucky and ended up in detention barracks, sweating out their crimes.

Unfortunately, the Selous Scouts eventually took Bob on because of the experience he had gained in the Paras, serving in the Vigilante anti-tank platoon. The Scouts somehow thought they could benefit from his service. He went on numerous ops with the Scouts, but while he was with them his rebellious ways got worse. One evening, in town, he was picked up by the military police for shooting up a Selous Scout party in Avondale. In view of his previous record, the charge seemed quite serious and we thought that that might be the end of Bob. Again he was released, only because he gave out information on the whereabouts of all the unlicensed weapons he knew of, namely, war trophies that other members of the SAS and the Selous Scouts had brought back from operations. Most of us were lucky enough to be warned and we managed to hide them.

An outcast in Special Forces, Bob then joined Special Branch and was involved in training surrendered enemy personnel. He didn't last long and was arrested after throwing a hand grenade at a taxi on the Beitbridge Road, just outside Salisbury. Incredibly, with the aid of a good lady lawyer, he even got away with that. But he was declared a prohibited immigrant and was kicked out of the country.

Just before he left he came around to my house one night to try and pick up my wife, thinking I was away on ops. Sheila spoke to him in the driveway and I confronted him through the curtains of my bedroom window. Before long, an argument ensued, with unguarded threats levelled at one another. When he eventually threatened to shoot me with the .44 Magnum he carried, I told him to try his level best as I had my service rifle on me. I waited for him to move and levelled my loaded FN at his head. I was fully prepared to blow his brains out at that point and I feel I would have been justified in my actions. If not for me then for the unarmed men he had murdered which I knew about and I'm sure there were others.

I think Bob knew I was serious and he backed off. Even his demented mind realised I would get away with killing him after all his silly antics and run-ins with the law. As he left, I told him that if he ever set foot on my property again, I would be only too happy to slot him. The next day he visited Sheila at work and had the cheek to ask her if I was angry with him. He added that it was all a joke and enquired whether I was actually serious about shooting him. Sheila told him about the FN and said that I had the front sight lined up between his pickles, my finger taking up pressure on the trigger.

We didn't see Bob after that.

I heard about him sometime later. He had apparently fled to Spain with the same lawyer who had got him off the hook in Rhodesia. There he got into trouble with the law and was sent back to the UK.

An interesting footnote: When I served in the Paras at depot, I was in 343 Platoon. Bob Pyke was in 346 Platoon with Costas Georgio (Callan), Nick Hall, Mick Wainhouse and Charley Christodoulou (Shotgun Charley). All of these men were deranged psychotic killers. I used to wonder whether some form of experimentation was done on that platoon in particular. Why was it that all of them turned out as they did? Mates from my Para days and I, joked that they were given a guinea-pig drug to make them into harder, more aggressive soldiers. They were all cooked in the head, that's for sure! Whatever had happened, something went wrong!

Funny, apart from those already mentioned, who got their just deserts, I've heard that most of 346 Platoon are now dead.

CHAPTER 16:
STEMMING THE TIDE

While the war escalated around the country, with an increasing number of Fire Force call-outs, B Troop got down to its real business of harassing and killing terrorists across borders. From captures in the field it was learnt that most incursions were coming from Tete Province in Mozambique. ZANLA were digging in their heels and intensifying their campaign of murder and brutality in the Hurricane operational area.

Under the inspired leadership of Lieutenant Martin Pearse and SAS Intelligence Officer Scotty McCormack, 20 members of the Troop began preparations for a two-week operation to harass enemy supply routes and lines of communication. We were to walk into Mozambique to a remote road, north of the border, beyond the Luenha tributary of the Zambezi River, where ZANLA were happily going about their business, ably assisted by FRELIMO. There we were to lay mines and ambush targets of opportunity.

Many in the Squadron at that time thought that mines were an unacceptable method of delivering a blow to the enemy. Left in place to harass particular routes, we could never be certain that they would actually be detonated by those we were targeting.

Laying mines is a very indiscriminate and cruel method of warfare. It must be said that all the mines we used were of Chinese and Soviet origin, captured from terrorists, or found in caches across the border. If we didn't destroy them, or use them, then they would only be used against ourselves, or against civilians in the country. In the war we fought there were no Queensbury Rules.

Rehearsals for the operation began near Goromonzi, east of Salisbury, where we found an area that best simulated the type of terrain in which we would be operating. We carried out an exercise to infiltrate the area without being seen and lay dummy mines on the access roads, to target the vehicles that would be collecting us.

I was unfortunately appointed to lug one of the heavy Soviet TMH46 mines, in addition to my own gear, which added an extra 20 pounds (9 kilograms) to my overall weight. Even on the exercise, walking into our target area, I felt the strain of the cumbersome mine and had to constantly shuffle my gear in order to gain a little comfort.

After the marathon infiltration haul, we arrived at a farm road where we knew our uplift vehicles would be passing. Martin Pearse designated early warning groups on the approaches and I and another operator carried out the task of removing dirt from the road, in two places, so we could lay our mines.

The knack to laying mines is not just digging a hole and covering it: it's an intricate and carefully planned procedure. Firstly, measures have to be taken to avoid leaving obvious spoor on the trail around the site of the mine. This was achieved with the utmost care taken in approaching the vicinity of where we wanted to bury the mines and then laying a groundsheet on the last metre or so of earth to the target area.

Lying on the groundsheet, dirt has to be removed in a pattern so that the dryer topsoil can then be replaced as it was, stacking it up on the side of the hole, separate from the darker, moist under-soil.

It is important not to dig the hole with vertical edges, but to bevel them, otherwise a vehicle tyre may pass over the mine, jumping from one lip of the hole to the next. Bevelled edges make the tyres ride into the hole, placing pressure directly onto the mine's MV-5 striker mechanism and MD2 detonator.

This may sound trivial but the TM46 and TMH46 mines only detonated with 396lb (180 kilograms) of applied pressure. Bevelling the edges could spell the difference between disaster and success – or, in the case of a mine, success and disaster.

Once the mine is laid you then have to disguise it, filling in the spaces around it with the undersoil and compacting it into place. This is necessary so that the mine can remain in situ for an extended period and the earth won't settle around it to reveal an obvious depression in the road. Once the soil is satisfactorily compacted, the topsoil is then replaced, ensuring no tell-tale signs of raised ground or scuff marks. For this we used a small branch, much like a feather duster, to wipe away any man-made signs. On occasion, if time permitted, we even went to the elaborate length of creating an artistic impression of vehicle tracks over the earth where the mine lay. Naturally, this was done only if we had chosen to site the device on well-used roads, where there was an abundance of vehicle tracks. Any excess soil was then removed from the area in a small bag or sock, which I used on occasion.

Withdrawing from the mine, you crawl backwards to the opposite end of the groundsheet and carefully raise it, again ensuring that no marks are left behind; then, backtracking over your own spoor, you clear the area in front of you with the same leafy branch.

All of this takes time and it is a dangerous game, particularly when you are concentrating on the job at hand. The worst that could possibly happen during this process would be if a vehicle came along while we were laying the mine, although we always relied on the early-warning groups to alert us. Even then, a tactical withdrawal is not possible in the rush to clear the road and the only course of action is to pick up the groundsheet and get the hell out of there, hoping all the time that the enemy would not notice anything amiss.

Should the mine be seen, then depending on circumstances, the main party – lying in ambush – must put down as much fire as possible, do as much damage as it can and bug out. Unfortunately, such an action means the mine-laying task could be compromised, placing the entire operation in jeopardy.

Half an hour later I finished laying my dummy mine and withdrew from the road. Under normal circumstances, we would put as much ground between us and our handiwork as we could but, for the exercise, we hung around, concealing ourselves in the long grass not far away. A few hours later one of the early-warning groups warned us of a vehicle's approach.

Ducking behind cover, we waited as it apparently drove directly over our mines. From where we were concealed, we could not tell this precisely, but once the vehicle had passed, it was flagged down and we retraced its tracks.

Had the first 'mine' not gone off when the truck passed over it, we would have been unlucky, but as it was, the tracks led straight over the second 'mine'. I doubt that anyone in the world would have had that much bad luck and our transport drivers would have been blown sky high. The TMH46 is a powerful weapon containing over 12 pounds (5 kilograms) of TNT. With that much bang the average vehicle stands little chance of escaping intact.

The exercise was a complete success, but Scotty insisted on further practice. A key word to success, and this was drummed into us, was 'repetition of training' and it stood us in good stead on future operations, and me personally later on.

As it was the rainy season, we expected to forge rivers in full flow on the operation, so we used the RLI swimming pool at Cranborne Barracks to practise river crossings.

It was no easy task carrying two weeks of supplies, as well as ammunition and the mines, but we got it down pat after a few attempts. Being a squat little fellow I provided much hilarity as I floundered in the deep end under an enormous weight; but with each one of us helping the other, our umpteenth pool crossing went without a hitch.

The actual operation commenced, with B Troop being dropped at the cordon sanitaire, a large minefield protecting Rhodesia's eastern border, about 20 kilometres away from our target. The trucks that delivered us, took back the engineers who had already breached the minefield, demarcating it with sand bags to indicate a path of access.

Before the operation I had spent a lot of time juggling the contents of my Bergen, to find a happy compromise between important items and superfluous ones. Mission-specific equipment was the priority but there was just never enough space. I never did find a happy medium and ended up discarding most of my rations, to make up for ammo, grenades, batteries, mines and other necessities. I didn't know it, but I was to pay for it dearly over the next two weeks.

The infiltration, although hot tiring work, was relatively easy and we reached the tributary during the final hours of the first afternoon, setting up an OP to observe the river. It was disturbing to note the frequency of FRELIMO patrols along the opposite bank, which appeared at regular intervals and we were left in no doubt that the entire area was saturated with enemy personnel. Our task, it seemed, was going to be made that much more difficult.

From our position, Scotty McCormack sent out two-man, close-target reconnaissance teams to check on the numerous villages in the area. When they returned, we learnt that every inhabited village contained a complement of FRELIMO troops, quite distinguishable from ZANLA by the uniforms they wore, who were there to assist in protecting their erstwhile brothers.

That night the Troop tried to cross the river and reach the road on the other side. Half way across, at about 23:00, there was a sudden flash flood and the water around us swelled, rising about two feet in as many minutes. The swift flow of the river, already a hindrance, increased to about double the speed and we all lost our footing and were dragged away by the current, submerging all our kit in the process. We managed to reach the other side, not without half drowning, soaking wet and chilled to the bone. A couple of guys, dragged under water, had unhitched their packs and nearly lost them, but they were retrieved from the low-hanging branches that had caught them.

The next day we hid out in our LUP and dried all our kit. My rations, the meagre few I'd bought, were virtually destroyed by water and were next to useless. I hadn't packed much canned food because of its weight and had carried only a high-energy breakfast cereal as well as maize meal and biltong. The dried meat was pulpy and sodden, while the powdery meal and cereal were swelled and ruined. I knew that I was in trouble and dreaded having to scrounge from the others which was considered the ultimate sin. We were all expected to look after 'number one' as a priority, before extending a hand elsewhere.

The following morning, having dried ourselves out, we started heading north to make our rendezvous. We hadn't been under way more than 20 minutes before the point man came across a village and signalled a halt. Ducking low, we crawled around the perimeter trying to avoid detection, moving at snail's pace through the thick elephant grass.

I can't adequately describe the feeling that comes over you when you realise the game is up. It's a kind of panicky, rushing surge as the heart beats faster and your sphincter muscle tightens. Training then kicks in and takes over the senses.

The mortar, when we heard it, was a distant popping sound, unmistakable for what it was. FRELIMO, it appeared, had either seen or heard us and were engaging from the centre of the village.

Lieutenant Pearse issued quick orders, telling us to get down and not return fire. I pressed myself into the earth, knowing that any second the bombs would drop among us. The TMH46 in my pack did little to comfort me as I knew it wouldn't necessarily need a direct hit to set the thing off. If it detonated it might take a whole heap of us with it.

Some 20 metres behind us, the bombs impacted, exploding harmlessly, although I could see the shrapnel shred the bark off nearby trees. We continued to lie still, without response, for about three minutes and listened to FRELIMO yelling and firing their AKs in our direction.

It takes a lot of discipline to be fired at and not return fire but after what seemed like an age, we moved silently from the area. Half-an-hour later we stopped and formed up for a quick briefing on the situation. We knew we had been compromised and FRELIMO would be on our tail.

It was decided to send a small detail back on our tracks to harass any potential follow-up and Clive Mason was sent with his modified .303 sniper rifle along with an RPD (a light Soviet machine gun) gunner.

Clive, like me, had trained as a sniper while he served in the British Army as a Royal Marine Commando and unofficially became the guru on sniping in the Squadron. Under the directive of Major Robinson, the CO, we had started a sniper cadre course in the Rhodesian SAS. I helped set it up and we both ran the course between bush trips and training.

On one of the courses that Clive ran he failed the whole class, officers included. Robinson was not too enamoured and arraigned Clive before him. Tim Callow, alongside whom I would later serve in the Selous Scouts, was one of the officers who failed and he was furious. The CO informed Clive that he could not fail an officer without exceptional reason. Clive stuck to his guns and reiterated that no-one had deserved to pass. As far as he was concerned, none of his students was sniper material.

The course was cancelled a short while later and Clive was so dejected he transferred to the Selous Scouts. Sadly, he was killed in action towards the end of the war when a stray RPD round caught him between the eyes as he withdrew from a contact.

Wherever Clive went, he dragged along his scoped rifle, forever in search of a long-range shot.

About half an hour after they left, we heard four rounds in quick succession, followed by intense automatic fire as the RPD gunner engaged.

The din that followed was short lived, but voluminous as a sharp battle raged. The rest of B Troop hit the deck, went into all-round defence and waited for Clive's return. He showed up 15 minutes later, closely followed by the gunner, legging it through the bush as if he had a hornet on his arse.

Clive told us that they hadn't been in position for longer than five minutes when they noticed two groups of FRELIMO hot on our tails, about 300 metres apart from one another. One group of about 20 was taking up the pace in hot pursuit and the other was trailing, doing 360-degree circles to find our spoor. From his position, centrally located to the front of the enemy, Clive opened fire on the lead party, taking down three men with his four shots. The other Freds dived for cover when the RDP rounds kicked up dust in their midst.

The battle we had heard was one FRELIMO party engaging the other, as they thought that each group was the remainder of B Troop. Clive didn't hang around to assess what damage they caused to each other and left them to their own devices. At least it bought us a bit of time.

Leaving FRELIMO in disorganised disarray, we fled at pace to increase the gap between us. Because of the constant danger of running smack into another village, due care was taken with a point group, advancing 50 metres to our front. Hopefully, if they ran into trouble, they could take care of themselves while we went to ground to await their return, or possibly to support them if necessary. We could then all book off in another direction, which stood us a better chance of survival if we ran into a really heavy punch-up.

I still carried all my kit, in addition to the mine and the exfiltration that day was murderous. We couldn't afford to let up the pace, as FRELIMO had been quick off the mark in launching their follow-up. The weight of my pack seemed to increase with each hour that passed and none of us had the chance to sustain ourselves since the previous night. I, for one, had eaten virtually nothing after my rations were spoiled in the river crossing.

We marched the whole day until sundown and lapsed into exhausted sleep after posting hourly piquets. The night passed without incident and we commenced our flight at sunrise, marching again until midday.

It's on operations like this that you begin to appreciate what selection is all about. Overloaded and underfed, lesser men would give up after the first few hours, right when it's imperative to keep up the pace. If one of us went down, it would let down the entire team. I suppose not letting down your mates is what keeps you going.

At 15:00 that afternoon we took up the slack again although I appreciated the small respite in our pace. Again, an RPD gunner was deployed on our back trail with instructions to follow up at a distance after observing our trail.

An hour later, while feeling quite certain that we had lost our pursuers, the RPD suddenly opened up behind us and all hell broke loose. As we dived for cover, leaves started to rain down on our heads from machine-gun rounds that were fired high through the trees.

Instantly, 81mm mortar bombs began to land all around us, bursting in orange flashes, while pinging shrapnel off obstacles and branches. The RPD gunner sprinted into our midst yelling that we must get up and make ourselves scarce.

Behind him the firing died down when he told us that FRELIMO had walked right into his position. He had taken down the lead scout with a long burst of fire. As he spoke, we heard FRELIMO in the distance, yelling out in English: 'What are you doing in Mozambique? Get out, you are not welcome here.'

The intrusion of civilised speech was ridiculous among the bloodshed and killing. It was quite absurd! Funny the things people say to each other in war.

Contrary to standard operating procedure, we went looking for a fight. Spreading ourselves over about 50 metres, we advanced in an extended line. We decided we had run far enough. The buck stopped here. It would probably have been better to put in a troop ambush on our trail but instead, we went looking for trouble.

Some 15 minutes had passed by the time we arrived at the scene of contact. The lead scout, who was taken out by the RPD in the initial burst of fire, was nowhere to be seen but there were signs of blood where he had fallen. We figured he must have been picked up when FRELIMO retreated, as there was no sign of them at all. I think they'd had enough with four guys already down to our fire and heaven knows how many casualties due to their own.

In retrospect, the shouting should have given us a clue that they were tired of the pursuit and were on their way out. We left the area and headed north, hoping to continue with our mission; but every time we stopped for a break we saw signs of FRELIMO, or ran into civilians. The bush was thick with every man and his dog scouring the countryside looking for us. The odds were not in our favour and Lieutenant Pearse decided to abort the mission and head south for the border. Freddie was always close on our arse and we had lost the initiative to ambush and mine the roads.

We all agreed that to abort was the best plan of action, but I didn't look forward to the tab-out. Not only was I suffering from lack of food and heat exhaustion, but I still had the bloody mine to carry back to Rhodesia.

It took us one-and-a-half days to reach the border, by which time I was on the verge of collapse. I appreciated the supply of fresh rations when the trucks collected us, but I still had to be treated for heat fatigue.

We were driven to Mary Mount mission station where we holed up for a few days in order to get our strength back. While there we were debriefed and learnt that we would be going back in to Mozambique the next day. This time it was payback for our aborted operation. We would attack the FRELIMO camp which had harassed us and give them something to think about.

The following morning we crossed the border via the same breach in the cordon sanitaire. Every precaution was taken to ensure that no-one had left any surprises for us during our absence. The engineers gave us the all clear and we commenced our walk into the heart of enemy territory, laden once again with full kit, although we left the mines behind.

This time around, we pretty much knew the way straight to our objective so we made headway in single file, with wide enough gaps between us in case we were ambushed. We didn't want to expose too many of us in the killing ground when the enemy fire came forth. On reaching the Luenha River we sat about until darkness fell, then crossed over, fortunately without incident this time.

A kilometre or so from the village, Lieutenant Pearse sent a reconnaissance team forward to ascertain FRELIMO's presence; we settled down to await their return. Dependent on their findings, we would approach the village at first light and sweep through.

The sun was just rising when we stepped forward in an extended line, weapons at the ready, expecting certain action. I carried my usual AK-47 assault rifle, as did many of the B Troop guys.

Several members carried RPD machine guns, chambering the same round as the AK. Some of them were cut down to give them an overall shorter length and some had their return springs lengthened to increase their rate of fire. One or two members preferred the trusty FN with its 7.62 x 51mm NATO cartridge and although it was a superb weapon, I desisted from carrying one, mainly because the AK's shorter overall length made it more manageable, particularly on parachute ops.

Nearing the village we could see a few FRELIMO soldiers sitting outside a guard room, listening to a radio. They appeared to be very relaxed, unaware that B troop were about to descend on them. It was a relatively easy approach and we made no sound at all. The long grass, which had given us away before, was covered in millions of tiny dew drops which sparkled like diamonds in the early light. As we stepped forward the grass gave way effortlessly, slipping apart like eels in a barrel.

About 50 metres outside the camp we all went to ground when Lieutenant Pearse gave the signal. We still maintained the element of surprise, as we watched ahead and witnessed more FRELIMO troops ambling out of their quarters, a few approaching the guard room. A fire flickered delicately as someone shifted a log, bending over to warm his hands.

The attack was initiated with a 42 Zulu rifle grenade, which landed smack in the fire, bowling over the few who sat there in a chorus of screams and shouts. Then we poured fire into their midst as we continued the advance, searching our arcs for targets and picking them off.

Early into the contact I had a stoppage with my AK, the very last thing you want to happen in the heat of battle. I cleared it and commenced firing but after a few more rounds from a fresh magazine the damn thing jammed again. The second stoppage was harder to clear and I dropped to my knees. No amount of physical force would budge the cocking handle, so I removed the magazine, pressed the butt into the earth and kicked the handle with my heel. Eventually it gave and cleared a round from the chamber, but I couldn't for the life of me see what had caused the problem in the first place.

I fed a new magazine into the receiver's recess and continued with the advance a few metres behind the others.

In fire-and-movement drills, practised a thousand times, we moved forward, giving covering fire to the next group as and when we went to ground. Those of the enemy who didn't fall in that initial furious minute, fled through the camp and ran into the bush on the other side.

One group of guys was given the task of clearing all the buildings, while another set up our 60mm mortar. We used the weapon as an impromptu stop group, landing bombs in the enemy's flight path about a hundred metres beyond the camp. We hadn't dedicated stop groups earlier, for risk of being compromised. There were just too many enemy personnel milling around.

After sweeping through the camp, some of us regrouped at the guardroom where Lieutenant Pearse had taken up station. We began gathering up what we could for intelligence purposes and piled captured weapons into a heap.

As we bought more and more weapons to the guardroom, Lieutenant Pearse was removing the magazines and making them safe. A few of the other guys assisted him, as the haul was immense.

I settled down and stripped my AK. I was thinking that the river crossing may have interfered with the weapon's action, by depositing sand in the chamber or in the working parts. I couldn't figure it out as I'd cleaned the rifle 20 times since then. At Mary Mount, it had been thoroughly stripped and oiled.

There is no need to harp on about the attributes of the AK-47 rifles, as they are generally totally reliable and need no vindication. My weapon had just let me down at the most inconvenient time.

Just when the weapon was stripped and all the parts were lying on my scarf in front of me, automatic fire peppered into the walls of the guard room. It came from an area of dense cover just outside the camp. Everyone dived for cover and I ran to the pile of captured weapons to replace my own. Picking up a fresh rifle I must have touched the trigger and it went off; the round punching into the dirt behind Lieutenant Pearse, having passed between his legs. At such close range the impact of the bullet billowed up a huge cloud of debris, showering the lieutenant with dust as he took cover.

After the little shootout which was quickly dealt with, the brave defenders emptying their magazines and joining their comrades on the run, Lieutenant Pearse stood up, shook himself free of dust and bellowed 'Who the FUCK nearly shot me?'

I could have kept my mouth shut, but I owned up and explained that it was me. I told him that the rifle concerned was one that he had just cleared and there must have been a round in the chamber. There was no magazine on the weapon, luckily, and it was in the pile that was supposedly safe.

If the rifle had been charged with a full 30 round mag, I have no doubt that I would have shot the shit out of the B Troop commander as the fire selector catch was in the fully automatic position. The one flaw with the AK-47, in my opinion, is that the fire selector moves from safe to fully automatic and then to single shot. This is what Soviet military doctrine dictates, but is contrary to western military practice where the most effective type of fire is rapid, well-aimed single shots.

I think the lieutenant realised his mistake and the matter was dropped. He saw my personal weapon lying stripped on the ground and he swallowed his pride. That was the first and only negligent discharge I'd had in my life and it gave me a wake-up call. I've always felt a little guilty about it and don't know what would have happened if I'd wounded, or possibly killed, the lieutenant.

Unfortunately, Lieutenant Pearse would die within three-and-a-half years of that incident. The charge he had thrown into a building exploded, bringing down a wall on top of him. I was serving in the Selous Scouts at the time, but his death brought back memories of that operation and instilled in me a deep-rooted respect for premonition. Before he left on the fateful mission, Martin Pearse, a captain by then, told another Squadron member that he knew he was not going to make it back. Three days after his death he was to be awarded the Silver Cross of Rhodesia, the country's second-highest gallantry award, for his part in another operation called *Bastille.*

Standing under the shade of a bluegum tree, during rehearsals for the operation on which he was to die, he whispered, 'Wouldn't it be strange if I copped it before I got my medal?'

A brave man was Martin Pearse and a soldier of whom Rhodesia could be proud.

From intelligence gleaned on the scene, we decided to attack another camp the following day, after returning to Rhodesia for resupply.

My previous eagerness for getting into the thick of things was proving far in excess of what I had hoped for and we were all totally knackered. The tempo of war had increased and the Rhodesian Army battled against time to get a foot in the door and to stem the flow of terrorism. The dirty job fell on only a few thousand individuals, from a handful of units which were constantly hampered by manpower restraints, while ZANLA and ZIPRA mustered tens of thousands to their cause, often through the barrel of a gun.

Our tab into Mozambique began much the same as the previous two and we marched on a compass bearing for most of that morning. By noon we were exhausted and keen to get the operation over and done with. As we neared the camp area, a burst of automatic fire raked through us from our left flank, barely 10 metres from where I stood. Fortunately the fire was ineffective and everyone went to ground unscathed, throwing off their Bergens as they did so. A few rounds were returned in the direction of the ambush but, true to form, the attackers emptied their magazines and fled.

Our mortar man managed to get a couple of rounds down the tube and we heard the bombs explode in the distance. Given our proximity to the target, time became crucial and we feared we had run into a clearance patrol who would warn the camp.

We dusted ourselves off and resumed the march with care, hoping that the noise of battle had not forewarned our enemy.

When we arrived at the camp, 30 minutes later, it was deserted. From its outskirts, we mortared the village and put down effective fire into buildings and places of concealment, but there was no response.

We set fire to the place after going through it, sifting the buildings for documents and were exfiltrating when we were again ambushed at close range. A small skirmish took place and the guys ahead of me outflanked the enemy position and killed two terrs who had concealed themselves in the grass.

From the appearance of things it seemed as if most of our foe were not keen to joust and the walk out was without incident. Only weeks before, the area had teemed with enemy, intent on causing our demise. For the next few days, from Mary Mount, we sent out patrols to gather intelligence and ascertain the whereabouts of other ZANLA/FRELIMO camps. It was exhausting work with no reward and eventually we gave up.

A couple of months later we were to return to the area, confident that FRELIMO would once again be settled. There had not been much activity at all in the vicinity, as the Selous Scouts were operating a ‘frozen zone’ there, which was off limits to other security forces.

Thankfully, this time, there were no God-forsaken tabs and we took off from Mary Mount in two Alouette helicopters, carrying two callsigns of men with an 81mm mortar apiece.

We were dropped about a kilometre from particular camps and stonked them with mortar fire while the choppers acted as eyes and ears overhead, directing our bombs onto targets of opportunity. The missions were relentless over a two-week period and we rained mortars across a vast swathe of enemy territory. I drew on my experience from the Paras in Kenya and the after-action reports indicated our fire had been largely effective, thoroughly demoralising the Freds.

Within weeks of that operation, radio intercepts picked up intelligence that hundreds of FRELIMO troops were deserting the army because they were tired of being stuffed up by the Rhodesians.

CHAPTER 17:
LOSS OF INNOCENCE

Back in Salisbury, Sheila was getting a bit pissed off with my increasing absence. When I did get to see my family, I was overjoyed and home life was good, but there was rarely any time to be a real father and husband. The boys were growing up and were in that period of life when a father figure has a crucial bearing on the outcome of their character. I was hardly ever around, with most bush trips lasting between six and eight weeks. My longest trip lasted 11 weeks, which equated to almost three months that the family had to do without me.

When I did get leave it was never for more than a week, but mostly just a few days. Even then it was spent on bar room operations with the boys, frequenting pubs and clubs like Le Coq D'or, Oasis, the Terreskane Hotel, Lions Den, the Windsor and the George Hotel. It was 15 cents a beer then and cheap enough to forget our worries in the bush, even if our sorrows were drowned in liberal amounts of alcohol.

Sheila often accused me of being married to the army and she was quite right. She never did understand that my time on leave was needed to unwind from the stress of constant operations. The guys who were with me on ops at least went through the same thing I did and I felt they understood me.

In hindsight I feel very sorry for Sheila, as she went through hell when I was away, constantly expecting a knock at the door that would deliver bad news. I know she used to listen to the radio every day, waiting for the force's communiqué, half expecting to hear the words 'Combined Operations regrets to announce the deaths of so and so and so and so in action'. She told me that every single day she prepared herself for the worst. Now that must be hell!

I was certainly not the best father or husband. I think, if circumstances had been different, that might have changed, but as it was I was caught up in a game of survival. Like others, I had joined the army to see a little action, but I ended up fighting for my life and for my mate's lives.

I had been in the military for nearly eight years, in two combat zones, before I was certain I had killed a man. That is to say, before I knew I was personally and irrevocably responsible for a man's death.

On other occasions it was easier to allow someone else to take the credit. There were countless operations where I had fired on enemy personnel, but in the confusion and din of battle, with everyone else firing as well, it was hard to claim a kill – and one was probably better off that way.

Killing is not a pleasant experience and I abhor those who claim otherwise. Some are psychotic, deranged killers, who think that their audiences will be impressed by their tales of death and dying. The rest are cowboys; Walter Mittys who have never seen a day's action in their lives. These chairborne commandos rile me to the point of being sick!

On numerous occasions, in the heat of battle, I fired upon an enemy fighter and watched as he miraculously escaped – impervious to my bullets, it seemed. I am a good marksman and it defied logic that I should miss so frequently.

A few times, when I was shooting at my enemy and he was shooting back at me, it was easier to say that one of the others had hit him than to personally accept responsibility. It does funny things to the mind, knowing you have taken another man's life.

I've often been asked how many men I've killed, but these questions come from people who have never been there. I would rather be asked how many people I'd saved, because that's how I justified it. If I killed one terrorist in combat, wouldn't that be saving other people who might later become victims of his murderous ways?

To sum up, I can't say I never killed a man, as I'm sure there were many, but it's easier for me to cope, thinking it was someone else who did the dirty work. It's my little way of maintaining some sanity in the crazy world we live in. When the day did come and there was nobody else to blame, it was somewhat different to how I had imagined it.

I was on another operation into Mozambique in late 1976. This time we were to drive in, combining two Troops of SAS, about 40 guys and 20 or so RLI personnel.

It is strange how I remember least about that operation, as I am usually good with that sort of thing – not so much times and dates, but events.

Rehearsals for the operation started at the Inkomo Barracks firing range, where we mounted captured DShK 12.7 heavy machine guns on the back of 25 trucks. They were mounted on their tripods and although a little unwieldy, they afforded 360-degree fire over the cab of the vehicles. At the time 12.7mm ammunition was scarce, so our practice was limited.

A few other trucks had Hispano 20mm cannon mounted on them. The cannon had been taken from the wings of Vampire aircraft and were immensely heavy, cumbersome weapons. Used in the ground role they were devastating and brought to the battle a new dimension of firepower. Bob Pyke manned one and I recall him laughing maniacally, as he loosed off round after round down range; the high explosive projectiles decimating the targets on the butts.

Rehearsals over, we drove the vehicles to a remote airfield, that bordered Mozambique in the Tete area. We made final preparations there and waited for the engineers to arrive.

When we breached the cordon sanitaire, it was as a flying column of 10 vehicles, rolling across the border in the late hours of darkness. The excitement of the unknown bit at my stomach. Nothingness filled my mind. Everyone was purposefully driven to get the operation underway successfully. As we crossed the border, I could sense the other SAS men around me, mentally running through last-minute preparations. Is my camouflage cream running, did I bring that extra battery, will we need air support and the big question, what if I get wounded? Although, by this time, combat was second nature, that question always came up. Personally, I would discard the thought as soon as it came. It did no good to dwell on the worst.

Through the night, we drove directly to our target, which was another FRELIMO/ZANLA camp, about 60 kilometres into the country. For purposes of operational security the vehicles kept their headlights off and we drove in complete radio silence. Some areas of the road were in a state of total disrepair. The Unimogs handled it well enough, but some of the smaller vehicles needed a bit of physical prompting. Despite the setbacks, we arrived as planned during the first minutes of sunlight.

On the way in, we dropped a mortar team in position and waited for them to initiate the dawn attack, raining bombs in a predetermined target pattern. After the long drive, it was incredible how things changed so rapidly. We were given a half-hour notice on standby, while we deployed stop groups around the camp and the next thing, we were in among the enemy, the column of vehicles driving straight in, blazing away with cannon, heavy machine guns and small arms fire.

It was a fantastic sight, witnessing the 20mms in action as they evaporated walls and targets in their path. After the mortars, the camp was in confusion and disarray, people running everywhere as they tried to escape the merciless slaughter. Some of the stop groups later complained about overshoots from the heavy weapons. The cannon shells apparently tore through the bushes above them, as they lay in wait in their ambush positions.

It didn't take long to rout the camp and the 'body count' was impressive, although not to the usual standard of Rhodesian attacks. Rhodesians, like the Americans in Vietnam, were preoccupied with the benign military term that defined battles won, by the pile of bodies at the end of them. The difference was that in Rhodesia, it mattered. If we could kill enough of the enemy, we could stop the steady flow of terrorism into the country.

Riding on our success, we hung around in Mozambique the following day, looking for more trouble. We were confident of safety in numbers, as it would have to be a brave, or stupid enemy to take us on, considering the firepower we carried. Not only were we well armed, but we had the advantage of mobility to strike as and when we pleased, or, for that matter, to get out if we chose not to fight.

As we approached a small village, the vehicles pulled alongside a dirt track and we dismounted to sweep through. We had been involved in a few skirmishes since the previous day's attack, with small pockets of resistance that hid out in the bush, or in the safety of huts and buildings.

We had cleared a few huts, all of them built slightly raised off the ground, when I rounded one of the structures and saw a foot disappear underneath another, about 15 metres away. My first instinct was to drop on my knees and double-tap two rounds from the FN I carried, in the direction of the movement.

A small groan came from under the hut, followed by a wheeze and a death rattle. I approached cautiously, bending down and used the barrel of my rifle to brush aside some grass that grew on the hut's verges.

When I pulled the dead man out from under the building, guilt immediately welled up inside me. The poor old devil was 90 in the shade, a cripple and it was obvious he was only there because he couldn't move anywhere else. Dark, frothy blood oozed from wounds where my rounds had punctured his lungs. There was a look of fear and disbelief on his face. He hadn't known what fury had come to find him that day. It felt like I had somehow lost my innocence, although in reality it had long since fled me.

One of the guys next to me, perversely rubbed it in saying, 'Shit Jake, you're a real killer!'

As if his words weren't bad enough, the others joined in jeering and cajoling.

I really felt shit. Here was this poor, old, defenceless man and I'd plugged him, without a thought or a care in the world.

I've thought about that day often since then and I've never been able to justify it in my mind. The British government had spent thousands of pounds, training me to defend the UK against the threat of a Russian onslaught. The Rhodesian government spent thousands of dollars training me to defend Rhodesia from terrorists. And here was my first confirmed kill – there was no-one else to blame – a crippled old man going on a hundred. I don't like to think about what other horrors he might have lived through, in order to attain that ripe old age – until I came along, that is.

After my 'blooding', I did my first parachute deployment into battle. When we returned to Salisbury, we were given a warning order that we were to be used on a short operation, parachuting into a ZANLA camp in Mozambique, just south of the Cabora Bassa Dam, near the Mukumbura border post.

At New Sarum air base, we were briefed on the operation and settled in, confined overnight, to commence the attack the following morning. The air force would arrive at the camp before us in Canberra bombers and drop Alpha bombs on the target before we jumped in. The Alpha bomb was an ingenious weapon for its time and was designed by Rhodesian engineers specifically for attacking large base camps. In essence, it was a bouncing bomb with a proximity fuse, designed to bounce to 4.5 metres and then explode, showering shrapnel in a downward pattern, which no other bomb could do.

The small, 15-centimetre spherical container that housed the bomb, was made of thin steel, under which lay a bed of 'super balls' (the rubber toy) on top of another smaller sphere. Around that lay ball bearings for shrapnel. Contained in the smallest sphere, was the charge and fuse. Ostensibly it was like a round, bouncing Claymore mine, only more lethal. When hundreds of them were dropped at a time from drum-like canisters underneath the Canberra's wings, there was little chance of escape.

We left New Sarum at 04:00 the following morning in two Dakotas, with 18 troops in each, which would put us on target at 05:30 as the sun came up. It was an A and B Troop operation and each of the Troops stuck to their own aircraft.

Only when we were five minutes out from the camp did we see the Canberras sweep past below us, to drop their ordnance on a low-level bombing run. The timing was worked out so we would be jumping as the last bombs were exploding.

On the signal we stood up and hitched our static lines, shuffling into place by the door. At times like these there is little room to worry about what lies ahead, as there are numerous equipment checks to process, not only for yourself but for the trooper in front of you.

The green light flashed on over the target and the first man stepped out of the door, followed by a steady rhythm of paratroopers until the last man had gone. My canopy deployed above me flawlessly and I looked around at the open space below. For a moment there was silence, only the occasional ripple of wind whistling through the rigging. It could have been quite peaceful if we weren't at war.

As I descended, I could see the dust clouds in the camp off to my left, as the Alpha bombs cut down their harvest, followed within seconds, by the last delayed sounds of the exploding ordnance.

The wind was very calm that day and there were no injuries on landing, unusual for such a low-level drop. I was in a callsign that was deployed north of the camp as a stop group and I remember being quite miffed that I was not the callsign commander. Without a radio it was hard to figure out what was going on around me and I just went with the flow of things.

No sooner had we landed and got into position, than battles erupted all around us, as stop groups engaged fleeing terrorists. My callsign was 20 metres off a huge anthill, when three terrorists rounded the red earthen tower, hurtling towards us. The pace at which they ran was too fast for them to slow down and I saw them see us, resigning themselves to their fate as they did so. I had come to recognise the look on men's faces who know they are about to die.

In a hail of fire, all three men tumbled over, one taking a side step, his forward momentum stopped instantly by the impact of numerous rounds, before spinning a few times and flopping over like a cartoon character that had just been shot. If there were merits for drama, then this aspiring actor would have got top marks.

The callsign waited about five minutes before the radio crackled into life, calling us forward to advance on the camp. I slapped the base of the magazine on my weapon, as I always did, to ensure a snug fit and stepped over some brush, my foot scraping the head of one of the dead terrs.

As I touched him the dead guy stirred. Normal procedure would have been a double tap into the guy's chest as we passed, to make sure he was dead. Others had learnt from their mistakes when they were shot in the back by terrorists they had supposedly already killed.

Something stopped me this time and I covered the injured man with my rifle. At first I could see no sign of a wound as he was turning towards me and I thought he might be a good capture. He was side on, his good side facing me and his rifle safe in front of him, but I couldn't be sure if he had a grenade or a pistol under his body.

When he did face me I saw the damage we had done with our bullets. Half his face was blown away and his left eye socket was totally gone – no sign of the eye-ball at all – revealing a deep cavity into the plasma matter of his brain. Chips of skull and brain clung to the torn, exposed flesh of his cheek. I was ready for him, if he made a sudden move, but the horror of it numbed me momentarily and I stood there looking at him.

The propensity of humankind to cling to the barest thread of life has always astounded me and this was an unbelievable example. No human being should be able to survive a 7.62mm through the face.

If what happened next wasn't so macabre it might have been funny.

Raising himself on one hand the terrorist shook his head, bits and pieces of him flying off his face like a dog shaking off water, sticking to the ground where they landed. Wiping his forehead with the back of his hand, as if to indicate the source of pain, he reached out with a cupped palm and asked, out loud, in English, 'Please boss, can I have an aspirin. I've got terrible headache.'

I couldn't believe what I heard. We all stood there unwilling to accept what we had just seen, unwilling to believe that we were responsible for this apparition in front of us. This bloodied human being seeking out one last chance for survival. That's another image that has stayed with me always.

We left the injured terr with one of the Squadron medics and continued with our sweep. I heard later that he had died of his wounds, but I have a sneaky suspicion that he was put out of his misery. Live captives were extremely valuable to the Rhodesians for obvious reasons but an injured captive in that state was of little use. I would never condone the execution of prisoners in the field, but I know that on occasion it happened. Outside of Geneva Convention parameters, or sound military ethic, a few guys realised the massive drain that an injured enemy soldier would be logistically and thought it better to save the trouble. In many cases, as this one could well have been, shooting an injured man was the compassionate thing to do.

One thing that did get to me on this operation happened just before we left. The commander of the operation, who had orbited above in the K-car directing the attack, landed by the secretariat of the camp and decided that a weapons test was in order.

The Squadron had toyed with the idea of replacing the FN rifle with the American M16, available to equip the whole unit through sanctions-busting methods. The Americans in the unit were enthusiastic about the idea and one or two already carried their own M16s on operations; Captain Bob McKenzie was one of them. The Rhodesians, to the man, preferred the FN over the tinny and less powerful M16. The commander happened to be carrying one in the K-car and he arranged for a few of the dead terrorists to be set up as targets. Maybe he wanted some form of vicarious satisfaction, having missed out on the actual fighting. At various ranges, a few of the guys put rounds into the bodies, alternating between single shot and fully automatic.

The commander wanted to see what the 5.56mm round was capable of as we had all heard stories of the round tumbling after it left the barrel. The standard round at the time was the military SS109 and we discovered for ourselves that it indeed tumbled beyond a range of 100 metres, keyholing through targets. I felt that the exercise accorded no honour to the dead. I suppose we were all numbed with the amount of horror we saw. When we couldn't take bodies back for identification, we left them to rot in the sun. There's not much honour in that. We just didn't have the time for issues like burials.

I didn't stick around to witness the effects of bullets on deceased human targets but nevertheless the Squadron stuck to their guns, so to speak and retained the FN after that little demonstration. I'm sure there were other reasons for the choice, but the test seemed to clinch it.

After sweeping the camp area, we tabbed south and slept in the bush not far from the border. Early the next morning we heard the Alouettes coming in to uplift us and take us back to Rhodesia. Aside from the misery I witnessed, it was operations like that which I loved. In, out and home in time for breakfast.

There were many operations that were fruitless, in an attempt to chase the war. Acting on intelligence gleaned on site, we would often deploy by parachute to achieve maximum surprise when the enemy least expected us. Having hit one camp, we could be sure that news would travel and the terrs believed we were incapable of hitting two camps on the same day.

Before an attack went in, sometimes a reserve force would be deployed to a forward airfield and stand by for news of additional targets. This was not always the case, as manpower was short and often the call-outs were lemons (false alarms) or the enemy had fled. Sometimes we would land at a deserted camp and find fresh spoor which we would follow relentlessly for days on end. Rarely did these kinds of operations meet with success.

CHAPTER 18:
APACHE COUNTRY

The war didn't pause for us and after a week-long R&R, we crossed to the extreme south of the country for an operation mounted from the Chipinda Pools area, just inside Gonarezhou National Park, into Gaza. We travelled by convoy in 25 trucks, arriving at Chipinda Pools while the bridge was still under construction. We crossed a shallow section of the Lundi River, continued on our way and were soon met by another 25 truck, which came bearing down on us from the opposite direction. I was in the passenger seat of one of the cabs and from where I sat, I could see a motley crew in the back of the oncoming truck, hanging over the sides, waving scarves and veils at us. Some carried 'shake shake' containers and waved them above their heads as if conducting a victory incantation. Other's heads were completely wrapped in combat scarves. There were no threatening gestures, or reason for alarm and it appeared that the bunch of reprobates was excited to see us.

As it came near we recognised the vehicle's passengers as 'coloured' men from the Rhodesia Defence Regiment. Always excitable, without casting all as a stereotype, they were an entertaining bunch of fellows. The coloureds continued to gesticulate, while shouting out loudly, as our vehicles drew to a halt.

A few of them clambered out of the back of the truck and ran over to speak to us. One particularly comical-looking character leaned in the window: 'Are you *oeuns* our relief column, *ek sê*?' he asked. 'It's about time you white *oeuns* gave us goffels a break.'

We were told that they had been forgotten – which was quite apt, considering the Defence Regiment's nickname was 'The forgotten army'. Units such as this, manned mainly by coloureds, with a few white officers and coloured officers, were primarily used to guard installations across the country, such as bridges and power lines. It was a boring task, meant for reserve troops, although on occasion they did get revved by terrorists which resulted in a bit of action.

It was the funniest thing to see a coloured, as I did once, boasting about his and his buddies' prowess in combat. As happened on this occasion, very few shots were fired and yet they would go on about it as if it had been the ultimate confrontation. You couldn't begrudge their character and it would leave you in fits of laughter witnessing their mannerisms and figures of speech. Much of which ended up as RLI slang, a language in itself, originated from coloured euphemisms.

The Defence Regiment coloureds were disappointed when we told them that we weren't their relief. One of our Troop commanders vowed to report their situation over the radio and get them replaced as soon as possible. They seemed to appreciate our gesture and asked us if we were interested in some shake shake. This foul concoction is a mixture of ingredients, home brewed to dangerous and sometimes volatile levels. We declined their offer but invited them to a brew of our own and told them we were going across the river into Mozambique. They were awed at our gumption and told us that we were mad. Only madmen would cross the border into Apache Country, which they said was inundated with terrorists and landmines.

We spent a couple of entertaining hours at Chipinda, teaching the coloureds how to strip and clean their Bren gun. The weapon, until we arrived, was rusty and seized up.

The reserve types of units in Rhodesia were always issued with inferior weapons. I'm not saying that the Bren gun is a shit weapon, but it was a little outdated compared with the MAGs and FN rifles of the frontline units. As a standard service rifle, the coloureds carried G3 assault rifles, unfortunately not the Heckler & Koch variety, but copies made by the Portuguese. In Rhodesia these weapons gained a reputation for stoppages and malfunctions and were frowned upon by many. Apart from their tinny feel when compared to the FN, I must say I never had a complaint about them. As a reserve weapon they were more than satisfactory.

I had just finished boiling water on my gas burner, when one of the coloureds, a lanky, skinny fellow, walked up to a group of us and engaged us in conversation. He related a story from his deployment that had us rolling around on the ground, choking with laughter. Vernon Conchie, a strapping, tough, well-respected B Troop member, was virtually crying as he fought to gain composure.

It's very hard to capture the humour of the incident, in writing, as much of it was in the telling, particularly the language used, as mentioned before, and I've never been good at drama. Never the less here is the gist of it: On one particular night, while guarding the bridge, a certain coloured was on gun piquet with the Bren gun when he noticed a firefly passing by, then another one. Whether it was the effects of the shake shake, copious amounts of marijuana (which the coloureds always smoked) or genuine mistaken identity, he mistook the glowing insects for incoming tracer rounds!

Letting rip with a magazine of 7.62, he screamed the alarm, yelling: 'Tracer incoming! Tracer incoming!' rolling his Rs and accentuating his Cs and then dived for cover. The firefight that ensued was a one-sided affair with the insects and a lot of other things coming off second best. Other coloureds, asleep in their tents, woke up and fired straight through the canvas walls at everything and nothing.

The whole camp opened up, thereby ignoring the principles of aimed, directed fire and emptied magazine after magazine on fully automatic. The pyrotechnic display was apparently quite a thing to see and it took a full minute to realise that they were not under attack.

Our enthusiastic storyteller finished off by saying, 'It was quite a firefly fight, *ek sê*'! We were even shown the tents that were perforated with hundreds of ragged holes.

The following day, still suffering the effects of humorous over-indulgence, we crossed the Lundi, once again back in Mozambique's Gaza Province and found out that the coloureds had not been lying about the mines. Every 500 metres a huge crater loomed before us on the dusty dirt road. Around the holes lay piles of twisted scrap metal that had once been vehicles.

I had just been afforded the privilege of becoming B Troop storeman, which I hoped would allow some leniency when the Squadron was in Salisbury. I figured that, as store man, I would not be posted on active operations as much and I could see more of my family. I thought that a six-month break would do me a world of good, but it was not to be that way. All I achieved was accumulating extra duties on top of my operational status.

My versatility was obviously noticed and so I continued with deployments across borders, much as I'd done before. The B Troop commander considered me a good option to send out with new members of the Squadron to show them the ropes. So much for my idea of a swan in sunny Salisbury!

There was another problem with being store man. When I was not present at the base camps, the stores tent would be pilfered and I would arrive back, hot and sweaty, to find the ration packs opened and all the best food items stolen. Toilet rolls were a favourite among the troops and I always had to account for those that were missing. It really seemed pathetic to me when I consider we were fighting a war at the time. That the number-crunchers could get so upset about a missing bog roll defies logic!

Once happily across the border we were ordered to patrol and cut for spoor. Intelligence reports revealed that large incursions were taking place from the region. We patrolled for two days, uncovering absolutely zip and at the end of the second day, were ordered back to an airstrip just inside Rhodesia.

The return journey through Apache Country was devoid of Indians, or any sign of them. We had a little trouble when one of the vehicles sank into the shifting sand of the gently flowing Lundi, but we were helped out by our new Defence Regiment friends. They were more than surprised to see us in one piece and I was told that they had even conducted a ceremony, after our departure, as they thought that was the last they would see of us. I'm sure it was just another excuse to bring out the marijuana and the shake shake, but it was a stirring gesture.

At the airstrip we were greeted by the sight of a Dakota and three Alouette helicopters, one of them a K-car with a 20mm cannon. The terrorists we had been looking for had been spotted by a Selous Scout OP in the area and we were to action the Fire Force.

The Troop was allotted callsigns and mine was to be on the Dakota, parachuting into the contact after the heliborne troops had been inserted.

By now the air force personnel had the Fire Force concept down to a practised art and we were soon equipped and in the air. It was only 20 minutes' flying time to the scene of the terrorist sighting, so the Alouettes took off before we did.

When we arrived overhead, the battle was in full swing. I recall standing in the door of the aircraft, as first man out and above the drone of the engines, hearing a great deal of noise as the K-car's 20mm cannon pounded away in the distance. The 20mm was soon joined by rifle fire and I realised that the aircraft was being shot at. Even in the hazy light of day tracer fire was visible as it zipped past the aircraft.

There was no time to think about dying and the green light distracted me, signalling my exit into oblivion. I stepped out of the aircraft into the slipstream which dragged my form rearwards, out of reach of the menacing tail structure. Above me my canopy opened and I checked the rigging for twists. Using T10 parachutes rigging twists translated into twisted ankles, broken bones or broken bodies.

Below me I could see ant-like figures running all over the show, some of them stopping to look up at us. Only they weren't just looking, they were shooting. Although I was below 400 feet (122 metres) I could not make out any detail but I was acutely aware of streams of grotesque green 'hornets' reaching up, highlighted against the dark earth backdrop, searching for me. The fire continued until the ground came into focus and rushed up to meet me.

On landing I jettisoned my harness and brought my rifle to bear from where it was strapped down my side. I couldn't have been too far away from the enemy and I expected a burst of fire to come my way any second.

Behind me, I glanced over my shoulder and noticed Vernon Conchie executing a perfect parachute landing about 20 metres to my right. Flaring just before he hit terra firma, he touched down on both feet – running in mid-air – anticipating the ground before him. His canopy folded as he turned and gathered up the lower rigging. Milliseconds passed and in one swift move he unbuckled both harnesses from his shoulders, his parachute billowing behind him with its new-found slack.

Before he even grabbed his rifle Vernon unhitched his trousers, dropped them to his ankles and squatted to take a dump. In seconds, having released his bowels, he ripped off his pockets, then his lapels and wiped his arse. In a follow-through motion he hitched his trousers and fastened them, then swiftly gathered his rifle and was potting off a few shots at some distant terrs before you could say presto. The way it unfolded I could see that he had rehearsed the manoeuvre during the descent. It was the most perfect defecation under fire that I have ever seen. In fact, I don't imagine there have been too many others like it.

Our callsigns moved forward, with small actions taking place around us. To my left I saw some of the lads cut down a group of terrs as they ran through the bush, firing wildly. It was a slow battle, as the enemy were spread across a wide area and it was hard going, winkling out groups of two or three from the dense undergrowth in which they had hidden.

After about two hours we had accounted for a few terrorists, no more than eight or nine in fact. We continued to search the area while the choppers flew overhead, also eager for the kill. Once in a while we would hear the 20mm, or the twin Brownings on the G-cars as they fired into enemy positions.

Eventually it started getting late and an eerie twilight settled around us. It was dangerous fighting in the half-light as everything took on the same tones. There were no tell-tale dense shadows to give away a terr's position under a bush. Some of the guys would just pump a couple of rounds at inanimate objects they were uncertain of. This practice saved many lives during the course of the war and often an object would keel over, spilling a primed weapon before it, revealing a terrorist lying in wait.

With impending nightfall the heliborne troops were flown back to Chipinda. We were unlucky and had to spend the night in the bush, accompanied by our new but very dead friends.

It's incredible how a body deforms so quickly. Rigor mortis sets in within the first hour and within an hour of that the body bloats, as trapped gases well up inside it. Fortunately it was dark and there were no flies. They came in the morning, attracted by the putrefaction of rotting flesh.

Hyenas were a problem that night. In the distance we heard them cackle, the scent of death already permeating the lowveld as they planned their approach. Crafty animals, the hyena were always aware of our presence, as our sweet odour was foreign to the natural smell of nature.

In ones and twos they would skulk forward, distracting us, as their cohorts snuck in behind and tried to drag the bodies off into the bush. Only a few well-aimed shots would drive them back and even then it was a battle of patience to see who would ultimately win the prize.

When we finally returned to Chipinda, after loading the bodies the next morning, we didn't feel so bad about spending the night in the bush. The guys who had flown in the previous night had to wash out the choppers after they had been piled high with dead terrs. The mess was appalling.

That afternoon I asked Conchie about his defecation under fire. His simple answer summed up all our feelings during that parachute descent. 'I just shat myself' he said. 'I thought I was going to get zapped before I landed.'

CHAPTER 19:
RAT-CATCHERS AND ROOM CLEARERS

There was always rivalry between the foreigners and the Rhodesians in the unit. Initially all the British members were called the Rotvangers (rat-catchers), a nickname coined for British POWs in Japanese prison camps during World War II. In order to survive, they caught rats for food.

With time the term Rotvangers was applied to all the foreigners, whether they were British, American or European. The Rhodesians never really got on with most of these guys for various reasons. The main bone of contention was that many of the foreigners were quite happy to sleep with the local black women and frequented black bars and night clubs.

It was not so much a racial distinction that pissed off the Rhodesians, as a class distinction. Rhodesians in general got on with blacks, but they were raised apart, in different social circles. The few blacks that did go to public and government schools were generally accepted as equals although they were a rarity.

For the most part white Rhodesians never slept with blacks. They fought and died alongside them, but to sleep with them was a social disgrace. Aside from that, associating with blacks, in their domain, was considered a breach of national security. It would have been unwise to ignore the fact that the nationalists had eyes and ears in the cities, particularly in the pubs; and it was in the pubs where men dropped their guard and spoke about things they shouldn't, aided by liberal amounts of alcohol.

Another cause for contention was the resentment the Rhodesians felt for the foreigners' experience in places like Northern Ireland and Vietnam. The foreigners always thought they knew better and boasted how they had done things here or there.

Having said that, most of the differences were trivial and each group gained from the others' experience. There were many hard, professional soldiers in both camps.

I was very fortunate and got on with most people. I was originally considered an outcast until the Rhodesians in the unit discovered I had been raised in the country. The likes of Bob Pyke hated the Rhodesians and he would often call me a sell-out when I camped in their corner. Bob was very vocal and was always scathing about men like Andy Chait, Koos Loots and Paul Fisher, all of them good men and entirely professional soldiers.

The South Africans in the unit generally hung out with the Rhodesians. Together they were labelled 'The Club Tomorrow boys' because of their habit of frequenting the night club of the same name. Additionally, a few Australians and New Zealanders were accepted into this circle as they had more in common with the white Africans. Coming from a continent and an island with more similarities racially and geographically, they blended more easily into the social scene.

On R&R the Rhodesians would always head off to Club Tomorrow, while the Rotvangers drank elsewhere. Many of the officers whiled away their time at the club and cliques developed between the non-commissioned and the commissioned ranks.

There was definitely favouritism shown by the predominantly Rhodesian officer cadre. They always considered their own kind first when good operations, such as camp attacks, came along. I was told that the Squadron CO had issued a warning that all nicknames should be dropped. If anyone was heard mentioning either of them they would be kicked out of the unit.

It's a pity that such rivalry existed. Although it never really got in the way that we fought the war, I feel that it maligned the Squadron in some way. How much better a fighting force would we have been had everyone forgot their differences.

Mavonde is about eight kilometres inside Mozambique, east of the Honde Valley. Terrorists were using the small town as a staging point to infiltrate Rhodesia and the valley was becoming an extremely hot area. The crunch came when the Ruda police station was attacked in force by a large group of ZANLA terrorists, who pressed home their offensive and caused much damage to the station, although nobody was seriously injured.

Then, just before Christmas 1977, 27 African workers were massacred at the

Inyanga tea estate while they went about their business of reaping a crop. Their hands bound, they were forced to lie on the ground and then were systematically executed with automatic weapons fire. It was one of the most brutal acts of terrorism in the war.

The SAS hierarchy sought permission to attack Mavonde and were given the all-clear in late December. We were to stage the attack from Grand Reef air base, near Umtali, utilising the usual mix of heliborne and parachute troops. It was to be the first time Rhodesian troops engaged in heavy house-to-house fighting and many lessons were learned from the raid.

At Grand Reef we were introduced to the new bunker bomb. As the name implies, it was developed by Rhodesians to neutralise bunkers. The bomb was designed after a previous attack on Rambanayi, when Ian Suttil, a former Royal Marine, was injured after entering a bunker which had already received the attention of numerous grenades. The device was nothing more than a glorified grenade really, containing a kilogram of PE4 plastic explosive. This was contained in a brown plastic, preformed box, to the top of which was affixed a standard grenade handle, firing mechanism and detonator.

The difference was the amount of oomph it packed. Normal grenades were useless when clearing bunkers and it was on numerous occasions that terrorists emerged, none the worse for wear, after sustaining one, two or even three grenades tossed into their subterranean lairs. Mavonde was to be the testing ground for this new equipment and it didn't disappoint us.

The day after arriving at Grand Reef we geared up for the raid. Awaiting our departure on the apron stood two Dakotas and the usual compliment of Alouette K-car and G-car gunships. Once again I was to be in the para role, manning one of the early-warning stop groups, jumping on the periphery of the small Mozambique town. Our task was to keep an eye out for escaping, or approaching, FRELIMO and ZANLA personnel. The real worry was that FRELIMO might provide relief in the form of BTR (Soviet armoured personnel) vehicles, equipped with heavy machine guns. Or worse still, they might react with tanks.

The flight into Mozambique was no different from the norm. My pulse raced when we arrived on target and the aircraft circled the town before levelling out on its drop-off run.

With practised efficiency, our ETA over Mavonde was timed to coincide minutes after the air force had already been through, softening up the target with bombs and cannon fire from Canberra and Hunter aircraft. Following the bombing, the choppers touched down on the outskirts of the town spewing out their troops who, when we landed, were already hitting Mavonde with full force, firing off RPG7 rockets and saturating the place with small arms fire. Our descent under canopy was pretty much the same as the previous one and once again we were engaged by small arms fire while still in the air. It was a terrifying thing to be shot at when we felt most vulnerable although we were told that hitting a paratrooper in descent was almost impossible. I'm sure that was more of a morale booster than hard fact.

Our landings were a mixture of piss poor and perfection, as some of the guys landed in trees and were having fleeting fire fights while they were still hung up in the branches. I was more fortunate and touched down gently some distance from the fracas.

Once in our callsigns, we made way to our designated areas, my own being on the high ground overlooking the town. It was a memorable sight, watching the guys below fighting room to room. If you didn't know the Rhodesians had limited experience in this sort of warfare you would never have guessed it. I watched in awe as callsigns moved systematically from building to building, covering each other's arcs, clearing each structure as they came to it.

At one of the buildings, after a brief exchange of fire, I noticed a trooper using a bunker bomb to clear a room of enemy. While a mate put in a burst of fire, to keep the terrs' heads down, he lobbed the bomb through a window and then ran to take cover at one of the building's corners. It was always safer to take cover where the structural integrity of a wall is greatest – or else the whole thing might collapse on you. When the bomb detonated, it lifted the whole roof off the walls before settling it down in a thud of dust and debris. It was a fantastic sight and a resounding success!

As we watched, an intense battle developed between FRELIMO troops and the Rhodesians. Separate contacts were taking place all over the show with an enormous amount of small arms fire and grenades being exchanged.

My callsign stayed in position, alert for enemy reinforcements, or stragglers trying to escape the town. I was positioned about 20 metres away from the rest of the callsign, when something caught my eye about 200 metres west of our location. In a small gully that led away from Mavonde, a few terrorists were crouched over, bent double as they hurried along a path away from the firefight. One of them was attempting to take a light-coloured shirt off in an effort to change his appearance. Wearing numerous layers of clothes was common practice among the terrorists, inside and outside Rhodesia and enabled them to blend into the rural environment after being spotted by security forces. True believers in Mao Tse-tung's doctrines of living to fight another day they often changed, dumped their weapons and melted in with the local populace.

In the gully, I could see that one of the terrs was armed with what appeared to be a bolt-action rifle. The others carried AKs and SKS rifles. I tried to attract the attention of the other guys, but short of a piercing wolf whistle, they were too absorbed in the goings-on around them to notice. Sound travels far on the open air between two hill features and I didn't want to warn the enemy of our presence.

They were half way up the gully and approaching a ridge, beyond which they would be in dead ground, so I opened fire. I was in the kneeling position and took a lead on the guy carrying the long gun, squeezing off one round from my AK. He dropped as if he was pole-axed and the rest of them went to ground. By now the other guys had seen what I was firing at and directed a volley into the re-entrant. The terrs legged it, experiencing charmed lives as they dodged and weaved uphill, geysers of dust erupting around them.

The weight of fire was far too heavy for them to escape and eventually we had them pinned down in a shallow depression. I got on the blower, informed the Troop commander of our predicament and was told to use top cover to winkle them out.

I called in Yellow Section; a Cessna 337 (called the Lynx by the Rhodesians), was circling a few kilometres from the town. The pilot told me to lob white smoke and direct him onto the enemy.

Crawling from cover, I unfastened a smoke grenade and pulled the pin, tossing it about 10 metres from my position. My eyes strained upwards to get a visual on the aircraft while I stood by, radio in hand, to correct its flight path. For a long minute I couldn't see a thing, but when I finally did, I was horrified to recognise the frontal silhouette of the Lynx, as it dived out of the sun, heading straight for the white smoke.

There was little time to mull things over, but I do recall having the silly thought that the aircraft looked quite graceful, in a menacing sort of way, as it loosed off a couple of SNEB 37mm rockets. I even followed the smoke, trailing behind the missiles, before I dived for cover. The earth around our position shook and erupted into a deafening fire ball, hurling fist-sized rocks in a wide radius. Suddenly I knew what it was like to be on the receiving end of close fire support. I expected to turn around and find the rest of the callsign a bunch of crispy, fried critters. Squinting through the dust, I was relieved to find them all in one piece, although a little panicked. One of them lunged at me, screaming to call off the attack. It was kind of like stating the obvious – as if the thought had not already occurred to me!

I managed to raise the pilot before his next salvo blew us to eternity. There was no time to bicker about the error and I directed him off our mark to put a few rockets into the gully. This time his trajectory looked good and following the white smoke, we witnessed a direct hit on the enemy position. Whether it was the rockets that were ineffective, or a continuation of the terrorist's charmed existence, it really didn't matter because as the dust settled we saw the remaining terrs disappear over the ridge. We all put down fire but without the success of my previous shot. It's not the easiest thing to hit a running target at the best of times, let alone with the recent shock of almost being incinerated by your own side. Like us, the terrs were pretty lucky to escape with their lives.

On clearing the area we found one slightly charred corpse. The guerrilla's weapon was an antiquated K98 Mauser of German origin. I couldn't tell what state it had been in because of the damage the rockets caused, but a weapon is a weapon and I should hate to have been shot by the powerful 7.92mm cartridge that the rifle fires.

We swept forward to the town in case more terrs were hiding in the gullies. Our trek downhill revealed no more signs of the enemy and I think our lucky trio were the only ones to escape. A body count in the town revealed 44 enemy dead for the loss of none, which on the scale of Rhodesian successes was only a mediocre day's jousting. The operation had taught the Squadron a thing or two about fighting in built-up areas and the bunker bomb was a resounding success.

Before we left Mavonde, we placed some TMH46 mines on the approach roads, boosted with PE4 and anti-lift devices. We could be sure that FRELIMO would enter the town as soon as we left and we wanted to leave a surprise for them.

There was a large haul of captured weaponry and documents, which had to be ferried back to Rhodesia. When the air force arrived to collect them, we were told that the military police were waiting at Grand Reef, ready to nab anyone with souvenirs of war. I didn't snaffle anything that time round, but I know plenty of guys who did. I would have kept the K98 had it been serviceable.

When we arrived back at Grand Reef, Lieutenant Bob McKenzie was having nothing of it. We all viewed the military police with outright disdain. They would swoop in like vultures to ruin our fun after we had returned from fighting the war. The lieutenant stormed off the helicopter and was right into them, shoving and pushing and telling them where they could get off. The MPs, it seemed, realised they had roped in the wrong stallion and we never heard another thing about it.

After Mavonde, there were numerous small-scale incursions into Mozambique to harass ZANLA and FRELIMO. One rates a mention because it was a Squadron operation and the first time the entire unit, virtually to the man, crossed the border. Given the expense of training the average SAS trooper, it was a high-risk operation which effectively put all our eggs into one basket – we would have been a grand target had the enemy caught us short-footed. We therefore put in extra effort on rehearsals, themselves a time-consuming but necessary activity.

We used a farm in the Mount Hampden area and simulated the entire operation from start to finish, going over several elements time and time again. The first quest was moving such a large force, about 80 guys, undetected through the bush at night. Not only would visibility be restricted, but numerous problems develop at night which are not serious during the day. The availability of technical equipment, so relied upon in today's elite units, was not available to us except for a single pair of night-vision goggles.

Our main predicament was the number of domestic dogs that abounded in the area that we were to walk into. A barking dog could easily spell an instant compromise, so we practised walking with as much stealth as possible. When it comes down to it, despite methods of foot placement to eradicate noise, it's quite different from the stealth one sees in movies. The truth of the matter was that if we walked within earshot of any conscious person or animal, we would be heard.

When the moon was right, we deployed to an area just east of Nhamatanda on the Mozambique border. We breached the minefield and began our long march, in single file, to the target area. We were hard pressed maintaining disciplined formation and gaps kept appearing in the line as we yo-yoed to and fro.

At 04:00, on reaching the target, we were halted by the incessant yapping of dogs. We cowered in cover but the animals kept up their chorus for at least 10 minutes. Word was passed down the line that the operation might be compromised and we prepared for an about face. With so many operators, by the time word reached the end of the line, new decisions had been made and orders changed.

We backed off from the area, while the dogs continued to yap at unseen ghosts. Circumnavigating the threat, we arrived at the mortar base plate position and dropped off the bombs we were each carrying. By this time I was absolutely knackered and just wanted to get on with the attack.

The callsign I belonged to was posted to the far side of the camp once again as a stop group. We snuck into position and awaited the sunrise which would bring with it the familiar sound of mortar fire.

To the minute the mortars opened up, dropping bombs on target from a preconceived range card. It was crucial to follow directions to the T as Rhodesian SAS men made a habit of punctuality and would soon be sweeping through dangerous ground. Seconds off and a mortar man would risk killing or wounding his own team.

The operation was a total swan for my callsign and nobody at all fled in our direction. We listened like impartial bystanders as the battle raged. It seemed distant except for the odd intercept on the radio, when we knew our mates were fighting for their lives.

An hour later we commenced our sweep forward to the centre of the camp. Not even a bird stirred and the area was totally devoid of life. Those enemy who had lived moments before were now lifeless heaps that adorned the bare, swept clay of the FRELIMO village. Their life's essence had leaked from their corpses to blend with the red soil.

As far as results go, it was the worst operation I had been on. A few enemy were accounted for but the rest had somehow snuck by the stop groups, escaping with any documentation they had, as a search revealed nothing.

Later that afternoon we were uplifted by chopper and flown across the border. The thankless task of having to walk was avoided and I appreciated the relief.

The Rhodesian Security Forces continued to fight a brave battle across a wide front. Looking back, it was kind of like sticking our fingers into the holes of a dyke, trying to stem the flow, but new holes kept appearing. We lost a few good men over the years, but we never lost a battle. The professionalism in the unit remained stalwart to the end, but the magnitude of the threat could never realistically be contained.

It saddens me now when I think of the lives lost, including all the innocent people who died at the hands of Robert Mugabe's ZANLA terrorists. They were victims, caught up in a quagmire of violent rage.

I'm saddened too when I think of the lives I took. Most were unavoidable and I justify my actions because they took place in the heat of war. One or two might have been avoided, but I don't like to think about those.

My war was to carry on. I was still young and fashioned of the same stern stuff that most men I served with were made of. It was not for us, at the time, to question the rationale of our actions. We fought to survive so that our mates and our country would survive too.

We were back in the north of the country, conducting operations against ZIPRA, in Zambia, from the idyllic environs of Lake Kariba. A small team of B Troop operators were to deploy by Klepper canoe, to carry out a reconnaissance on the main Livingstone-Victoria Falls road, which ran in a north-easterly direction to meet up with the Lusaka road.

We infiltrated the area and set up an OP on a small hill about 60 metres off the main drag and spent an entirely boring week doing nothing. Other than a few pedestrians and civilian traffic, on the fifth day we noted two Zambian Army BTR armoured vehicles as they rumbled south-west, oblivious to our presence. There was no indication of ZIPRA so we exfiltrated a few kilometres and were uplifted back to Binga in Rhodesia.

After a few days' swan we were deployed internally to the Sibungwe Narrows – a part of the lake, west of Binga, where, as the name implies, its width steadily decreases to form the closest point between Zambia and Rhodesia.

Virtually every territorial serviceman in Rhodesia knows the place, as it was a popular posting where troopies could take advantage of the sun and even catch a few Tigerfish if they wished. I mention the place only because of what we discovered there during that patrol.

Debussing our 45s, we approached the lake shore, sweeping the sandy terrain for terrorist spoor. It wasn't long before one of the guys found extremely wide tyre tracks of an unusual military-type pattern, where they shouldn't have been. We followed them to the water's edge, where they vanished as the soil changed to pebbles. We knew the Zambian Army had in their inventory a few amphibious vehicles and a report was filed indicating the area as a possible uplift point for Zambian patrols. It was a stark realisation that we weren't the only ones sneaking about in enemy territory and the Narrows was put on high alert as a result. Nothing ever came of it but every soldier posted there thereafter was a little more subdued when he went about bronzing his youthful body.

Kariba was a nice change of scenery, regardless of the relentless patrolling, but after a couple of days we were recalled to Binga and briefed on a possible camp attack. An OP had identified a ZIPRA camp ten kilometres into Zambia and it was decided to strike while the iron was hot. For the purpose of the operation, the *Sea Lion* ferry was appropriated to deploy the entire Squadron across the lake. From there we would tab to the enemy camp overnight and attack it in the morning. Funnily enough, for those with a sense of military nostalgia, the ferry still operates in Zimbabwe today under the same name as part of Kariba Ferries. Many a tourist to Zimbabwe may have travelled the Milibizi-Kariba route on this ferry and been unaware of the history attached to it.

It was a long wait while the ferry travelled from Kariba, almost 220 kilometres distant, but it arrived on schedule late that night. We boarded the craft and headed on a north-west bearing to a suitable landing point on the Zambian shore, which had been previously reconnoitred. On reaching Zambia, the whole Squadron disembarked, formed up in single file and headed off following the lead scout elements. Behind us, the ferry initiated reverse thrust and disappeared into the milky gloom. Our objective was to reach the target before sunrise so the attack could commence and we shuffled slowly, negotiating the dense bush, while we made positive headway. I began wondering, as did some of the others, why the vegetation didn't thin out as we got further from the water, when suddenly, after an hour on the march, we were ordered to stop. From the front came a directive to turn around and head back to the collection point. Discipline had to be maintained as we were still in enemy territory, but you could see the puzzlement on everyone's faces as they begged to know what had transpired. It was only when we got to the beach that we learnt the Squadron had managed to traverse a large island, the point elements arriving on the other side with Zambia still a few kilometres off. So much for articulate navigation skills! It must be said that it was largely an error on the driver's side and not much to do with ourselves.

The ferry was radioed and returned to collect us, but by then our timings were off and the operation was cancelled. To further our woes, after we boarded, the ferry's diesel engines emitted a final wheeze, belched out smoke and cut. We were stranded, sitting ducks as the entire Squadron floundered in open water, vulnerable to enemy attack. I dread to think what might have happened if the enemy were switched on and launched aerial reconnaissance patrols looking for Rhodesian security forces. We might have been wiped out in one fell swoop!

The operation was abandoned finally after that. Maybe it was felt that the compromise could have been too costly, had we been compromised at all. Or maybe the enemy had scattered from the camp, or possibly lay in wait for us, after the bungled attack. More than likely it was the embarrassment it caused at high levels. We never heard anything more of it.

CHAPTER 20:
Babysitting blues

There were more operations into Zambia from Binga. A new lieutenant, JD we'll call him, had recently passed selection from the RLI, where he had been wounded on operations and spent a long time convalescing. When he joined us, because of his inexperience, the Troop commander appointed me to watch his back. I was to point him in the right direction if and when he strayed.

My first operation with the lieutenant was as part of a four-man callsign, deployed by Klepper canoe, into Zambia, opposite the Binga area. Once again we were to set up an OP and watch for ZIPRA and Zambian Army activity on a road servicing a camp that mirrored its Rhodesian counterpart.

The infiltration was successful and we were dropped, by Squadron coxswains, in the Kleppers, under the dense overhang of a recently fallen tree at the water's edge. The bay in which we had landed had steep sides and offered perfect concealment for the covert insertion.

With the lake behind us, we patrolled toward the target area, taking advantage of the last hours of darkness. A few hundred metres from the water's edge the bush began to thin and the terrain became featureless and flat, pockmarked occasionally by a cluster of trees. Things always look completely different at night and when first light came, the terrain was worse than we had imagined. As far as we could see, there were open, grassy, gently rolling plains with less dense cover than we had thought.

Whenever we operated in Zambia, carrying out recce patrols or manning OPs, we wore the same plain green uniforms as the Zambian Army and painted our faces with 'black is beautiful' cream. From a distance, if we were lucky, we might pass as a Zambian patrol and hopefully not raise any suspicions. Most of the time we were aware that we were operating in the enemy's back yard and that things we might take for granted, the enemy might not. The thicket we might hide out in, for instance, could very well be a familiar hunting ground, or possibly even the enemies' very own lover's lane. Many of the ZIPRA camps housed male and female occupants and sexual fraternisation among the enemy was common. It wasn't unusual for recce teams to witness a couple straying off into the bush for a bit of slap and tickle.

We always had to be careful when approaching an area and look for signs of human disturbance. The more obvious ones would be an overpowering smell of urine, which might indicate a bush toilet, or simply an abundance of dog spoor indicating that a tip or disposal area was nearby.

Less obvious signs, to the uninitiated, would be the presence of birds, like Marabou storks circling overhead. Carrion eaters and scavengers, Marabous were always a sure indication of human habitation.

When we arrived at our target area, the Lieutenant chose the only hill feature for miles around to place our OP. I advised against it and told him that any hill feature was a likely place for the enemy to look if they suspected they were being watched. Without a doubt, the terrorists always searched the hills, having learned from experience that the Rhodesians normally placed their OPs there. I said that a far better choice would be a raised knoll somewhere less obvious. I must admit we didn't have much of a choice, but the hill we were about to climb stuck out like a pimple on a baby's bum. Unfortunately, the lieutenant pulled rank and went ahead with his decision anyway.

We settled into a depression on the top of the hill, right next to a big boulder and did our best to camouflage it. In Zambia, we couldn't just go around throwing up camouflage nets and the like, which might change the overall silhouette of a feature when viewed from the low ground, so most of our hides were open, taking advantage of hollows and natural features. We were always careful not to disturb the surrounding brush.

After settling into our new home for the day, a distant bush fire emerged on the horizon, steadily creeping our way. The wind was not favourable to us and the fire raged with alarming speed in our direction, eventually reaching the base of the hill and edging up to expose our meagre concealment. Fortunately, the grass thinned as the ground got higher and the fire petered out, burning everything around us, to leave a three-by-three metre island on which we perched. The fire then edged its way down the opposite side of the hill, gaining momentum, before veering off, carried away by the prevailing wind. I was a bit concerned about what had caused the fire and advised we move position. The lieutenant wouldn't hear of it and we stayed where we were.

Toward evening JD told two of us to remain behind, while he and another operator crept forward to conduct a close-target reconnaissance, taking with him an A63 (VHF communications set) so we could remain in comms. We retained the TR48 (HF communications set) and another A63 at the OP. He told us that he would collect water on the way back, to ensure we had our fill for the duration of the operation, arriving back at our position three nights later.

My companion was a trooper and I organised a roster, in which one of us could get our head down, while the other was on watch. I made myself comfortable to get some rest. Setting up my mini gas burner I got a much-needed brew on the go.

Within a few hours darkness was upon us and the lieutenant and his companion disappeared into the night. The following day he contacted us and gave us a situation report. From his vantage point he could see a hive of ZIPRA activity, including well set defences and gun emplacements protecting the camp and its approaches. I hoped, above hope, that ZIPRA didn't have the equipment to pick up our radio communications.

The second morning, after talking to him at about 06:00, I cautiously moved around our OP informing my companion of the latest news. I had just returned to my spot and was brewing up again, when I heard a commotion. The noise grew louder and I identified it as human voices speaking an African dialect. My heart raced and I was on my feet in seconds to investigate. My companion needed no warning and froze, pressing himself into the ground. Taking up my FN, I tiptoed around the big boulder and peeked in the direction of the noise. About a hundred metres away, at the base of the hill, a hunting party of eight Africans, dressed in an assortment of military uniforms, trudged up to meet us, with purpose in their pace as they steadily climbed. They carried a mixture of machetes and SKS rifles in extended line and ushered before them a pack of ravenous-looking dogs. The other operator stood to, while I hurried into my webbing and packed away my gear, burning my fingers on the stove as I blew to extinguish the flames. The enemy were almost upon us when I rounded the boulder with my rifle into my shoulder, pointing it at the nearest man's chest.

When they looked up, the shock on their faces was almost as much as ours. I quickly put two and two together and realised that our unwelcome guests were searching the top of the hill for game that they had hopefully flushed, ahead of the man-made fire a few days before. The soot-stained earth would readily give up any animal spoor that led to our position. The only edible vegetation, for miles around, was right where we sat comfortably watching the ZIPRA camp.

I didn't fire my weapon as I didn't want to draw the entire neighbourhood onto our position, but I advanced steadily yelling at them to fuck off. Even the dogs seemed to notice the seriousness in my demeanour and the whole hunting troop turned and raced down the hill, stumbling and tripping in their terrified flight to safety. There was no time to procrastinate so we gathered up our gear, sharing out the Bergens that the other two operators had left behind. We were bearing an incredible load and we strained under carrying the added weight. A hurried effort was made to hide any signs that would reveal how many of us were in the OP, but it was impossible to hide everything, given the circumstances. After a few days of living in an area there are too many telltale signs of a human presence.

While my companion went to his knee in front of me I called up the lieutenant and warned him of the compromise. I then got hold of the base at Binga and requested a hot extraction. It would be about ten minutes before the whole ZIPRA camp was on top of us and we needed no encouragement to bug out. Saddling up, we headed off at a half run and jogged down the hill, heading toward the lake.

We hadn't gone far when I looked behind me and noticed our trail through the burnt grass. We might as well have poured buckets of red paint behind us, as the ashen vegetation crumbled, revealing bright red soil beneath it. I knew the choppers would be airborne already and only 20 minutes' flying time from our position, but it did nothing to calm my frayed nerves. I was sure the camp would have been alerted by now and a search party would be hot on our tails.

Some 20 minutes had passed since the compromise and we had been legging it for about half that time when the radio came to life. The chopper pilot told us that he was about two minutes out and we should find a suitable LZ. I was looking around at all the open space when I heard the helicopter and then saw it heading towards us in the distance. I dropped my pack and jumped in the air, waving my arms like a ground controller on a caffeine high, in an attempt to attract the pilot's attention. He bore down right on top of us and settled 30 metres away while we cowered from the swirling rotor wash. Debris and ash covered us from head to foot – but rather that than an encounter with a numerically superior, not to mention highly pissed off, enemy.

I had just clambered aboard the chopper and looked over my shoulder at the distant hill when it disappeared in a puff of smoke. The entire top of the feature billowed up in dust clouds as 82mm mortar bombs saturated our previous location. Had we still been there I have no doubt we would have been killed.

We flew west for a minute and then started to head north back into Zambia. I asked the gunner/technician what we were doing and he said: "We were going in to pick up the lieutenant and his companion by the ZIPRA camp." I yelled in his ear that he must be mad and motioned for the pilot's attention. When he looked at me I tried to let him know about the gun emplacements and the anti-aircraft batteries. Above the noise of the engine he just shrugged his shoulders and continued to head into the lion's den.

Fortunately the lieutenant got hold of the pilot when he heard us approaching. He warned him that the AA positions were manned, ready and waiting. He told the pilot that uplift was a negative and he would find his own way out with the other operator. In my view it was a redeeming gesture in light of his prior ignorance which had landed us in this muddle in the first place!

The chopper turned south-west and headed home. The lieutenant and the other operator managed to get away from the camp later that morning, while ZIPRA's attention was focused on searching for us. He was uplifted late in the afternoon and flown back to camp for debrief.

If I wasn't impressed with JDs initiation, the Troop commander was furious. I mentioned a few critical errors that led to the compromise, in the main, that we should have moved after the bush fire and we all agreed. It was a close shave and we could have found ourselves in a very sticky position. The lieutenant was cautioned and told to rely more on the experience of his senior NCOs until he learnt the ropes. The Troop commander might as well have been pissing in the wind as it came back to haunt him on other operations. One of them was in the not too distant future and I would pay for it with my soul.

B Troop moved west of Binga to the Victoria Falls, where we based ourselves at a tented camp next to the Victoria Falls International Airport. The facility was used as a forward base to conduct operations internally in the Tangent operational area, as well as a staging post for clandestine ops into the western regions of Zambia.

Once again I was designated babysitter for JD, whose callsign was given the task of conducting another reconnaissance on a suspected ZIPRA camp, north-east of Livingstone. I was absolutely guttered and feared that the lieutenant's antics would eventually lead to a whole lot of trouble. I didn't feel like dying just yet, but at the same time, I couldn't leave the rest of the callsign's fate in his hands. To add to my woes, were my additional duties as troop store man. Other store men were never deployed on ops and remained on base, carrying out administrative tasks. I'd been through this before, so I won't harp on about it, but suffice it to say that things were not going to change for me throughout the war.

Our insertion method on this operation was deployment by helicopter through the Zambezi River gorge. It was a fantastic thrill flying at low level between the towering rocky cliffs and quite a sight to behold. After take-off, we headed north until the falls were in sight and then dipped east, into the gorge, dropping to meet the water surface, as the white walls of spray tumbled into the middle Zambezi behind us. Flying under the Victoria Falls Bridge, we continued on for 20 minutes, skimming the cascading river as it fought its way through boulder country, tossing and turning in an effigy of the world's largest washing machine. It's bizarre to think now how people while away their recreational time white-water rafting on that stretch of river these days. It was a relatively new sport back then and certainly the furthest thing from our minds as we made our way to wage war on an unsuspecting enemy.

After an exhilarating flight, the chopper ascended to an open area by the river's edge. On either side of us the cliffs widened to form a bowl, narrowing ahead as the river continued to cut its way through solid rock. Touching down momentarily, we deplaned, laden with equipment and the Alouette continued on its way; its rotor blades hardly missing a beat to give the impression that it had never landed.

In a defensive perimeter, we hung around the LZ for about an hour. If we had been heard we didn't want to emerge over the precipice on the Zambian bank immediately, as someone might be watching. The lieutenant reached for his map, a huge monstrosity of a thing and plotted his course, fumbling with it in the powerful wind that funnelled through the gorge. He may as well have waved a big white flag to signal our presence as he spread the 1:50 000-scale map across a huge granite boulder, weighing it down with smaller rocks on the corners. How the whole of Zambia could not see it I will never know.

Our course should have been pre-plotted and I told the lieutenant so. He offered some lame excuse, but I wasn't really listening. All I wanted was to ensure we all came back from our little adventure alive.

After having heralded our presence to all and sundry, we moved west, pacing it slowly, until the light faded. We found an LUP among some rocks not far from the river and slept, posting piquets on lookout. At first light, we were out of our LUP and heading in an easterly direction. I was quite familiar with the ploy of throwing the enemy off our tracks, but this was ridiculous and besides, we made no effort to anti-track. At mid-morning we found a path that led in the general direction of where we were headed. It was well used and the earth was packed to form an unbreakable surface, over which lay thick, fine sand, blown in from miles upstream. Behind us, the path obviously led to the river and was used to fetch water, or was used by fisherman. The lieutenant decided to use it and casually ambled north-east, once in a while consulting his compass. I was in the tail-end Charlie position and sent a message forward that we should get off the path, or at least try to anti-track. My advice was once again ignored in the lieutenant's haste to get on with the task at hand.

The terrain around us was fairly open and I worried that we would be seen. It wasn't hard to realise that our luck would run out eventually and that we would either stumble into civilians, or worse still, the enemy.

I was thinking that perhaps I was being too cautious, when I glanced to my right, just off the beaten track and a coppery reflection caught my eye. Brushing aside clumps of grass, I picked up a few AK spent cartridge cases. This was certain evidence that the enemy hunted in the area and I passed on another message that we should be tactical and be more careful. The lieutenant, however, continued his stroll down the increasingly widening – thus well-used – path, which was becoming more of a road by this stage.

A little further on, one of the other operators stumbled across an AKM bayonet which lay hidden among some fallen leaves. I was becoming decidedly flustered as it became clear that we were indeed on a guerrilla path. The lieutenant was delighted with the little trinket, a fine addition to his collection back home and he just plodded on. Any minute I imagined, we would walk into either a well-armed ZIPRA or Zambian Army patrol.

At midday, JD finally decided to leave the path, signalling us to move off to his left and I delightedly followed. Entering the verge of long grass where the others had turned off, I was stunned when he suddenly dropped his gear to the ground 30 metres ahead and announced that it was time for a brew. If he didn't have a thick Rhodesian accent I imagined his words would be something like: 'I say chaps, jolly good spot for afternoon tea, wouldn't you say?' in typical colonial British officer drawl.

It was the most flagrant misuse of common sense I had ever seen. Behind our picnic area, a sheer cliff loomed, running the length of the path as far as one could see in front of us and behind us, leading into a gully which ended in a cul-de-sac. If we were attacked from the path we would be sitting ducks, bottle-necked in a natural trap and unable to flee.

We took turns to brew up, while one of us always focused on the path. When it was my turn, a soft whistle sparked my attention and I looked up to see a civilian ambling down towards us, cane fishing rods over his shoulder. He wore a set of blue overalls and as he approached I recognised the insignia of the Zambian Railways on his left breast pocket. The man was in his mid-fifties and oblivious to our presence until he drew closer. Noticing us, his pace slowed before he picked up his step, hoping that we weren't a threat. JD barked out orders to apprehend him and a couple of the guys stepped onto the path and motioned him over at gunpoint. I could tell he was getting worried when the creases on his face deepened as he gulped, wincing at his fate.

Hesitantly he walked towards our position, his frail legs wobbling as he shifted the fishing rods on his shoulder. I soon realised that this old man of Africa was the type one could learn from and wondered how many things he had already forgotten about the bush that we hadn't yet discovered.

In among us, the old boy shuffled, staring imploringly, begging for an answer as to what we wanted to do with him. After a few attempts to get some information out of him it became apparent that he didn't speak a word of English. The lieutenant was keen to glean some intelligence from the old man and told one of the guys to sit him down and blindfold him. When he was told to sit, he didn't understand, but his legs buckled out of fear before he was forced to do so and he collapsed in a heap on the ground. He must have thought he was in trouble when he recognised us as white men under our greasy black face paint.

I was already worrying about what we were going to do with him and despised the lieutenant for having put us in this position. If we had done what was normal and stayed clear of the paths, then we wouldn't have had to decide this man's fate.

In this sort of predicament it is hard to make the right choice. Being a blatant compromise, the militarily sound thing to have done was to have disposed of him, but that was easier said than done. From a purely moral point of view, it is never easy to murder someone in cold blood and on top of that you have the predicament of getting rid of the body satisfactorily, where it would not be discovered, or attract birds and animals when it decays. In this particular circumstance, the best thing to do would be to let the old man go and we could take our chances that he wouldn't run off and report us to the nearest patrol. Or we could have called the whole operation off, as we'd probably be discovered anyway, if we hadn't been already. Another idea, with more risk, would be to take him along with us, releasing him at the conclusion of the operation.

Half an hour later we had extracted no information at all from the hapless soul. He had no idea what we were going on about and at this point, thank God, no-one had been rough with him. He was simply an old villager, living off the land and was unfortunate enough to be wearing Zambian government garments – probably the only clothes he had and which came from a bygone era.

The lieutenant called me over and said we were moving at 16:30 and the old boy wasn't coming with us. Did I have the silenced .22 pistol with me? I saw where he was heading and argued that it was his responsibility to organise mission-specific equipment. He should have brought a silenced weapon along, or delegated someone else to. Then I argued for the man's life, suggesting alternatives to slotting him in this lonely part of Zambia. I suggested taking him with us, or tying him up in the gully out of sight and gagging him so he could make no noise. When my words fell on deaf ears, I got to the point of telling the lieutenant that he was a complete wanker. He had compromised the operation already, I said, so we might as well call it off.

The lieutenant was adamant that we should kill our captive. Short of a mutiny, we could do nothing. He ordered me to slit his throat – a ghastly way to kill someone. He had obviously never done it before; neither had I, but I had heard about it and it's a messy, bloody thing to do. The victim hardly ever dies when he's supposed to. It's not like in the movies. I told the lieutenant that if he wanted him dead he must do it himself as I wasn't prepared to mar my soul with the old man's needless death.

I wish I had been stronger back then, but I eventually succumbed and began to look for ways to end it quickly for the old guy. Rather I kill him than have someone else botch it up and cause him pain. I thought about taking him back to the river and drowning him. As frail as he was it would be easy to hold his head under water, at least with two of us keeping him down.

We were all still sitting there at 16:00 when the lieutenant looked over and got pissed off with me because I hadn't killed the guy yet. The old man just sat there, knees raised off the ground and his back against a thin tree, wondering what was going on. His eyes were wide with fear and the odd tear rolled down his face.

Staring me down, the lieutenant once again ordered me to kill him, adding that it had to be done in the next ten minutes. If I didn't follow his orders he would put me on charge for insubordination when the operation was over. It's only in hindsight that I realise I might have had a leg to stand on if I'd refused the order, but I can't gloss over that. I wasn't a cold-blooded killer, but I felt indebted to slot the guy as a kind of mercy killing, just so it was done properly. How lame that sounds in retrospect!

Right then I would have happily killed the lieutenant over the row concerning the old man, but I made a decision that would live with me for the rest of my life.

Another operator saw the desperation in the situation and came over to help me. While he went up to the old guy, to distract him, I crept around behind the tree with a piece of para cord in my right hand. The old guy saw me and I tried to act as if nothing was out of the ordinary – that nothing was premeditated – but he knew he was going to die. The other operator, Trooper X, lunged for him and pinned his arms to his side. I swung the cord around the tree and grasped it with my left hand, pulling back on it against his neck to impede his breathing. With a foot firmly pressing into the base of the trunk I leaned back with all my strength, throttling the guy, his eyes bulging as he gasped for air that wouldn't come. With each minute that passed, his snatches at life became less desperate until finally he was still.

I released my grasp and the old boy slumped to the ground, a grey pallor over his face.

Trooper X dusted his hands on his jeans and looked up at me. We'd both crossed a line that day and recognised the feeling in each other's eyes. I just stared at him and hated myself for what I'd done. I hated the lieutenant for his incompetence and the thought crossed my mind of putting a quick two rounds through his head. The act of fragging an officer, a term I'd recently heard from the Vietnam War, suddenly made sense.

I was contemplating my second murder in a day, this time premeditated, when a loud gasp for air resounded from the old man's throat and he came back to life. As it happened his head lifted from the ground where it lay and arched back on his shoulders. I launched myself at him, wrapping the cord around his throat again and squeezed the life out of him. My accomplice to the crime, Trooper X, grabbed for him, straining to keep his frenzied bodily thrusts down.

When he was finally motionless I checked his pulse to make sure he was gone. Satisfied – that's hardly the word – I sat back breathing heavily.

Glancing at Trooper X, I saw tears in his eyes and I turned quickly, raising a hand to my face, to wipe away my own. Although it was a while before I realised it, with the old man's dying throes, a little piece of me had died also.

JD ordered us to throw the old man's corpse over a cliff into the gorge. Trooper X and I grabbed the lifeless heap by the ankles and wrists and dragged him back down the path from where he'd come. As we stumbled under the weight his clothing snagged on a stump and a branch here and there. A determined kick to the offending limb freed it and let us get on our way.

I wondered who was waiting for the old boy at his kraal – how many wives he had and how many children. I wondered what form of cruel fate had intervened, to bring this man to a lonely death while he went about his daily ritual of catching fish to sustain himself and his family. If it was fate that intervened, then what despicable death lay in wait for my sins?

When we got to the cliff, I looked over the rocky precipice as it tumbled into the river below. Swinging the body, we counted to three and launched it unceremoniously into open space. It fell a few metres, bouncing off boulders before snagging on a ledge about halfway down. It wasn't exactly out of sight, but only if you were looking for it would it be noticed.

We had walked for about half an hour when NT decided to camp just off the beaten track again! Tactically, it was absolute madness and I let him know as much. The animosity that grew between us was more than evident now and the tense atmosphere could be cut with a knife.

I didn't sleep that night, haunted as I was by the old man's image. My lack of shuteye was probably the best thing anyway as we were literally in ZIPRA's back yard.

The next morning, at 05:00, the lieutenant told me to take one of the guys and go back to our last position. He wanted assurance that the old man was really dead. I just couldn't believe the madness of his proposal! I knew he was dead as it had been at my hands that he died. I just hoped that the same ghost that had haunted me during the night had paid the lieutenant a visit also.

I did as I was told, retracing our obvious tracks – and they stuck out like bollocks on a bull – and as sure as church on a Sunday, the body was still hanging on the ledge exactly where we had left it. I had a chilling feeling looking at the old man's corpse. It's as if he leered at me, like he knew my turn was coming. I'm not too superstitious, but the look on his face haunted me for weeks afterwards.

I returned to the callsign and we continued to march down the well-used path.

Sarcasm has never suited me, but I felt like grabbing the lieutenant's hand and skipping off merrily into the sunset singing 'The hills are alive with the sound of music' or something equally silly. We might as well have done so, as by the signs we were leaving behind us we could have very well attracted as captivating an audience as Julie Andrews once did.

We walked most of that day, stopping occasionally to entertain the lieutenant with one of his tea parties. When we rallied at about 17:00, the bush thickened and the path meandered left, becoming a strip dirt road well capable of taking vehicle traffic. The road headed in a northerly direction into the interior of Zambia and the lieutenant decided to head south. It wasn't a conscious decision. It just looked like he preferred to go that way as it was an easier route. As far as I could figure out, we were about 30 kilometres east of Livingstone, well out of the area we were supposed to be in to conduct the reconnaissance.

Once again, we walked in the open along the track until, up ahead, a sharp bend revealed a bunker-type structure, its apertures covering the direction from which we came. Freezing instantly, we shot off the road and advanced cautiously, reaching the bunker from its flanks. Inside, there was a bed made up from wood and grass but it was deserted. The floor was swept and on one of the low side walls was hanging a uniform. I told the lieutenant that it looked like a guard room, the type of which one would find at the entrance to a camp. For once he agreed with me and instructed me to get onto the TR48 and send a coded message informing base of what we had found and our future intentions. His idea was to continue to follow the track and see where it ended. I quickly drew up the message and sent it. Our reply told us to advance with the utmost of caution until evening, when we would dog-leg and set up an OP to watch our own tracks.

We had just pushed on past the bunker and hadn't walked for five minutes, when I saw someone about a hundred metres away watching us. From his actions he appeared puzzled as he stood, hands on hips, observing our advance. I whistled softly to alert the others and with hand signals, on my blind side, I indicated that we should carry on walking, trying not to cause alarm. I was not certain of what our commander's intentions were, so I slipped off the safety catch on my AK. Firing a shot now would alert the entire base camp, if there was one and the last thing I felt like was legging it through the bush with not much daylight ahead of us.

Staring in the stranger's direction I raised my hand and waved. The guy looked nervous and it appeared that he wasn't convinced by our pseudo antics. Instantly I dropped to my knee and swung my rifle into my shoulder, aiming in his direction. He shrunk away immediately and I waited for a minute with my weapon poised. The others had followed suit by now and the next thing we saw was the guy burning it through the grass at about 90 kilometres an hour, heading away from us.

I ran forward to tell the lieutenant that the guy had webbing on and was obviously ZIPRA, or belonged to the Zambian Army. He seemed unarmed, but we were no doubt compromised for the second time in as many days.

Well out of his element the lieutenant finally lost it, panicking and asking me what we should do. It really seemed as if he had come to the end of his tether. Although we were in a muddle, I felt that he was finally out of the command equation and I could take charge. Pointing in the direction of the Zambezi, I inferred that we'd better get the hell out there while we still had a bit of daylight. We had about 15 minutes until nightfall, when we would be stumbling around the bush like blind men on a merry-go-round. The lieutenant didn't argue and took up the pace at the lead. So much for a captain going down with his ship.

I brought up the rear and we backtracked down the path, leaving it after we passed the bunker and legging it into the thick bush. In view of the weight we carried, we did pretty well, taking our mark off our erstwhile leader who couldn't get to the Zambezi quick enough. When darkness descended we were a relatively safe distance away from the area but not out of danger. We continued to walk, as we knew that when morning came, we would only have a half-hour head start. If our enemy were to mount vehicles, they could well be at the river when we reached it.

At 24:00, while we took a break, the lieutenant ordered me to send another message, using Morse code, telling base that we had been compromised and would be heading south in the morning. At first light we were up and raring to go, but instead, he headed west for some high ground. I asked what he was doing and he said we were putting in a dog-leg to watch our spoor. *Now* he was trying to be tactical, at the most inopportune time! Our best interest at the moment would be to get out of there. What did he suppose we should do when we found the entire Zambian Army on our trail?

I stated my mind, but the lieutenant told me to go back on our tracks and set up a Claymore mine. He would go with the others to the high ground and wait in ambush for the enemy to arrive. Now he really wasn't making sense. How would he follow through with the ambush when I initiated it from another point? Tactically, he was so far removed from reality that he was now becoming a real danger to his men. Sure, we often took on insuperable odds, but that was when we had the advantage of surprise. The enemy would be expecting us to booby-trap our trail and would be on the lookout for anything out of the ordinary.

I couldn't make sense of the madness, but followed orders anyway, disappearing alone toward a certain contact. The rest of the callsign left for the top of a hill, I supposed, so they could watch me single handedly take on the enemy.

Half an hour later, as I moved stealthily along the verge of the path, I looked up and saw a company-sized patrol scanning for our spoor up ahead. I moved off to the left, putting about 80 metres between the path and myself and pressed my body into the hard earth underneath a cluster of bushes. I was in a slightly raised position from the enemy and I watched them as they ambled straight past me. It seemed as if they weren't having much luck tracking us on the hard, sun-baked ground.

Relief is an emotion I learnt well that day and my heart resumed beating normally once they had passed. I decided to stay in my hide and watch the trail for more activity, as it was too dangerous to move. The enemy was between us and the river and I stayed in position until 16:30. At that time I peered down the trail, in the direction the patrol had gone and noticed the rest of the callsign led by the lieutenant, rifles at ease on their shoulders, coming towards me. How they had missed the enemy defies explanation, but I was certain it had a lot to do with luck.

We spent another night in Zambia, before being uplifted back to Victoria Falls. At the debrief, JD got a huge bollocking for his actions after being compromised. The OC informed him that he should have got completely out of the area and requested an immediate hot extraction. He also got a bollocking for carrying his personal identification card on an external operation. Had we been killed or captured, fingers would have been pointed directly at Rhodesia – something the government was not too enthusiastic about, considering we weren't yet at war with Zambia.

Unfortunately, not much was said about the needless death of the old man. His demise was forgotten, as just another casualty of war. It will live on with me for eternity and remains one of the scars I bear from my war days.

I submitted a report to the OC that JD was a danger to his own men and should not be given the responsibility of a callsign. In the report I stated that – through stupidity alone– he would get his men killed. Further, I added that I would not go out with him on any future operations, come hell or high water, irrespective of the disciplinary action resulting from my insubordination. I was lucky. No more babysitting missions were given to me.

Sadly, JD was killed a year later, while still serving in the Squadron, when a landmine he was laying, detonated prematurely. Unfortunately, two other SAS men were also killed in the blast.

CHAPTER 21:
CHIOCO

On 24 March 1977, A and B Troops attacked the Chioco Garrison in Mozambique, a ZANLA stronghold, containing over one hundred enemy personnel. The garrison was built by the Tanzanians, who had pulled out, leaving an excellent facility with electricity and running water for FRELIMO. Situated so close to the border, it now housed ZANLA terrorists as a last staging point on their way to cause havoc in Rhodesia.

The FRELIMO and ZANLA personnel in the camp had the advantage of a well-placed trench system around the barrack blocks, which was protected by bunkers with heavy machine guns. Not far from the camp, at the Chioco police station, there was a 75mm recoilless rifle which would be countered by our 60mm mortar. It was to be a tough nut to crack and we expected the enemy to put up a fight.

I can't think of an operation that took place, where numbers were in our favour, as most of the time we were vastly outnumbered by a well-equipped enemy. Our main advantages were always surprise and the thorough ruthlessness with which we carried the war to our foe. The planning that we put into operations was second to none and better than anything I had ever seen.

We deployed to Mtoko forward airfield to await a briefing for the operation. As B Troop store man, I was tasked with issuing equipment, ammunition and rations to the 22-strong team who were to be driven to Mary Mount and from there, deployed by chopper to a point about 16 kilometres from Chioco. A factor that would determine the outcome of the attack, was the weight of firepower we carried, so every man was issued with additional ammunition which would hopefully sway the battle in our favour.

Imre Baka, another Squadron store man, was inundated with ammunition requests and although he knew little about the actual operation, it didn't take long for him to realise that something big was in the offing. Generally a base soldier, Imre was thrilled when told he would be deploying with the mortar team to assist in the assault.

The overall commander of the mission was Captain Graham Wilson, an excellent soldier who was to become the most decorated man in the Rhodesian Army, winning the country's three highest valour awards during the course of the war.

Captain Wilson gave an excellent pre-operation briefing and ran through the tasks of each callsign that was to take part in the attack. During the briefing, I was surprised to find my name on the notice board as one of the mortar team. I had expected a bit of a swan, remaining in base camp while the others were inserted into Mozambique. With operational security so tight, it was only at the last minute that we found out our exact role on operations. I was to be the 60mm mortar man, carrying the weapon as well as two bombs. Each man on the operation would carry an additional two bombs which would be dropped at the base plate position.

The other callsign commanders were briefed on their missions, and learnt that they were to infiltrate the camp during the pre-dawn hours and place Claymore mines against the corrugated iron walls of the barrack buildings. After harnessing them together, with a hurriedly jimmied cable, the Claymores would be detonated simultaneously, heralding the start of the attack.

Every conceivable contingency was run through, utilising a model of the camp, built with the aid of aerial reconnaissance photos. Ration-pack boxes were used as buildings; on them was marked the material, out of which each structure was made. Bunkers, trenches, hills and gullies were depicted with mounds of sand and papier-mâché. It wasn't the best model I had seen in the Rhodesian SAS, but it served the purpose well and detailed everything immaculately. Later, on bigger external operations, members of the Surveyor-General's mapping department were bought in and models were made out of papier-mâché, using photographic overlays to depict contours, ridges and gullies.

They were fine models, accurate to the last detail and would have been more at home in the offices of a reputable architectural firm, than being an aid to the war council for executing external camp attacks.

After the briefing, we moved to the end of the airstrip and ran through a couple of dry runs of the attack, putting into practice what we had all just learnt.

I was given a mortar range card and had to practise firing off imaginary mortars on a preconceived grid pattern; three bombs, move and three bombs again, repeating the performance once the firing had started. It didn't take long before I had it down pat and I was confident in my part of the raid.

As time was crucial, after a brief lunch, we boarded the trucks and headed for the mission station at the border.

The first callsigns deployed into Mozambique late that afternoon in three Alouettes, flying low and level over dry scrub, straining underweight as they approached the top of the escarpment. I waited at the airstrip with the mortar team and another callsign for the choppers to return and deliver us to the insertion point. We flew low over the Ruya River where it meets the Mazoe River, banking sharply as the pilot adjusted his course. The pilots, always professional, delivered us directly to the other members who could just be seen as we approached a tree line.

The terrain was not conducive for a landing, so we had to make a jump for it, with all our equipment, as the choppers hovered a metre or so above the ground. With the added weight of the mortar tube, I landed violently and was almost instantly out of the operation. A quick check ensured my legs were still in one piece and we moved off to join the others.

Captain Wilson brought us all together and informed us that we would use the remaining daylight to find an LUP for the night. We would wait for the onset of full moon and then march on a bearing for Chioco, arriving nearer our target during the early hours of morning. I slept little that night, as did most of the others and it wasn't long before word was passed down the line to prepare to move out. It was an agonising march, but we made headway by the light of the moon. Before the sun came up, we found an area of thick cover and went to ground again. Sentries were posted and we all got as much shuteye as possible, hiding out during the daylight hours.

Towards midday we heard the sound of distant rifle shots, but soon realised they came from hunters who posed no threat to us. As long as we lay low we were safe, blending in with our surrounds while we waited for nightfall.

The second night's march was worse than the first. Forced to lie low during the hours of daylight, my muscles had seized up and my shoulders had become raw from the weight of my Bergen. It took a couple of hours to get into rhythm, but soon we walked like automatons, driven more by will than want.

Andy Chait led the column, using our lone pair of night goggles and led us past a generator that groaned away to our right. We had just passed the machine when it rattled and coughed to a halt, and a deadly silence settled about us. Either it had run out of fuel or it had been turned off by someone who was awake when he shouldn't have been. We went to ground and hoped for the former.

At 23:00 we came to a footpath. Our maps told us it led straight to Chioco. Two separate, single-file lines were formed and they moved out on either side of the path. Within 20 minutes, the unmistakable sound of African music reached our ears from up ahead. We had arrived at our target before schedule and formed up into a defensive perimeter. A close target reconnaissance (CTR) detail, scouting forward, confirmed we had indeed reached Chioco.

Captain Wilson came over to me and told me to follow him with the rest of the mortar team. Imre Baka fell in behind me, with my callsign commander and we made our way through a maize field to a position, centrally located in the rows of corn. The position was as good as we'd find and the head-level corn stalks would not impede the flight of our bombs after they'd left the tube. The ground seemed a bit soft, but it was ideally situated between the garrison, behind us and Chioco town to our fore. When the firing commenced we would be afforded excellent cover from view.

The captain gave us a final briefing before he left to join the assault teams. They would pass us, on the way to their positions and drop off the bombs that each member carried. Our task was to mortar the FRELIMO-dominated Chioco town, one kilometre from the camp, focusing mainly on the police station with the 75mm recoilless rifle.

Sergeants Andy Chait, Iain Bowen and Captain Wilson, would lead the assault teams, while Nick Breytenbach's four-man stop group would make their way to the northern side of the camp, set up their Claymores and await the fleeing enemy. Initiation of the attack would be when Nick and Iain, whose Claymores would be against the buildings, detonated their mines simultaneously.

As the mines went off, another member of Nick's callsign, Frank Booth, would lob two grenades into an occupied bunker. He would approach it from the north, once he had reached the position with the four-man stop group. When the grenades went off, he would high-tail back to his position, while the other three four-man assault teams would sweep through the camp from the south, driving the enemy towards him, like hounds baying a pig.

It seemed like an eternity while we waited. Everything was going according to schedule and the assault teams had positioned themselves in their respective areas. There was still about half an hour until H hour, when Sergeant Chait approached our position, looking for someone to replace a member of his team. The member had a hoarse cough and Sergeant Chait feared it might compromise the operation.

He asked me if I would join him and I was quite willing, but the mortar team commander refused. I had learned the bomb patterns in my head during practice and I was considered too valuable to the operation. In my place, Imre Baka was selected. Firstly, he was thrilled to have been brought along on a real operation and now he was overjoyed that he would actually be taking place in the assault. It was a fine day for him and one he would speak of for eternity.

I heard later that Sergeant Bowen had almost been compromised when he set up his Claymores. Stringing them out along the length of the structure, he had approached the concrete stairwell that led to a door servicing the building, when a naked black man, cigarette dangling from his lips, stepped outside and proceeded to urinate a metre away from the SAS man. Iain froze, as he watched the glowing cherry draw nearer and he was ready to initiate an early attack, but fortunately he was not seen and returned to rest out the remaining minutes until dawn.

At 05:00, H hour, there was an almighty explosion, as eighteen Claymores detonated simultaneously. The disturbance was followed by an incredible volley of small-arms fire, as the assault teams stormed the camp. I began to fire the mortar, remembering to adjust the range after each salvo. The soft earth became a problem and the mortar was digging deeper with every bomb. That meant the bombs weren't going to land where they were supposed to; if anything they would be falling short, so I did the only thing I could and packed the base plate with soil, assisted by one of the other guys stamping it into place with the heels of our boots.

After firing about nine rounds of 60mm, an 82mm mortar opened up on us from a position to the north-west. Their bombs were landing way off and it was apparent the enemy had no idea of where we were. The 75mm recoilless rifle soon accompanied the mortar fire from more or less the same direction, but the rounds where whistling overhead, in places cutting their way through the highest corn stems and exploding in the bush 50 metres behind us.

There was also an impressive amount of tracer fire, most of the luminous green trails arching straight into the air. We began to worry that the assault teams had bitten off more than they could chew. With the amount of red tracer, from the SAS FNs and green tracer from the SAS and the enemy AKs, it looked like we had run into a battalion of enemy troops, rather than the hundred we had expected. We were in no real danger, in our position, as the enemy fire was inaccurate and ill disciplined, but it was an anxious period as we waited to hear news of the attack.

The battle lasted for 20 minutes and the firing stopped. Assisted by the sergeant next to me, I began to dig the mortar out of the soft earth where, despite our best efforts, it had sunk in by more than a foot. As we worked, the maize field parted and a few members crashed towards us, carrying Sergeant Chait, cradling him between them as they ran. He was still conscious, but they were fighting to keep him alive, as he was losing an enormous amount of blood.

It transpired that Andy and his assault team had swept through, on the right-hand side of the camp, winkling out and neutralising ZANLA defenders as they manned their weapons in the trench system. Imre Baka was right in his element and followed orders like he had been fighting this sort of battle all his life. When they came to a particularly well-defended trench, Andy ordered Imre to throw in a white phosphorous grenade, which he did, effectively taking care of the stubborn terrorists who were directing a huge amount of fire at them. When the grenade detonated, globules of white phosphorous sailed through the air, like white hot streamers at a fairground fireworks display, followed by the terrified screams of dying men as the chemical burnt into their skins.

When the callsign reached the position they were to remain in until the commander's team had finished their sweep, an RPD opened up from the base of an anthill that formed part of the trench system. Andy screamed for Imre to toss him another grenade, while the rest of his callsign poured fire into the position. Andy had expended his supply of grenades in the heavy fighting that led the team this far. Imre did so, unhitching a grenade from his webbing and lobbing it underhand to his commander. He was watching Andy when the earth erupted around him, spitting dirt into the air and all around the defenceless sergeant. Andy's weapon had been placed by his side while he pulled the pin from the grenade he had just been given. Somewhere in the trench system a lone terrorist raised his weapon above the earthen embankment and fired shots in the direction of the attackers. It was a last-ditch effort to save himself and he fired wildly. Suddenly Imre heard a loud slapping noise, like a bamboo cane hitting wet cardboard and he saw Andy's camouflage jeans split open. The sergeant, yelling that he was hit, tumbled into the trench for cover, the grenade rolling in with him.

Andy realised his wound was life-threatening and immediately called Captain Wilson, now fighting his way towards him, to the trench. He told the captain that the bullet had severed an artery, typically understating the obvious, as blood gushed in streams from his wound. The terrorist, who had inflicted the damage, still had to be neutralised and 30 seconds was lost before a tourniquet could be applied by a medic. It was to be a very expensive 30 seconds and would ultimately cost Andy his life.

Imre Baka retrieved the grenade from where it had fallen, pulling the pin in one swift motion and throwing it – as one would throw a baseball – at the terrorist who was still firing at them. When the grenade exploded, silence fell over the trench and the dying groans of the enemy soldier were heard from the position where he fell.

By the time Andy was carried to the LZ, directly next to the mortar position, a tourniquet had been applied and a casevac chopper had been called for. Sergeant Bowen, on the opposite side of the camp, sprinted across open ground, bullets punching into the dirt at his feet, trailing behind him his medic to offer assistance. A bed was brought to the LZ to make Andy more comfortable, while we waited for the chopper. Captain Wilson called in the Hunter fighter-bombers to put in a strike on Chioco, if there was trouble during the uplift. A couple of well-placed golf bombs should definitely deter any follow up.

The uplift passed without event and Andy was loaded aboard the chopper. Overhead, our top cover screamed through the light cloud base as they awaited our request for support. Behind us, the firing had died entirely, but we expected a FRELIMO quick reaction force (QRF) to be hot on our tails. With the amount of damage inflicted on the enemy, it was decided to get out while the going was good and head back to Rhodesia. More helicopters were on their way to collect us, as we walked to meet them.

After counting through the members of all the callsigns, I fell in and took up the tail-end Charlie position. We had only tabbed for about an hour when we were informed that Andy had died aboard the helicopter on his way back to Rhodesia. Despite the best efforts of the medic, who had administered several drips, he had lost too much blood.

It was a sobering loss to the unit and put a damper on our success. Andy was the epitome of what you would expect of a Rhodesian SAS man. Well respected, he was entirely courageous and a thorough, professional operator.

Overall, 38 enemy were accounted for, but the figure might have been a lot higher. Nick Breytenbach's stop group alone was responsible for killing 25 terrorists. One of his callsign was so close to the fighting, that a dead terr tumbled onto him after he was shot through the head.

Intercepts that came to light later revealed that a party was going on in Chioco town at the time of the attack – which may have explained the music we had heard when we were infiltrating. As a result, the garrison was relatively deserted when we hit it. Lucky for ZANLA!

Nick Breytenbach was eventually awarded the Military Forces Commendation for his part in the raid. Frank Booth, who had waited out a hair-raising 15 minutes with primed grenades in each hand for the attack to commence, was also decorated.

CHAPTER 22:
FREEFALL AND FIREFORCE

In October 1977, the Squadron began preparations for the largest freefall operation of the war. The Gaza Province had been somewhat neglected by the SAS while they focused on FRELIMO and ZANLA in Tete.

In Tete, the SAS ruled the roost and FRELIMO dared not move. The Squadron's harassment programme had been going on for so long that terrorist incursions into Rhodesia from there had decreased by 75 per cent.

Previously, the Selous Scouts had been operating in Gaza, applying their skills to ambushing the rail route between Mapai and Barragem. In addition to those 'shoot and scoot' operations, they also attacked Mapai, routing the enemy, blowing up buildings and taking over the airfield. Their only advice to the SAS, when they departed the region, was that Gaza would be a tougher nut to crack than Tete.

The way Major Robinson saw it, given the amount of FRELIMO activity in the area, as well as a large hostile civilian population, the safest method of entry would be a HALO (High Altitude Low Opening) parachute descent deep into the interior of the province, to ambush and harass lines of communication and supply. Edging away from the rail link, which would surely be under closer scrutiny by enemy forces since the Scouts' last visit, he felt we should pay attention to the road system, which ran parallel to the railway between Malvernia and Barragem. Not only was the road used to transit ZANLA forces to staging points closer to the border, but it also provided a life-line for ammunition supply to FRELIMO.

Rhodesian artillery units, using antiquated 25 pounders of World War II origin, had been bombarding areas around Vila Salazar, duelling with FRELIMO artillery and Stalin Organs, in an effort to break enemy morale. The Freds always ran out of ammunition in these duels and would usually be supplied by road from Maputo. The Squadron hoped that with a bit of luck, a juicy target of terrorists, or ammo-laden vehicles, would offer itself while we waited in ambush.

If anything was Apache country, Gaza was it. Not only was it saturated with unfriendly forces, the terrain also had similarities to those which one would expect to find in parts of the American Wild West. Featureless, sandy and dry, we expected problems right from the word go. Everything we would need to sustain ourselves would have to be carried in on our backs, including water.

Once again, the mission commander would be Captain Graham Wilson, in charge of a mixed bunch of A and B Troop soldiers, 24 in total.

Nothing like this had ever been attempted before, so in-depth rehearsals took place at a drop zone in Seke, just outside Salisbury, taking off from New Sarum. We would be jumping from two Dakotas for practice, but when the real operation commenced we would use the services of a DC-7, owned and piloted by Jack Malloch. He was a Rhodesian entrepreneur and the man responsible for a large proportion of the sanctions-busting operations carried out by his freight airline, Affretair.

Our operational jump height was to be 12 000 feet, just below the oxygen depletion level, with each of us carrying enormous weight, comprising mortars and mortar bombs, weapons and additional ammunition for the AKs, FNs and RPD machine guns, as well as stores and provisions. Extra ammunition and water would be crated and dropped first, under parachutes utilising the Kap 3 Automatic Opening Device (AOD).

We were all ordered to use the Kap 3 in case we blacked out when we exited the aircraft, a frequent occurrence at high altitude. Some of the operators were against it, but it paid off on the day.

On the night of our first rehearsal we boarded the aircraft, uncomfortably trying to adjust our positioning as we shuffled like penguins under a huge burden. Captain Wilson blew a fuse when he felt the weight of our Bergens. To be honest, it was such an effort that many of us had skived, replacing the heavy objects we were supposed to carry, with lighter ones. Always a man to get things down to the finest detail, the captain felt we were not serious about the task at hand and gave us a severe bollocking, threatening to kick us off the operation. Being a first-off operation, most on us were excited at the prospect of becoming pioneers in this diverse rendition of freefall.

There were many operators queuing up to take our places and an early dismissal was the last thing any of us wanted. Not only was it the biggest HALO jump of the war and would remain so, but it had other factors which made it unique.

Firstly, we were to jump out of the Douglas DC-7, a much faster aircraft than usual, on a very dark night with no moon, unusual for our standard operating procedure. The commander of the operation felt that the darker it was, the less chance there was of being seen. Secondly, the amount of equipment we would be carrying was unequalled by any previous HALO descent or static-line insertion. We would be forging new methods of operation that would go down in the history books of the Rhodesian SAS.

With the bollocking out of the way, we got on with the jump, assured that any further short cuts would be severely reprimanded. There was no time to replace the weight in the packs and Captain Wilson begrudgingly let it pass, warning us that we would pay for our indiscretions during the final jump.

The rehearsal jump went without a hitch. The interior of our Dakota was not the same as the DC-7, (which was complete with rollers to help move the equipment boxes to the door) but we managed anyway.

Our pre-operation briefing dictated that we all strap penlight torches to our helmets, facing backwards, which we did with masking tape. Half of the freefallers would use green filters in their torches and the other half red. The equipment boxes had filtered strobe lights attached to them and the idea was to jump straight after they were launched through the door, following our respective loads. Opening our canopies at 2 000 feet, we would then follow the crates to the ground in two staggered columns, landing, we hoped, not too far away from each other. On the practice jump, when we jumped over Seke, the two streams of coloured lights looked like an aerial view of dense highway traffic at night, as they meandered in swaying lines after the crates. It was a perfectly executed simulation and we were all confident that the operation would go smoothly.

The day of the operation was soon upon us and we ran through final checks and briefings. The crates still had to be packed, so I assisted in loading ammo, mortar bombs and water, arranging it so no damage would occur when it landed. There was a little room left in the crates so we packed the extra space with additional rations to absorb some of the impact.

I carried out a personal equipment check, ensuring that my AK was in good working order. My webbing, custom-fashioned from an Eastern bloc chest webbing pattern, was reinforced where it had frayed and my magazines were stripped and cleaned with a lightly oiled rag. In most areas of operation, over-oiling could result in dust-fouled weapons and malfunctions. In the Rhodesian SAS we used oil sparingly, unlike what I had been taught in the Paras.

One advantage of carrying an AK and in fact most of the Eastern bloc weapons, was not only the overall shorter length, but the availability of ammo. While some guys preferred the FN, in reality a far more powerful and accurate weapon, I knew that if I ever ran out of AK ammo on ops I could re-supply from captured guerrilla weapons – and there were always plenty of them.

Late that afternoon we all laid out our kit on mats, in the Para School hangar. There was not much more to do, so we ambled about chatting and joking. It was a nervous wait for most of us, the fear of the unknown creeping in while we were inactive.

Two hours before our scheduled take-off we ran through a final briefing, covering among other things escape and evasion plans, in the event of any of us becoming cut off or lost. It was thought that the best place to head for would be the South African border, 40 kilometres south-west of our drop zone. The South Africans had been briefed, without giving the game away, to be on the lookout for Rhodesian stragglers.

We emplaned at midnight and sat on benches that had been fitted along the sides of the aircraft for the occasion. Under the benches were oxygen bottles and masks in case we passed out. As Captain Wilson predicted, we were already paying for our lack of thoroughness in not preparing ourselves properly for the weights we carried. Our packs and parachutes were an enormous strain and it was a relief to flop onto the seats once we were aboard.

When we took off there was deathly silence about us. The pilot headed for the border, flying on a south-east route which would take him over Mabalauta Forward Headquarters, where an operator was waiting to fire a flare. The visual reference would help the pilot correct his course as he flew compass bearing only, on a pitch-black night. The atmosphere in the aircraft was tense. In silence I mulled over the drop and went through everything in my head. I was wary about jumping with such weight, about 45 kilograms in all and I hoped the extra would not upset my balance in freefall. If I blacked out, my Kap 3 was primed to open at 1,500 feet but I knew – if that happened – that my drift would take me far away from the LZ.

The apprehension was immense. It was one of the few times, just like after depot training in the Paras , when I was sent directly to Northern Ireland, that I wondered why I had put myself in this position in the first place. There were a thousand other things I would rather be doing than throwing myself into pitch black nothingness, deep inside enemy territory.

We flew at high altitude and everyone just sat there waiting for the order to go. My equipment was huge, sitting between my legs and I worried that I would not be able to strap my Bergen in, tucked behind my legs under my bum and get to the door in time, when the green light came on. It was small consolation that everyone around me looked like they were in the same state of terror that I was.

Approaching the DZ, one of the operators passed out from lack of oxygen. A dispatcher rushed over, reviving him with an emergency oxygen set, before the man vomited into the mouth piece. While this was happening, the red light flashed on at the door. The man was too ill to proceed with the operation and it was decided to leave him behind, meaning that we were now already one short. My goggles were misting up from my heavy breathing and I strained to get my balance. Raising myself to my feet, my knees buckled under the weight. With my Bergen in place I joined the steady shuffle of human traffic to the door. A PJI passed by each of us to ensure we were not suffering from oxygen deprivation.

We were still five minutes out from the target and it was the most tiring five minutes I've spent on my feet. The order came to check our equipment and I just sat back on my Bergen, momentarily relieving the draining burden on my legs.

I was positioned second in my stick, about 18 from the door and I remember watching the red light – wishing it to change, to get this over with – when the green light suddenly came on. Instantly, the crates were pushed out the door and I stumbled forward as if in slow motion when compared to the practice jump. We were literally snowed under with gear and it was barely possible to move. The others in front of me tumbled out the door with the decorum of elephants pissed on marula fruit. It was an unco-ordinated amble to drag ourselves out of the aircraft and into the weightlessness of freefall that would bring relief.

When I came to the door there was no finesse in my exit. I couldn't manoeuvre my legs to a comfortable position to jump so I just fell sideways through the opening. I was whisked away by the slipstream, tumbling for a few seconds as I struggled to get my bearings. Stabilising myself was another thing altogether. Opening my eyes I recall the darkest black enveloping me and I wondered if it weren't a dream. Maybe I'd passed out and this was my subconscience taking over. It took a few more seconds to realise I was actually upside down and falling with my back to the earth. The weight of my Bergen created a bottom-heavy effect and tipped me into the most natural flight pattern for my ungainly form. It took a huge effort to arch my body, but I eventually came around and stabilised my fall. Below me, red and green lights mingled like decorations on a Christmas tree far from where they were supposed to be, unco-ordinated in their descent. Further away I could make out the strobe lights on the crates as they fell into the darkness below. Between them and my own position, a stream of assorted lights concertina-ed as operators fought to gain control. I watched with horror as one green light passed by, appearing to fall directly to earth, no control in its 90-degree dive, tumbling and spinning like a Catherine wheel.

Just then my goggles lifted off my face and I grabbed them with my right hand. The sudden disposition threw me into a head-down spin before I lost control again and tumbled through the open space of blackness. It was a dizzying roller-coaster of queasy insanity before I found my feet. Around me I couldn't see the horizon. I faced the strobe and craned my neck against the force of Gs to read my wrist compass and my altimeter.

Making sure there was nothing below me, I reached deployment level and pulled my rip cord. The canopy blossomed above me, rippling as small pockets of trapped air escaped the opening folds. I again searched for the strobe and followed it to ground. The horizon was still distinctly absent and fearing an early landing I released my Bergen, catching its straps on the toes of my boots before dropping it to dangle below me.

I had the briefest glimpse of the horizon and was able to take a bearing on my compass, when all hell broke loose beneath me. The terrific noise of branches breaking was magnified as I tumbled through them, glancing off one to the other, before doing an about face and landing upside down. I came to a halt bouncing about a foot off the ground on my tangled rigging. A brief pause to collect my thoughts and I reached for my wrist knife. I hacked at the para cord and fell the short distance to terra firma, landing with a thump on my shoulder blades, my head tucked into my chest. I then started to cut and pull the parachute from the tree so as to leave no indication of my presence.

I didn't know where the other guys were and I was still wrestling with my canopy, when another operator stumbled over to me. My trousers, the only pair I had, were lying in tatters around my ankles, ripped to shreds as I fell through the tree. I didn't have another pair so I stitched them up with safety pins. Although the Rhodesians often went to war wearing shorts, I think it may have bordered on insanity to attempt fighting naked.

I was in a lot of pain and my skin was stinging from numerous scratches all over my body. A particular burning sensation throbbed from where my arsehole should have been.

I had little time to think of my aches, so I gathered up my kit, packing the ruined parachute on top of my Bergen with the help of my mate. When we started walking out to meet the others, the pain really hit me. I stopped and angled my head to look at my backside, but I couldn't see much. It felt like someone had rammed a red-hot poker up there and twisted it a few times just for fun. The stinging sensation grew with each step. Twenty minutes later, with me in burning hell, we reached the crates. They had all landed within about 80 metres of each other and were in good order.

Settling my arse on the ground, I winced at the pain and rolled over onto my side for relief. Not only was I sore, I also had an unquenchable thirst which inhibited further movement. The sun was coming up and already the heat was scorching. I drank as much as I dared but it did nothing for me. I felt I was in a really shit state and groggy from the over-exertion and painful injuries. It was only when a medic checked out my injuries that I discovered a branch had penetrated deep into my buttocks. It wasn't a bull's eye, but it was close enough to my shit chute to warrant a shiver. An inch south and I would have been crapping into plastic bags for the rest of my life.

Of the 23 operators who exited the aircraft, 22 dribbled in over the next few hours. Sergeant Iain Bowen was carried in with a broken leg and two others had twisted ankles. Then there was me with a stick up my arse.

Jan Greyling had passed out on exit from the aircraft and fell to the earth unconscious. His was the green light that I had seen tumbling below me on a collision course with terra firma. One of the men who had argued against carrying the Kap 3 AOD, Jan was extremely lucky when his parachute automatically blossomed at 1,500 feet. When he came to, he was more than seven kilometres from our position and it took him a 15-hour marathon, using the bush craft skills the Squadron had taught him, to finally link up with us. Had he not found us he would have hit out for the South African border.

The DZ was situated about 13 kilometres from the target road, only three kilometres off course when we were dropped. An amazing feat on the pilot's part, given the complexities of the operation.

We spent the day in an LUP, organising our callsigns and preparing to march that night. As time progressed, my injury stiffened up and it became evident that I would have to remain with the injured party while the others put in the ambush. An immediate casevac was out of the question, even for Iain Bowen's broken leg, as it would have compromised the operation. The four of us were left behind, having been patched up by Greyling, the Troop medic. Poor Iain Bowen was in a serious amount of pain, but he bore it with the professionalism that he was made of. It was a good call that I stayed behind, as the next day my wound was a pus-filled trench of sceptic rot. I kept an eye on it, but in the field there was not much I could do to keep the injury absolutely clean.

There was some humour among the boredom. Iain and I laughed when we envisaged the four of us being stumbled on by an enemy patrol. It would have been a set-to engagement, as combined we could not have run very far if we tried.

It was five days before we heard news of the others' success. Having set up a successful ambush, in which three ZANLA trucks loaded with ammunition and personnel were fired upon, 20 enemy were killed and two of the trucks turned and fled. Captain Wilson called in a Hunter strike which ended their flight and they too were destroyed.

During the ambush, Trooper Dave Collins, lying in his firing position, was shot through the head by sporadic AK fire from ZANLA. The terrorist was quickly neutralised but not before he hit another two operators, shooting one through the foot and creasing another's skull. All three were lying in the positions they were when the firing commenced. Captain Wilson, who was already on his feet in among the injured men, escaped unharmed as bullets whizzed about him.

Miraculously, when our medic Jan Greyling raced over to Trooper Collins, he was still alive. His injuries were severe and life-threatening, but an immediate casevac and first-rate field medical attention ensured he would live.

We, the injured party, were uplifted and flown to Malapati airstrip where the

Squadron were based. It had been an exceptionally boring bush trip for us after the extreme highs of the insertion phase.

At Malapati my injuries were treated by draining the laceration and disinfecting it before I was told I would be returning to Mozambique.

I was to be part of an airborne assault group that was to conduct a classic assault parachuting behind enemy positions and hitting the FRELIMO Stalin Organs. In our SAS role it was the same sort of thing we had trained for in the Paras; inserting behind enemy lines and hitting the enemy hard from the rear. I was enthusiastic about the operation but, for unknown reasons, it was called off at the last minute. Instead we were to reinforce the original HALO patrol by static-line insertion near Mapai.

Just when 18 paratroopers were lined up and ready to go, I was called off the operation entirely. My injuries, although not severe, were considered enough to hamper the speed at which the group could move, conducting ambushes, bugging out and hitting other areas in rapid, hit-and-run guerrilla-type operations.

My injuries healed and after a few weeks, the combined A and B Troop saboteurs returned. Their efforts had been rewarded with successful ambushes on the Mapai-Barragem road link, but the Squadron did indeed find out that Gaza was a tougher nut to crack than Tete. FRELIMO appeared to be far more aggressive in that region, perhaps as a result of the Russian, East German and Cuban advisors, who were prevalent. In one or two encounters, the Rhodesians came face to face with these communist soldiers and although they were no match for our ability, their professional expertise did hinder operations in the south.

Elsewhere in the country the RLI and RAR were hard-pressed manning continual Fire Force call outs. The pace of the war had intensified to the stage where some men were being parachuted or heli-inserted into as many as three contacts a day. The SAS were called upon to bolster the limited manpower reserves and remain on standby at Malapati for Fire Force duties.

From my experience of these sorts of operations, my hat goes off to the men who conducted them every single day. Usually short, sharp, high-octane battles, they were terrifying in the extreme and had the ability to rattle men's nerves after a relatively short period. The first one we took part in from Malapati was just like that.

When the siren screamed it caught me unawares. There is no getting used to the ominous wail of the alarm that tells you you're about to go to war. It's like an orchestra of outraged demons, the ascending and descending tones penetrating your entire being, signalling your destiny to meet the enemy.

My injury was all but healed when we deployed to the sighting of a large band of terrorists in the south-east region of Rhodesia. For a change, I was in the direct sweep role, inserted by helicopter in the first wave of troops to go in.

Fire Force is much like a quail shoot when the birds shoot back. Advancing in extended line, the onus is on the individual trooper to be alert at all times, peering into areas of possible concealment where a terrorist may be hiding in thick bush, or waiting to initiate contact by firing on us in the open. It's almost like begging a reaction from the enemy by yelling out: 'I'm here'.

Of course, we did have the advantage of support in the form of Lynxes and K-car gunships. The K-cars, aboard which was the fireforce commander, could shoot into the tops of trees and dense cover with their 20mm cannon; the solid and explosive shells either penetrated the treetops or burst upon them, thereby raining shrapnel down on the enemy and flushing him out into the open.

When we knew a group of terrs were holed up in a particular area, we would call in a Lynx with its rockets or Frantan bombs. The Frantan, or frangible tank, was the Rhodesian version of napalm and was a horrific weapon to be exposed to. On impact in the target area, a rolling ball of jellified petroleum would scorch a burning path through the contact area, sucking the oxygen from the air.

After insertion, this particular operation was typical of many. As the callsign I was a part of advanced, small contacts took place around us as other sticks engaged targets. When there is so much battle going on around you, you know that it is going to be your turn soon. My heart was in my mouth and we were not disappointed.

A trooper on my right flank suddenly opened up with his MAG, putting down fire into a bush five metres to his front. No sooner had he pulled the trigger than I watched an inoffensive bundle roll out into the open. All eyes strained ahead searching out more terrorists. Meanwhile, the trooper reached the man he had just shot and put a quick burst into his chest.

Some 20 metres further on I heard the distinct metallic clunk of a grenade-arming mechanism. Where it came from I wasn't sure, but the others followed suit as I dived to ground. A few seconds later the grenade exploded three metres to my front with a hollow thump. The terrorist who had thrown it crashed from hiding, certain that his grenade had done what was intended. I was on my feet and recall looking at the man as he fled, when I noticed two holes punch into his back. It wasn't a long shot but it was good, instinctive shooting – the target going down instantly. I recall looking around for the shooter when I realised it was I who had shot him. I didn't even think about the actions that spelt out his instant death. I was becoming cold.

It was a successful contact and six terrorists were killed overall. A lieutenant in A Troop was injured when a guerrilla shot him through the elbow.

On another Fire Force operation, we weren't so lucky. They were dark days when the Squadron stood in for the RLI at Buffalo Range while they went on R&R. Reacting to the usual Selous Scouts callout, we deployed as usual in helicopters, with paratroopers waiting in reserve.

During the initial sweep, a switched-on terr, lying in wait with an RPD machine gun, opened up and downed three operators. Lance-Corporal Nel and Trooper Seymour were killed in the initial burst of fire and my good friend Torty King was severely injured.

The terrorist, although wounded, managed to escape after putting down effective covering fire, thereby also warding off immediate medical attention for the wounded. If the medic had been able to react sooner, a life might have been saved.

It's not nice watching your mates die – and just as chilling to think that it could have been you. None of the dead and wounded were any less effective operators than we were. They were just unlucky. Maybe it was their time.

Fire Force deployments were a harrowing experience and required nerves of steel. The men of the RLI and RAR, I commend you!

B Troop was soon back in Tete, this time for six weeks, deploying to Chioco once again to harass the road routes and attack the town. After the initial attack, where we lost Andy Chait, the garrison was rendered unserviceable and ZANLA and their FRELIMO cohorts had moved into the once magnificent Portuguese villas that lined the town's avenues. When the SAS hit, they overran Chioco and Captain Wilson became mayor for a day, celebrating the little victory by sipping

Manica beer out of china teacups, served up on linen tablecloths. The celebrations were accompanied with fresh rations from a storeroom that was discovered nearby. Overall it was a jolly little affair.

The town had been deserted at the time of the raid. Unbeknown to the SAS, its inhabitants slept in the bush, retiring there each evening for fear of further attacks by Rhodesian forces.

The only casualties of the raid occurred, when a few unlucky ZANLA awoke in their sleeping positions only 20 metres from the SAS mortar team. When they opened fire, an unobserved mortar operator spun the tube in the direction of the upset and loosed off a bomb. The tube was almost vertical and it was magnificent instinctive shooting. The firing died immediately and the team learnt they had scored a direct hit. Later they found a terrorist limping around with one foot; his other one having been neatly severed by mortar shrapnel. Around the impact crater were sets of blood-soaked webbing, indicating other casualties who had been carted off.

While this was all happening, I was finally afforded my swan and remained at Mtoko Forward Air Field in an administrative role. The Squadron sergeant major was in charge and it was a charmed existence, making sure ammo and provisions were available to the troops at all times. I was a bit jealous when continual reports of constant action came in from my mates in the field, but I enjoyed the break considerably, in particular the evenings spent in the air force bar across the airstrip.

After a particularly active few days, a chopper came in to collect supplies for B Troop. Aboard was a pile of captured weaponry which included AK and SKS rifles. I was told by the SSM to have the weapons tagged and bagged for storage, which I did, instructing a driver to deliver them to a tented storage facility at the base.

That night in the bar one of the air force technicians asked me if he could procure an SKS rifle. I said no, as it would be in contravention of military policy. The driver who had helped me that afternoon, sipping a beer quietly by my side, then enquired as to whether he could have one. He said he wanted it for his dad's bar at home, where it would make a fine conversation piece adorning the mantle. I brushed off the enquiry, saying that it had nothing to do with me, the weapons were army property and besides, I told him, they were all in a shit state.

A few weeks passed and I was back in Salisbury, when I was picked up by the military police and questioned about a missing weapon. I learnt that the driver had stolen an SKS from the cache and was caught lurking around Club Tomorrow, trying to pot his girlfriend who had left him for another man. When questioned, the driver told the policeman where the weapon had come from and he lied that I had given him permission to take it.

Ultimately, despite my defence, I was accused of selling captured weapons and I went through the rigmarole of having unwelcome intrusions in my house as the MPs searched for more evidence. Sheila was not amused at all and despised the arrogance of the policemen who went about their business ripping the house apart, acting as if I was already convicted.

After coming up with plum, I was placed under base arrest. Vernon Conchie, sympathetic to my predicament, entered the military police cells at Cranborne Barracks one night to search out the troublesome driver. When he was found he was warned that the truth had better come out and that he would have to change his statement, or else he would end up on the missing persons list. I must say, it could not have been pleasant, having Vernon breathing down your neck trying to exact vengeance.

Needless to say, the driver changed his statement. I attended his court-martial where he pleaded guilty to the theft and I was excused.

It was not the last I heard of the issue. When I returned to the Squadron, Major Robinson, the CO, wanted to bust me for gun-running. As far as he was concerned I was guilty and the outcome of the court-martial was only as a result of Vernon's intervention and his terrifying demeanour. As the CO put it, anyone would admit to stealing the crown jewels under Conchie's interrogation.

I refused to accept any further punishment, but the CO initiated another court-martial, despite my lawyer conversing with him and reiterating that the charges had been dropped. Not good enough for the CO, who had me convicted of fraternising with junior ranks, after which came a severe reprimand and a R$30 fine.

At the end of the hearing, it was held that I should have taken responsibility for the weapons and not delegated the driver. What didn't get mentioned and what made a lot of people angry, was the SSM's negligence in passing the task on to me when it had really been his responsibility in the first place. He was as guilty as I was of sub-delegating and not ensuring the weapons were properly stored. Shit only runs downhill, I suppose!

I really felt like a scapegoat and the incident marred my enthusiasm for the unit at the time. I suppose something had to go pop and I was the cracker at the party.

After the way I was addressed at the orders committee, I resolved to leave the SAS and try my luck in the Selous Scouts. Besides, my three-year stint was almost up and the recruiting vultures had already knocked on my door in a bid to get me to defect.

I made my views known to Major Robinson but he insisted that I had to go on another operation before I could leave. I was ordered to report back to B Troop, where they were waiting with the rest of the Squadron at New Sarum, to mount an enormous operation against ZANLA bases in the Manica Province of Mozambique. The operation was a combined air/ground assault by the SAS and the air force on the terrorist bases at Chimoio and Tembue, designated Zulu 1 and Zulu 2; the largest concentration of terrorists identified during the course of the war.

I had only one foot in the door. It wasn't the people that counted who had ruffled my feathers, but I felt that some of my brothers had let me down when I needed them most. It was as if those who were responsible for my well-being had left me deserted on a small fucking island without so much as a coconut. My time in the army was over and the powers-that-be wanted to send me on an operation where I would most likely be slotted. Under normal circumstances, soldiers were given a reprieve when their service time drew to a close. I told Lieutenant Ken Roberts, the new Troop 2 i/c, of my woes and his typical response was a shrug of the shoulders, followed by a curt 'shit happens'.

As it turned out, I arrived at New Sarum late and the Squadron had already departed to Chimoio. I caught a transport to Grand Reef airfield, but they had left there also and I missed out on the initial attack.

Eventually I flew into Chimoio by chopper with a re-supply of ammo, but the fighting was all but over by then. The Rhodesians had swept in during the early hours of the morning, neutralising the camp's defences with strike aircraft, before inserting heliborne and parachute troops in the biggest Fire Force operation of the war. Militarily, it was a resounding success and given the shortages of aircraft, equipment and manpower, the results were out of all proportion to what was expected.

It has since been queried whether any other army in the world would have been able to conduct an operation in the face of such enormous odds, let alone muster the big brass balls that were necessary. But the Rhodesians carried it through successfully, pitting a mere 185 troops against the 9,000 guerrillas who were expected to be in the camps.

Of the 9,000 personnel stationed at Chimoio, 4,000 were fully trained terrorists and the rest were either in training, or somehow tagged by association to the guerrillas. Many of them may have been quite innocent victims, having been in the wrong place at the wrong time. It was a ploy that ZANLA often used when they housed civilians and family members at military training camps. They could always turn around later, throw up their arms and cry foul at the Rhodesians' cruelty, claiming that the camps housed refugees. It was only much later that Zimbabwean politicians, former ZANLA leaders, admitted that Chimoio was indeed a terrorist camp. Nevertheless, it really was a turkey shoot.

When the Rhodesians attacked, the camp hierarchy had bravely legged it, leaving the masses to die by bomb, bullet and bayonet. I witnessed the slaughter at Chimoio. The enemy bodies were piled high. Many of them were unarmed, caught napping when the Canberras and Hunters came in to drop their Alpha and Golf bombs. Hundreds of corpses bore the telltale puncture marks of the six-inch flechette darts from the 500-pound (227 kilogram) anti-personnel bombs. The others were gunned down as they fought last-ditch battles to survive, or they were shot while they fled in terror from the onslaught of the Rhodesian war machine.

Immediately after Chimoio, Tembue, or Zulu 2, was attacked, using the same troops who had already fought at Chimoio. This camp was thought to house up to 4,000 guerrillas, but by the time the Rhodesians arrived, many of them had fled. Tembue was also a military success although nothing compared to Chimoio. Combined, at both camps, more than 2,000 enemy were killed, with thousands more injured. Had the Rhodesians been able to muster more troops, the figure might have been much higher. As it was, very few of the many sub-camps were actually attacked. The cost to the Rhodesians: two dead and eight injured. A remarkable effort when you think about it!

My war in the Rhodesian SAS was over, but the country still fought hard for its very existence. During my time serving with the unit, I had gained considerable experience and my overall impressions were good. The Rhodesian SAS remains, in my opinion, one of the most effective little bands of fighting men the world has ever seen. During their battle, on three different fronts, the Squadron managed to inflict damage upon the enemy out of all proportion to its size. At any one time, including national servicemen, the unit at its peak could muster only about 200 individuals.

There were no supermen among the men I fought with. What made them stand out from the rest, were the qualities of meticulous planning, repetitive implementation of rehearsals and professional adherence to given tasks. Add to that personal fitness discipline, an intricate knowledge of weapons, equipment and tactics and we were ready to take on all comers.

Of course, there were one or two incidents that did mar my outlook of the unit and there were a couple of characters I would rather have never met. One of them ultimately paid the highest price for his country, so I won't harp on and dishonour that sacrifice.

Inside of me something still ticked, yearning for the adventure that comes with soldiering. Another part of me sought a compromise where I could be in two places at once – looking after my family and fighting my own little war.

With hindsight, I can see now why I never found that happy medium, but at the time I had it all worked out in my head. Given my background, I had more to offer the military than my fighting skills alone and I felt that a change was in order, for me to progress as a husband and a father, as well as a soldier. If I could get into the operations room, or perhaps the intelligence section of the Selous Scouts, as during my Para days, then that would be just fine. My family neglect would be over and I would also be doing something that I really loved. Something which, I hoped, would keep me occupied and not be an anticlimax to the pace of operations I had experienced in the SAS.

My mind was made up and I would leave, but my battle was far from over.

Map of Rhodesia (Zimbabwe) showing areas in which Jake operated whilst serving in the SAS and Selous Scouts.

CHAPTER 23:
Masters of Bush Craft

After the SAS returned from the Chimoio raid, my feelings of despondency had not changed and I sought fulfilment elsewhere. In December 1977 I approached Chris Schulenburg, a serving Selous Scout whom I had met in the Squadron and asked if a transfer could be facilitated. Chris was a highly decorated soldier and was awarded the Silver Cross of Rhodesia while still serving in the SAS. Already he was a legendry figure in the military, for the close-in reconnaissance operations he conducted deep into enemy territory. Among the Selous Scouts he was viewed with awe, by officer and soldier alike, both black and white. Later he would become the first recipient of the Grand Cross of Valour, Rhodesia's highest gallantry award.

I felt encouraged when I was informed that the Selous Scouts would readily accept me. An interview with the unit's commander, Lieutenant Colonel Ron Reid Daly, was organised for a few days later. In truth, the Scouts always waved a contract in front of Squadron guys, like dangling a carrot in front of a donkey.

The Selous Scouts had been formed in 1973, at the directive of the Prime Minister himself, after experiments had taken place utilising pseudo tactics developed for use against ZANLA and ZIPRA guerrillas. The concept itself was not new and had been spawned many years before from an amalgamation of ideas from different minds. Among the more prominent of these were Allan Savory and Brigadier John Hickman, who toyed with the idea, after leaning on experience the latter had gained in Malaya, when he was part of the British deployment of pseudo-gangs.

Allan Savory was a bushman par excellence and a Territorial Army officer. In civilian life he worked as an ecologist. He too saw great potential in fielding highly trained tracker/combat pseudo-gangs. Savory ran the first course on bush survival techniques; a very necessary discipline if one was to pass off as a terrorist.

Others, who were involved in the initial experiments, were seasoned soldiers with experience in pseudo-operations from Kenya during the Mau Mau days and SAS men with incredible imagination and a flair for something different. One of them was Andre Rabie, after whom the new Selous Scouts barracks would be named. He was a brilliant bushman and a superb soldier, although his interest in pseudo work leaned towards fanaticism. He once even tried to dye himself permanently black, in an effort to better fit into his role as a terrorist! Unfortunately, Rabie was killed in an accident during the early days of experimentation.

Although 'frozen' zones (areas denied access to other security forces while pseudo-gangs operated there) had already been established, a map-reading error was made and the price of the mistake was high. Andre and his team of operators were cooling off in a pool below a small farm dam wall, oblivious to danger, when they were fired upon by an RLI patrol which, understandably, took them for terrorists. Andre died in the opening fusillade and the rest of his team scattered. Fortunately, no one else was injured.

An investigation revealed that Andre was to blame for the map-reading error, mistaking one dam on his map for another. His loss was severely felt by all who knew and worked with him; and the importance of correctly establishing 'frozen zones' was pressed home.

Collectively, these men brought together a wealth of knowledge that would eventually lead to the formation of the Selous Scouts.

Ostensibly, the whole pseudo-concept involves masquerading as the enemy to infiltrate his support network, gathering intelligence and thus closing with him. It is a multifaceted concept and relies heavily on up-to-date intelligence from fresh captives.

To really fool the adversary into thinking that you're someone you're not, requires an infinite knowledge of his habits, tactics, rituals and structures. To best understand this, it is essential to emulate him down to the finest detail.

Whereas in Malaya, whites and native troops could pass for the enemy, Africa posed a different problem. To pass a white man off as a black man was virtually impossible, given the intrinsic differences in mannerisms and cultural backgrounds. The best way to combat this was to use black troops at the forefront of pseudo-operations. Thus, 70 per cent of those who operated in the Selous Scouts were black. Even so, as the war developed and the Selous Scouts became notorious to the enemy, further ploys had to be devised in order to retain the upper hand. Thus, turned terrorists were incorporated into the rank and file, who could then be armed, trained and sent out to kill their former comrades. As must be obvious, it was a very risky business.

In doing this, however, it was possible to keep ahead of the game by employing techniques and devices that the terrorists developed, to identify genuine guerrillas from their pseudo-counterparts. For instance, when meeting another gang of guerrilla fighters, certain handshakes were employed, or identifying objects, like bangles worn. These devices changed periodically and thus it was important to have a large rural intelligence network, or access to fresh captives on a daily basis, who could keep the security forces informed of any changes. The ground coverage for intelligence purposes for the unit was run by Special Branch, an integral part of operations, as it had been in Malaya with the British. Without Special Branch there is no doubt that the Selous Scouts would never have achieved the success that they did.

To the Rhodesians, pseudo-operations were a novel idea and nothing like it had ever been attempted before. The only inter-racial unit in service at that stage was the white-officered Rhodesian African Rifles and it was not known whether white and black troops would mix successfully. Given the cultural diversities, it was a long shot, but in reality it panned out well. Rhodesians of all colours were able to live amicably together when fighting for the same cause.

Initially, to outsiders, the Selous Scouts were publicised as a combat tracker unit of the highest calibre. On the inside, however, there was another darker side to the unit which only came to public attention towards the end of the war. This was the pseudo-operations element conducted by black and white Rhodesian soldiers, turned terrorists among them, infiltrating genuine guerrilla gangs and gathering intelligence, or directing combat troops onto their positions to neutralise them. Some men, who served in the unit at the time, mostly national servicemen, had no knowledge about this side of operations and they were used mainly on external assault ops, or internally manning observation posts and tracking the enemy.

My initiation to the unit was a rather privileged introduction and I was made privy to a lot of classified information. Meeting Ron Reid Daly in person was an interesting experience in itself and his initial reaction to me was one of hesitancy as he glanced over my paperwork. Raising his eyebrows he sized me up quizzically upon recognizing my name.

'Harper Ronald' he said. 'Weren't you that troublemaker in the Rhodesian Light Infantry back in '65?'

The lieutenant colonel had then been the founding regimental sergeant major of the RLI and he knew my brother well. He remembered clearly his antics, which resulted in numerous headaches for the exasperated RSM. He was a unique man and despite the mistaken identity, he probably would have given Ian a chance anyway, seeing, as he did, rebelliousness as something that could be moulded into a useful asset in the type of soldier he was looking for.

During the Malayan emergency, Reid Daly had served with C Squadron SAS (Malayan Scouts) after he had volunteered for service in the east. His wealth of knowledge had been gleaned there while conducting deep penetration missions into the jungles against communist rebels. When he returned from Malaya, he continued to serve as a regular soldier in the Rhodesian military and took up a post in the RLI. He was the first choice as commander when it was decided to form the Scouts.

With the formalities out of the way, I was introduced to Major Neil Kriel, a bull of a man and the OC Reconnaissance Troop. Recce Troop, as it was called, was made up almost entirely of ex-SAS men and was considered an elite within the elite. Ostensibly it was the CO's private little army and many of those who served in its ranks were veteran guerrilla fighters and decorated soldiers. It was considered an honour by anyone in the unit to serve alongside the likes of Chris Schulenburg, John Gartner, Martin Knight Willis, Rich Stannard, Tim Callow, Aaron Mlambo, Steven Mpofu and Martin Chikondo. These men were the reconnaissance experts of the Rhodesian Army and penetrated deep into enemy territory to observe enemy camps and send back intelligence.

Major Kriel informed me that a place was open under his command for an Intelligence Clerk to help him with the planning of operations. It suited my needs perfectly and again enthusiasm welled up inside me after the recent upheaval I had been through.

I would be taken on by word of mouth which would negate the selection procedure and incredibly, on a month-to-month contract. I could leave the unit at any time, with a month's notice and request an RTU to return to the SAS if I was not happy.

My initial job description made me as happy as a hippy on LSD. I would be responsible for attending intelligence briefings at army HQ, as well as identifying recce jobs for the teams. Thereafter I would help plan operations, obtain maps of the areas concerned and brief the personnel designated to the mission. As far as I saw it, I had landed with my bum in the butter and found exactly what I was looking for. I just couldn't wait to tell Sheila and the boys. They were a bit young to understand my enthusiasm, but the way I felt I just wanted to tell everyone.

I took a short break before joining the Scouts at Andre Rabie Barracks. It was a blissful period, spending time with my boys and sifting through the problems that had developed between Sheila and me. I hadn't been purely monogamous in my marriage and I suspected Sheila hadn't been either. Rumours abounded in Salisbury, as close knit as the community was and any news of mischievous activity outside of marriage spread like wildfire on an open prairie. I remember hearing that Rhodesia boasted the highest divorce rate in the world during the bush war. Statistically it was said that one in three marriages was destined to fail. I could well believe it, having witnessed the promiscuity that prevailed in social circles while husbands were away in the bush. It was a very sad situation, but one I could almost understand, considering the loneliness that wives must have felt when their men were away for increasingly longer periods as the war intensified.

What did get me and I've really no right to complain, was that promiscuity among married couples was not only restricted to strangers. I knew of many instances where best mates were shagging each other's' wives while the other was away. I did it myself once and I'm really not proud of it. I suppose these excesses were the spillover of the pressure the country was under. I have mentioned the veneer of bravado in an earlier chapter and promiscuity, along with drinking and other things, was the outlet for this frustration.

Sheila and I managed to resolve our differences and we went through a brief period where we had never felt closer. The past was behind us and we looked forward to a future that could be spent as a family, despite the ongoing war. Richard and Paul were normal young boys doing normal things, like playing with toy guns. Cops and robbers, or cowboys and Indians, were the popular games of choice. Paul always came off second best in those shenanigans.

To those not in service, or to the uninitiated, the subtle differences to living in a country at peace were only really noticed when one left the environs of the cities. Sure, by the numbers of uniformed men walking around, it was obvious that the country was at war, but the cities always maintained a defiant, jovial air. Leaving Salisbury, or any town for that matter, it was the armed convoys of vehicles that gave the game away; housewives sitting in passenger seats with Uzi sub-machine guns pointing out of car windows while young children played 'I spy with my little eye' in the back seat.

A day's outing, like a picnic, to one of the beautiful lakes or national parks in the country, was exactly that, a picnic. The difference was that someone had to be covering you with a machine gun while you uncorked the bottle of champagne, or buttered the bread rolls for the braai (barbecue). Looking back, we lived in a 'pretend' society of calm, unwilling to believe that our little war could impede our lifestyles. It did, but we got on with it anyway and made the best of the situation. And what a time it was!

When I started operations with the Selous Scouts, things didn't turn out as I imagined they would. Major Kriel did all the groundwork and preparation for the reconnaissance teams and I pretty much became the Reconnaissance Troop lackey. My unofficial title was camp commandant although I was still a corporal. My earlier charge in the SAS had precluded any promotion for a year.

At Andre Rabie Barracks, Recce Troop was sectioned off from the rest of the Scouts, billeted at the bottom of the base's grounds where they did their own thing. During my first few months I was given the responsibility of drawing ammo, rations, requisitioning ration money and looking after stores and equipment. Additionally I was sent as a forward party, in charge of 14 base staff, to set up camp in the areas of impending operations.

Dave Scales, another ex-Squadron member, was Chris Schulenburg's right-hand man and the Troop signaller. He always accompanied me on these forays into the remotest of areas to establish a communications network and generally lend a hand. The teams would follow a few days later, once we had set up a comfortable camp and by personal example, cleared the roads of landmines. On our little forays we did not have advanced mine-detecting equipment simply because it was hardly available. Driving in first, we always stood the risk of running into mines, or being ambushed, but at least we were well armed. The forward base defences, of which I was in charge, consisted of a 12.7 mm Degtyarev DShK heavy machine gun, two 7.62 mm Goryunov medium machine guns, two 60 mm mortars and a couple of RPG7 launchers.

It was my responsibility to site the weapons, dig pits and trenches, keep all the weapons clean and work out guard rosters while we were in the bush. Once this was all done I would set up personal accommodations for Major Kriel and the teams, ably assisted by the staff.

It wasn't a terrible job, but it also wasn't what I had been expecting.

My first operation with the Selous Scouts rates a mention because of what happened there. A terrorist base had been identified in Zambia, not far from the small town of Feira – where I had operated before with the SAS – at a place called Kavalamanje. Combined Operations had assigned the SAS, RLI and the RAR to attack the camp, but the pre-operation reconnaissance was to be carried out by the Recce Troop of the Selous Scouts – led by Chris Schulenburg and Martin Chikondo.

The attack was to take place sometime during March and Dave Scales and I left a week early, with our forward entourage, to set up a forward base at Kanyemba on the Zambezi River, in the extreme north of Rhodesia. It was a relatively deserted area, manned only by a few Customs officials and a police post to provide early warning of border trouble as well as protection.

After we had arrived at Kanyemba air strip we found a suitable location and set about readying the camp. While Dave got secure HF communications up and running, I delegated staff to erect the operations room and accommodations for Major Kriel and the operators, who would arrive by fixed-wing aircraft the following day.

While the staff busied themselves, I sited the defensive weapons and built covers over the gun pits to provide protection from the weather. The rainy season had set in and our activities were hampered by perpetual guti (fine ongoing drizzle), sloppy wet mud and extreme humidity. If the rain didn't soak us through to the bone our sweat would have!

My own home, for the duration of the operation, was a shell scrape which I sited next to one of the machine guns. It didn't perturb me that my home would be a lair in the sodden wet earth while the operators lived in tented comfort. If the camp was revved, at least I would be below ground with a modicum of protection.

Recce Troop flew in without incident and settled into the forward base. On 1 March 1978 Chris and Martin were deployed by helicopter into the hilly terrain west of Kavalamanje, making their way to a high ridge overlooking the town. There they set up a powerful spotter scope and attached a 35mm camera with home-made clamps and tape. We never did have access to the technical equipment available to other armies at the time and had to make do with our own improvisations.

Over the next few days the reconnaissance team sent in a pile of detailed reports confirming a ZIPRA presence in the town and based at numerous camps on the outskirts. So detailed were Chris's reports that they included not only numbers of personnel and weapons carried, but dress detail down to the smallest observations. One report indicated that the enemy seemed alert, but the majority of them roamed around with their bootlaces untied.

From the OP, they were able to capture a clear picture of the goings-on below them and formulate a battle plan that would be most advantageous to the security forces. There was also a Zambian Army presence nearby and the team plotted positions of defensive weapons and anti-aircraft emplacements. When the Rhodesian Air Force swept through, these would be the first targets they would take care of.

A few days before the raid was to commence, a Selous Scout Troop drove in by road in case assistance was needed. The staff made them as comfortable as possible in accommodations by the airstrip and I made sure that ammo and provisions were supplied.

On D-Day minus one, further OPs were set up on the Rhodesian side of the river in case anything was missed. I was posted with a callsign to an advantageous point that gave us a clear view when the battle commenced.

Based on the information provided by the recce team, the attack was scheduled for 6 March 1978, utilising two commandos of the RLI and one company from the RAR as the assault force. The SAS would drop further north, with anti-tank weapons, to negate a response from a large Zambian Army contingent situated 10 kilometres away.

When dawn of 6 March came there was a gloomy, overcast sky with heavy rain sweeping the entire area. Because of the weather the attack was delayed by two hours and so the Hunter and Canberra aircraft swept in with their cargo of

Golf and Alpha bombs at 10:00. It was a fantastic sight watching hundreds of alpha bombs rain in on the designated camps. Through my optics it was possible to follow them and watch them bounce to about four and a half metres, before exploding on their proximity fuses. The hail of shrapnel that splintered downwards had a satisfying effect, neutralising some of the enemy as they ran; their hapless figures suddenly going limp and falling into lifeless heaps.

To the south of Kavalamanje, the shock troops commenced with their advance on pre-plotted positions, taking care of any resistance in their way. Despite the delay, surprise was complete and most of the enemy scattered inland. Small battles developed below Chris and Martin's position across a vast panoramic vista. The recce team directed troops onto hiding guerrillas who had sought sanctuary in the flood plain behind them and most were winkled out and killed. Unfortunately, due to the heavy summer rains, the bush surrounding the area was a lot denser than anticipated and the advance was hindered. By late afternoon many of the enemy were unaccounted for and had fled towards a natural bottleneck between the river and the flood plain. Had we placed troops there our coup might have been complete.

When darkness fell, we were called back to the airstrip and given a warning order that we would cross the river the next morning and assist the other troops with the sweep. The SAS were withdrawn from their position also, leaving behind them a small team in case the Zambians intervened.

The Zambians were not too much of a problem, as radio intercepts revealed that they weren't worried about their ZIPRA comrades at all. Calls for help from Kavalamanje had been ignored, with the Zambians preferring not to get their feet wet.

The following morning we were ferried across the river by helicopter and joined up with the SAS, RLI and RAR troops for the sweep. I managed to corner Major Kriel and air my reservations about the sanity of our deployment. As far as I could see, we might be vulnerable to mistaken identity by some of the other troops, dressed as we were in an assortment of terrorist-type clothing. Looking about the Selous Scouts, we could very well have been a bunch of terrs.

Some of us were adorned with Stetson-type hats – which the guerrillas often wore – and an amazing assortment of guerrilla dress and weapons. The other units were attired in standard Rhodesian disruptive-pattern uniforms which were easy to distinguish. Whether the major took in my concerns or not, I don't know, but we continued with an uneventful sweep towards the flood plain. During the night, those enemy who were still alive, had found their way to safety and were long gone from the area by the time we arrived. Overall, the attack had been a success, with 42 ZIPRA accounted for and a large quantity of weapons and ammunition destroyed. Except for a few minor wounds, the Rhodesians had so far escaped unscathed.

Toward lunchtime we were recalled to the Rhodesian side of the river to join the remnants of the SAS, who waited while their demolition teams put charges on a small bridge that crossed the Kalulu River, a tributary of the Zambezi. With the bridge blown up, any attempts to intervene from Feira would be greatly hindered.

Back across the river, we walked in our callsigns to a designated rallying point. A few of the chaps and I lagged behind and brought up the rear. As the lead callsign rounded a bend in the road, an SAS early-warning team opened fire, thinking we were the lead element of a terrorist follow-up patrol and two of the Scouts went down with severe injuries. The Squadron guy who opened fire, Rogan Brown, a mate of mine, realised his mistake late but just in time. He ceased fire but the damage was done. As a result of the friendly-fire incident, one of the Selous Scout operators had to have his leg amputated and he forever held a grudge against the SAS. I really felt like saying that I had warned Major Kriel about putting us into the field, dressed as we were, but I supposed that would just be rubbing it in and would make no difference to the two guys whose lives were messed up.

Another strange thought occurred to me on that particular bush trip. After Kavalamanje, we were withdrawn to Kanyemba, where we broke camp a few days later and returned to Andre Rabie Barracks at Inkomo, just outside Salisbury. A number of the vehicles we drove back in were homemade armoured fighting vehicles. Built by Selous Scouts technical personnel, they were based on a West German design over a Mercedes Unimog engine and chassis. They were quite unlike anything the Rhodesians owned and for all intents and purposes could very well have been mistaken for Eastern bloc amphibious vehicles. To add to the confusion, unlike the standard Rhodesian armoured vehicle family, which were all daubed in green-and-earth camouflage patterns, ours were plain green, much like the green that the Zambians used on their military vehicles. This was an intentional design function that would hopefully con the enemy into thinking that we were friendly when we operated across borders where, I must point out, they were mostly used. To further complicate matters, as we drove into Salisbury, the armoured vehicles were crowded with Selous Scout operators perched all over them and bristling with Soviet weaponry. Most of the Scouts were black operators and those of us who were white were blackened up anyway, hiding our obvious white features. Most of the traits that distinguish whites from blacks are only discernable from a distance when walking, or running and not when sitting casually among mostly black soldiers. These characteristics display themselves to the watchful eye, in mannerisms and in different stride patterns, and are not that obvious when men ride on vehicles.

And here we were, driving into the capital city looking for all the world like a bunch of ZIPRA commandos on a raid. It struck me that we weren't once stopped, or challenged, on the 270 kilometre journey from the border. A team of enemy personnel armed as we were could have wreaked havoc in the capital city!

The Rhodesians were good, but there were serious security shortcomings and I dread to think what could have happened if the enemy had the same big brass balls that we did, when we drove unchallenged into neighbouring countries. It was a lesson I learned well, but for the duration of the war we continued to go where and when we pleased, dressed as enemy personnel.

CHAPTER 24:
Dirty deeds

Later, some months into my transfer, I was put in charge of a Quick Reaction Force in case one of the reconnaissance teams got into trouble while deployed externally. In the event of hot extraction I would fly in there with my own little army and get the unfortunate operators out of harm's way. To this end I trained some of the staff, not all of them badged Selous Scout operators, in weapons handling and tactics. Some were no more than bottlewashers and cooks, but together we formed a tight-knit band that was always ready for deployment. In effect, we became the Selous Scout's personal Fire Force and we were raring to go.

Rarely did anything happen, although I ended up being away from Salisbury on bush deployments more often than I had been in the SAS. After all the headway Sheila and I had made in resolving our disputes, the pressure began to mount and we were soon back to square one. I couldn't really blame her and she probably thought that my absence had a lot to do with my planning. From her point of view, it must have appeared that my initial idea of joining the Scouts only to spend more time together, was just a ploy to indulge my own military passions.

`At this time, Sheila was working as a checkout operator at the TM Supermarket in Avondale. For Rhodesia, the brand-new supermarket was an immense shopping facility. It had recently been owned by the Checkers supermarket group. Her boss was an ex-Rhodesian who had lived in South Africa, also working for Checkers and he took over as manager of the Avondale branch. Over the ensuing months RT became a close family friend.

A former officer in 5-Rhodesia Regiment, on his return to the country he received his call-up papers requesting his attendance at the unit on a six-weeks on, six-weeks off basis. This did not tie in with his civilian occupation, so he sought my advice. Fortunately for RT, one of the TM general managers was a Territorial Force officer who worked in the Selous Scouts operations room. The officer managed to pull some strings and a vacancy was opened for RT, who during his six weeks call-up, would report to Andre Rabie Barracks and man the operations room at night. It was an arrangement that better suited his full-time job as manager of TM Avondale. The ops room was manned by various personnel, standing by the radios and phones to receive information from the operators in the bush. On duty, the officer in charge had a bed and he could sleep, only to be woken if anything critical arose. Within a few short weeks of RT taking over the night shift in the ops room, an incident occurred which was very costly to the regiment.

Corporal Obasi was one of the Selous Scouts most valued pseudo-operators and had received the Bronze Cross of Rhodesia for his exploits in the Urungwe Tribal Trust Lands (TTL). There, in a sector of *Operation Hurricane* in which both nationalist factions operated, he was able to play ZANLA gangs off against ZIPRA gangs and effectively gain control of a huge area.

After his award and a brief resting-up period, he returned to operations in the Selous farming area when he learnt that a group of ZIPRA terrorists had slipped through his net and were basing themselves near Hartley. Corporal Obasi made immediate preparations to move there and establish communications with the genuine guerrillas, outfitted as his group were as pseudo-terrorists.

Before his deployment, the usual 'freezing' signals were sent from the ops room to inform all the Joint Operational Commands (JOCs), and Sub Joint Operational Commands (Sub JOCs) that a Selous Scout team was working in the area. It was the JOC's responsibility to send a return signal, acknowledging that no other security forces would be allowed to operate there.

RT was on duty that night and when the signals were sent, he failed to notice that a small part of the area in which Corporal Obasi's group was operating, extended into the JOC Grapple (Midlands) operational area. He informed JOC Hurricane, but omitted to 'freeze' the other area. It was to be a grave omission indeed and was the only mistake that was made by the ops room during the course of the war.

For the most part, the Hurricane and Grapple operational areas were farming lands and relatively densely populated. In the white farming areas PATU (Police Anti-Terrorist Unit) patrols, manned by reservist policemen who farmed in the area, were very quick on the trigger and over the course of the war they were responsible for many successful contacts with terrorists.

As a result of RT's error of omission, Corporal Obasi and three other excellent operators, oblivious to danger, were ambushed and killed by a PATU stick. They were operating in the small slice of land that formed part of JOC

Grapple, in the extreme west of their area. In one fell swoop the Selous Scouts lost four of their best pseudo-operators. The result: the loss of control in the area Corporal Obasi had worked so hard and bravely to gain.

For unknown reasons, RT escaped the wrath of the CO, who gave him some leniency. He was new to the job and, we were told, didn't quite know the ropes. As far as many people were concerned, he should have been fired outright. When a mistake costs the lives of four valuable men, surely that is as heinous an error as could be made? Certainly, he shouldn't have been kept on in the operations room, as he was. Fortunately for the Selous Scouts, nothing of that magnitude ever happened again.

I felt a bit resentful towards RT after the tragedy, but with the close ties between Sheila and himself, he remained a family friend. He was a bit of a braggart and loved to boast about his Selous Scout status to those who weren't quite aware of the facts. He had never been in Special Forces and was really just an officer attached, but with the growing fame of the regiment he swanned around with the airs and graces of a seasoned Special Forces operator. He never seemed to take note of the fact that the actual operators were mostly reserved characters in public society and didn't run around bragging about who they were.

When I was away in the bush RT used my car around town and as transport to the barracks. Sheila didn't have a driving licence so it made sense to lend him the car so it wouldn't remain idle. Additionally, he could help out if Sheila needed to go shopping, or in an emergency like getting one of the boys to hospital.

Despite our differences RT and I used to confide in each other and we became quite close. During my leave we would drink together at a few of the watering holes in town, where we both, but particularly me, unleashed our pent-up tension. During these excursions RT often spoke about classified information that he was privy to in the operations room, or at army HQ. They were really stories that should have remained confidential and not mentioned in places where there might have been prying ears.

I first got wind of the internal strife within the regiment from RT. Accusations had been made about certain operators using 'frozen zones' for their personal benefit – poaching elephant for their ivory. To cut to the chase, a row developed in army HQ and a lot of mistrust was placed in the Selous

Scouts. Certain senior officers were not happy with the regiment's autonomy and rows developed at the highest levels of military control. These would eventually seep into the very core of Selous Scout operations and create a disruption that was to mar the unit's record. The most senior officers of the regiment, the CO and OC Recce Troop, would be involved.

RT also spoke about the dirty-deeds section of the Selous Scouts. This referred to certain operators who conducted operations to discredit the nationalists of both factions. I could never be certain which was fact and which was fiction, but some things he mentioned were definitely true. One night at the bar, after RT had spent the day with Special Branch personnel attached to the Selous Scouts, he gave me a warning. Leaning across the table he muttered into my ear that I should avoid certain things if I was to go on any cross-border operations with the unit. He had been told that elements of Special Branch had lifted and doctored, enemy stores and provisions, and placed them back in their original caches. I was warned never to eat any captured canned food as it had been poisoned with strychnine. Enemy grenades had been tampered with so that they would detonate immediately the pin was pulled. Small-arms ammunition had been doctored with powerful charges, that would burst the breach of the weapon when fired and clothing had been laced with contact poisons that resulted in the wearer's long and painful death.

I wasn't surprised by what I heard, as I had read of similar operations conducted by the British Special Branch in Malaya and elsewhere. In Malaya, aside from the already mentioned dirty deeds, rice caches were laced with ground glass and many other crafty methods of rendering the enemy inoperative were spawned from fertile imaginations.

I can hear some readers saying things like 'despicable' and 'unacceptable'. When compared to the atrocities committed by the nationalist forces, these things almost seem acceptable. Not for me to have parts of my body cut off me when I'm alive and force-fed to my family members.

I heeded RT's warning and actually heard of a few cases where raiding Rhodesian troops fell sick after eating from cans of pilchards, captured across the border. And there were instances of terrorists being tracked after a farm-store raid, in which the culprits stole laced clothing, being found emaciated and weak after the poisons had taken effect. I knew that such dirty deeds were always conducted with a high degree of responsibility. It sounds odd to talk of responsibility when the intention is to kill people but, as I've mentioned before,

Special Branch ran a very organised ground intelligence network and they operated only on the most reliable information.

In the case of clothing being laced at a farm store, for instance, the articles would only be moved there prior to reliable intelligence that the store was going to be raided by terrorists. Once there they would be controlled by a handler, or someone who had been informed, and it was impossible for them to end up in innocent civilian hands. Such was the nature of the dirty-deeds war.

The straw that eventually broke the camel's back in my relationship with RT, occurred one night after I returned from the bush where I had set up camp for another Selous Scout reconnaissance operation. After greeting Sheila at home, RT popped in and invited me for a drink on the pretext of 'business'.

The reader will have gathered by this stage that I was no saint, and I don't mean to infer that I was. I was quite keen to visit one of the clubs and sink back a beer or two, not to mention the opportunity of checking out the talent. As my car was in for a service at the time, RT had borrowed another from a friend. We left together and hit the town in full force, ending up at Le Coq Dor and partying the night away. Before long, RT and I had picked up two stragglers; young women keen to get it on with servicemen. The one who attached herself to me was a pretty thing wearing a long green flowing dress. A dozen beers later and as many gin-and-tonics for the ladies, RT approached me and asked how I was shaping. I told him that the young lass wanted me to take her home, but I had declined as I had no vehicle. Dangling the car keys in front of me he egged me on, declaring that he had a headache and would get a taxi home. With that, he left and the two women and I continued to drink and dance the night away.

Unbeknown to me, RT did not go home. Instead, he pulled into my place, leaving the taxi running at the gate. Knocking on the front door, a startled and sleep-deprived Sheila opened up to find RT looking forlornly at the ground. With the pity of a bulldog begging for scraps, he glanced up and declared: 'I'm really sorry, Sheila, but I felt I had to tell you. Something terrible is happening.'

The look on Sheila's face begged for an explanation and he continued: 'I tried my best to stop him, Sheila. I swear!' he paused for a moment. 'Your faithful husband is at Le Coq Dor shaping up with some woman. If you don't believe me there's a taxi waiting at the gate that will take you there.'

I can understand that Sheila was deeply hurt. After the recent misunderstanding with my transfer and the relationship hassles we had so nearly surmounted, this was the final straw.

‘Oh, by the way’ RT added, ‘she’s wearing a long green dress.’

Sheila didn’t go to Le Coq Dor that night. As far as she was concerned her boss and confidante had no reason to lie, so she took his words at face value.

I wasn’t aware, until sometime later, that RT was madly in love with Sheila and it had been his ploy to set me up the whole time, using to his advantage my weakness for the company of women. Yes, of course I was not innocent in the affair, but it did bug me that one of my own chums would turn against me and be so conniving. I began to have my suspicions.

Sheila confronted me about the situation and told me what she had heard and how she had discovered my near infidelity. It created a huge stumbling block between RT and myself and we never saw eye to eye thereafter. On a professional level, back at base, it was an uncomfortable situation to be in. One which would ultimately have far-reaching effects on my life.

CHAPTER 25:
Recces and rockets

Wherever the Selous Scouts operated in Rhodesia, it was from the sanctuary of secure forts. At the peak of the war, there were six of these forts in the various operational areas that could be used as forward staging posts for internal and external operations. The forts were large structures and were surrounded by high corrugated iron walls to dissuade outsiders from looking in, and to provide security for the pseudo-operators returning from the bush. The regiment's methods of operation were still very much top secret.

I left for Mount Darwin early one morning, during July, to establish a temporary camp at some buildings alongside the old Selous Scout fort in the town. The fort had been closed for various reasons but was still off-limits to even regimental personnel. A few days into the deployment, Major Kriel summoned me and asked me to pass on word of the fort's status; it was out of bounds because it contained stores of captured enemy provisions that had been earmarked for the dirty-deeds chaps. Tinned food had been laced with poisons and Major Kriel didn't want any accidents happening, with hungry operators pilfering the supply. I spread the word among those who were there and we waited for the remainder of Recce Troop to arrive.

Tim Callow was a tall, wiry fellow who didn't really look the part of a Selous Scout reconnaissance operator. His outward appearances belied an intense professionalism and he was ultimately to win one of South Africa's highest gallantry awards after he left Rhodesia and joined the Special Forces there.

Intelligence had revealed that Tembue, or Zulu 2, which had been attacked by the SAS just prior to my departure from the unit, was again being used to train ZANLA terrorists before they staged into Rhodesia. The camp had sprung up over a large area and six different sub-camps had been identified from aerial reconnaissance.

Tim Callow's two-man callsign, along with a two-man callsign under Captain Schulenburg, were to penetrate the periphery of the camps and observe them from two different locations. Operational security was vital – if the reconnaissance confirmed the intelligence reports, then the Rhodesians were to attack it immediately.

I was briefed on the operation to man the Quick Reaction Force if either of the teams were compromised, or had got themselves into a spot of trouble. In view of that, I would soar in with my bottle-wash commandos and extract the teams from the jaws of death.

The four operators were deployed to within 20 kilometres of the camp by static-line parachute and made the approach to establish their OPs without incident. A few days into the deployment it transpired that the teams were short of water and a decision was made to fly in a fresh supply. As luck would have it the stores were fresh out of containers, so I was asked by Major Kriel to travel back to Inkomo to the quartermaster's stores and fetch some jerry cans. For the journey he lent me his white, civilian-registered Land-Rover, which was the only vehicle available at the time.

At 05:00 the following morning I grabbed my AK rifle and made haste to Salisbury, aware of how treacherous the route was that I would be travelling alone. In order for the choppers to make the scheduled drop, I had to be back no later than mid-afternoon the same day. For the purpose of the trip I wore civilian clothing and carried my rifle across my lap as I drove. The journey, most of the way, was relatively peaceful as the road was entirely devoid of traffic. No-one travelled unless in convoy or with armed escort, as the north-eastern areas of Rhodesia were a hive of terrorist activity. At the time, ambushes occurred on the route at frequent intervals.

I had almost reached Bindura, the halfway point to Salisbury, when I crested a hill and my heart sank. About a hundred metres below me, in a dip on the road, a group of armed men stood at ease casually chatting. They were all black men and carried an assortment of AK rifles and RPD machine guns. When they saw the Land-Rover they moved off into the bush. As far as I was aware, there were no pseudo-gangs operating in the area and I correctly assumed they were terrorists. I was half-way down the hill when I moved the fire selector switch on my rifle to fully automatic and was second guessing my decision to accelerate through a probable ambush, when I saw them again. My mind screamed at me to turn the vehicle around and disappear in the direction I'd come.

Driving a hundred metres downhill, at great speed, doesn't take long and I was glancing through the trees and grass on the side of the road when the group again came into view. There was nothing for it at this stage but to continue on my way.

I don't know who was more shocked when I passed them at 110 kilometres an hour but the blank expressions on their faces summed up their mood. They stared quizzically as they realised I was not who they thought I might be. Foot to the pedal and head down, I willed the vehicle up the opposite hill, expecting to hear the familiar sound of rounds whizz by any second. No fire came but it was with much trepidation that I sped on to the next town.

Some ten minutes later I careened into the Selous Scout fort at Bindura to report what I had seen. There I was told of my good fortune as the facts became clear.

A Roman Catholic priest, who was stationed nearby, often travelled the road alone in his white Land-Rover. It was suspected that he was sympathetic towards the terrorist's cause because not once had he come to grief when others about him were ambushed and killed. In other parts of the country Missionaries, in particular, were targeted as enemies of the people. We could only assume that I had been misidentified as the priest by the terrorists. A close shave indeed!

The ops room put in a call to ComOps to report the terrorist sighting. I left to continue with my journey and made an uneventful trip to load up with jerry cans in Salisbury.

On the return journey, as I passed by where I had seen the terrs, a Fire Force action was in full swing about a kilometre off into the bush, at the base of a small hill. The staccato boom of 20mm cannon, as it engaged targets, was heard above the roar of the helicopter's engine. I heard later that it was a successful contact and several of the terrorists had been killed. Some of the choppers that took part in the action were those that were based at our forward area at Mount Darwin, right next to the Selous Scout camp.

I always got on well with the air force personnel with whom I came into contact. The relationship between the 'blues' (the air force) and the 'browns' (the army), was tight-knit thanks to the fireforce concept which brought them together. Without being demeaning to our air force pals, it was a similar relationship to that which a cavalry man develops with his horse. Each relies on the other to achieve best effect in combat.

While we waited for reports from the recce teams to come in, there was little else to do but twiddle our thumbs. We took it in turns doing radio stags on a 24-

hour basis, in the event of trouble, as the choppers stood by on the apron.

During our nights off we were able to wander down to the BSAP (British South Africa Police) camp and have a few drinks at their bar. It was a welcome relief from the boredom and many an affable relationship was built between policemen, soldiers and air crews. There were normally two Alouettes based permanently at the airstrip, along with a Lynx fixed-wing aircraft for fire support. This meant that there were five 'blues' personnel around at most times: a pilot and a technician for each of the choppers and the pilot of the push-pull Lynx.

Bored to wits' end one day and after a few friendly challenges in the bar, the 'blues' and the 'browns' decided to square off and have a rocket-building competition. There would be three teams and the winning team would be the recipient of a crate of beer bought by the losers. The competition rules were to design, construct and fly a rocket which would be judged by the policemen. We had a day to come up with our designs and we were to convene on the apron at 15:00 the next afternoon to show off our efforts. Points would be awarded initially for getting our contraptions off the ground and then for which rocket flew the furthest. Additional points were given for any unique design features.

I was paired with the two chopper techs, Kevin Nelson and another man whose name I can't remember. The pilots, François du Toit and his compatriot, were in another team. Major Kriel, Dave Scales and another operator and close friend by the name of Butch Atkins, were in the last. We all set to building our rockets in the greatest of secrecy, comparable to the planning of a cross-border operation.

At 15:00 the next day we gathered on the airstrip. I was surprised to see the lengths that the other teams had gone to in building their rockets. Ours was a simple affair constructed from the inner tubes of toilet rolls taped together to form a body, with a cardboard cone taped to the nose. At its tail were affixed flights, not dissimilar to those of an arrow and it was painted blue and adorned with US Air Force markings. The entire thing was just over half a metre long, taped to a stick and its boost came from a nozzled, reinforced fuel bay containing cordite, which we had removed from .303 machine-gun rounds. Ignition was simple and by means of a fuse entering one of the bottom nozzles. We were quite proud of our design, but it was nothing compared to the other two.

Major Kriel's team had built a three-stage ignition rocket utilising Icarus flares taped together. It was an impressive sight, only a little unwieldy if anything.

The 'blues' design took the cake, however. When they revealed their monster it was not hard to see from where they had cribbed the design. Wheeling out a 37mm SNEB rocket – taken from one of the pods on the Lynx – with small design changes and mounted on a purpose-built launcher, we all took a step back and began to wonder about their sanity. We were assured that the high-explosive warhead had been removed and replaced with a homemade nose cone. Other than that, there were few changes to the rocket at all.

My team drew the short straw and we launched first. The launch pad was a dustbin in which we inserted the contraption which pointed menacingly skywards. One of the techs stepped forward and lit the fuse, hurrying away in case the thing went bang before it took off. The nozzles emitted an enormous whooshing sound and the rocket shot straight into the sky before burning out at about 200 hundred feet. We didn't do too badly, considering our rocket was tiny compared with the opposing teams' monstrosities.

Major Kriel's Icarus adaptation was next and we looked on expectantly as they provided ignition. With the major holding the rocket aloft, his head cowering in anticipation of launch, Dave Scales snuck up behind him and pushed the firing device. Instantly both men were hidden in a huge cloud of white smoke as the ungainly device lifted off. Struggling into the air, it wobbled on its axis as stage one found thrust.

At about 60 feet, when the fuel from the first compartment was spent, it had been intended that stage two would ignite, carrying the rocket to a higher altitude, where the ignition of stage three would kick in and carry it higher. Instead, like the Apollo disaster, it snaked left and right and then exploded in mid-air with a deafening crump. Fortunately, the designers had taken all the magnesium out of the flares or otherwise we might have been showered by its burning-hot contents.

Unfortunately, as planned, the other two stages did ignite; the tape that harnessed them together not having the integrity to hold true and they shot off horizontally all over the place. Stage two was a real peach and rocketed in the direction of the two Alouettes parked on the apron. As it raced toward them, trailing white smoke, we cringed at the thought of a direct hit and the resultant damage. The 'blues' were screaming their lungs out although I don't know what good it might have done. Luckily it passed over the nearest chopper and burnt out in the long grass beyond. When we turned around we saw stage three rounding a nearby hangar and heading straight for us. We all dived for cover and it passed over us with feet to spare until it skidded harmlessly to a halt in the dirt. Meanwhile, the body of stage one had spun into the bush on the side of the apron which erupted into a raging bush fire. With the tenacity of bulldogs on a bone we set to beating the flames into submission with branches and whatever else we could find.

I couldn't help thinking, while he was at the forefront of the battle against the flames, that Major Kriel would have had a hard time explaining the loss of two valuable helicopters. We eventually controlled the inferno after 15 minutes of madness, but with only metres of open ground to spare before it did any real damage.

Obviously shaken, we were a little hesitant when the 'blues' wanted to fire up their 37mm. We stood back, as they erected the monster on its beer-crate launcher and prepared a car battery to provide ignition. They attached the rocket's wiring to the battery, the electronic ignition fired and the projectile soared heavenwards. The last we saw of it was its vapour trail disappearing into the clouds as it raced toward outer space. It was a sobering ending to an unnerving experience.

Needless to say, the 'blues' won. They drank well in the canteen that night, but I still think they cheated by using the SNEB in the first place.

The day after the Mount Darwin rocket competition, the Alouettes that were based there were commandeered for an RLI operation into Mozambique. Sadly, on the return journey, after dropping off troops, one of them was shot down as it flew over an enemy-occupied village. The pilot, Francois du Toit, having recently beaten us to the crate of beer and his technician, Kevin Nelson – my compatriot and team mate – were killed when it crash-landed. As it was nightfall, the remaining chopper returned to Mount Darwin and a team was sent in the next day to recover their bodies. It was a sad conclusion to an otherwise jovial time and we celebrated the lives of the two lost men over a few drinks.

Not far from Tembue, Tim Callow and Aaron Mlambo were also running out of luck. They had managed to establish an OP on a hill feature to the west of the camp, while Chris Schulenburg and Martin Chikondo set up a position somewhere to the north-east. A few kilometres away, the water provisions had been stacked in the jerry cans I had fetched and camouflaged for later use.

For the duration of the reconnaissance, both teams sent back detailed reports of enemy activity in the area. So far, the numbers of terrorists that intelligence reports had said were in the camp, had not been assessed and there were fewer than originally thought. After being established in their hides for over a week, the command elements decided to attack the camp anyway and began preparations for the assault.

A week before the attack was to go in, an emergency request for hot extraction was received from Tim Callow. His position had been compromised and he was on the run. To worsen matters, given the amount of time and money invested in the operation, he had left behind his Bergen containing crucial information and maps which could fall into enemy hands. Quite inexplicably, he had also left his radio and personal weapon. It was assumed that the enemy might have heard the helicopter when it brought in the water supply and they were patrolling the general area.

I assembled a Quick Reaction Force for their first operation since I had been in the Selous Scouts. From Mount Darwin, we were moved by helicopter to a feature in Mozambique called the 'Train' where the Rhodesians had set up a forward fuel collection point. Flying towards it, it was not hard to see why the hill had been dubbed that – it loomed on the horizon looking much like a train engine with stacks and carriages. It was a long hill feature with steep sides and a flat top, which was considered a relatively secure place to situate the fuel dump.

When we landed, my team leapt out and went into all-round defence. The pilot called me over and told me that there was a change of plan. As the two operators on the run were in light order, they were to be hard extracted. This meant they would be plucked to safety using the harnesses they wore. We were to remain at the dump and prepare fuel for the return journey. In addition, while we waited, I was requested to do an audit of the fuel left there, so that it could be re-supplied if short.

The choppers lifted off and left us on standby while they extracted the two fleeing men. I deployed piquets and sent the MAG gunner to watch the most obvious approach. I was just settling in to count the drums of fuel when a long burst of fire sent me diving to the ground. I looked around to see where the commotion had come from and noticed the machine gunner bowing quite sheepishly.

'Sorry *Ishe*!' he said, jumping to his defence. 'I just put the gun down on its bipod and it went off!'

I was enraged from the shock of sudden panic. I bellowed at him and demanded to know what the fuck he was doing. But then I saw where he had twisted the ammunition belt to diffuse the accidental discharge (AD). The gunner showed me what had happened and it became clear that it was not entirely his fault. I had seen a similar instance while I was in the Paras, when one soldier was killed and another injured from an AD. In the British military, all the MAGs are marked with a small white line behind the cocking handle. When you pull the working parts to the rear, the handle has to pass the white line or they'll spring forward, picking up and firing a round. This is why we were taught always to cock the MAG while the butt was into the shoulder: you can exert more control on the cocking handle that way.

In Rhodesia all the MAGs were daubed in camouflage paint, hiding any obvious mark, so it was possible to make an error. The gunner had simply not pulled the cocking handle far enough to the rear. I resolved not to report the incident, but gave him a stern lecture. He was a good operator otherwise and I didn't see a need for him to be charged.

As it turned out, we were not needed and the extraction was a success. The chopper flew in carrying the escapees, haggard, but with huge grins on their faces. The relief of being safe was obvious from the way they beamed smiles down at us as we cowered under the wash of the rotors. Tim Callow unfortunately sprained his ankle while departing the area, but other than that they were okay. We flew back to Mount Darwin so they could recuperate and be debriefed. During the debrief the full facts of the compromise became clear.

While looking through his telescope, which was mounted at their position, Callow noticed a ZANLA clearance patrol searching for them. He warned Mlambo and they both ducked low, hoping they wouldn't be seen. The next time Callow peeped over the lip of the crest a fusillade of rounds came whining into the dirt around them. Both operators, under Callow's orders, legged it down the opposite side of the hill, grabbing the telescope as they fled. Halfway down the hill Tim fell and sprained his ankle. Not able to carry their Bergens, on which were left the inflatable water bladders they'd filled from the cache, they hid them among some rocks where they hoped they wouldn't be noticed. Callow leaned the Austrian sniper rifle he carried against his pack and departed, limping along behind his partner.

The terrorists followed them but exercised a lot of caution. The rest was history, although it was feared that the incident could compromise the entire operation, particularly if the Bergens and the radio had been found.

Despite the predicament, the powers-that-be decided to go ahead with the assault anyway, acting on information from Schulenburg's position which was still in place. On the day of the attack, 30 July 1978, I was ferried back to the hill feature to try and recover the lost equipment with Mlambo. Callow stayed behind because of his sprained ankle.

For the operation I was told to prepare for a four-day patrol, so we took along rations and ammunition for the duration. As we were a sub-section, with only two men, I opted for superior firepower and drew a cut-down RPD machine gun from the armoury. To quench its thirst, should we run into trouble, I carried two 200-round belts of ammo and a 100-round belt, already in the gun, slung in a bag beneath its receiver. If we could find the Bergens it would obviously mean that the compromise was a false alarm and we had nothing to worry about.

The attack commenced at 08:00 and a short while later, Mlambo and I caught a lift in to Tembue on a re-supply chopper. As Mlambo had recently been there, it was not hard to find the feature and the pilot dropped us in a clearing about 20 metres from the OP. In the distance, the attack was in full swing and as we climbed, we gained a clear view of the circling helicopters as they engaged the enemy, or directed troops onto stubborn pockets of resistance. It was grandstand view indeed, but it was not the first time I had witnessed a battle raging from afar.

The slope of the hill feature was quite steep, as we tactically moved to its peak. On reaching the crest I could see where the OP had been sited and it looked untouched. ZANLA, who had been in the area, as I could tell from the tracks which I saw lower down the hill, hadn't even found the OP and had seemingly been on a routine patrol.

Leaving the vantage point behind us we went in search of the deserted equipment. Half way down the hill we came across the Bergens which, not surprisingly, lay exactly where they had been left. However, one could never be too careful and I checked them out thoroughly before moving them. I was worried that anti-personnel mines may have been hidden around them, or worse, the whole thing was a set-up and the enemy were lying in ambush. After observing the area for a short while we moved in. The immediate vicinity seemed clear, but nevertheless I attached a length of para cord to each of the packs and crouching at a distance, pulled them over. Callow's rifle clattered to the ground and came to rest on one of the water bladders.

We recovered the radio, still set on its frequency although the battery had died, and continued back up to the OP. I had never been more knackered in my life as I carried Callow's Bergen, rifle, my own Bergen and the RPD. It was a steep climb up rocky ground and I lapsed into a lung-burning amble way behind Mlambo.

Back at the top, when I looked through my optics, I couldn't tell what the observation team had been looking at. The camp was hidden from view about five kilometres distant – and spread over a large area. All I could see were the helicopters above tree level as they went about their business. With the heat of summer, the haze alone negated any advantage the OP would have. Perhaps a week before the haze was less evident and the view unrestricted.

The helicopter arrived to ferry us back into Tembue, where we would wait until the mopping-up was over. The choppers were still busy ferrying callsigns all over the show, in pursuit of fleeing guerrillas. With the amount of equipment we carried, there was no seating room inside the chopper's cabin, so I stood on a strut outside the door. It was a hair-raising, but exhilarating flight, as we left the edge of the hill and the ground fell away beneath us. My legs were shaking after the scramble to the top of the hill and for a moment I worried that I would fall off.

Overall, the attack on Tembue 2 was a disaster. Much inter-unit bickering resulted and certain officers even questioned whether the camp contained terrorists in the first place. Many excuses were made from other arms of the military, about communication problems and wrong frequencies used, which resulted in a miss drop of paratroopers. Regardless of the excuses, the terrorists had flown the coop. Chris Schulenburg later said that he had seen the enemy running past his OP like ants when the attack first went in.

When Special Branch flew into the camp to gather intelligence, they were appalled by what they found. Some of the foreign soldiers in the RLI had tied a terrorist's body to a tree, cut off his genitals and shoved them into his mouth. SB fumed and called an emergency meeting with the Fire Force commanders, warning them that they would come down hard on anyone caught conducting that sort of practice. It gave us a bad name in some circles, as it should have done and I dread to think what the terrorists would do, having witnessed an atrocity like that, if they ever captured Rhodesian soldiers. On the other hand, I felt the SB were a little hypocritical, considering the tactics they themselves used in their war against terror.

While at Tembue, one of the Alouettes flew over another one on the ground while its rotors were winding down. The down draft forced the grounded helicopter's rotor to cut itself in half, neatly severing the tail boom from the front section. It was an interesting spectacle and fortunately no-one was injured. For the Rhodesians it was a very expensive accident as the South Africans had withdrawn many of their Alouettes which had been on loan to the country. We could not afford the loss of a single helicopter as they were irreplaceable.

Later in the afternoon, we were flown back to the base at Mount Darwin. At the camp I ran into Sergeant John Gartner, a good friend of mine in Recce Troop. John was a brilliant operator and had once served with the Australian SAS.

I always felt that there were operators like John Gartner, who never received the credit that was due to them. As often as Tim Callow and Chris Schulenburg were manning OPs in the heart of enemy territory, John Gartner was out there doing the same thing. And what of the black operators who hardly got a mention? Among them were fine soldiers who displayed the highest degree of professionalism. Some were decorated, but in the case of others, their stories will never be told for fear of reprisals, as they still live in the country. Some gave their lives for a unit and a cause they really believed in.

All I'm really saying is that when a try is scored on the rugby field, there are 14 other guys who also made it happen. War is a team sport. I feel it's important to give some credit to other men who gave the best of themselves.

I really began to question my reasons for leaving the SAS after Tembue 2. I was not content with the way things had turned out and I was anxious to get back to Salisbury to sort out issues with my wife. It does a man little good when he's constantly thinking about the skulduggery that might be going on while he's away. In the last few days at Mount Darwin, aside from my duties, I caused an upset that was to buy me a short reprieve.

A bit of a cartoonist, I've always doodled away my free time, coming up with caricatures of people I know. Apart from doing my illustrations, I did little else but run errands for Major Kriel all the time. One day, to vent my frustration, I did a cartoon depicting a temporary ops room, with speech bubbles coming out of the doors and all the windows. Each bubble contained the words 'Jake do this … Jake do that' and it was obvious that they belonged to the major. He was not too amused after he saw it, but I think he got the picture that I was disgruntled and he gave me a small break by softening up on his demands over the next weeks.

It was a short-lived reprieve and in retrospect, I think I should have drawn more cartoons!

Major Kriel had an inventive imagination and would have been well suited to the design department of an armaments manufacturing company. On a brief deployment to Grand Reef, he came up with an ingenious plan for a six-barrelled 60 mm mortar which could be buried in the earth after attacking a terrorist camp and then detonated remotely, or even by a delayed fuse, some time after the raiders had left. The idea was to cause alarm and mayhem when those terrorists who had escaped unharmed, came out from hiding to assess the damage of a raid.

The contraption he designed had six mortar tubes facing in slightly different directions, much like the smoke grenade dispensers on a tank. On initiation, the bombs would fire from detonators at the base of each tube, landing all over the terrorist camp. On test day, the major and I went around the base and told everyone that we were trying out a new weapon, so they wouldn't be alarmed when they heard the bangs. The Fire Force troops were warned to remain near the billet side of the airstrip and not to venture onto the runway.

After walking to the end of the airstrip we dug a small hole and buried the tubes with earth, covering them until only the tops of the barrels were sticking out. The major then boosted each one with additional gunpowder from ammunition and secondaries from 60mm bombs, before putting in the bombs. We attached an electrical wire to the cluster of individual detonator wires and then moved off a safe distance so testing could commence. Some 50 metres off Major Kriel turned, quite satisfied with the distance between us and the mortar. I had my doubts and suggested we move a bit further and possibly take shelter in one of the bunkers on the edge of the strip. He heeded my reservation reluctantly and moved away until we settled into a bunker and peered out of a large aperture. To add ceremony to the occasion, the major initiated a small countdown before attaching the wires to a car battery we had with us. The ruckus that followed was not the recognisable sound of simultaneous mortar fire, but an enormous explosion that sent dirt and debris flying for hundreds of metres. Even within the safe environs of the bunker I was suddenly stung by flying shrapnel, which zinged through the aperture and buried itself in my upper body. The wounds were superficial, but they were enough to remind me of how lucky we were to have retreated this far. Had the major fired the device from where he originally intended, I have no doubt we would have been mincemeat.

It took a few seconds for both of us to recover from the shock of the explosion. Staring out of the bunker I watched the dust settle and shook my head. A long whistle sounded from the major's lips as he too just stared out vacantly. More seconds passed before we ventured toward the remnants of the multi-barrelled mortar where we found a crater in which you could have hidden a donkey. In the distance, clods of earth could be heard raining down on the corrugated iron roofs of the billets. Glancing in that direction we could see the air force personnel with their hands on their heads, panic-stricken. Before long they were running to their aircraft to inspect what damage had been caused.

Needless to say, Major Kriel was not popular for some time afterwards. The experiment had been a flop and any intimations of further attempts were shot down in flames.

On another small operation in Kariba, Major Kriel was in his element showing off to a few 'blues' the customised weapons we used in the Selous Scouts. One of his favourites was the cut-down RPD machine gun. The modifications made to this weapon made it easier to carry and wield in a contact and also gave it a slightly higher rate of fire. Ostensibly the barrel was shortened to just above the gas piston housing and the return spring was lengthened and hardened to increase the rounds per minute.

Butch Atkins was sitting in a Land-Rover outside the Recce Troop ops tent, when all of a sudden a burst of fire sent him sprawling for cover. Bullets punched into the soft-skinned vehicle and a huge commotion was heard from inside. When I heard the firing I ran in the direction of the ops tent to see three air force men appear, visibly shaken at the tent's opening. I then learnt what had happened. While the major was toying with the weapon, he fed in an ammunition belt to demonstrate how it functioned. How the negligent discharge came about I don't really know, but the next thing, bullets were whizzing between the 'blues' and punching through the soft canvas into the vehicle in which Butch was sitting. Fortunately, no-one was hit, but Major Kriel felt like a real wet biscuit. His embarrassment was evident by the different shades of red he turned as he profusely apologised to his 'students'.

I suppose a major is a major, so nothing ever came of the incident. I did do a cartoon of it, which Butch has to this day. Major Kriel saw it sometime later and once again he was not too impressed with my artistic expression. I think I may have received top marks if my cartoons had been judged elsewhere.

CHAPTER 26:
INFIDELITY

I had been a member of the Selous Scouts for almost a year when I found out about Sheila's affair. Returning from Mount Darwin, I was surprised to find her bags packed on the front porch, along with suitcases with the boys' clothing and boxes containing their toys and other belongings. My suspicions had nagged at me since the incident with RT some time before and my male intuition, which I've always believed was as good as or better than the female variety, told me that something was going on. I couldn't put my finger on it but I suspected an affair between my wife and the senior officer. With his position in the Selous Scouts, he was a man I saw quite regularly and it incensed me that he could possibly be shagging my wife and have the balls to carry on with me as if nothing was happening.

Sheila had obviously given the matter some thought while I was away and immediately confronted me, informing me of the affair and telling me that she was leaving. My suspicions were confirmed and I bit down hard on my lower lip, as I fought a battle to control my rage. RT, I was told, was to collect her the next day and take her and the boys to his farm just outside Salisbury where they would live together. I wasn't too enamoured with the prospect and an argument developed. Sheila stood her ground and the rest of the night was spent in a gloomy atmosphere with me taking the couch for a bed.

The following morning, at sparrow's fart, RT arrived to steal my wife from me. I knew that since he had driven in from the farm he would be carrying his FN rifle and for the second time in that driveway (the first being with Bob Pyke), a standoff developed between two armed men. Walking towards the gate, my own FN cradled in my arms, I approached RT for a confrontation. I was aghast when he shoved out his paw and tried to shake my hand. Brushing his genial attempt at truce aside, I told him to get the fuck out of my driveway before I shot him. I was well aware that I was addressing a senior officer, but the facts negated his position of seniority. Within the code of military conduct it is a serious offence to fraternise with the wife of another rank.

I think RT knew I held the ace card because he heeded my warning, spinning on his heel and driving off in a flash. Sheila, inside the house, knew I was well capable of losing my temper and she watched passively from the bedroom window.

If ever our marriage was on the rocks it was now. The breakdown had been both our fault, partly as a result of the incredible strain on the country, but it had much to do with our own actions.

RT and Sheila continued to see each other while I was away fighting the war. It became common knowledge that he was shagging my wife behind my back and I often drew comments, or just stares from the men I operated with. I finally came to the end of my tether and resolved to settle the matter once and for all. I went to the director of legal services in Milton Buildings to air my grievance. An affable and understanding lady, she wrote a letter to RT stating that he had contravened military law and if his actions did not stop immediately, he would be court-martialled.

A few weeks later word got to me that RT thought my gesture was a joke. He bragged that they could court-martial him, but it wouldn't make a difference to his secret liaisons with Sheila. I was infuriated and a part of me wanted to rip his throat out, but I was determined to keep the situation within the bounds of civil or military law. I knew he was goading me toward a confrontation so that he could charge me with assault and thus have me incarcerated out of the way, or possibly kicked out of the army altogether.

One morning, while I sat deep in thought, having tea in the sergeant's mess, I was snapped back to reality by the scraping of chairs. The Selous Scout RSM and CSM sat down in front of me with contemplative frowns on their brows.

'Jake.' the RSM said. 'Is it true what we hear about RT and your wife?'

I nodded, but cast aside their concern with my own remembered aggravation.

The two of them just sat there contemplating matters for a while, reclining and taking in my anger. The next thing the CSM swore out loud, revealing his true feelings about the ops room officer.

'Fucking idiot! That arsehole is responsible for the deaths of four of our top operators. He shouldn't even be in the unit in the first place!' he said, stating what we had all been thinking. The RSM shuffled in his chair, leaning towards me. His right index finger came to rest on his upper lip and the creases between his eyes deepened.

'Jake' he whispered. The tone in his voice was serious. 'Here are my keys on which is the key for the armoury. Could you bring them to me in the officers' mess in about an hour? Just say you found them.' He paused, letting his words sink in, then continued: 'What I want you to do is take a landmine from the armoury and go and put it on the road outside RT's farm. It's about time we did something about that fucker!'

It was the closest reference to fragging that I ever came across in the Rhodesian Army. Here were two senior NCOs advocating my illegal killing of another Selous Scout officer and they were quite prepared to help. I loved the fact that they cared, but it was a bit too excessive – even for me.

Almost begrudgingly I turned down the offer for assistance. The RSM was adamant that I do something about it, even after I had said that the landmine may be too indirect a method. It might take out a civilian, or some innocent person travelling down the road.

'Ah, come on Jake. There are plenty of terrs out where he lives. Just borrow an RPD and machine-gun the fucker. You can't be more direct than that!'

I was almost taken in, particularly when I realised how serious he was. The little evil streak that resides in all of us tugged at my conscience, daring me to snatch the keys. I thought about it long and hard.

Fortunately for me sanity prevailed and Sheila's best friend came to the rescue. She had witnessed events from the sidelines and approached me a few days later with startling news. I think she felt a bit sorry for me and although she wasn't entirely on my side, she sympathised with my predicament. Unbeknown to me, or Sheila for that matter, RT had been a naughty boy and was dipping his wick on the side. Not only was he cheating on Sheila, but the recipient of his wick happened to be her best friend. She agreed to approach Sheila and come out with the truth. While RT was saying he loved my wife, there was at least one other woman that we knew of whom he was promising the world.

When Sheila found out the truth she was horrified. I think she genuinely thought that things might pan out between herself and RT. She stayed on with me, but only because I was the lesser of two evils. It would take a long time to resolve our differences, but I don't believe we ever did put them behind us.

Major Kriel was lost without me but he had problems of his own. At the end of the day I felt I had been conned and I wasn't content. Around Inkomo, I was a glorified taxi driver, ferrying base personnel between forts and to army headquarters. On one occasion I was ordered to drive Chris Schulenburg to Bindura and made myself ready for the journey. When I arrived outside his billet, he stepped out attired in a full-body armour suit looking much like a Samurai warrior. The bulky trauma packs of the time, cubed on his chest and dangling from his waist, gave him the air of that historical figure. When I asked him where *my* body armour was, he retorted that I was expendable and therefore didn't need any. I never did work out whether he was joking or not.

The Selous Scouts were going through a rough time and many officers were leaving. Major Kriel left, after a row developed at army HQ when Lieutenant Colonel Reid Daly found his phones were bugged. He was understandably infuriated and the incident was a major breach of operational security. Some time before Major Kriel left, he asked me if I could assist him with a problem. The Selous Scouts were planning to attack Chimoio again after the SAS's previous success and the major thought the top-secret files the SAS possessed would be a great help in planning the operation. The files were a full account of the reconnaissance operations conducted by Rich Stannard when he was in the SAS, as well as the debriefs after the attack on the camp and other intelligence information.

I left for the SAS barracks and drew the necessary files, returning them to Chris Schulenburg and Tim Callow, who were to be responsible for the latest reconnaissance. Leaving it at that I didn't hear much about it until sometime later, when the operation commenced.

Back at Inkomo, Major Kriel again asked for my assistance. He had tendered his resignation and was about to leave the unit to take up a post with the South African arms manufacturer Armscor. In reality his post was a cover for work he would undertake with the South African Special Forces, but that we would only find out later.

Tossing a few boxes my way he ordered me to take them out the back of the camp and burn them. They were files, he said, that were no longer needed and contained highly classified information pertaining to Recce Troop. In view of the inter-unit row that was developing they should not get into anyone else's hands.

I did as I was ordered, but not before approaching John Gartner whom I wanted as a witness to my actions. It seemed odd to me that I was burning top-secret files when there was no immediate threat to them being breached. John stood by me as I loaded the files into a 44-gallon drum and incinerated them with the aid of some petrol. By the time the flames died there was nothing at all left of them.

A few months later, after Major Kriel had left the country, SAS HQ contacted me to retrieve their Chimoio files. I told them that they were no longer in my hands but I would investigate the matter. After conversing with Chris Schulenburg and Tim Callow, all fingers pointed back to Major Kriel. I left for SAS HQ where I informed them that he had the files, or at least would know their whereabouts. SAS headquarters made a call to South Africa and traced Major Kriel to Armscor. He said that he wasn't sure of the whereabouts of the files, but he thought that they may have been burnt. He told them that he had given them to me and that I had burnt them.

Once again I was contacted and in light of the recent information, I was asked about the files. I insisted they were not among those I had destroyed as they had had black lever-arch covers and were designated top secret, unlike anything I had thrown into the fire.

No-one could understand why Major Kriel had ordered any files to be burnt to start with, but I had to make out an affidavit with the assistance of Rich Passaportis, a captain who served in the Selous Scouts, to verify my claim. And so begun a long-winded investigation which indicated that Major Kriel had 'borrowed' many files and documents and passed them on to the South Africans.

Later we discovered the truth behind Major Kriel's rapid departure from Rhodesia. Maybe he had an inkling of what lay in store for the country, given his own experience of internal strife within the Selous Scouts and so expedited his own safe passage in advance.

The South Africans were setting up their own covert organisation to deal with 'super sensitive' operations as early as 1978, a date which coincided with the major's departure. To this end they were recruiting experienced personnel from Rhodesia, to run a 'deep penetration reconnaissance' capability. Called D40 originally and then Project Barnacle – Neil Kriel was the obvious choice as founding commander.

After a brief spell at the Bluff with 1 Reconnaissance Commando, he was called in by Major General Fritz Loots, the general commanding South African Special Forces and briefed on the top-secret mission of the unit. The rest is history. On subsequent visits to Rhodesia, he and other operatives recruited serving members of the police, the army and Special Branch into their ranks. If and when independence came, they would be well placed to serve the South Africans.

It is probable that Neil Kriel was recruited while he was still serving in Rhodesia. Intelligence revealed later that Armscor was often used as a cover for such recruiting. Paid out of government slush funds, the foreign operatives of Project Barnacle were listed as 'procurement officers' and paid from their books. It was only later that Armscor got cold feet, after thinking about the implications if an operative was caught by one of the Frontline states and labelled a spy. Thereafter, all Project Barnacle operatives were inaugurated into the South African Permanent Force.

While Neil Kriel ran Project Barnacle, the organisation's duties were expanded to include the neutralisation of enemy and own-side liability assets. If and when a member became a liability and posed a threat to operational security, then he/she was rapidly disposed of. The most common method was poisoning and the bodies were thrown out to sea. Our Major Kriel, who possessed a private pilot's licence, was known to have dropped many 'liability assets' off the coast of South West Africa (Namibia) flying a light aircraft.

It may have been his way of securing his position in Armscor when things fell apart, but we will never know. Major Kriel's way out of it, I feel, was to draw me in as a plausible excuse if his actions were ever uncovered.

The government initiated proceedings to have Neil Kriel returned from South Africa to answer these allegations. His new country, however, looked after him and ducked and weaved around every effort that was made to bring accountability to his shoulders.

A short while later a friend, who operated from South Africa, having recently spoken to Neil Kriel, passed on a warning: 'Watch your back, Jake' he said. 'Kriel's got it in for you.'

After more than a year in the regiment, I went back to visit my SAS mates at Kabrit Barracks, which the Squadron had moved into during my absence. I wanted to see if the grass had turned greener on the other side since my departure. On 5 January 1979, a special open day ceremony was held to award 55 operators the honour of wearing their wings on chest rather than on their right shoulder. It was an award that signified the wearer as a distinguished operator and had its origins in the Western Desert during World War II with David Stirling, the founder of the SAS.

It was a disappointing visit after it became apparent that the SAS had turned into a glorified parachute regiment, bolstered as it was with an abundance of recently selected school-leavers. It was still professional to the core and there were few other choices when it came to recruiting manpower into its ranks, but overall it had changed from the SAS I once knew, when its ranks were swelled with hard, older men with a wealth of experience under their belts.

As an ex-member I was invited to the open day and I attended in my Selous Scout colours. Some freefallers were doing an exhibition of HAHO (High Altitude High Opening) jumping and all of them landed in a small area in front of the spectators. There were stands showing all the various goodies that the Squadron used on operations and one displaying captured terrorist weaponry, which drew a large crowd.

Billy Grant, a mate of mine, was there, dressed up in his diving gear, looking a bit like a fish out of water. Some of the kids who attended were enthralled by the frogman because, in Rhodesia, a landlocked country, they would not have seen anything like it. There were slide shows of operational deployments, desensitised obviously for the faint of heart. Many of the pictures shown were ones I had snapped on operations while still a member of the SAS. Overall it was a grand affair, at the end of which there was a braai with huge steaks, chops and boerewors sizzling away over the flames.

I had just made the rank of sergeant after a year had passed since my reprimand and I wore my rank for the first time in public. After watching the parade, quite a long and emotional affair, I mingled with my mates from B Troop in the sergeants' mess and caught up on the latest news. It became very evident that the ceremony actually caused a great deal of despondency among them once everyone got talking. Many believed that it was the worst thing that had happened to the Rhodesian SAS, as in the run-up to identify recipients for the award there was a sudden rush of backstabbing and favouritism towards different individuals. Looking at the big picture from outside the Squadron, the allegations appeared to hold some truth.

In a few instances there were guys who received the award who, in the opinion of others, should never have got it. Then again there were others who didn't get it who truly deserved it. It may sound like a case of sour grapes on my part, but honestly, the sour grapes were rife among everyone that day, especially among the Rotvangers. As I said before, you can't score a try in rugby without 14 other players helping.

Another gripe that someone pointed out to me was the severe lack of foreigners who qualified for 'wings on chest'. Most recipients were Rhodesians who, as I mentioned before, had the chance to prove themselves on the best pick of operations. The Club Tomorrow boys were in the majority when the men marched smartly forward to receive the honour from the CO and from Rhodesian President John Wrathal.

I was making plans to return to the Squadron but the wings-on-chest ceremony changed my mind. Being at Kabrit Barracks reminded me too much of Depot Para in Aldershot. The unit had become too big and ungainly and there was too much bullshit going on. I resolved to just carry on in the Selous Scouts. My job description hadn't turned out as I thought it would, but I had little other choice.

Six months before the parade, C Squadron SAS had become 1 Rhodesian SAS Regiment, expanding the unit from squadron to regimental status. Then and now I believe that instead of incorporating national servicemen into the SAS, a new parachute battalion should have been formed for use on camp assaults and the like, allowing the SAS to focus on their reconnaissance missions, intelligence-gathering, specialist raiding and ambushing skills, while the RLI and RAR focused on internal fireforce operations.

The new battalion could have been called 1 Rhodesia Parachute Battalion, with its members wearing the famed maroon beret. To me it would have made more sense to maintain a small hard-core unit of professionals who were a cut above the rest. Firstly, because operational security could be maintained a lot easier and secondly, more time and expense could be devoted to individuals in the unit to turn them into better operators.

I am not saying that standards were dropped in the Rhodesian SAS selection procedure. However, I do think that something was lost when young, inexperienced operators were bought into the ranks of the Squadron. An integral part of choosing the right individuals lies in scrutinising their maturity levels, which, in my opinion, almost guarantees a more calm and collected operator. I know that many others shared my views.

Sometime after the parade I ran an errand, to collect a Selous Scout operator from the airport who had just returned from South Africa. While I was waiting for him to collect his baggage, I bumped into a few SAS lads who were standing around in a group waiting to depart the country. They were all trained divers and I assumed they were going on an operation in Mozambique – which meant they had to fly to South Africa first and deploy from there, courtesy of the South African Navy. It wasn't difficult to figure that one out.

Weeks later news broke about the fuel-depot attack in Beira on the Mozambique coast. Saboteurs had raided the depot, firing RPG7 rockets and saturating it with machine-gun fire. The resultant inferno caused a major set back to the country.

A month afterwards I ran into Billy Grant, one of the SAS divers I had seen at the airport and happened to mention the incident to him. 'Well done.' I said. 'You guys did a terrific job in Beira!'

Billy was flabbergasted and insisted I tell him where the security leak had originated. He was certain there had been a major breach, as only a handful of people were supposed to know about the operation.

I told him the truth, namely, that I had seen them all leaving Salisbury airport. On hearing the news of the raid I had put two and two together and had come up with the obvious answer. He was a bit stumped, but eventually admitted that I was right. It just goes to show, it's so easy to breach national security even when you're not thinking about it.

CHAPTER 27:
LEGENDS

There were many men in the regiment who preferred to operate alone. Chris Schulenburg was one of them and he would often detach himself from his sub-section and set up his own OP away from his team-mate. He preferred it that way as then he had only himself to rely on and be accountable for. I have only the greatest respect for such men, who on operations, not only had the threat of the enemy to deal with, but who also had to face the hardships of the African bush as well – often a very real danger. Despite that, there were only a few instances of trouble when Rhodesian soldiers crossed paths with dangerous game.

Another incredible man, Martin Chikondo, Schulenburg's second, was a marvel of an operator who gained my utmost respect. Adept in Nature's surrounds, he too would live for weeks on end in enemy territory conducting military operations on his own.

Think about it. Most men are a little uncomfortable sleeping outside alone, even in a peace-time environment. Take away the tent and the modern conveniences of camping and then throw in the necessary disciplines that are crucial to survival in a hazardous operational environment: no fires, absolute silence and no immediate support. Add a few hundred enemy personnel to the equation, possibly searching for you and for good measure throw in a herd or two of buffalo, a few elephant and a lion. To deal with that takes a thorough knowledge of the environment one is operating in – and a fair share of balls!

The first time I worked closely with Chikondo was some time after Major Kriel had left the Selous Scouts. Recce Troop was in a bit of a quandary, as no-one had been directly appointed to command it and Schulenburg, the obvious replacement, was unwilling to take up the reins as he had more important war-waging matters at hand. The troop was deployed to Wafa Wafa, the Selous Scout training camp on the shores of Lake Kariba, under the temporary command of Tim Callow. Once we had settled in we undertook retraining exercises which included diving and the use of Zodiac inflatable boats. It was a casual time and I thoroughly enjoyed it. We even managed to get in a little Tiger fishing, all the while drinking ice-cold beers under the hot African sun. This was the lighter side to soldiering and part of the reason I had returned to Rhodesia in the first place.

It was all becoming a bit of a swan, when Lieutenant Callow volunteered the Troop to take part in a selection course which was being run at the time. I had a feeling that some of the operators resented the fact that most of Recce Troop had not done Selous Scout selection, as they had transferred from the SAS.

Not one among us were too enthused with the prospect of sweating our arses off all over again, but we agreed that if ordered to do the selection course, we would do so willingly, just to prove a point. I for one felt the fittest I had ever been and believed that the course, although difficult, was well within my capabilities.

Collectively we managed to talk some sense into Tim Callow. As confident as we were, the process was an embuggerance and it would have been disastrous, not to mention embarrassing, if one of us had actually failed. I have often wondered if any of the DS on the course would have failed us on purpose, just to rub things in. It could have made for good conversation spreading rumours of the tough SAS men failing Selous Scout selection. Fortunately, the idea was dropped.

My relief, however, was short-lived when Lieutenant Callow called me in for a briefing. An operation had come up and he craftily used that as an excuse to pull us out of the selection course.

Chikondo and Mlambo were to be deployed to an area on the shores of Lake Kariba, where it was thought the local population were aiding and abetting ZIPRA terrorists. Dressed in pseudo-terrorist garb, they would approach a particular village west of Bumi Hills and while masquerading as the enemy, would try and make contact with the genuine guerrillas. Failing that, they would say that their party had been ambushed and they were the only survivors. Could they find out when the next ZIPRA deployment to the area would occur, to enable them to get back to Zambia?

I was to command the operation and deploy them by Zodiac to the area they were to infiltrate. We were to leave that afternoon but we were not to pass Bumi Hills before 16:30, after which the area of operation would be 'frozen'. At that time an OP overlooking the lake, set up in Binga, would be watching us to make sure that all was as it should be. If there were any hitches we would be contacted by radio and the operation would be called off.

That afternoon we kitted up the Zodiac with provisions and ammunition for a couple of days and headed west. It was a windy day but the breeze brought relief from the sweltering heat. We were dressed in regular Rhodesian camouflage, looking typically like Special Forces operators with our communist AKs, but we all carried terrorist clothing to change into on the move after crossing the designated mark.

A few hours later, at about 16:40, we passed Bumi West. Something niggled me and I was keen to make sure the area was safe before continuing. I called the OP on the radio and given the all clear, I set the boat on course toward our rendezvous. As far as I could see across the vast expanse of water, we appeared to be the only boat on the lake. No other craft were allowed west of Bumi due to the troubled times.

About fifteen minutes later, I gave the order to change and we fumbled into our terrorist kit. Chikondo and Mlambo shifted around the boat as they stripped off their camouflage denims and put on the dirty rags more common to the enemy. I was having a little difficulty controlling the tiller arm of the outboard but still managed my transition into terrorist apparel, when I glanced behind and noticed two boats rounding the bend at Bumi. Rooster tails of water shot out behind them as they closed the gap between us.

They were still some way off, but the steady thump of fibreglass hitting water could just be heard as the hulls cut the choppy surface. Our faces were all struck with immediate concern as we wondered what was happening.

The gap between us was narrowing fast when I realised that the boats were fast patrol craft of the Army Boat Squadron. As they raced towards us I could vaguely make out camouflaged figures manning the MAGs mounted on the forward decks. Other men held FN rifles and all of them pointed menacingly at us.

Many rude expletives raced through my mind as I glanced at my compatriots. Dressed as they were they could have convinced even the most suspecting ZIPRA guerrilla of their bona-fide terrorist status. I wasn't far off the mark either with my blackened-up face and hands, blue denim drag and RPD machine gun. I expected a hail of copper-plated lead to puncture the soft hull of the boat and our even softer skins at any moment.

My initial thought was that Callow had screwed up and had forgotten to send in the right signals. If that was the case, then we were in dire straits indeed!

Similar inflatable craft to ours had been captured in ZIPRA stores, on cross-border operations into Zambia, so it wasn't beyond the realms of imagination that we were terrorist operators commencing a waterborne infiltration. I imagine the fact that we might have been doing so in broad daylight wouldn't quell an excited trigger.

At the last minute I had an idea: Chikondo and Mlambo were already trying to change back into their Rhodesian uniforms at double time, when I ripped off my shirt, exposing the bronzed, but obviously white skin underneath.

The inflatable had come to a dead halt in the water and I jumped up waving my shirt above my head maniacally. My team-mates had their clothes off by now and were fastening the buttons of their Rhodesian smocks. The first fast-patrol boat reached us and sped around us like a hornet, all weapons trained on us. I yelled above the noise as our little craft pitched on the turbulent wake of the motor launch, trying to make our visitors understand that we were Selous Scouts on an operation and that this area was 'frozen'.

The Boat Squadron guys had heard nothing about it. They told us to hold steady while they got on the radio. I cranked up the communications set and called Callow, asking him if the area was clear. I told him we were being detained by the army who could very well have slotted us.

I was waiting for a response when next thing a voice came in loud and clear. It was Sunray himself, the CO from Inkomo, wanting to know what was going on. He had picked up the transmission and didn't want another cock-up like RT's, when four of our best operators were cut down. Quickly he snapped a command asking our position. I replied telling him to wait before I answered in code.

While I was busy the CO got on the blower and asked Callow if he had 'frozen' the area. The boats continued to hound us like wild dogs circling their prey.

Three minutes later, fortunately for us, the commander of the lead patrol boat gave the thumbs up and they turned in unison to head back to Bumi, leaving behind them a giant wake for us to contend with. It was a close call and could very well have turned disastrous.

After the near mishap we headed for a group of small, rocky islands in the vicinity of our target village and beached on the northern side as the sun went down. We settled in for a couple of hours and ate a quick compo meal washed down with hot tea.

With final preparations over, we boarded our craft and headed back to Rhodesia. A kilometre distant, the lights of cooking fires could be seen as we approached carefully through a maze of submerged trees. The last thing we wanted at this stage was a punctured pontoon and a sunken boat. The crocodiles were numerous in the area and would gorge themselves on an easy meal of prime human flesh.

To muffle the sound of the motor it had been fine-tuned, but we put doubled-up hessian sacks over the housing to quieten it even more.

Approaching a secluded bay I cut the engine a hundred metres offshore and paddled inland. At knee depth I jumped out and dragged the boat into a cluster of half-submerged rocks. There I would stay until the pseudo-operators had made contact with the village. Before they left we agreed on a signal which would warn me of their return. Chikondo's imitation of a cricket chirp was superb and would fool anyone listening closely.

My wait was long but uneventful. Three hours had passed when I heard a noise off to my left. I ducked behind cover when I noticed two men walking along the shoreline towards me, their silhouette stark against the moonlit sky. Loose gravel beneath their boots crunched together – the noise loud from where I sat in silence.

A short distance away they stopped, sank to the ground and one of them bought his hands up and cupped them to his face. My RPD was trained on them, but the cricket chirp came and precluded its use. I returned the recognition signal and the two came in.

The operation had been a success. The villagers were only too happy to contact the terrorists across the water. They told the operators that communication was via fisherman in dug-out canoes who liaised mid-water and passed on messages.

Our little island, where we had made home earlier, was to be our camp for the night. We returned and bedded down before setting off in the morning.

Some time later the guerrillas were engaged by our security forces. In the ensuing battle, all of them were killed, which effectively discredited reliable support from the entire area of the fishing village.

It was a successful operation and one that highlighted the typical work of the Selous Scouts. We weren't all about killing and 90 per cent of our time was actually spent in bringing the terrorists to close in battle; lengthy operations of establishing communications and then winning trust.

Another operation undertaken by a particular black Selous Scout operator required balls the size of grapefruit and was a sure indication of the calibre of man he was.

Infiltrating one of the tribal trust lands, he roamed around the area alone and unarmed, visiting different kraals and villages. All he carried was a 60 mm mortar tube along with a few bombs in his magazine pouches. After establishing his credentials with the locals he was eventually introduced to a genuine guerrilla group. His cover story was that his own group had been in a contact with security forces and he was the only survivor. He asked if he could join his new acquaintances until such time as they returned to Zambia for rest and resupply.

With the enemy convinced of his bona-fide status, he accompanied the gang while they headed towards the border, a journey that would take over a week. Along the way, as they settled in for each night, our operator made excuses to relieve himself, borrowing an AK or personal weapon from one of the terrorists and sneaking away into the night to do his business. Safely in hiding he then removed the firing pin or a fundamental part from the weapon and returned to camp with a huge grin on his face, to convince his comrades that he had satisfactorily emptied his bowels. Handing the weapon back, he thanked the man who had been kind enough to lend it to him and settled in for the night.

The following evening and each thereafter, after a hard day's slog, he repeated the performance with a different man and weapon, until only one functioning firearm remained. On the last night he borrowed that weapon and after a final Oscar-winning performance of relieving himself, he arrested everyone at gunpoint. The quick-off-the-mark naturally went for their firearms, but on pulling the triggers they heard a very distinct and disappointing click. A short burst of fire from the functioning weapon cut short their confusion and discouraged them from attempting to escape.

It was an operation fraught with danger and problems. At any given time his identity could have been discovered, which would have spelt his instant death. Fortunately for the operator, the terrorists were not conscientious about cleaning their weapons and his ploy was undiscovered. That the AK, AKM and SKS rifles, the most common weapons among the enemy, could still function after long periods of abuse is a great credit to the weapons, but was also a factor that worked in the Selous Scout's favour on that particular operation.

It was a brilliant demonstration of what pseudo work could achieve and testimony to the professionalism of the man.

A black operator and member of Recce Troop, who deserves mention, was Steven Mpofu. Steven worked closely with Chris Schulenburg much of the time until he was seconded to my mate John Gartner.

On one particular reconnaissance operation, while operating with Schulenburg, Mpofu became a bit wary about their tracks being followed. He raised his concern with his commander, but was largely ignored. Mpofu decided to put in a dog leg on his tracks and returned to where they had come from, leaving his commander on his own. It was nothing new to Schulenburg who preferred the anonymity of solitude.

The commander settled in for the night and Mpofu left to investigate his sixth sense. He had not travelled 500 metres, when he ran straight into a FRELIMO patrol. Fire was exchanged and Steven legged it back to the LUP.

When he got there the commander had already fled and was heading to Rhodesia with the radio. Mpofu chose his own flight path and managed to elude the enemy who were hot in pursuit. By this time Schulenburg was already home, having called for a hot extraction and been uplifted back to Rhodesia. Alone, Mpofu faced a long walk through dangerous territory and one that would take many days.

Back at Bindura, when the Selous Scouts' ops room had heard nothing of their lost operator, they were about to give him up for lost. From Schulenburg's account, the last they knew of him was the commander's recollection of an immense weight of fire being heard before he bugged out.

A few days after the incident the police telephoned the Selous Scouts ops room and said they had in custody a man who claimed to be an operator. He had walked into a shopping centre on the Rhodesian side of the border, dressed only in his trousers and had given himself up to a policeman, informing him of the whereabouts of his weapon and clothing. Had he remained fully dressed he might have been shot on sight as a terrorist.

We were ecstatic to have found Mpofu, as his loss would have been sorely felt. Over a few days he had managed to escape and evade an unrelenting enemy, as well as unsympathetic civilians who would have readily given him up, and cover a marathon distance back to Rhodesia.

It's only now, when I read books, or hear of other incredible escapes, like British SAS man Chris Ryan during Operation Desert Storm, that I think of the amazing intestinal fortitude that our own operators displayed on so many occasions. I only wish they too could have received the honour that was due to them.

Unfortunately, history records that the new government under Robert Mugabe purged many of the fine operators I served with, particularly those who had been former terrorists themselves. Many were sought out by the new Central Intelligence Organisation or Secret Police and done to death in despicable ways. A sad truth indeed!

CHAPTER 28:
BLUNDERS, BOREDOM AND BOTTLE-WASH COMMANDOS

The remainder of Recce Troop deployed to Mangula to join the others. John Gartner's callsign was operating in the Hurricane operational area, where they had set up OPs on known terrorist routes.

As there was always a shortage of helicopters, we had to share the few available to us with an RLI Fire Force on standby at the Mangula Country Club. It was a deployment highlighted by sleep deprivation as the young troops of the RLI partied each night away in the club's modest bar.

By this time a temporary officer commanding Recce Troop had been appointed. An ex-air force pilot, Captain Mike Borlace was a thorough man who had been wooed by the legend of the Selous Scouts. After serving with distinction in 7 Squadron, where he had been awarded the Silver Cross of Rhodesia, he sought fulfilment elsewhere and passed selection with flying colours. Among the RLI troopies he was legend and known for his fearlessness in deploying them into the midst of raging battle when necessary.

As a chopper pilot he certainly came close to the fighting on many occasions. As the temporary Recce Troop OC, while we were stationed at Mangula, Captain Borlace attended the briefings that were held every day between the air force and the RLI. There he advised both parties on our status and our requirements in the field.

John Gartner's callsign had met with relative success and were extracted from the bush by helicopter. They arrived at the country club looking very much like terrorists and were ushered into our own quarters where they could not be seen. After their brief, we prepared to break camp and return to Inkomo. Captain Borlace left for the afternoon meeting while the rest of us began to relax and look forward to the end of another bush trip.

Just when we had resigned our fatigued bodies and minds to several days of rest and recuperation, the captain called us into the ops tent. Plans had changed and we were to make haste to Sinoia where he had volunteered us to man a Fire Force. From there we would be deployed that evening to the Urungwe TTL, where there had been a terrorist sighting by another Selous Scout OP. Undermanned, the RLI were unable to action the operation alone and needed more manpower. The addition of our two callsigns would give them more than a fighting chance.

The drive to Sinoia was hard on the kidneys as I mounted the back of a Crocodile MPV (mine-protected vehicle). We weren't breaking any land speed records, but the heavy suspension felt every dip and bump on the open road. Then the heavens opened and drenched us to the bone. The vehicle with its angled sides had no roof and the rainwater swashed around on the floorboards, obstructed only by heavy sandbags.

The Rhodesians were pioneers in producing this type of mine-protected mobility. The heavy iron, angled sides were meant to deflect most of the blast in the event of the vehicle hitting a mine and the tyres, filled with water, would contribute additional weight and absorb most of the blast. The sandbags were added protection should shrapnel and debris penetrate the armoured floor.

A few jarring hours later we pulled to a halt outside a service station on the outskirts of the small town to await orders. We were joined there by another vehicle carrying two callsigns of RLI troops. From there we drove further south, eventually turning west onto a farm track. At the farmstead where we were to wait, we received a typically warm welcome from the owner and his wife. Ice-cold glasses of refreshing lemonade were brought promptly to satisfy our thirsts. To the west, the sun settled behind a rolling green landscape. It was too late to go to war, so a decision was made to attack the enemy the following morning.

After a restless night's sleep we were up at sparrow's fart to await the arrival of Cyclone 7. When the choppers arrived it was with the news that the RLI had gone in already and were engaged in a running battle of mini-contacts over a wide area. I deployed with an eight-man team; four men per helicopter to form a line north of the contact area. We were to sweep south looking for terrorists and also conduct a bomb damage assessment for a new type of Golf bomb that the air force was using. As there had been a large group of terrorists, the Hunters had been called in for extra support and the more powerful bombs had been used for the first time.

Captain Borlace insisted that I be the MAG gunner in his callsign. In a contact you couldn't want a better weapon, but when not in use, lugging it around can be a real pain. It was a terrific effort, being as lightweight as I am.

We had not been on the ground for 15 minutes when our callsign was fired upon from a small grove of trees. I hit the ground, burying the weapon's tripod a few centimetres into the damp earth. I heard return fire around me as the other operators opened up and I squeezed off a short burst into the tree line before finding a steady rhythm. On a 20-degree arc I put down a heavy weight of fire into the target area. I didn't know what I was shooting at, but whatever it was, was shooting back at me. I knew where the enemy fire had come from and keeping their heads down, was better than lying and waiting to be shot.

These contacts were usually so short it was only when they were over that you thought about the event. I saw a couple of the other operators get to their feet and dash forward before I became aware that the fire had subsided. Not long afterwards I became acutely aware of a stinging sensation on my left cheek. I had had my right cheek firmly tucked into the gun butt, but my left cheek had been exposed to hot brass from one of the operator's FNs.

I clambered up and moved forward with the gun at my hip. Even with the smallest of efforts my breathing resounded in my ears as if I was wearing a crash helmet, the hoarseness of it overpowering the high- pitched tinnitus that rang in my ears. Covering the 20 metres to the tree line passed as if it were in slow motion. My senses were focused to a sharp edge, willing the vaguest of discrepancies to show.

At the tree line two dead terrorists lay at the base of an acacia tree. When I arrived, the captain was already sifting through their pockets and their webbing, looking for documentation. Other than a few ragged holes in the blue denim jackets that the terrs wore, there was no indication that life had departed them. They could have been taking a morning siesta if one didn't know better.

After searching the bodies Captain Borlace called in the kills to the command chopper. On new orders we swept forward to meet with an RLI callsign at the outskirts of a village in the area. We approached cautiously and were soon greeted by the sound of gunfire. Captain Borlace screamed 'contact front' and we edged forward in a broad sweep.

A small battle was raging when we reached the village. From our vantage point we could see some of the RLI guys taking cover behind the mud walls of a few round huts. I could tell that they were veterans by the way they moved. There was no panic in their actions as they casually sought out the enemy. One of the troopies, closer to the fray, held a grenade in each hand. He left his rifle leaning against a wall and ran forward to one of the huts. The others gave covering fire through the building's doors and walls. I imagined the fear the terrorists must have felt inside. I could envisage lasers of sunlight crisscrossing the dusty environs of their lair as the 7.62 mm punched through.

At the hut the young trooper pressed himself into the wall. Pulling the pins of both grenades he paused for a moment and then with his right boot kicked in the feeble door frame. A moment later he lobbed his grenades inside and retreated for cover. 'Grenade' he yelled as he dived behind a water trough a few metres away.

Inside the hut a terrified scream was cut short by the muffled crump of high explosive. The door swung inwards once more as the air inside was consumed by fire, and then suddenly outwards as a dress-clad figure lurched into the daylight clutching at its stomach. Several FNs boomed and the figure went down, motionless after a few twitches which spasmed through the body.

The trooper, back on his feet, retrieved his weapon and ran back to the hut. Approaching the door from the lee he stepped into the opening but his weapon was already kicking at his hip. He entered the hut and a few more shots were heard. Umpteen seconds later he returned, dragging the messy carcass of another dead terrorist behind him. He had two AKs slung over his shoulder.

On the far side of the village, another dress-clad figure lay alone in death. The floral blue of the dress she wore stained dark with crimson. It was apparent that she had been a victim of the air force strike. Only on closer inspection did we discover that 'she' was in fact a 'he'. The dress he wore, as was the case with the other 'she-male', was a disguise to throw us off the scent. They had figured from experience that Rhodesian troops would not fire on women unless they were being shot at. The alert went out to watch out for other terrorists who may be disguised as women.

Apart from the one bomb victim, we didn't find any other trophies for the air force. When we searched the area the only indication that bombs had fallen there were fléchettes buried deep in the trunks of trees.

Later we had another small contact when a lone terr opened up on us. I must have fired a hundred rounds into the bush in which he was hiding, but it was a pretty one-sided affair and over in seconds.

After mopping up we were uplifted and taken back to the farm. We drove back to Sinoia for a good meal. I guess it was the norm back then, but when we entered the motel foyer, blackened up and messy, the few people sitting at the bar, farmers of the area, gave us only a casual glance before attending to their more important beers.

The next day I arrived back at Inkomo and saw John Gartner. I told him about our Fire Force action and aired my disgruntlement at being used in the wrong role. I just hoped that Captain Borlace would not volunteer us for any similar actions in the future. He never got the chance.

When Mike Borlace was captured in Lusaka, he was carrying out a reconnaissance for Recce Troop, masquerading as a tourist. After the second Air Rhodesia Viscount was shot down in February 1979 by Joshua Nkomo's ZIPRA, in which all 59 people on board perished, orders were received from the highest echelons of government for Nkomo's immediate termination.

The Selous Scouts were originally accorded the honour of master-minding the operation and Captain Borlace was the man who carried out the final reconnaissance on the ZIPRA leader's residence. On his say-so, the sending of a secret code word to verify if the target was at home, an assault team in two newly acquired Bell helicopters would fly into Zambia and liaise with the captain, who would then drive the assault troops to Nkomo's residence to commence the attack. Previous successful recces had already been conducted by two other operators, Chris Grove and Anthony White, but it was Captain Borlace who would give the signal to move.

White had, in fact, failed in an attempt to kill Nkomo and certain African members of the regiment, who were privy to the operation, were beginning to think that witchcraft was at play. If it wasn't witchcraft, then reliable old Murphy must have had a hand in things, as everything which could possibly go wrong, did. When Captain Borlace sent the first confirmation that Nkomo was at home, heavy rains prevented him meeting up with the assault team as two bridges on route to the rendezvous had been washed away. The assault team was uplifted and returned to Rhodesia.

On the second attempt, having found a new rendezvous, the assault team was landed in the middle of a Zambian Army brigade exercise and a hot extraction had to be called for. It seemed that Nkomo was indeed living a charmed life! Aside from the numerous logistical problems the Scouts ran into, every time conditions looked favourable to recommence the operation, Nkomo was lucky enough to be boarding an aircraft en route to one of his many overseas destinations. The operation would then have to be delayed as further setbacks occurred.

The captain was in constant need of financial re-supply, his vehicles were having problems and it was feared that he might be attracting some unwanted attention. On the third attempt to assassinate Nkomo, this time by means of the assault team parachuting in to rendezvous with the captain, the mission was called off after a failure to contact him by radio at the LZ. The team returned to Rhodesia once more, concerned that some fate had befallen the temporary Recce Troop commander and waited for news. The next day word was received that Mike Borlace had been arrested at the airport by the Zambian police.

I had very little to do with the operation until after Borlace's capture. He was interned in the Lusaka prison and a plan was put forward by Lieutenant Colonel Reid Daly to mount a daring rescue attempt. For reasons unknown, every idea he came up with was stonewalled or put on ice. It began to look like the Rhodesian government had deserted Mike Borlace in his time of need.

Recce Troop, by now attached to Support Troop because of our leader's capture, was based at Forward Air Field Kariba (FAF 2) at this time, next to the civilian airport. The camp was manned by the Police Escort Patrol, who ran the gauntlet to Karoi every day escorting civilians. I had been to FAF 2 several times before when we deployed Chris Schulenburg and other Recce Troop operators into Zambia. At the bottom of the airstrip there was a permanently stationed Lynx aircraft to provide better communications between the Scouts' ops room at Inkomo and the teams when they were in the field. During April 1978 the aircraft was also conducting night reconnaissance missions over Zambian roads trying to pick up movement of ZIPRA conventional forces, as they moved to the border before launching attacks on Rhodesia. Nkomo's plan had always been to mount a conventional assault on Rhodesia, taking over the towns as his forces drove on to Salisbury.

Unbeknown to us, the SAS had also been planning an operation to assassinate Joshua Nkomo. The first I knew of it was when my old buddies rocked up at FAF 2, complete with a convoy of disguised Sabre Land-Rovers painted to look like Zambian Army vehicles. The Trojan horse-type operation was to comprise a bold drive into Lusaka, having been deployed by the *Sea Lion* ferry onto the Zambian shore complete with vehicles, right into the heart of the beast where the assault team would barge Nkomo's gates and attack his residence with complete surprise and magnificent firepower. The Land-Rovers were all equipped with MAGs and the operators all carried sufficient personal weaponry, RPG7 rockets, grenades and bunker bombs.

I caught up with my old pals and was invited to join them when they left on the journey across the lake, for the night deployment a day later. I jumped at the chance as we were still awaiting orders for Mike Borlace's rescue operation. It was believed that the hierarchy at Combined Operations were hesitant to approve any immediate attempt which might interfere with the SAS operation.

On the evening of 14 April 1978, I accompanied the SAS to the lake shore where I watched the ferry edging out into the waters of Kariba. Although I was not going on the operation, it was a tremendous feeling of excitement to be part of such a daring plan and I bid my compatriots farewell and good luck as they sailed from Rhodesia.

A few days later they were back, full of stories of their adventure although they too had failed to kill Nkomo.

Arriving in Lusaka unchallenged, the attack had gone ahead almost as planned, with all the guards and those who were in residence being neutralised. One of the two gates to the residence had proved a problem when the padlock didn't give to the ramming. Using a breaching charge, the SAS were soon inside. A systematic cleansing of the house then commenced with bunker bombs thrown into each room, starting with Nkomo's, then the entire place being hosed down with RPG7 and machine-gun fire. After physically clearing all the rooms, an inspection of the corpses was carried out, but Nkomo was not among them. Unfortunately for the SAS, he was not in residence that night. He later claimed to have escaped through a toilet window above the cistern of the lavatory. Given his immense size, almost 150 kilograms, his claim was highly doubtful and it was more probable that luck, more than anything else, had saved his bacon. Reports later indicated that he was warned of the attack through a leak in Combined Operations, but nonetheless, he was a very lucky man.

One of my mates was unfortunate to be one of three Rhodesian casualties in the assault. Shot in the backside, I visited him a few days later in the Kariba hospital and managed to smuggle in a few steaks and beers past the nurses.

Poor Mike Borlace languished in prison for a long time and ultimately was only released when the war was over.

Leaderless, we were deployed to Grand Reef once again, on the other side of the country, where we were to meet our new commander, Captain John Early. He was an American, who had only recently come to the regiment from the air force, where he was a parachute jump instructor. A veteran of the American Special Forces in Vietnam, he was a bit of a cowboy, but a very likeable man. However, Early was not happy with the new posting and sought combat deployment rather than command. It wasn't long before he was out of the picture completely and we returned to Inkomo Barracks for yet another introduction.

Captain Andy Samuels, or Captain Devil as he was known, was a former RLI officer and more suited to the task of commanding Recce Troop. He was good at his job but if anything, seemed a little laid back. As a result of the upheaval concerning Captain Borlace, we ended had up being temporarily seconded to Support Troop under Captain Rich Passaportis. In fact, he ended up running Recce Troop and we were mostly deployed with them, something which none of us really liked.

While Mike Borlace was rotting away in his cell, Recce Troop accompanied Support Troop all over the country. We were mostly deployed to Kariba and Victoria Falls, from where we mounted operations into Zambia and Botswana. It was a very unhappy time for me as I had slowly become more of a camp lackey. Sergeant Major Willie Devine, also ex-SAS, took over my role in Recce Troop and I found myself without a job description.

A slight interruption in the monotony of camp life came when we deployed into Zambia by Klepper canoe, in order to put in taps on the telephone lines from Lusaka. At the time we weren't too sure why we were doing it, but it came to light that ComOps was trying to ascertain the source of various intelligence leaks. These were simple operations, fraught with danger, but it was the promise of action that made me tick. At least I was doing something.

Shortly thereafter, we finally got word that Mike Borlace was to be rescued. OpSec was extremely tight and very few members of the Scouts knew about the operation. My part in it was to be a member of the team that deployed the rescue force, across the river by canoe. The team would then make its way to the main Livingstone-Lusaka road where they would be met by a truck, driving into Zambia from Botswana via the Kazungula border post and using the ferry. The truck had been rigged by Scouts technical personnel and was complete with a false floor over a shallow compartment that could hide the entire rescue team. Once in Lusaka they would break from their secret compartment and assault the prison where Mike was detained. The plan called for much élan and thorough preparation.

On a sunny afternoon at Victoria Falls, a few other operators and I prepared to mount a reconnaissance on the Zambian shore of the Zambezi River. For the task we were outfitted as tourists and Special Branch had booked our places on a sundowner cruise which would take us close to the Zambian bank. It was probably the easiest recce I ever took part in. We had all the trappings of holiday-making, including copious amounts of beer, all to look the part. We were to board the cruise, resplendent in tropical Hawaiian shirts and look out for a landing site on the Zambian shore, being careful to choose our landmarks properly. It was critical for us to get our bearings right, as things can look very different at night. It was to be a relatively easy exercise and we were told that there should be no opposition force of concern, as the landing site was to be well in the middle of a game park.

The cruise was soon under way and beers in hand, we made mental notes of the opposite bank. It was the skyline that we had to look out for because by the light of the moon, when we were actually deploying, it would be the only recognisable feature. An hour later we had identified a small bay, that was evident by the huge ivory palms that surrounded it. With their height they stood out above the other trees and should thereby be easily recognisable on the night of the operation.

A few beers later we docked and were comfortably merry with alcohol. We weren't pissed, but I must say I never thought I would be sipping cold beers while conducting a reconnaissance. I made notes of our findings and sketched a quick drawing of the Zambian horizon.

As the sun rose the following day, we loaded four Klepper canoes onto the back of a 45 truck, ready for the evening's move to the river. They were safely tied down and we covered them with tarpaulins, being careful to disguise their shape, by throwing in a few sandbags and other military kit. Operational security was vital and we didn't want anyone guessing what we were up to.

Captain Devil then sent me to the airport to see if I could obtain some inner tubes from spare aircraft tyres. Butch Atkins and I set off in one of the Land-Rovers. Most of the black operators couldn't swim, so the captain thought it best we take the precaution of making them buoyant should they fall out of the canoes if these were to capsize. An inflated tyre around the neck should do the job.

Our search was not in vain and we returned with the tubes. The black operators looked a sight with the bulbous life-savers festooned around their necks. In any other part of the world it would almost be ridiculous to include non-swimmers in the ranks of Special Forces, but I can verify that what the black operators lacked in the aquatic department, they certainly made up for in bush craft, weapon handling and courage.

At the launching site that evening, I set up two 60 mm mortars in case the landing was opposed, sighting them on the far bank. Butch Atkins would remain with the comms vehicle and in the event of trouble, he would bring the mortars into action. A couple of operators would man them and await our return from Zambia. The bombs, if correctly placed, would be sure to spoil any reception party waiting to welcome us.

We slipped the canoes into a small backwater and a white froth eddied around us. The river above the falls is beautiful and is one of my favourite places. But all that beauty escaped me while we were waging war.

The Kleppers were really loaded down with ammunition and provisions for the operation. The assault team didn't take their Bergens as these would only be additional weight. The meeting point with the truck was not far off and thereafter they would be well taken care of. I was in charge of the boat callsign and I insisted we must all be in direct communication. I verified that everyone's comms sets were in order, then pushed off for the Zambian bank.

Although it was dark already, across the way, I was able to identify the cluster of palm trees I had chosen for the landing site the previous evening. They stood out starkly against the moonlit sky.

Dipping our paddles gently into the water we moved off as a group without a sound. Soon the current caught us and it became more of an effort to stay in line with our landing site. I pointed my canoe's bow into the current and paddled upstream at an angle to intercept the drop-off point; but it was hard going given the weight in men and equipment that we carried. Despite my best efforts as lead canoe, the current was dragging us downstream faster than we could make headway. It took a marathon effort, battling against the powerful surges of fast water, to get anywhere near our objective. The previous night's swan on the booze cruise was a distant memory.

Aside from our paddling efforts, we worried about hippos, which had been known to overturn canoes when stumbled upon. Hippos are very dangerous animals and their incisors are capable of tearing through the toughest of fibreglass, let alone the flimsy canvas covering of the Kleppers. Once in the water we were exposed to their attention and reaction – that's if the crocodiles didn't get us first.

Half an hour later, after paddling upstream, we were within 50 metres of the Zambian shore and the ivory palms came into view again. Against the powerful dipping of paddles, the sound of my breath seemed incredibly loud and for an instant I worried that we might be heard. Fortunately, the current waned in a sloppy backwash and the paddling became easier – just the sort of place one might find crocs on a July evening. Although we were in a tropical zone, the gentle breeze, combined with the water, made us shiver and even our physical exertion did little against the cold.

The radio communications had not come into their own yet as the four Kleppers had miraculously stuck close to one another. A short whistle signalled a 'huddle' and the three other coxswains closed with my canoe. A brief 'Chinese parliament' was held and we were all in agreement that we had found the correct bay. A quick dig of the paddle and my Klepper slid into the still water beside the drop-off point. Gently I dug into the river with deep strokes, controlling the paddle so as to make the least noise possible. When the paddle touched sand, I gave the order for the operators to disembark. The other canoes slipped in on my starboard side and they too disgorged their cargo of heavily-laden soldiers. Four men moved steadily towards the bank and formed an all-round defence. The remaining operators shoved the canoes off by the bow and we drifted into the darkness. Within seconds I could make out no detail of the shoreline at all. As quickly as we had come, we were gone, the night closing in around us.

The return journey to Rhodesia was as difficult as our departure had been, despite the lighter weight. Each of us had dug deep into our reserves of energy, to deliver the operators to the opposite bank, but suddenly the much lighter craft were whisked away by the current. All I knew was that I had to keep a bearing of roughly upstream if I were to reach our entry point or anywhere near it. I paddled like mad, with the other three boats closely behind, but it appeared we were getting nowhere. With no horizon to work on, the fast-running water gave the impression that we were standing still. At best, we were going backwards.

When I was about to give up and let the current take me, the radio crackled into life. It was a callsign from the bank in Zambia that we had left behind 15 minutes before. The news they carried was a massive let-down and my heart sank. For all our trouble we had to return and collect the operators, as we had landed them on an island. Flashes of my previous experience in the SAS, when we had mistakenly achieved the same result, shot through my mind and I wondered if I would ever live it down. Certainly the operation would rate high on my 'most embarrassing incidents' list. I rallied the other coxswains and gave them the news.

Going back to Zambia proved more taxing than it was worth. We had already made one mistake and it proved as difficult to find the operators, as it had been to find the correct drop-off point in the first place. After we had gone way beyond the palms, we paddled against the current until we thought we were in the right spot. Another 10 minutes of futility proved us wrong and I decided to call the lads on the radio requesting the flash of a torch or a strobe light. OpSec would no doubt be broken, but I figured we were better off taking the chance than leaving them deserted in Zambia.

As it turned out, we were not far off the mark to begin with. A couple of flashes guided us to the right point and the rendezvous was successful. The island in question was only 40 or so metres from the real bank, but as the black operators couldn't swim and we had taken the tyre tubes off them, crossing the narrow stretch was impossible.

Fully loaded once again we canoed the dividing water and redeployed the men. This time our navigation was on the mark and the operators melted into the bush after a quick shove-off. Mike Borlace was finally a step closer to freedom and the operation was under way.

Back at our base camp, we waited for news of the rescue. Almost a day had lapsed when the team came over the radio to inform us that their lift, the modified truck with the false bottom, had not arrived. Could we deploy by Klepper the following evening and uplift them?

Most of us were somewhat confused until we found out what had happened. Unbeknown to us and a sure sign, if the only one, of where the Rhodesian military machine broke down, was the communication gap which existed at high levels. Everyone seemed to have their fingers so far up their arses that information was often not shared. Of course, operational security was vital, but the entire reason for having the combined operations headquarters in the first place, was to guide all arms of the military toward one objective so that each arm would complement the other. Many at ComOps were so stingy with sharing information, for unknown reasons, that even though they knew what was happening, their lips were sealed.

My former buddies in the SAS had different ideas from those of the Selous Scouts. While we were planning Borlace's release, they were planning to sink the Kazungula ferry, on which our success rested. The ferry had been identified as a means of transporting both terrorists and weapons between Zambia and Botswana, so that the enemy could infiltrate Rhodesia. It was purely bad luck that they sank it at the precise time when the truck had been waiting in Botswana, to board the ferry and cross into Zambia. If information had been shared, our captive may have been a free man much sooner. As it was, he spent over a year in jail and was in and out of the High Court of Zambia being tried for treason, the penalty for which was death. It was only through legal counsel, backed by Special Branch funds, that Mike Borlace was eventually deported to London. By that time Rhodesia was no more. Maybe it was his good fortune that he didn't get to witness the dying throes of his country.

During this period, while we were playing 'cockleshell heroes', my QRF team, the bottle-wash commandos, had their first and only contact with terrorists. I was extremely pissed off that I missed out, but was highly proud of the men at the same time. On returning to the Victoria Falls airport, I was astounded to learn there had been a terrorist sighting quite nearby. The only choppers and troops available to man the Fire Force were the QRF at the base, who were quickly assembled and deployed. In the following action, the cooks and bottle-washers did us proud, killing three terrorists for the loss of none. The chopper's twin-barrelled .303 Browning was also responsible for a further kill. Our return to camp was marked by a high-spirited revelry of war stories, that grew out of all proportion to what they were. Nevertheless, the men had done a sterling job, so it wasn't for us to scoff at them. I'm sure I wasn't the only one who felt a surge of jealousy turn my body green.

CHAPTER 29:
AUDACITY

After the bungled attempt to rescue Mike Borlace, I was once again tasked to deploy Martin Chikondo, five kilometres west of Livingstone, for an operation into Zambia. Chikondo and a section of seven men, posing as a Zambian Army patrol, were to mount a roadblock on the main Livingstone-Lusaka road and capture some high-ranking ZIPRA officials who were known to use the route. Failing a successful capture, the second prize was elimination of the officials who formed the command element for ZIPRA's Northern Front - 1. Their primary task, en route to man the roadblock, was to check out the Livingstone airfield to confirm whether the Zambians had sited surface-to-air missile batteries there, Rapiers supplied by the British.

After a fruitless search, the section left the airfield and walked five kilometres to Sindi Plots, next to the main road. A radio intercept had provided precise information that some of the ZIPRA command element were to pass through, driving a Land-Rover, on their way to a logistics base in the area. With the road block set up, it wasn't a long wait before the ZIPRA vehicle came into view. In order to establish their bona fides, the section let the vehicle pass unhindered, as they stood by on the side of the road. Sometime later the Land-Rover returned and Chikondo stepped into the road and ordered it to halt. Approaching the driver, a coloured man and somewhat a rarity in ZIPRA, Chikondo demanded his credentials and asked him where he was going.

In the back of the Land-Rover Bob Dongo, the deputy commander for the Northern Front - 2, became suspicious when he noticed the length of Chikondo's sideburns. The Zambian Army was entirely clean-shaven and the deputy commander reached for his pistol. Chikondo was quicker off the mark and opened fire with his own weapon. In the mêlée, Bob Dongo was wounded and another officer, the ZIPRA logistics officer for the region, was killed. Sam Wright, the coloured driver, was taken captive along with another two ZIPRA terrorists.

Chikondo's section immediately called for an uplift to secure their captives and a chopper was soon on the way. So vital was the information that the ZIPRA men carried, that the helicopter had been circling in wait above the falls, for word from the operators. Dongo needed urgent medical attention, or the value of the operation would be lost.

As the chopper was landing, one of the captives made a break for it and was gunned down. The others were trussed and thrown aboard for the flight back to Rhodesia. A short while later another brave ZIPRA member tried to sabotage the operation by throwing himself onto the pilot. He was shot in the back by one of the Selous Scouts on board. His body was retained for identification purposes by Special Branch.

Unfortunately, Dongo died en route to the Wankie hospital, but not before he disclosed some valuable information. He was able to collate the location of Zambian Army units and the whereabouts of the Lusaka Intelligence Section. He was also able to pinpoint infiltration routes into Rhodesia, across some of the narrower sections of the Zambezi. These were ambushed by other units in the military and resulted in some credible kills.

If it wasn't for Martin Chikondo's incredible courage, on this and other operations, a wealth of information would have been lost and severe setbacks felt.

Being a member of the Selous Scouts was not all about roughing it in the bush, carrying out pseudo operations dressed as terrorists. Much of our work might seem sublime in comparison, almost criminal sometimes, but nevertheless was a very important part of waging war against the enemy and against those who gave him succour.

After one of our uplifts from Zambia it was noted, as we flew over the Victoria Falls Railway Station, that an abundance of trains were parked there waiting to cross the border, carrying materials north to Lusaka and even as far as Tanzania.

One such train was decked out with two levels of brand-new Volvo vehicles, which were no doubt going to one of the many aid organisations that actively assisted the terrorists. After we landed, Captain Devil put in a report to Special Branch to inform them of our findings. It seemed odd that an air of normality existed on the trade routes, while the two countries were quite literally at war.

Special Branch were intrigued by the information and provided two operatives to accompany us on a close target reconnaissance. Like the booze cruise recce, this reconnaissance was an easy one, conducted in the train yards of Victoria Falls, within the safe environs of Rhodesia. After establishing an infiltration route into the yard on the first night and checking out the goods, we returned to the FAF to formulate a plan. We couldn't just go blowing up commercial goods inside our own country, so another means of denying our enemy's access to the Volvos had to be found.

We came up with a simple plan. The following night we retraced our steps and arrived at the Volvo-laden wagons. We had bought several 20-litre containers of linseed oil, along with a few funnels, which we planned to put into the vehicle's oil reservoirs. A half hour later, every single vehicle in the yard, destined for the trip north, was contaminated with the oil and we departed. We never did hear anything of the results of our sabotage, but there must have been several highly irate dignitaries flustering over seized engines. Pity. I would have loved one of the Volvos for myself.

After the Kazungula ferry was blown up by the SAS, much of the commercial traffic on its way north passed through Victoria Falls. There were other similar operations conducted by Special Branch that I heard of, but the Selous Scouts' work in the area had been seriously affected by the loss of the ferry. No longer did we have a convenient means of inserting agents or recce teams into Zambia and Botswana, so our operations in the area dried up for a short period.

One interesting operation, which did come up, was a raid on Sindi Plots just outside Livingstone, to attack a South African, African National Congress (SAANC) base situated there. The ANC, then South Africa's enemy, had been known to assist ZIPRA actively, often infiltrating Rhodesia together. At the height of the war, Joshua Nkomo's ZIPRA were backed by at least three companies of the SAANC who always had more in common with the Matabele than the Shona, being as they were an offshoot of the South African Zulu tribes. Traditionally the Shona were an historic enemy, which so caused a lot of in-fighting.

The original intention of the SAANC was to infiltrate sections of 10 men into Rhodesia, who would make their way to South Africa and conduct terrorist operations there. What actually happened was, by the time they got to Gwanda, half way between Zambia and South Africa, they were halted in their tracks and redirected to fight ZANLA, who were encroaching on the west of the country, the Matabele's tribal base. The end result - more problems for the Rhodesians to deal with.

Whatever the reason Rhodesia assisted South Africa – be it because the fuel and ammo-starved Rhodesians were over a barrel, or be it for more in-depth, political or sinister reasons – the Selous Scouts were tasked with raiding the SAANC base as part of Operation Dice. This major operation included other tasks that were designed to sabotage ZIPRA's conventional war ability and hopefully bring it to its knees.

Virtually all Rhodesia's front-line forces would be involved in the operation. North of Kariba the SAS, accompanied by a small team of Selous Scouts, made available to monitor road activity, would blow up bridges that were vital to Nkomo's forces if he were to invade. They had already severed several road links which would effectively hinder ZIPRA's plans. The gloves were finally off and Rhodesia, in order to boost her standing at the Lancaster House Conference, being held in London at the time, would gain considerably if she could aid in Zambia's economic collapse.

Elsewhere, teams of SAS, Selous Scouts, RLI and RAR soldiers, would conduct raids and lay ambushes on known terrorist routes.

During the briefing for the attack on Sindi Plots, I was tasked as an assault team member, to sweep through the camp, as well as carry a 60 mm mortar to provide backup in the event of Zambian Army intervention. The assault force, always small by international standards, was to fly directly into the camp in two Bell helicopters and bring the SAANC to battle.

The Rhodesians often carried out raids with limited resources; resources which generals in other armies would consider too meagre to accomplish an objective. I remember, when I was once on an infantry minor-tactics course in the Paras, I was told that in order to raid an enemy defensive position effectively, when he has the advantage of digging in on his own turf, the raiding forces should outnumber the defenders by at least three to one. The 6 June 1944, D Day invasion, was based on a strategy of numbers. It was all about who could get the most troops where and when. That's all conventional military reasoning, but the textbooks, out of necessity, were often thrown out of the window when the Rhodesians went to war.

A reconnaissance, conducted by African members of the troop, had alerted us to the camp's defences and we expected a fight when we landed. There would be no softening-up of the target by aircraft or artillery prior to its commencement and we were to attack with total surprise. We were to fly in there like the airmobile infantry, strafing the tree line with door-mounted machine guns as we landed, advancing to contact under fire. Before the operation, a couple of guys from South African Military Intelligence, flew in to liaise with Special Branch. They would accompany us on the raid and sift through any documentation we found. This sort of co-operation was common and we often had our friends from south of the border hanging around.

I was suddenly filled with an immense euphoria. Although I had always been operational, I had somehow lost myself since leaving the SAS. I think there were many contributing factors to my wandering spirit, not the least of which was my disintegrating marriage. The prospect of going into battle again, pitting myself against greater odds, was like finding my feet for the first time. On top of that, the overall feeling in the country was one of doom and gloom and I had let myself get caught up in it. It was infectious. After all, we were fighting for our very right to have an identity. I can't imagine what indignation would reign, if all of a sudden an Englishman could no longer be an Englishman, or a German a German. Why then would some have it that a Rhodesian could no longer be a Rhodesian?

Were we that bad? Were our leaders really the manic despots like others who have been portrayed in history? I can hear some answering 'yes' to that question, but I beg to offer a defence. The United States of America, Australia, South Africa and Rhodesia all have histories which started within a few hundred years of each other. In the grand scheme of things, that's a pretty small margin.

Of all of those countries, only one can honestly say that it never purged the natives on the land in their early histories. Sure, the Rhodesians fought battles against the natives in the first rebellions and they may even have been one-sided affairs. But the Matabele also have a proud warrior record and in their historical footnotes they look back on those times with righteous pride. The rebellions were an important part of establishing their warrior heritage, not events which they weep and whine about because they were oppressed by the foreigner. I can remember reading a *National Geographic* late seventies edition. The author asked one RAR soldier if he minded fighting and killing people of his own race. The wording of the article, if I remember it correctly, was: 'A mirthless smile and an emphatic answer lay in wait for that question. 'What do you think we have been doing for the past thousand years'?

It's a lot more than the Aussies can say for their Aborigines. In Australia's early history, the colonial immigrants were successful in wiping out 75% of all Aborigines on the mainland and 100% in Tasmania. When they couldn't kill them fast enough, they interned them in camps and introduced smallpox to eradicate them. Most early Australians were convicts, some of whom were given a free pardon if they went out into the bush and returned with the scalps of 10 Aborigines. Now is that something to be proud of?

I don't see the Aussies, or the Yanks, having to fight protracted guerrilla wars for their right to be who they claim to be. And I needn't go into detail about the Yanks' record with their Indian natives.

Let's look at the Commonwealth countries as a separate entity. Only one of them can ever claim to have bought their right to self-governance from the British. The Rhodesians paid the princely sum of £2-million for that right, back in 1923. Realistically, the Rhodesians had governed themselves for longer than the Australians had, or any British annexed colony for that matter. And they did so with representation of blacks in parliament.

The government's policies might have been archaic, but what is really wrong with the educated vote system? There was no apartheid. Blacks could vote if they had achieved a certain level of education. I'm sure a white, below the acceptable grade, would have been turned away from the polling station, although it is probable that he would never have been asked. Should any country be run by naïve people? That's where real tyranny comes in. Look where Zimbabwe is today.

Suddenly I was a patriot and nothing else besides. I was a patriot for all the people of Rhodesia, both black and white and I owed something to them. I wasn't going into battle because it was a game, as when I first arrived back home. I no longer begrudged my mates because they might be having more fun than me. I had finally identified the feelings that had been smouldering away inside me, unchannelled and unbridled. I once again had a cause to fight for. My country, my family and my mates.

We left for Sindi Plots early, riding Pegasus to war. Boarding the Bell helicopter was a bit of a strain, loaded up as I was. Aside from my AKM assault rifle, the 60 mm mortar was strapped to my Bergen and its side pockets were loaded with bombs. A few of the other lads carried extra ammunition for the tube, but were quite limited in what they could take due to their own extraordinary firepower. An assortment of communist weapons was distributed among the lads, including the regular AKs and cut-down RPDs. As was the norm, a few preferred the FN for its greater accuracy and power.

The Bell helicopters had mounted .303 Browning machine guns, pointing out each door. That equated to four Brownings in all and an impressive rate of fire of 3,400 rounds per minute.

The flight from Victoria Falls took no longer than eight minutes and we soon came to the outskirts of the camp. Behind us the spray from the falls rose on a hazy horizon.

Mosi Oa Tunya (the smoke that thunders) is what the Africans call it in their local dialect, but we were speaking in a different tongue that day. The machine guns spoke vehemently as they strafed the tree line and the choppers pitched to land. The terrain was as flat as a pancake, with open fields and thickets of dense undergrowth. In one of the open fields, I leapt out along with the others into an all-round defence. The choppers lifted off under the cover of 20 automatic weapons which threatened outwards, pointing like the rigid tentacles of an iron octopus. We were the body of the creature and moved as one into a sweep line the moment the aircraft had left, running headlong for cover toward the camp.

Surprisingly there was no return fire so far. Above the noise of the Bells it had been hard to hear anything on landing. I looked into the tree line and the tell-tale muzzle flashes that I expected to be silently winking at me were nowhere to be seen. Maybe the enemy were holding their fire, drawing us into the killing ground and would open up when we closed on them. Maybe. But it didn't come.

On the verge of the camp, we were met by a maze of zigzag trenches, camouflaged with grass and shrub. Whoever had sited them had made a good job of it and they were well placed so they could not be detected from the air. As we cleared each outer ring of trench it became apparent that the camp was deserted. Where was all the gunfire we had expected? Where was the resistance?

An inspection of the camp revealed that the enemy had fled as soon as they heard the choppers. It was really apparent when we got to the buildings and the central commissariat. Evidence pointed towards a hurried departure when we found half-drunk cups of hot tea. I found and kept a nice Russian watch which had been left behind next to a bed. Another operator appropriated a Singer sewing machine for his girlfriend.

At the main HQ we found a combination safe which was locked. The maker's name, Chubb, revealed that it was Rhodesian, made in Salisbury. Warrant Officer II Charlie Krause wanted to search it for intelligence value and ordered us to carry the iron monstrosity to the LZ for uplift to Rhodesia. It proved far too heavy and he decided to blow it instead. Getting it out of the door was a task in itself, but we managed by rolling it on its sides. The WOII then went to work, packing the area of the locking mechanisms with a ribbon charge. This shaped charge is designed to cut through metal, but its effectiveness relies on knowing how thick the metal is. With the safe closed, it was impossible to gauge the door's depth, so an educated guess had to be made. We ignited the detonator and took cover. The results of the explosion showed that the WOII's assessment had been somewhat over-ambitious. When the dust and debris settled, it was still raining money. They were South African rand notes, but most of them were burnt or damaged by the explosion. Regardless, we gathered up the destroyed notes and bundled them into a plastic bag. I'm not sure what happened to them after our return to Rhodesia, but I have a sneaky suspicion that some of the operators tried to pass them off on their next holiday down south.

A further search revealed a couple of branch-covered Gaz trucks of Russian manufacture. The demolition experts went to work on those and blew them up also. One operator found a suitcase in a hut filled with marijuana cobs – so named because they were wrapped in maize leaves, each one about the size of a corn cob. There were about 500 of them after a quick count.

The commissariat was paid due attention and was destroyed with PE4. I still have photos of the before, during and after results, which appear in this book.

While we were in the middle of sifting through the camp, one of the early warning groups contacted us on the radio. A Zambian Army relief column was inbound on the main access road to check out the disturbance. WOII Krause ordered me to set up the mortar and give them something to think about. I moved to the edge of the camp with another operator and was about to fire my first bomb when he screamed at me to stop. Giving a sitrep, he was informed that the Bells were on their way back to deal with the Zambians. The 'blues' didn't want any ordnance flying through the air when they swept in on the strike.

After they had strafed the column, the choppers returned and we flew back across the Zambezi to the Victoria Falls airport with our contraband. The Zambians had suffered a few casualties in the aircraft strike and decided that discretion was the better part of valour.

In Peter Stiff's book *Selous Scouts, Top Secret War,* there is a picture of me running towards one of the choppers, with the 60nmm commando mortar on my pack. The picture was taken by my good mate Wally Insch. The photo also shows that I was carrying a bag containing a vehicle jack. I had discovered it in one of the Gaz trucks that were destroyed. I was down one jack in the Scouts MT section and I was going to get charged for it, so I commandeered the new one for a 25 Unimog. The guy in front of me is carrying a couple of suitcases. One of them was filled with the marijuana cobs and the other with the burnt money, and assorted spoils of war.

For all my trouble, my Russian watch lasted only a year.

Operation Dice was a bit of a let-down after I had regained my senses and sought something to fight for. I found what I was seeking, but the enemy would not entertain my passions and proved unenthusiastic about joining us in battle. The raid was not an entire loss. A great deal of intelligence was gained, which identified the whereabouts of SAANC guerrillas within Rhodesia. That aside, where else in the world could you go to war and within five minutes be back at one of the country's premier resort towns?

Recce Troop continued to be attached to Support Troop, an attachment which did nothing for our frayed moods. In defence of Support Troop, I don't think that they were too happy with the arrangement either, as we still suffered the legacy of Major Kriel when he had his nose so far up the colonel's arse.

In April 1979, Bishop Abel Muzorewa's party won the first integrated elections and Rhodesia became Zimbabwe-Rhodesia. The British Conservatives declared the elections free and fair, but international recognition for the new government was withheld.

The war continued in earnest and by the end of March all white males in the 60-65 age group became eligible for call-up. Later in the year the government appealed to the United States for recognition, but it was withheld also. More people died.

By June 1979 the first black dominated government was installed and still the USA and the international community turned down an immediate lifting of sanctions. It seemed as if it wasn't only the terrorists who wanted all or nothing.

By the time the Lancaster House Agreement came, everyone was squabbling over scraps: ZANLA were fighting ZIPRA, ZIPRA were fighting ZANLA and both nationalist movements were fighting the Security Forces… and so on and so on. More people died.

After Operation Dice, in September 1979, the Zambian government mobilised its country for full-scale war against Zimbabwe-Rhodesia. And yet more people died.

By late October 1979, after Sindi Plots, we had moved back to FAF 2 in Kariba. We continued to deploy recces and assault teams into Zambia, to counter the increasing incursions into the country. To the north and to the east, ZIPRA and ZANLA respectively were making their last stand. By this stage it was estimated that over 9,000 terrorists were inside Rhodesia's borders. A settlement agreement was approaching and both nationalist parties wanted to bolster their support in the Tribal Trust Lands. The end result – terrorists were pouring through the border!

The country had fought a courageous battle and was ostracised by the rest of the world. The 30,000-strong Rhodesian military was stretched thinly on the ground. When one bears in mind that any army is made up of over 80 per cent rear-echelon soldiers, then it's obvious that there very few who actually did the fighting. Despite a Herculean effort, the tide of war was changing and attrition was weakening Rhodesia's resolve.

I had toyed with the idea of returning to the Squadron once again but the prospect didn't really grab me. I was settling into a few beers one day, sitting at the round-table bar in Carribea Bay, one of Kariba's resorts, when I was made an offer I couldn't refuse. Special Branch was looking for experienced operators for ‘wet’ work.

‘Wet’ work described the type of operations that governments like to deny. There was much to be done to bolster the government’s standing in the upcoming settlement. Rhodesia’s hand needed to be turned to more devious tasks if there was to be any chance of survival.

A plot began to formulate in my mind. No longer was I the naive young man who arrived in Rhodesia so many years before. Through what I had seen and done, a temperament of resilience and solitude had developed within me. Whereas I thought I had already taken the gloves off, they were only half removed. Finally, I thought my hands would be free from the restrictive bounds of covering. Finally, I could throw down the gauntlet in front of my enemy and challenge him to battle – even if it was not entirely with the honour I would normally accord him.

CHAPTER 30:
INTO THE FIRE

Special Branch Callsign 24 was the designation of a top secret, elite group of ex-Special Forces operators, based on a smallholding at Helensvale in Salisbury. There were other similar callsigns, designated 25 at Borrowdale Police Station and so on. All of them fell under SALOPS (Salisbury Operations) conducting pseudo-operations and black ops, mostly in the outlying TTLs working closely with Police Ground Coverage.

I arrived at Helensvale in late October 1979 on attachment to Special Branch. At this late stage of the war, our main task was to determine how close the terrs were to Salisbury, and if they had effectively infiltrated and cowed the local population, many of whom were working in the environs of the capital city. Meanwhile, the number-crunchers were trying to estimate the outcome of probable elections.

My transfer was facilitated, after resigning on a month's notice from the Selous Scouts, but a small problem had arisen before I departed. When I checked out of Andre Rabie Barracks it was brought to my attention that another weapon was missing. This time it was a MAG and two liners of ammunition which were signed for by me at the armoury.

I had no intention of a repeat performance of my last days in the SAS and I resolved to get to the bottom of the issue. There was no denying the armourer's claim, as there it was in front me – form 1033 – an army-issue receipt voucher with what appeared to be my signature on it.

My attempts at recollection were futile and I was released to commence with Special Branch operations. Before I left I was told that an investigation would be launched into the matter and charges apportioned on the severity of the findings. Once again it looked as though I could be in serious trouble.

In the meantime, I was fined R$2,000 as a replacement fee for the weapon and this amount was docked from my army pension. Two thousand Rhodesian dollars was a lot of money in those days!

It was many years later after the transition of government that the facts became clear. A good friend had signed for the weapon, forging my signature, on behalf of Major Kriel when we were on a bush trip to Mount Darwin. Unbeknown to either of us, Major Kriel had lent it to a farmer in the Centenary area for protection. When my mate checked out from the Selous Scouts six months before my departure, he had asked me about the machine gun, something I had clearly forgotten. Quite innocently I told him that I knew nothing of it except that the major had it at Mount Darwin and he had left the country. Somehow my mate managed to escape the Selous Scouts unscathed, but left the problem to ambush me on my departure.

The enquiry was ongoing and Captain Devil offered his assistance in the form of a false statement. We conspired to say that the weapon was lost overboard during an operation on Lake Kariba. Some careful thinking precluded our plans, as we envisaged what trouble would reign if the machine gun actually pitched up one day – miraculously grew fins and rose from the murky depths. I had little choice but to accept the fine.

I saw the Selous Scout armourer, Bugs Marang, some time after the war and he told me that the farmer had eventually handed in the weapon. I tried to claim a reimbursement by going to the Selous Scout's (by this time Zimbabwe Parachute Battalion) pay and records office, but in vain. Army HQ couldn't give a rat's arse. So much for fair play!

Callsign 24 was made up of four ex-SAS members. I took over from Gary Lewis who had left the army for greener pastures. The callsign's commander was Ian Suttil. The others were Billy Grant, Jannie Meyer and me. Suttil, a former Royal Marine, was the unfortunate soul who was shot when entering a bunker at Rambanayi. He had already given the bunker the attention of a few grenades, but one of the occupants had lived through it and shot him several times in the backside. Suttil always had the luck of the damned. He was wounded several times during the war.

On pseudo-ops we deployed mainly to the Chiweshe TTL, where we would send in our black operators to the villages dressed like terrs. There, they tried to gauge the reaction of the locals. Not surprisingly, at this stage in the war, they were always welcomed, fed and given shelter. The terrorists had indeed infiltrated the very core of the masses, through some genuine support and a large amount of intimidation.

In all the TTLs there was a 6 pm-to-6 am curfew. This was in effect to dissuade civilians providing support to the terrorists, who moved around mainly after dark to escape Security Force patrols. There were severe penalties for fraternising with the terrs and we would often set up ambushes on likely routes in and out of the villages. Anyone seen after dark was dead meat.

I took to carrying the MAG again. If we did get into a contact I wanted the fire power. I ended up lugging the cumbersome weapon all over the place and it did a lot for my fitness, but the ambushes were all in vain.

KK was our sergeant, who led all the pseudo-operations into the villages. He had been in the BSAP, or associated with them, for most of his life and he was a veteran SB operative. Sometimes when KK and his callsign entered a village, they would run into genuine terrorists and receive the same treatment as they did. Often they would eat from the same bowl and share the same beer. KK was always wary of meeting the terrs, as he thought they might be Selous Scouts. Occasionally the terrs said the same thing about his callsign.

On one such incident in the Concession area, a pseudo callsign, led by KK, approached a village and asked for food. They ate their fill, entertained by the locals during the meal and said their goodbyes. On the way out, in view of and hearing distance of the village, we carried out a simulated ambush on them. The idea was to give the collaborators a scare and we entered the village at first light, acting as a normal Security Force patrol, to let them know how miffed we were. We told them that we had killed all the terrorists in our ambush and we knew that the villagers had fed them. We slapped the males around a bit, but it was nothing too serious and we sent them all off to the Concession police station to face charges. In view of the evidence they could hardly deny their collaboration with enemies of the state.

When they climbed into the back of the covered 25, they were shocked to find KK and the other operators sitting there with huge grins on their faces. Such was the surprise at finding their former comrades still alive that some of them began to wail praise at the divine. Their shock was even more evident when they discovered that they had been duped for so long.

KK headed off in one direction with our captives, while five of us, combining SB and BSAP callsigns, left for the farm on which we were staying. It would only take about 15 minutes in the armoured Land-Rover as it was no more than five kilometres away.

The whole operation had taken an hour, but unfortunately, while we were interrogating the villagers, the real terrorists had been watching us. Knowing full well that we would return the way we had come, they mined the road with a TMH46.

Pete Lawrence was driving when we rounded a bend and the front left wheel hit the mine. Fortunately, I was sitting in the back of the vehicle and I got blown clear, flying metres into the air and landing on one of my arms and on my knees. I didn't feel anything at the time but there was an instant hush around us as everything went silent. Through the haze and confusion I really didn't know what had hit me, but I felt like I might have felt the morning after a serious night out.

It seemed as if everything was in slow motion, as I crawled to the side of the road looking for the others around me. Huge clods of earth were raining down and the acrid sulphur of explosive was stinging my nostrils. I distinctly remember looking down the valley and watching a huge black cloud drifting away with the prevailing wind.

When I realised what had happened, my first instinct was to prepare for a follow-through ambush. Surprisingly I was still grasping my rifle in my left hand and I was trying to switch the safety catch to fire but struggling to do so. I couldn't feel my right hand but there was no other pain. I placed the rifle between my knees and fumbled with my good hand and was eventually successful.

When I looked up I could taste blood and grit in my mouth. The smoke had cleared and there were bodies lying everywhere. A high-pitched drone hummed in my ears. There was a huge crater from the explosion and the vehicle was lying next to it, half in and half out the hole. I got up to ascertain the damage.

Suttil was walking around in a confused state. He was holding his arm and there was blood and snot hanging out of his nose in huge balloons. Every time he breathed a big snot globule would expand from his nose like the bulbous throat of a croaking frog. From head to toe he was covered in thick black soot. He didn't have his weapon as it had been crushed in the blast. We would later discover that he had crushed ribs and a broken collar bone as well. He was lucky to have been in the back with me.

The three guys in the front were really messed up. Gerry Webster of the BSAP had two shattered legs. As I approached him I saw bones sticking out of his tattered flesh and uniform. He was in extreme pain and grimaced bravely. I comforted him for a few seconds before I reached Grant.

He was under the vehicle. He had somehow managed to switch places and the vehicle had landed on top of him. Pete Lawrence was unconscious and was lying in the road next to him. Both his eyes were bulging like obese cricket balls, swollen and purple. He was covered in blood and thick dark oil. All of us were black from the residue of the blast.

Being the least injured I quickly gathered my wits. In a futile attempt, I looked around for the jack to try and lift the vehicle off Grant. He was conscious and moaning. I couldn't find it so I went in search of a loose log to use as a lever, but couldn't find anything suitable. Eventually I called Suttil to the vehicle and got him to hold under the hood of the engine. I told Grant that on the count of three we would lift and he was to pull himself clear. I counted to three and Ian and I strained with our injuries, lifting the Land-Rover clear of Grant while he inched himself backwards. With every centimetre he gained his face contorted with enormous pain. He had a broken pelvis, broken ribs, and a broken arm and nose. Lucky the terrs didn't ambush us after the explosion. I had managed to keep my rifle without letting go of it once, except when we lifted the vehicle, but with the concussion I was feeling, I don't think I would have put up a defence.

While we waited for a casevac I had to give Grant a Sosegon jab so he wouldn't go into shock and also to help him with the pain. When I'd sucked the ampoule dry, I flicked the syringe before stabbing the needle through his skin. For some reason I couldn't depress the plunger so I had to use my left hand. I got it in eventually, but it was a clumsy, uncoordinated fumble. I was distressed that I was causing him more discomfort but I was not as distressed as he was. Despite his pain he still found the humour to ridicule my attempts at nursing him: 'C'mon Jake, surely you are used to jabbing things with your prick?' I didn't find it funny at the time.

'You should get more used to your left hand, Jake. You never know when you'll be unable to use your right.' His inference was phallic. While I was acting medic, a vehicle arrived from the farm. They had heard the explosion and came to investigate. Luckily they had a radio and called for the medivac.

When the chopper arrived I was left behind due to the less threatening nature of my injuries. The other lads were carried, or climbed aboard, the helicopter and lifted off. A team of medical staff arrived from Concession and a nurse came over to me where I was lying on the side of the road. She put a cigarette in my mouth and told me it would soothe my nerves. I tried to tell her that I didn't smoke but she was insistent so the cigarette just dangled from my lips.

I eventually got a lift to Ian Fleming Hospital in Salisbury. When I got there I discovered my wrist was broken, but that was the worst of my injuries. Apart from tinnitus and a few bruises I was well enough to go home.

Later that day I learnt that it took four men to lift the vehicle from the crater. I still don't know how two of us had managed to help our mate. I have since spoken to paramedics who told me of instances where in an emergency they had managed to summon incredible strength far beyond that of the people who were on the scene of an accident. It must have something to do with the adrenalin surge that comes with near-death encounters.

The day we hit the landmine was 22 December 1979 – three days before Christmas. On 21 December a settlement agreement had been signed between all the feuding parties in the Rhodesian war and a ceasefire had been declared. Across the country, over 22,000 ZANLA and ZIPRA terrorists had convened at assembly points and now they were in the country legally. In truth, the larger assembly points were bolstered with mujibas, young men who served as the eyes and ears of the terrorists, while the genuine ones roamed the country and kept a check on the tribal populace.

Rhodesia was to have her first internationally claimed free and fair elections and the country, in the interim, was once again under British rule.

Callsign 24 got three weeks' sick leave. Pete Lawrence was in a coma for a couple of weeks and suffered very mild brain damage. He would eventually recover fully. The rest of us nursed our wounds, with very little to do except drink beer and cope with our anxiety attacks.

It was a frustrating period, as we waited to learn the outcome of the impending elections. Mugabe, we were told, would never win even if it became necessary to use military force to hedge our bets. In the event of him winning, however remote a chance that might be, plans had been made which would be triggered by a secret code word to attack the assembly points and neutralise the enemy.

In Salisbury, the University of Rhodesia and other buildings which housed the terrorist hierarchy, would be assaulted by the SAS using tanks, armoured vehicles, 20 mm cannon, aircraft and a heavy weight of fire power. To the south our South African brothers secretly supported the *coup d'etat* and had intended to provide both soldiers, already serving in Rhodesia under the guise of Rhodesian troops, as well as aircraft based across the border.

Ian Suttil was recovering slowly, as was I and we both felt a great injustice had been done to us. Sure, we were as ready as the next soldier to accept the consequences of our chosen profession, but it somehow felt different when we knew we were on the losing side. We felt there was a global conspiracy against our fledgling nation.

The waiting did us little good, leaving plenty of time to dwell on the possibilities of failure. If Robert Mugabe did win the election, what then would all our commitment have been for? What would lie in store for us?

Suttil was really champing at the bit to get his revenge for the landmine incident, although I had my doubts as the end seemed so near. He kept on uttering things like 'revenge is sweet' and 'we'll get those bastards'.

Just before the Rhodesian people went to the polls, I found myself at a braai crying into my beer with other operatives of Callsign 24. The feelings among us that day were of despondency and anger. Everyone felt we had been sold down the river by the international community and possibly by our own leaders. We had seen first hand what the nationalists were capable of and we had experienced 'terrorism' before it became a popular euphemism.

To make matters worse, while the country awaited its sentence, everyone stayed at home fearing the worst. The usual mix of people who frequented our braais failed to turn up. The veneer of bravado was wearing thin. The tumbler of cognac was replaced with local beer in sanctions-ridden Rhodesia.

A few hours later, just when we were going to call it a day, Inspector X, our liaison officer at SALOPS, drove into the yard. He told us that he was looking after a contingent of South African Police who were monitoring one of the smaller assembly points near Dombashawa. The vast majority of us who served in the military felt a great deal of resentment towards the British, Australian, Fijian and other troops who made up the bulk of the monitoring forces. There were also British bobbies, complete with helmets, wandering around with milky-pale skins oblivious to what was actually going on. We felt sorry for them. I was often witness to the ridicule they came under when being scrutinised by both tough Rhodesian troops and terrorists in the final days of the war.

On his way in, Inspector X had driven past the assembly point and noticed a party was in full swing. ZANLA, it seemed, were already celebrating their victory before anyone had even voted. According to him they were drinking, dancing and playing drums. Of more concern, were reports that a particular gang of terrorists had reneged on the conditions of the ceasefire and were roaming the countryside in the Dombashawa area armed to the teeth. It was suspected that the armed gang was in cahoots with the guerrillas at the assembly point and were there to ensure the people voted their way.

Inspector X had reported his findings to his superiors and was ordered to do something about it. Given the sensitivity of the times, whatever it was had to be deniable, or at the very least justified, even if it meant getting our hands dirty. With the international spotlight on the country there was no room for an incident that might make the Rhodesians look guilty.

As we had no idea of where to begin our search, Suttil suggested we gate-crash the ZANLA party. If anyone knew anything about the armed gang it would be them. As trust between the feuding parties was on a knife edge, we could expect either a hostile reception or even full-on battle. The way we were feeling, it was just what the doctor ordered. Looking back I guess it was fear of the unknown that bred within us a desire to lash out. After all, the best form of defence is attack.

The collection of buildings that housed ZANLA, also on an old smallholding, was about five kilometres away from our own headquarters. It was already late in the afternoon and much planning had to be done. Suttil scanned the police sitreps for the day to ascertain any other intelligence that might be of value. Other than the original report, there were only a few references of noise and public nuisance that came from the assembly point.

We could expect ZANLA to have posted sentries and decided that the best approach would be at night. I knew that all of us were kind of hoping that the darkness would add to the confusion, that we would encounter an over-skittish guard who would panic and get the ball rolling. We were uncertain of what weapons were stored within the facility, but we knew there would certainly be some. We each equipped ourselves with our own choice of firearms in the event of things going wrong. I carried the MAG again and I doctored the belts of 7.62 mm ammunition with extra tracer. One ball round for every incendiary. I did this often as I knew the fear that tracer put into people. I fitted a hundred-round belt to the gun and carried an extra two belts in my webbing pouches. I also carried a few M962 grenades to clear rooms.

Suttil called for a briefing and we decided how to approach the entrance. In an eight-man extended file, combining another callsign, we would walk up to the main gate and engage the security detail. If all went well, we would tell them that we were a security force patrol investigating the sighting of the armed gang of guerrillas. Could we speak to the ranking officer or political commissar?

Failing that, if things didn't go well, we would already be in the thick of it and conversation wouldn't be necessary.

On our approach I would take the centre position with the gun. An RPG7 operator would take the extreme right and another with a 42 Zulu rifle grenade the left. If and when the shooting started, the heavy weapons would engage the most obvious targets like buildings or groups of terrorists and the formation would advance to contact under an umbrella of small-arms fire.

At precisely 07:00, we boarded the back of a Crocodile MPV and headed to Dombashawa. All eight operators wore standard Rhodesian uniforms and were outfitted like a fighting patrol. If anything gave away our true identity, it was the abundance of communist weapons and hand grenades. At a point about a kilometre from the assembly point, we debussed on the main road and after a quick Chinese parliament, ensuring everyone was ready, we approached the revelry. From our position the sound of drums could be heard echoing off the huge granite outcrops in the area.

My left hand ached under the heaviness of the gun but I dismissed the pain for the obvious advantage of the firepower it would give me. As the gap closed between the patrol and the assembly point the noise grew. In the distance we could make out a few lights flickering through the wind-swept branches of trees. The feelings of nervousness I had felt suddenly departed and were replaced with a determination to get on with the task.

About 200 metres from the facility Ian called a halt. We melted into the bush around us and conferred for one last time. Ian said he would conduct a close target reconnaissance and we were to wait for his return.

He was back 20 minutes later. From what he had seen there was only one sentry armed with an SKS rifle. He could only just make him out in the moonlight, but he appeared to be not too much of a problem as he was mingling with other ZANLA cadres in the yard. Our plan remained the same as it had been and we extended ourselves across the road, with me taking up the centre. On command, we advanced at a steady pace toward the objective. As we neared the assembly point more detail became clear. The party and the drums were sited to the left of the main building, and around the yard rubber bush and cactus formed a crude hedge.

Then, 40 metres from the objective, the darkness no longer cloaked us. On my right I heard Suttil mutter something like 'time to rock 'n roll' in his best American drawl. At 30 metres the sentry challenged us. We continued toward the gate and the next thing green tracer rounds cracked overhead. It was the only signal we needed. The jittery sentry did as expected and opened fire prematurely.

From the hip I let loose fully automatic fire into the densest area of human habitation. With the predominance of tracer ammunition, my fire looked like one long laser beam, as its initial impact chipped away at the building's walls before drawing into the seething mass.

To the right, as I fired, I was faintly aware of the whoosh of the RPG7 as it engaged. The trailing smoke of the rocket entered my peripheral vision and it exploded satisfyingly with a thud against the closest wall. The 42 Zulu emitted a dull crump from my left, barely audible over the combined racket of small arms and machine-gun fire. Tracer arced and crisscrossed all over the show as the rifle grenade detonated to the left of the structure.

We were through the gates before we knew it and ZANLA were running everywhere. Many ran straight into the building but others saw their chance of escape and legged it to the back of the yard. I watched as one group ran through the cactus as if it wasn't there.

I dropped to the ground and fired short bursts. My machine-gun fire followed targets into the main facility, where I noticed tracer rounds emanating from the windows. Someone was putting up a fight. The smoke from the RPG7 inhibited our view but it soon cleared. The red tracer was stark among the green as it shot off at right angles to the walls and burnt out in the ground or high in the air. The fear had left me. I became acutely aware of the small things happening around me, like individual tracer rounds spinning out on the polished terracotta floor of the building's veranda, dancing like demons at some ritualistic sacrifice. I changed belts. A hundred rounds had gone in a minute.

We advanced again and started to clear the building. Through the glass of the windows, those that remained intact, I could see that all the rooms were inhabited. Jannie Meyer ran past me and called for me to cover him. With his back against the wall he systematically edged to each window and tossed a grenade in. The grenades detonated with a subdued crump amidst the screams of terrified terrorists. The lights faltered. Of those who lived through the explosions all I could see was the whites of their terrified eyes and the glint of teeth from mouths agape in horror.

It was very much a one-sided affair but the terrorists had initiated contact. I wonder now what his brothers might have done to him, if the sentry who opened fire had lived through the carnage; if they knew that the terror that beset them was the result of those first few rounds he had fired. It was what we wanted anyway.

It's hard to describe the end of a battle because it just ends. I think, when the adrenalin flow slows you become more aware of what's happening around you. You become human again after the automatic responses of training.

Just for good measure Suttil scattered a few AKs around the rooms to supplement those weapons that were already there. They were unregistered weapons and had been captured in a previous contact. He fired them with gloved hands through the windows and into the ceiling so it would look like the terrorists had fought back bravely. In one of the rooms we found sets of webbing, an AK and a PPSH sub-machine gun.

Inspector X called us on the radio to see what the noise was about. Suttil told him to wait-out as a contact was in progress. When he arrived 10 minutes later he was told that we had come under fire while searching for the group of armed terrorists. Suttil wasn't lying. A group from the SAP monitoring contingent had accompanied Inspector X and they checked through the buildings. I saw one young policeman vomit uncontrollably when he entered a room and saw the floor awash with blood and body parts. The wounded lay screaming everywhere. The South Africans were inexperienced then and for many their troubles were yet to begin.

The majority of terrorists had managed to escape. They were on the run in the granite countryside of Dombashawa. I'm sure many of them never turned up again until after the elections. To them it must have seemed that our attack was the beginning of the Rhodesians' devious plan to eliminate the entire enemy.

There were seven dead bodies that we accounted for among the numerous wounded. We left the carnage for the South Africans to deal with, but on the way back to Helensvale, we were stopped by a BSAP roadblock. The policemen manning it didn't seem happy with the situation.

Suttil told them that we had just come from the contact area and gave them a situation report. If they had any queries they were to report to Inspector X at SALOPS.

At the farmhouse we had a drink and celebrated our revenge. It appeared that all among us were ecstatic with the night's success. I do recall having a sense of foreboding. It wasn't at the forefront of what I was feeling but it was definitely there. Outside it was cold, unusually so for the time of year. A cold front had crept in from South Africa and was making things quite miserable. I could deal with the elements outside, but it was the coldness within that bothered me most. My feelings worried me intensely. Maybe I was becoming soft.

I fully understood the need for operations of a deniable nature. The bleeding-heart liberals will scream 'murder' and 'savage'. I couldn't quite grasp what we had achieved other than satisfying our own craving for retribution. It was only the next day that I began to wonder if the operation at Dombashawa had been sanctioned at a higher level at all.

Arriving at Central Police station, SALOPS HQ, the member-in-charge, Inspector Luca, was not impressed. He made it clear that he was not convinced about the facts of our story. Inspector X came under the spotlight too. He was crapped on from a dizzy height and allegations were levelled against him for conducting his own private war. Inspector Luca ended up by stating that he hoped he didn't discover that the operation was the making of an Inspector X 'Metro Goldwyn Meyer' production. If he did, we would all be charged accordingly. Maybe it was for show, but it left me with many nagging doubts. There is much to be said for conducting operations under the sanction of an organisation or government – as opposed to independent action. When an institution is behind you, its kind of justifies things however bloody or borderline legal they may be. I wasn't used to this sort of operation. It nagged me that I might have been involved in unlawful actions. Actions I could end up in jail for.

Ian Suttil was on a high the following day. He had 'killing fever' and was planning the next operation. On Enterprise Road, in the Newlands suburb of Salisbury, just where it meets Glenara Avenue, another assembly point existed where higher-ranking ZANLA personnel were housed. Suttil's plan called for two roadblocks to be set up in broad daylight on either side of the complex, in the event that the police might respond to an attack and come to ZANLA's rescue. In an operation that was estimated to last 10 minutes, we would drive through the front gate and slaughter everyone in the building.

The foreboding I felt began to chew at me. The nagging doubts hadn't left and I wondered if Suttil hadn't seen just a bit too much action in his lifetime. Was this an act of vengeance? Was Dombashawa the same? I was really concerned when his plan placed me at one of the roadblocks with a MAG and he told me that if the police did intervene, then I was to deal with them as well. Now we would be killing people from our own side!

Maybe I had seen a bit too much action myself because I began to panic and tried to think of a way out of it. I didn't want the rest of the team to think I was gutless but the operation didn't sit well with me. Fortunately, Inspector X called the whole thing off. After his last bollocking I think he felt he might not get away with it. Thank God for small mercies!

I've always wondered what we were doing back then and have since sought justification for my actions. Many people, even those I spoke to, who were privy to Rhodesia's last desperate throes, knew nothing of Callsign 24, let alone what we got up to. I think the answers are lost now and died with those who knew them. All records of events were smuggled out of the country, or were shredded or burnt before the new government came to power.

At 09:00 on 4 March 1980 it was announced that Robert Mugabe had won a landslide victory in the elections. Of the 100 seats in Parliament he had taken 57 and his victory was absolute. The unimaginable had come to pass. Mugabe was to become the first black prime minister of an independent Zimbabwe. Rhodesia was no more.

Callsign 24 waited unawares at the farm for the return of its commander. When Suttil raced into the yard from the briefing he had just attended, he told us to arm ourselves and prepare for the biggest battle of our lives. I can't remember his exact words but his speech was both motivating and stirring. Since that time, I have watched the Hollywood movie *Independence Day* starring Will Smith several times. Bill Pullman, the character who plays the part of the president of the United States, gives a motivating speech when the nation is faced with the wrath of alien invasion.

'We will not go quietly into the night' he says. 'We will not vanish without a fight. We're going to live on. We're going to survive. Today we celebrate our Independence Day.'

Suttil's speech wasn't quite like that, but it had the same effect. We psyched ourselves up and prepared to sacrifice all we had for our cause. We prepared to sacrifice our lives if necessary. At the farmhouse, we were to wait for instructions from Inspector X. If ZANU did win the election we were then to go on the rampage hitting predetermined ZANLA assembly points. If we ran into ZANLA in the streets while they celebrated, we were to take them out. It would be the biggest coup of the war and a final thrust that would render ZANU useless.

The waiting was the worst part of it. Dressed in civilian clothes and armed to the teeth, we boarded a couple of civvy-registered cars and headed into town. The announcement of the results was approaching and we wanted to be correctly placed when the news broke.

We were all hyped up for the killing spree, but I must say that Suttil was particularly so. If I didn't know better then I would have thought he was wishing for a ZANU victory just so he could get on with it.

The instruction never came. When we tuned into the news service it was to learn that the war was over. Emptiness filled the pit of my stomach and a strange numbness crept over me. Ian was furious and ordered us to drive the town looking for trouble. Maybe we had been left out of the loop and Inspector X had forgotten about us. With the shock of the election results it was highly probable.

We drove through Salisbury and found all was quiet. The suburbs were like a ghost town and no-one stirred. Inside the flats and houses we drove past, many people were packing, scared of the uncertainty ahead. I drove past my own place and wondered what Sheila was doing inside.

The fear that filled the community suddenly hit us and we pulled over on King George Road in Avondale. It was utter disbelief that reigned among the white community that day. There was a lot of disbelief among many of the blacks too.

When we gathered ourselves together and collected our wits, we headed for the Beefeater Pub in Strathaven. At the pity-party, other servicemen sat in their uniforms looking subdued. Blank expressions were common on faces. Some groups huddled around tables speculating as to what had gone wrong. Others made plans and encouraged each other that the word was still going to come. It was just a delay, they thought. Something was bound to happen! This couldn't be the end!

I found myself weeping into a beer again. Pete Lawrence, Jannie Meyer, Ian Suttil and I were too numbed to speak. For Suttil and me it was the end of the world. We were both professional soldiers who had developed a passion for the cause we fought. Fighting was all we knew. For eleven years I had been involved in constant action and there was little else for me to do. Would the terrs seek revenge? Were our families and loved ones safe? Would we have to leave the country? These and a thousand other questions raced through my mind.

A few beers later we had resolved to look out for each other. Our fear was replaced with anger. If the terrs got out of hand we would stick together like a band of brothers.

CHAPTER 31:
ARMS TO REST

Rhodesia's death was a quiet affair, easily forgotten by those who didn't want to remember the country. Before the war ended and after it, a slow attrition would creep in and drain the country of valuable white manpower. It would take many years for the problem to be recognised, but at first the new Zimbabwe survived on the remnants of a thriving sanctions-induced economy.

The flight of whites from the country, not a new occurrence but rapidly speeded up, was appropriately christened 'the chicken run'. It applied to those who didn't want to fight and who fled to places like South Africa and Britain on flimsy excuses such as having to further their education, or because it wasn't their war. They left behind a tribe of white Africans – people who had nowhere else to go and even if they had, wouldn't go anyway.

After the war, those who stayed behind remained disillusioned for quite some time. Men who served in units like the SAS and the RLI would eventually be afforded disbandment parades and thereby marched into the annals of history.

The Selous Scouts, the single most serious hindrance to the enemy and one which had struck fear into its very core, was accorded no such honour and its members scattered to the four corners of the world. It was to be the same for Callsign 24.

Many moved south and joined the military there. The South Africans welcomed them with open arms, but of course, they had ulterior motives. The wealth of experience the Rhodesians had gained in counter-insurgency warfare would serve them well. South Africa's own war was heating up in South West Africa (Namibia) and in Angola, presenting an opportunity that couldn't be missed.

For the black operators, their time was drawing to an end and they were sold out by neighbours seeking political favour with the new regime. Many disappeared.

Two weeks after independence, Callsign 24 had no home. Ian Suttil, Pete

Lawrence, Jannie Meyer and I joined the flight of frightened Rhodesians and travelled south. For the time being we left our families in Salisbury. Once we were in South Africa we would send for them. For the moment at least they were safe.

The country looked no different during our quiet drive from Salisbury to Beitbridge. We left the capital city amid a bustle of morning trade and it seemed as if nothing had changed. Outside the city the lush African bush, blooming from the recent rainfall, changed into the rolling greenery of thriving farms, petering out before Fort Victoria. I wondered how long they would remain that way.

After passing Fort Victoria, the traveller is rewarded with stunning sights of the most beautiful area in the country; sights that are purely Africa. The vantage point that the winding roads offer around Lundi, Rutenga and Bubye River are a vista to behold, particularly during the rainy season. I felt heartsore on that trip and didn't expect to see those areas again.

Arriving in Pretoria, we went straight to the South African Police HQ and offered our services as a SWAT team. The 'Slopes' weren't interested in what we had to say, but instead offered us positions as combat instructors. We couldn't believe it. Here we were willing to get our hands dirty; a highly trained team of special forces soldiers raring to go and they nipped our offers in the bud.

Two weeks after that, on 25 January 1980, there was an armed robbery at the Volkskas Bank in Silverton, Pretoria. A three-man team from Umkhonto we Sizwe, the ANC's military wing, stormed the bank with AK-47s and grenades and took 25 civilians' hostage. They then demanded the release of Nelson Mandela and other ANC activists from prison. To make sure the authorities knew they meant business, they executed a young, white, female teller. Sadly, the SAP had no means of dealing with it, having only just formed a SWAT-type equivalent called Task Force. They rushed the bank and managed to neutralise all three terrorists, but not before one of them had thrown a grenade which killed another civilian and injured eleven more.

It was a sad event, considering the SAP could have retained our services with as little as a warm smile. We weren't rampant killers or mercenaries seeking huge fortunes. We were highly professional soldiers and the orphans of a forgotten war. Our weapons were already in South Africa thanks to a quickly brokered deal and had been smuggled into the country in the SAP vehicles that were being used to monitor the assembly points. They were sitting right under our noses at the police-dog section in Pretoria. All it would have taken was a call.

When we finally collected our weapons we had little use for them. I gave mine to a mate, an ex-Rhodesian who lived in Pretoria. It was a fair cache he received that day: two AK-M rifles, thousands of rounds of ammo, pistols and webbing.

When I returned to Zimbabwe some weeks later I found myself in a very reflective mood. My time in the military had been the highlight of my life, not all good but certainly encompassing a greater splattering of adventure than I could have hoped for. An instructor job in the SAP would be a huge anti-climax to the excitement of the past and was not quite what I had in mind. Being in action, I imagine, is much the same as making money. The more you have the more you want.

As it happened, the SAP could not accept our services. They didn't want us because we had not been official members of the BSAP. Our own police force had abandoned people such as ourselves, as they didn't want to be part of any political finger-pointing. Blame had to be laid somewhere and they made sure it wasn't going to be laid on them.

Ian Suttil and the rest of Callsign 24 joined the SAS again. The unit had not yet disbanded and rumour had it that the South Africans were building a new base at Schiettocht farm in Phalaborwa, specifically for the Rhodesians. 5 Reconnaissance Commando would absorb the former Selous Scouts at Schiettocht, while the former SAS members would travel to Durban and join 1 Reconnaissance Commando at the Bluff. Once there, they would become 6 Reconnaissance Commando. I originally was going to make the move but I had my doubts.

It was Sheila who made up my mind for me. She told me to stop playing soldier, hang up my guns and get a real job. As she saw it, it was the only way to save our marriage. Her comment caught me unawares, but I could see how sick to death she was at my constant absence. I didn't want another RT incident happening simply because I was never at home. It was time to compromise. I had no other skills except those I had learnt in the military and there was no longer any scope for killing. I turned to photography as a means to an end.

I sought an interview with Johnny Gibson, my last boss in Police Ground Coverage. He was still working in Special Branch and I asked if there was any work for me. His initial response was not encouraging and left me feeling rather inadequate. In his words, what could I do besides kill people and blow shit up?

Could I drive a typewriter? No.

Did I have the necessary investigative skills to conform to civilian police work? No.

It seemed that all doors were closed.

As a last resort I mentioned that I had trained in Northern Ireland as a covert photographer with the Parachute Regiment. Could they use me in that field?

It must have been one of those small mercies again. Gibson told me that in the 'morning prayers' (their jocular expression for morning meetings) it had been mentioned that they needed a photographer at E Desk. All SB work in the photographic field was still being conducted by the CID. It was time for independence, autonomy and a degree of privacy. He told me he would speak to Geoff Price, member-in-charge of E Desk, Counter-Intelligence Division and get back to me the following morning.

I waited until lunchtime the next day, before my impatience got the better of me. When I finally got through to him I was asked to bring evidence of my previous work in the Paras, in the form of photographs, to back up my claim. An interview was set up with Geoff Price and I got the job.

Initially I would be employed as a research officer in SB as I was technically a civilian. My pay and expenses would come from a slush fund that had been set up to service others working in a similar capacity. I would operate from Central Police Station at CID studios. I would be supplied with cameras and film and would have a darkroom. Counter-Intelligence was across the road in Daventry House on Station Road**.** E Desk occupied the whole top floor of the building.

I was over the moon. Of course I didn't know quite what to expect, but it seemed like a happy compromise to me. Other than small irregularities, it would be an 8-to-5 job, allowing for more time with the family. Suddenly I felt I might be able to work with the new regime. I didn't agree with them, but reconciliation was the popular word of the day and I thought I might just fit in.

I contacted Ian Suttil and told him my news. He, Pete and Jannie had news of their own and had just received word that their departure to South Africa was imminent. At the end of February 1980, they would travel south where they would be absorbed into the ranks of 1 Reconnaissance Commando.

I sensed Ian was a bit nervous about the move. I couldn't figure out why, as there were a hundred other operators joining him. There is always safety in numbers. Only later did I realise that Ian was one of the unfortunate victims of the war. Like many others, he had become detached from society. His battle was not against an enemy, it was against himself.

Ian never got to see his first year through with the South Africans. He was killed in action in Mozambique less than a year later. On the 29 January 1981, during a night attack against ANC targets in the Matola suburb of Maputo, Ian was one of four casualties who died when a grenade detonated prematurely. Poor Ian – after being shot seven times and blown up almost as many, his luck finally ran out.

I've often thought about Ian's death and it struck a chord. Maybe it was my own demons playing up – the old man of the Zambezi, the even older man of Mozambique or the souls of Dombashawa – but I saw reparation in his dying. I don't know what kind of ghosts haunted Ian, but I wondered if mine would one day play out some vengeful act against me. I hoped, if they did, it would be quick.

Special Branch was made up of several desks. The Counter-Intelligence Division was one of them and was itself broken down into several more desks. There were specialty desks and desks for all the countries that Zimbabwe might have a beef with. There were even desks for those countries that enjoyed good relations with the government.

Ostensibly, for the first few years after independence, SB pursued a continuation of Rhodesian policy and objectives. For the first six months after independence, the division continued pursuing the same tasks with impunity that had been allotted to it by the former regime. It was as if there hadn't been a change of power at all. Certainly, with what I know now, the South African National Intelligence Service, or another of similar ilk, might as well have just set up shop slap-bang in the middle of Salisbury. Such was the confusion that reigned and the nature of tasks assigned to us, that I was often clueless as to why I was conducting certain operations. Until the new order stepped in, that is.

I ended up in Special Projects, E Desk, under the guidance of Ian Harries and Alan Bailey. Special Projects had several research officers attached to them from civilian occupations. They were all paid from 'slush funds' allocated to the particular department they worked for.

Research officers were in a different league to what paid informants might be in a police force. They were paid agents and were 'totally off the record'. They were people who were recruited by the organisation, in view of the positions they held in commercial society. It made sense to recruit people from where they work rather than go through the rigmarole of placing them there.

CI Division had well-placed people at the airports and at the post offices. The Central Post Office was manned by two research officers who worked at the sorting tables. There they were able to go through all the mail, while keeping a tab on listed targets. When they found a letter or parcel addressed to a target, they would surreptitiously open it, inspect its contents and possibly photocopy it. If they couldn't satisfactorily seal the package without raising suspicion, they would use Customs tape to make the breach look official.

There was Zimbabwean Customs tape, Her Majesties' Customs tape, Customs tape from China, Japan, Libya, Peru, the USA and Timbuktu. If you wanted Customs tape, CI Division had it. Thus, if suspicion was aroused, the breach could be attributed to some foreign post office or Customs service.

When I arrived, the two research officers at the Central Post Office had the best porno collection in the country. I know because I saw it. Porn going missing wasn't likely to raise eyebrows as it was illegal anyway. I can hardly imagine a complaint being filed by a civilian who had lost the latest video of *Debbie does Dallas*! However, one of the research officers was later relieved of his post in disgrace after a trap was set for him. Complaints had been filed of missing money and jewellery and the sticky-fingered culprit was eventually nabbed.

Special Projects Section covered a wide field of jobs in the division, ranging through surveillance, counter-surveillance, infiltration, electronic bugging and photographing targets. We liaised closely with most intelligence organisations in other countries and would often work together assisting one another on important operations.

It was a 'you scratch my back, I'll scratch yours' sort of deal, but there were always ulterior motives. Most CI operatives become well versed in the art of diplomacy. Retaining a warm welcoming smile, giving away all but nothing, was the way we operated.

My first introduction to Special Projects was covert photography work of mediocre intelligence value. I was assigned to tail people in the Bat Mobile. This was the organisation's version of the American Dodge van, so often seen in movies featuring the CIA or FBI. Ours wasn't as lavish, being a humble VW Combi, but it did have the smoked-glass windows. They afforded perfect cover for close-up shots.

All I had to do for good results, was upgrade my film in the lab and learn how to take photos with great speed and focus. Inside the Bat Mobile there were chairs, a desk and banks of battery chargers for the surveillance teams to use when mobile.

Our surveillance team consisted of 14 black footmen, SB operatives, who worked hand in hand with the VW mobile station. Their task was exclusively surveillance and they would tail targets on foot in teams. When one operative dropped the beat, he would signal another to take over. In effect, we could observe our targets 100 per cent of the time while they were on foot. If they hopped into a car and drove away, the Bat Mobile would take over or call in other mobile surveillance.

Skilled personnel from other professions were available to us as well. On the CI Division's payroll there were locksmiths, estate agents and hotel managers. Practically all walks of life were represented. There were teams of reservists who did call-ups in SB and were available at a moment's notice to do surveillance, using their own vehicles. Most of them were established businessmen or were members of senior management, allowing them to move around freely without let or hindrance from bosses and the like. They got a mileage allowance in addition to the cash sweetener they were paid and plenty of petrol vouchers to boot.

The reservists were never too popular among the permanent staff in SB. To us they were 'jam stealers' who never had to leave the comfort of Salisbury for bush trips. There were a few cowboys among this lot, sporting some mean firepower. One chap I knew carried an original Thompson sub-machine gun complete with drum magazines in the boot of his car!

Naturally, in order to fit in, there were more than a few women working for the organisation as well, some of them lookers. I had three lasses working on the same desk as me, which was an entirely new experience. Having been in the army my whole life, I had never worked with women before, so it was very exciting. One of them in particular was a real corker and among the guys she had the nickname of CSL. I won't attempt to offend by spelling it out; suffice to say we were lucky she never found out what it stood for. We'll just call her Kristy. If Sheila ever knew I worked with her, there would have been hell to pay. She knew me so well around beautiful women.

One of the first jobs I did was to photograph a certain Cuban gentleman, who was of great interest to our CIA American liaison. He had travelled to Zimbabwe alone and was looking for accommodation for the Cuban diplomatic corps, who would arrive later in the year. It had come to our attention that he was out to buy houses for the embassy and for its staff. After independence there was a sudden surge of diplomats from nations who had supported ZANLA during the struggle. Apart from the Cubans, there were North Koreans, Libyans, Chinese, Russians and many diplomats from the Arab states. It was a rosy posting for them. They could swagger about, making everyone believe they were the deliverers of peace and justice. The men would leave their wives at home and seek sexual favours from black prostitutes in the cities.

This particular Cuban gentleman was wanted for the murder of an American citizen some time back. Our primary task was to identify him and make sure, via shared information, that he was indeed the right guy.

One of our reservists was an estate agent from a large business in Salisbury. Kristy was assigned to him and they approached the Cuban for business, handing out cards that were both official and unofficial. The Cuban took the bait immediately, no doubt due to Kristy, who wore a tight low-cut dress, sported fantastic boobs, gorgeous legs and was irresistible. She had absolutely everything going for her, including an affable character and big inviting 'come to bed with me' eyes. Just the smell of her perfume drove men wild, but she always maintained an air of mystery. Even when her doe-like eyes beckoned you on, you somehow knew that she wasn't that easy a fish to land.

Our Cuban was booked in at the Meikles Hotel, where the introduction was made. It seemed plausible that estate agents would look for business at hotels in view of the recent influx of diplomats to the country. Over the next few days, Kristy met him at the hotel with the reservist and they drove all over town looking at properties. On his third day he was to attend a meeting with 'The Party' at Milton Buildings. 'The Party' was the name for the new government that had taken over the reins.

We were not sure of the time of the meeting, so Alan Bailey assigned Kristy and me to the Bat Mobile and we parked outside the hotel.

Other than the reservist, Kristy was the only one who could identify him at that stage, so she had to be eyes on. When the subject left the building I would photograph his every move and, I hoped, capture images of who he met and where he went.

Kristy and I sat in the vehicle outside the hotel from 08:30 onwards. Being in such close confines with her drove me crazy and it was difficult to focus on the task at hand. She kept crossing her legs and squashing her huge boobs against the desk when she leaned over to speak to me. By lunchtime I was a dribbling wreck and I had to leave the van for a breather.

The subject failed to show himself and we called off the operation. We found out later that he had changed his plans and was to meet 'The Party' the next day. Naturally, we were there the following morning and I was once again subjected to Kristy's magnetic charms. I soon got to the point where I couldn't control myself.

We built up a good rapport between us during that time.

Once again the Cuban evaded us and we dropped everything for more pressing matters. On the third day into the surveillance, we got worried. A few of our footmen had been placed around the hotel and we had deployed the other two women from E Desk, scantily dressed. Having covered all angles we still came up with plum.

An informer in the hotel told us that 'The Party' had collected the subject and they had departed via the back service entrance. It was suggested that he may have been informed of our presence. Or he may have merely decided to be careful.

When we got back to the office, the other two lasses asked what Kristy and I had been doing in the Bat Mobile the whole time. We never let on, preferring to leave it to their imaginations.

The rapidly disintegrating situation called for a new plan of action. That night I took Sheila to the Meikles Hotel for a drink. We entered the lounge and sat at a table where I could face the lift entrance. Sheila sat in front of me, which strategically placed her in the direct line of sight. I had my camera and hoped to catch the Cuban meeting Kristy for dinner: Kristy had contacted him and suggested they celebrate the purchase of the embassy property over a meal in the lounge.

If I was seen taking photographs I was sure I would look like a tourist, happily snapping away at my wife or possibly my girlfriend. It was a hard task to set everything up correctly without informing Sheila of my ulterior motive. Sheila wasn't stupid and picked up immediately that my attention was not entirely upon her. Unfortunately, she thought I was perusing other women and jumped to conclusions.

It wasn't long before the target showed up on the arm of Kristy, who led him past our table. However, the lounge was popular that night and I couldn't get a clear shot without giving the game away.

As Kristy walked past, Sheila leaned into me, a look of distaste on her face. 'Did you see that blonde woman walk by? She looked like a hooker!'

I'm sure my face flushed bright red. If only she knew that I had been locked up in the back of a vehicle with her for three days!

'No, darling. Which woman are you referring to?' I lied.

I knew that if Sheila ever saw Kristy again I would be waist-deep in shit. There's no doubt she would put two and two together and come up with four.

I felt as if I had failed my mission that night. It was the easiest thing in the world for me to take photos, something I was clearly good at. But the Cuban was proving elusive.

The next evening Alan Bailey and I did a 'wet job' on the Cuban's room in the hotel. He had left for dinner with 'The Party' and our footmen let us know that he was under surveillance. Kristy was downstairs in the lounge once again, with some fabricated last-minute paper work to seal the embassy deal. She would waylay him and warn us if he came back and we took the opportunity to sticky-beak his belongings.

In time I would become a real pro at 'wet jobs'. I was issued with a Polaroid camera which I used when I first entered a room. Once we had breached the door I would take a step inside and photograph the room across a 180-degree arc. Then I'd take another step and do the same thing. I would photograph ornaments on furniture, suitcases where they lay on the floor or inside cupboards and clothing that had been left on a bed. This ensured reference to instant images of the surrounds so as to leave everything as we found it. Crafty subjects would often leave traps.

As mentioned, CI Division had well-placed people everywhere. The hotel management, who were on retainer, provided us with keys and we had duplicates made for every room in every hotel in the country. It was a whack of keys but we only carried the ones we needed, after being provided with the relevant room numbers.

We successfully turned out the Cuban's room and I managed to take pictures of all the paperwork that lay about. Alan scrimmaged through his belongings and we left the room as we found it.

I never did find out the outcome of that operation. We furnished our liaison at the CIA with copies of the pictures and filed our own for reference.

The Cuban left Zimbabwe sometime later and we expected his return. Sources in the travel industry provided us with his entire itinerary. But he never did come back – and our CIA buddies weren't letting on either.

CHAPTER 32:
BREACH

There was more work to do on the Cubans before they moved into the plush residence that was to become their official embassy in the suburb of Belgravia. Time was short, with only a month before the embassy was fully operational and our CIA liaison had vested interests in its establishment. A meeting was convened with the Americans, and CI Division had to formulate a plan to infiltrate the residence and set up some sort of listening device. We had to move fast, to which end the American embassy expedited the arrival of a CIA team to work closely with us. After several joint night reconnaissances the operation was given the go-ahead and we sat down to work out a plan. I was assigned two CIA operatives who would carry out the task and was briefed to provide any necessary assistance.

Fortunately the building was empty. Nevertheless we utilised our surveillance assets to keep a tab on all the Cuban staff should they stumble upon us while we were at work. The staff were watched 24 hours a day and their movements recorded.

Once we were satisfied that we would not be disturbed, we entered the house late one night, where we spent hours mulling over our plan. It wasn't as simple as it may seem, as primarily we had to make an educated guess as to where the Cubans would site their offices. We had to establish where they would put the ops room, the communications room, the ambassador's office and the staff offices. My job entailed photographing every room and even the attic for future reference, so that we could strategise back at Daventry with our co-workers.

After careful deliberation, it was decided to put in two listening devices. One would be hidden in the lounge, which we thought the Cubans would use as a main office and the other would be concealed in the rafters above a room which we guessed would be used as the comms room. Each device would consist of a microphone, battery and aerial wire rat-tail, which could pick up conversations and then relay them to a listening post (LP) on which a transcriber was waiting.

The devices had to be disguised carefully, so as not to alert a vigilant staff member or security officer.

I began to learn the fine art of communications espionage from the masters. What I had already learned as a covert photographer stood me in good stead with my CIA counterparts and we worked well together. After photographing the wooden rafters, we spent a morning in town procuring identical wood from a DIY supplier in the industrial area. We were careful to match the grain and colour precisely and bought several beams.

Back at the embassy we made a perfect match of one beam to a rafter, hollowing it out to conceal the microphone and battery. From the base of the hollow, we drilled through to the outside of the beam, creating a minute tunnel for the rat-tail. Once the device was in place, the hollow was sealed over with wood of the same grain and colour. The beam was meticulously crafted into place, where it became part of the building's structure. The only thing that could be seen, when looking up, was a tiny pin-prick that wouldn't be noticed even to an observant eye. The other device was also set into wood, this time a length of heavy mahogany, which replaced the mantle on the fireplace in the lounge.

A couple of evenings on the trot were spent infiltrating the embassy to fit the mantle in place, each time ensuring that when we left, our unfinished work would not attract the eye of one of the embassy's own security personnel. The fireplace job was a masterpiece, with careful cementing and plastering concealing any signs of recent work. The paint to cover the job was mixed as an odourless concoction by one of our reservists in the paint industry. The final touch came on our last breach of the residence, when we sprayed attic dust in the loft to hide any signs of our presence. The dust I had hoovered out of my own attic at home. It was sprayed on using a modified bellows-type device.

The whole operation really was an eyeopener for me and raised my awareness a notch on the learning curve. The equipment was tested and worked beyond our wildest dreams. The LP was established at another CI Division member's house a few hundred metres away from the embassy and the devices were fitted with remote on/off switches to conserve battery life.

It was a great success for many years, until one of the bugs was compromised. An operative by the name of Doug, who had been privy to the operation, left on an intelligence course to Havana, with our Cuban counterpart, for a year. While he was there the bug was discovered. Strangely, the Cubans knew exactly where to find it and one of their representatives marched into the CIO HQ one day with the transmitter in his hand. It was an embarrassing situation, to say the least, but the source of the leak was left unchecked.

As member-in-charge of E Desk, Geoff Price expanded my duties. When I wasn't on surveillance I was working in the office under Alan Bailey, doing research work on subjects who had entered the country illegally. These were normally diplomatic people, who had taken advantage of their immunity status. We were concerned that some may have something to hide. It was our responsibility to investigate all facets of their lives, both inside Zimbabwe and out, utilising the services of our foreign liaison if necessary.

When it came down to it, I was supposed to know what my subjects ate for breakfast, their daily habits, who they met, their relationship to these people and sometimes even their bowel movements. This might entail phoning all the hotels to find out their whereabouts, or using the division's human assets to provide information for us.

Most of the work we did was called illegal work. Illegal work was exactly that and entailed breaking into cars, houses and hotel rooms in order to glean information on a subject. When necessary, we would stage the break-in to look like a petty theft, or something of a criminal nature. I guess it was one of the perks of the job. None of us complained when we were able to seize valuable trinkets in the name of national security!

I was thoroughly briefed that under no circumstances should I be caught. There was little recourse for error but I was informed that, in the event of being arrested by the police, I was to go with the flow, revealing nothing of my status and it would be dealt with.

I had to be careful. Diplomats and certain other people carried guns and would not hesitate to shoot if I was found fiddling in their affairs.

I was asked if I had an unlicensed weapon. One would think Division would supply one, but I had a Tokarev pistol that I had taken off a dead terr during the war. Geoff Price told me to keep it and to carry it on all my assignments as I might have to use it. If it was used, I was to dispose of it in a lake, or bury it and hope there would be no trace. It was a virtual licence to kill, but it was disguised with careful rhetoric.

In the event of using the weapon on a subject and killing him or her, I was not to get compromised. If I did, CI Division would claim no knowledge of me and I would be left to my own devices. If the circumstances were unavoidable or it became necessary to kill on behalf of national security and I was then arrested, an escape plan would be hatched to free me and alternate identities provided. I had to be patient as this might take a while. The greatest of all sins was to get caught in the act of espionage. I was not to embarrass the government by any means.

Once I had taken all this in, I was issued with an ID card for SB, a driver's licence in my name and a fictitious one, along with false identification documents in my own name in the form of a Press card, an immigration officer's card and an airport security officer's card. I didn't know at the time that the driver's licence was a fake and it caused many headaches later on in life when I had to present it.

A very revealing operation had its beginnings at this time. A party of 10 Libyans had entered the country using diplomatic means and were staying at Meikles Hotel. They had left the hotel early one morning on a shopping spree around town and our surveillance teams had them under watch continuously. When they were far enough away, Alan and I entered their rooms and started processing all their belongings. We made very good progress in the time available as there were so many rooms to go through – but we hit the jackpot in the last one.

Opening a leather attaché case, we discovered it was filled with crisp one-hundred-dollar bills amounting to US$18,000, amongst other paperwork. We counted and photographed all the money and then set about photographing some of the letters that we had found, that were addressed to the Libyans from local sources.

On our return to Daventry House we informed Geoff Price of our findings and he was flabbergasted. As far as he was concerned we should have taken the attaché case and walked out of the hotel with it! The Libyans would have no cause to report the incident, as they were not allowed to have that much undeclared foreign currency in the first place.

The real jewel in the crown came when the letters we had photographed were processed. One of them, from a certain gentlemen by the name of Arawatah, of Maori extraction, was a plea for help from the Libyans in joining the Palestine Liberation Organisation (PLO). In it he had references from ZANU-PF which he thought might help his application.

During the war, this chap had offered his services to ZANU after joining the Rhodesian Air Force where he worked in Milton Buildings in the communications department. Through his correspondence with the party, it was discovered that he had been responsible for many of the leaks about Rhodesian military operations into neighbouring countries.

Later we learned how severe the leaks had been, when we discovered that he had personally informed the ZANU hierarchy, Robert Mugabe included, about the Rhodesian's raid on Chimoio and Tembue (Zulu 1 and Zulu 2) in 1977. With this information, Mugabe made sure that all of his senior officers and commanders would be absent at the time of the raid, attending a so-called 'meeting' in one of the cities, in effect leaving the masses to die at the hands of the Rhodesians. I remembered the slaughter well. Chimoio was the camp I had flown into shortly after the raid.

More damning evidence presented itself upon further investigation, when we discovered, from other documentation, that Mugabe had planned to swell the population of the Chimoio camps with refugees, so that the Rhodesians would be blamed for killing civilians. He had left the poor people who had supported him to face the wrath of his enemy's onslaught!

It appeared that Mugabe had learnt well from the famous words of Winston Churchill: 'Sometimes the truth is so important that it has to be protected by a bodyguard of lies' except he took it a step further. With the truth, in this case keeping the identity of his mole a secret, he sacrificed his own supporters, setting them up for the kill in order to get the most mileage from the situation. He had to make sure it all looked normal and pretend to have no knowledge of the impending attack. If he had let on that he had been tipped off, there would have been an enormous witch-hunt in Rhodesia for the ZANLA agent, a valuable asset to his organisation.

Arawatah, our New Zealand friend, was responsible for many a blunder perpetrated by the Rhodesians. CI Division mounted surveillance on the New Zealander for months after our discovery, but I was never sure as to what we stood to gain. Maybe old personal vendettas were the order of the day, as certainly he would be held up as a hero by the new government and become almost a protected species, so it puzzled me why we were tailing him. All the reservists who worked on the case used to talk about killing him rather than watching him. Most of them had done their own fair share of service in the Rhodesian military and they were understably itching to bump him off.

I don't know what happened to Arawatah in the end. Whether he joined the PLO or was indeed taken out by a loner in the division, I'll never know. I never bothered to find out.

A task came up in which CI Division wanted one of their agents to infiltrate a cocktail party at Zimbank, a commercial banking entity, in order to meet the bank manager's secretary. Once a rapport was established with her, the agent was to turn on the charm and then gently break into the subject of his dealings in the illegal emerald trade. It was hoped she would talk about similar dealings her boss was involved in. Intelligence sources had revealed that this senior manager was involved in the illicit trading of emeralds with foreign partners. Our secretary was very close to her boss and we thought she might be in the know.

For some reason I was chosen for the task. I was told that it was because of my age and charm, but I suspect it had more to do with my reputation as a wandering eye and a womaniser!

By definition, it was not the type of work that one would expect counter-intelligence to be involved in. It was more up the street of the Criminal Investigation Department, but somehow we got involved. Maybe there were facts that I was never aware of, as with most jobs, we were only given enough information to allow us to achieve our objective.

I attended the party, arriving at the Zimbank head office in my Renault 4. It didn't escape me that in terms of popular folklore, I really should have been driving a Lotus or Aston Martin of James Bond fame. But reality bites and I went with what I had.

One of our reservists, who worked at Zimbank, took me inside and began introducing me to various guests. I had assumed the alias of a geologist and was furnished with accoutrements to lend credit to the ruse. Before long, and after mixing with the crowd successfully, I sidled up to the secretary and turned on the charm. Surprisingly, it was one of the quickest chat-ups I have ever undertaken and she was soon putty in my hands.

By the end of the night I readily accepted an invitation to accompany her home. As she was married, we drove to her aunt's house where we thought we might have some privacy. It was once we were there that the whole operation backfired. Entering the lounge, I was introduced to the aunt, who appeared to be no older than my conquest and almost as pretty. Pressing the charm, I got the formalities out of the way and left her glance to stare over at the gentlemen she was entertaining. My bottom lip dropped when I saw a familiar face. The gentlemen happened to be the husband of one of Sheila's best friends! We both stared at each other sheepishly until I excused myself.

I made my excuses and arranged to see the young lady the following night.

The next day, before the meeting could take place, I received a call from my wife enquiring as to my whereabouts the previous evening. My gut instinct told me that she knew exactly where I had been. The ruse was over. It seemed that her friend's husband had dropped me right in the shit. It didn't make sense that he would give up his own infidelity to get me into trouble, so I called him. The short of it was that he had used me as an excuse to cover himself, but he'd somehow slipped up and set the cat among the pigeons. His wife's investigative skills were right up there with Sherlock Holmes and he had little chance of remaining discreet.

I don't think James Bond ever had to beg his way clear of his indiscretions with women, but I did just that, explaining to Sheila that I was on assignment for the organisation. Short of lashing me with a cat-o'-nine- tails, she soon had me dutifully begging her forgiveness. When she asked just exactly how far I would have gone to maintain the deception, she had me. Sheila 1. Jake 0.

Needless to say, Sheila didn't believe me and convened a meeting with the other gentlemen in question. With his balls firmly in a vice she blackmailed him, saying she would reveal other secrets she knew of to his wife. I'd always thought that my wife might have been more suited to the dark side of an interrogation table, than work as a check-out girl in a supermarket.

The depth of shit I was in gradually rose and I sought a way out of it. The crunch came when Sheila grabbed me by the short and curlies the following morning and insisted I take her to Zimbank to meet the young woman whose name she'd squeezed out of her friend's husband. With events rapidly turning pear-shaped, I phoned Johnny Gibson and asked if he could resolve the matter. I handed the phone to Sheila, who was informed that I was on a mission of national security and she wasn't to intervene. He apologised for the misunderstanding, but said it was necessary for me to continue with the operation. It was unfortunate that the other gentlemen had compromised it in the first place. Could she see her way clear for another few days until the operation was over?

Sheila would have none of it and asked why I was used on operations where I had to chat up women. He gave the same excuse I had heard on my enquiry. I was the right age and I had the charm.

For reasons unknown, I never did meet up with the young lady again. When I reached the office the next day it was as if the case never existed in the first place. Sheila 1. CI Division 0.

Counter-Intelligence Division was given a mobile tracking unit. It worked by fitting a magnetic transmitter to the bottom of a subject's car. The receiver for the unit was fitted into the Bat Mobile. It made our surveillance a lot easier and we rarely lost a subject thereafter.

On one of the first operations with the tracking unit, we unknowingly followed a subject to a garage where he was taking his car for a service. We watched as an attendant drove the vehicle over a mechanic's pit, in preparation for checking out the undercarriage. We started to panic, as in those days, the transmitters were rather large and stuck out like balls on a bull. Fortunately, the subject had left by the time we intervened, and I crept in to remove the transmitter while another agent distracted the mechanic.

My good friend KK was one of the fortunate souls who remained in Special Branch, unmolested by the new order. We often used him on surveillance jobs to enter a subject's room, wearing a dust coat and disguised as a TV repair man. It's incredible how far a dust coat or a clipboard will get you when you behave in a manner that says 'I am'.

His main purpose was to identify the subject before we could. Knocking on the door, he would ask if the subject's TV or radio were working and that was all he needed to do. Once he had identified the target he would return to the foyer, change clothes and follow that person when he or she left the hotel. Outside he would contact us by means of a pre-determined signal like scratching his head, or picking his nose, when he was either directly behind or facing the target.

On one of the 'wet jobs' at the Monomotapa Hotel, the subject had left the foyer and was walking out of the door closely followed by KK. The pre-arranged signal was given and other footmen took up the beat, while Phil Hartlebury and I made our way upstairs to check out his room. No sooner had we entered the room than we heard a key in the door. I dashed into one of the cupboards, but left my briefcase on the bed. Through a narrow slit I watched Phil as he turned left, then right, looking for a place to hide. His actions were almost comical, but he wasn't quick enough off the mark and the door opened.

Phil stood back with his hands on his hips looking unsure of himself while a shocked subject walked in. They both just glared at each other with total surprise, before Phil recovered and took the initiative:

'Excuse me, sir' he said 'What the hell are you doing in my room?'

A heated argument ensued, which very nearly became violent. In the safe confines of the cupboard, I was fretting over the briefcase on the bed when Phil again took the initiative. With his chin in the air he turned toward the door and stormed out, declaring: 'There's only one way to solve this. Let's see hotel management.'

An enraged subject followed Phil, and I seized the chance to recover the briefcase and disappear via the fire escape. I heard the rest of the story later.

Meanwhile, Phil and the subject had entered the lift and were gradually descending to ground floor in angry silence. As soon as the lift hit bottom and the bell rang for the door to open, Phil didn't dilly-dally but legged it for freedom.

The last I saw of Phil, before we met at the office that afternoon, was when he made the hotel entrance and dashed into the park, closely followed by the fuming target. He told me later that it had taken about a kilometre to lose his follower, but he did eventually escape.

As it turned out, KK had identified the wrong man when leaving the foyer. It happened relatively frequently. Surveillance followed him around town the whole day, without being any the wiser.

I asked Johnny Gibson what we were to do if things went wrong in the room. His answer was that we would have to shoot the subject and toss the body out the window.

'Whatever you do, just don't get caught,' he said.

The next few jobs I did were a bit more interesting. One of the targets that had been watched since Rhodesian days was the Brickhill family. They operated

Aeroflot Airlines from an office in the centre of Harare, formerly Salisbury.

The Brickhills' involvement in dealings with the Russians had been ongoing since they had lived in Zambia during the war. In Zambia, Bulawayo-born Jeremy Brickhill had actively assisted ZIPRA by running their political publications office, printing propaganda for the nationalist cause. Under Dumiso Dabengwa he had helped run a very effective Department of Analysis and Research, plotting Rhodesian troop movements and controlling the flow of intelligence from ZIPRA agents.

This department was also responsible for organising assistance from foreign sympathisers, which is where the Russian contact came in. Other contacts we were aware of at the time included the ANC, the PLO and a consortium of Soviet-backed terror organisations. A self-proclaimed leftist nationalist, Jeremy Brickhill was one of a handful of whites who had helped the terrorist cause during the war.

Despite the change of government, to one whose members they had supported for so long, the Brickhills were still under surveillance for quite some time after independence. This was due in part to his ZIPRA connections – the losers among the nationalists and a credible opposition to Mugabe's ZANU.

We broke into the Brickhill's offices one night and sifted through all their documentation. Their homes were also on the agenda and we pulled in a huge haul of interesting intelligence. They also owned a bookshop called Grassroots, at the Fife Avenue shopping centre, which sold publications of a political nature. I got assigned the task of conducting a reconnaissance on the bookshop and formulating a plan to destroy it.

I came up with a simple plan to break into the shop at night and leave an incendiary device on one of the shelves among the books. A plastic bottle containing alginate and brake fluid would be sure to raze the shop to the ground.

Geoff Price wasn't happy with the plan as there was a restaurant next to the bookshop. He didn't like the idea of burning the entire shopping centre down and the operation was called off. Maybe Geoff knew something I didn't. It seemed odd that such an important target should suddenly be dropped.

Some years later an attempt to assassinate Jeremy Brickhill was made by former Rhodesian servicemen working for the South Africans. Having watched their target for many weeks, they established a pattern when he visited a popular Harare coffee shop in Avondale at the same time every morning.

On the 13 October 1987 they remotely detonated a car bomb, parked outside the coffee shop, as the target walked by. Unfortunately for them, but luckily for Brickhill, another car protected him from the brunt of the blast. Although he was seriously injured, with a ripped-open stomach, a ruptured spleen and a body peppered with shrapnel, he would live to sip coffee another day.

The next assignment I was given was to investigate an author who was writing a book about Robert Mugabe. CI Division conducted the operation under the pretence that we were making sure the book didn't contain any damning information about our new leader. The real objective, however, was to make sure it didn't contain anything damning about the Rhodesians. We didn't want any information coming out about the few isolated incidents of Rhodesian brutality, like the one at Tembue 2 where foreign soldiers in the RLI had cut off a terrorist's genitals and stuck them in his mouth.

The author of the book, David Martin, wrote *Struggle for Zimbabwe* from his experiences while living with the terrorists during the war. As far as we were concerned, it was bleeding-heart liberalism that might tarnish the Rhodesian's image, something which was only a memory away. If the evidence we found was damning enough, we were to destroy any copy of the manuscript and thus hopefully avoid publication. If the only means of doing so was by torching the house in which the author lived, then so be it.

Some investigative work led to information that David Martin was having his house painted, and Johnny Gibson and I arranged to meet the contractors. The paint company had been operating since Rhodesian days and its proprietor had served in the military. Being upfront with him, we managed to convince him of the importance of the operation and he agreed to employ me temporarily as a painter. I was to pretend I was new on the job and I was learning the intricacies of the trade.

I joined the crew on the weekend they painted the house and surreptitiously found my way into the study. Using the services of the proprietor, we closed the door once I was inside and erected a ladder at the outer entrance so no-one could disturb me.

In the study I found the manuscript and began to photograph as much of it as possible. Given its length it was not possible to record every page so I sifted through the chapters and took pictures of what seemed important.

Back at the laboratory, under closer scrutiny, we discovered that the book was in fact a pretty fair, if one-sided, account of ZANLA and their leaders' activities during the war. We could find no reason to destroy it and left it to run its course. The book was published much later, although it might have contained some additions after we had processed the manuscript.

I have often wondered if David Martin ever found out that CI Division had penetrated his household and very nearly destroyed his life's work.

CHAPTER 33:
Spy versus spy

In the 1980s a lot of problems were going on in the background of Zimbabwean politics. Many of them were the result of South African intelligence agents, some among us, who were trying to destabilise the country. Most of the agents, who were sent on these missions, were ex-Rhodesian soldiers who had made the trip south after the war. Only hindsight affords a modicum of compassion for these operatives, who were used to extend South Africa's secret influence across the continent. They were really pawns in a war that was being fought over policies that Rhodesians didn't agree with and knew little about.

What developed was a spy-versus-spy scenario where operatives from different agencies were constantly trying to outwit one another thereby, in effect, causing mayhem to those who lived in countries that bordered on South Africa.

All vying for a piece of the action, were the three South African agencies: The National Intelligence Service (NIS), Military Intelligence and the Civil Cooperation Bureau (CCB). The lack of communication between these agencies, all on the same side of the conflict, became so evident that at times they may as well have just fought each other.

For Zimbabwe, it was a tense period, highlighted by South African raids and sabotage. The most harrowing event of the period, although a highly guarded secret to most living in the country at the time, was Mugabe's campaign of genocide against the Matabele people. An offshoot of his former adversary ZIPRA, now called Super-ZAPU and ably backed by South Africa, was causing strife in the western areas of the country and this gave him the excuse to send in the North Korean-trained Fifth Brigade to quell the disturbance by so-called 'dissidents'. They rained terror upon the Matabele and launched a policy of ethnic cleansing, killing tens of thousands and dumping their bodies down mine shafts.

Much news of the massacres filtered in to the CIO, but even we were kept in the dark as the organisation wasn't trusted to be politically onsides, even with Danny Stannard, the golden boy, in the driver's seat. Main roads leading into the Matabele tribal areas were sealed off with army roadblocks and special passes were required, allowing only the most loyal party officials or military personnel through. We even heard of stand-offs developing between black police details (mainly ex-BSAP and mostly Matabele themselves) and soldiers when the police tried to carry out their rightful duties in those areas.

In the cities, the South Africans kept the authorities busy by carrying out raids against ANC targets. Although the Zimbabwean government claimed otherwise, it had allowed Umkhonto we Sizwe, the ANC's military wing, free harbour in the country and were actively assisting in their terror training. I knew this because we had carried out surveillance on Umkhonto elements, who were housed at Mbare Hostels soon after the war. Among the targets that were hit, were the ANC headquarters in Harare as well as their representatives in Bulawayo.

Another target, was the ANC's chief representative to Harare, Joe Gqabi, who was gunned down on 31 July 1981 in the driveway of his residence in Mabelreign.

The assassination of Gqabi, by a Project Barnacle operative, was one of the many blunders that caused huge headaches for whites who had remained in the country, particularly those in the security forces.

Project Barnacle, an arm of South African Military Intelligence, which incorporated ex-members of the Rhodesian forces, had no idea that Joe Gqabi, as deep into the ANC as he might have been, was a paid asset of another South African Intelligence organisation, the NIS.

A few weeks before someone emptied the contents of a 9 mm Uzi sub-machine gun magazine into his head, he had found an explosive device under his car, which was brought to our attention. He had obviously informed his NIS handler about this, but with things as they were, word never got passed on and he became another victim of a failure to share information.

Shortly thereafter, on 16 August, there was an enormous explosion at the former Selous Scouts barracks at Inkomo. The barracks had been used as an armoury to house ZANLA's weapons, which had been moved from Mozambique and from the assembly points after the war.

Another Project Barnacle operative, a former Rhodesian Engineers officer, who had remained on in the Zimbabwe military, sabotaged the stores and was caught for his trouble. In a daring rescue attempt, other operatives from Project Barnacle kidnapped the investigating police officer and forced him to release the saboteur.

The ongoing harassment by South African elements, caused huge problems in the new security forces. The hand of reconciliation, which had been dutifully extended at independence, was gradually withdrawn, as suspicion was laid on the whites. In reality, the new government couldn't really be blamed for this mistrust. There were so many behind-the-scenes shenanigans that it was impossible to tell Arthur from Martha, who was onside and who was not.

During the run-up to independence a number of unsuccessful attempts were made on Mugabe's life. Danny Stannard, an ex-SB officer and my boss, who would become the head of internal security, had a hand in foiling the most sinister of these. In recognition of this he would be awarded the country's highest decoration for valour, the Gold Cross of Zimbabwe, in 1990.

The most serious attempt to assassinate Mugabe, and one which would have had far-reaching consequences if it had succeeded was the planting of a series of massive explosive devices on the route his motorcade was to take when travelling to a state banquet at Meikles Hotel during his inauguration. A number of other VIP dignitaries who were to attend the banquet, including Canaan Banana, Prince Charles, Lord Peter Carrington, Governor Lord Soames and Lady Soames were also in the motorcade. The principal target was Mugabe, but the others would undoubtedly have also been killed or seriously injured if the explosives had been detonated. They were deemed expendable, collateral damage to the main objective of ridding the country of the ZANLA leader. Danny received information of the plot and foiled it by warning Mugabe before it could happen. A large claymore type explosive device was also recovered from Rufaro Stadium where the inauguration was scheduled to take place after the dinner.

After this Danny could do no wrong in Mugabe's eyes. He was the most trusted white in the security services, something which helped him later when other elements of the CIO tried to frame him to get him out of the way.

While South Africa was raining terror on the ANC, I was approached by an ex-member of the Selous Scouts who lived in Kariba. Although I wasn't fully aware of the circumstances at the time, it was obvious that he had South African connections. He was in fact a Project Barnacle operative. I was informed that certain people in South Africa were frowning on my continuation of service in the new regime and this they viewed as tantamount to treason. If I helped him out, he would clear my name with the relevant authorities.

What he wanted me to do was to infiltrate Joe Gqabi's funeral and take photographs of all the people who were there. He needed these to pass on to Peter Dew, an ex-member of Special Branch who now worked for the South Africans.

As it turned out, I was briefed by Geoff Price to infiltrate the funeral anyway. SB had their own interest in who was going to be there. I posed as a journalist and melted in with the other Press representatives. While I was snapping away, a particular coloured gentleman, also a photographer, noticed that I was taking close-up pictures of all the guests there. His suspicion aroused, he approached me to ask who I was and which press agency I represented. I paid him no attention and flashed my journalist ID but he kept on badgering me. Fortunately, Jack White, a *Herald* reporter, saw what was going on and came to my rescue. I knew Jack from the past and he had an inkling of what I was up to. Jack intervened and told the gentleman to mind his own business. He vouched for my freelance status and said I was a good friend of his. I was fortunate that Jack was well-known in Press circles.

After the funeral I passed on negatives of the photographs to a mutual contact who knew my Kariba friend and that was the last I heard of them. I told Johnny Gibson about Jack White's intercession, which had saved the day and he was highly impressed. We later recruited Jack as one of our reservist photographers. With his influence, he was able to attend and photograph many functions we would otherwise have had difficulty in penetrating.

I thought long and hard about what my ex-Selous Scout friend had said to me. It perturbed me that my buddies, people I had fought alongside, held more than a little malevolence toward me. With circumstances changing, things certainly weren't rosy for those of us who had stayed on in the services. Many had simply done so to secure the pensions they had worked so long for. Being a civilian attached, I had no pension. My reasons for staying were simply because I had no alternative and I was trying to save my marriage. I was trying to support a wife and two kids who really didn't want me to disappear on bush trips as I had in the past. Going south wasn't an option for me. Sheila refused to move anyway.

I gained immense satisfaction from my work. I couldn't for the life of me see how I was aiding and abetting the new regime, with the nature of the tasks I was undertaking. In those days, as I said before, much of the work we did was a continuation of Rhodesian policy, as the new government hadn't bothered to look in and see what we were up to. The new order was still jostling for power and conducting witch-hunts, seeking out their compatriots who had wronged them in the past. Their own national intelligence service was small potatoes compared to the larger fish they had to fry.

Johnny Gibson agreed with my feelings. As far as we were concerned, thank God there were whites remaining in the services. At least we lent a bit of stability to an otherwise trying and unstable period. If we weren't there, God knows what fate would have befallen the white community, as the Portuguese had experienced in Angola and Mozambique. In one documented incident, the entire community of a small Angolan town was convened by the new masters at a sawmill, under false pretences; then tied to planks at gun point and fed through the saws alive.

The whites who remained on in the service of Zimbabwe kept law and order. Together, with some rational members of the new regime, they managed to circumvent many threats to slaughter the whites en masse.

I met up with my old buddy, John Gartner, in Harare one morning. John was in the country secretly, as he was operating all over Africa for South African Special Forces with Neil Kriel, Chris Schulenburg, Tim Callow and the rest of the Barnacle boys. In the capacity of a businessman, he roamed the continent in a modified Peugeot 504 conducting long-range reconnaissance for his adopted country. The car was equipped with extra fuel tanks and had hidden in its boot two radios, a TR28 and a TR48. They were crafted carefully into the side arches behind the rear wheels. John was leaving the country under new orders and wanted to warn me what he had heard in South Africa. Rumours abounded that I and the other whites who remained in the services were sellouts, and something had to be done about us. John was genuinely concerned for my well-being.

Before he left, John handed me the keys of the Peugeot and said I could have it. The first thing I had to do was to remove the radios, have the car painted another colour and organise for it to be licensed and taxed. If I could do this, I was welcome to it as it was going to be dumped anyway.

Another friend in Kariba, also ex-SAS and Selous Scouts, pulled some strings and sorted out the car for me. It needed some work done to it, so we swapped the radios for an engine overhaul kit with a diver who worked at Kariba and fancied himself a radio ham. Through his brother, who worked at the government vehicle depot (CMED), we managed to get a brand-new log book and within weeks the vehicle was transformed and theoretically legal.

The Peugeot raised a few questions back at Daventry House but I told them the truth, or as close to it as possible. It was given to me by a friend I had served with in the Selous Scouts. When the Scouts were unofficially disbanded, many of the operators were invited to take items they might be interested in. Some took diving gear, some watches, cameras, telescopes, parachutes and some even weapons. My friend took a car, the Peugeot, which I told them had been used to do external reconnaissance.

The story didn't go down well with some people, who were jealous, but it seemed watertight at the time. Their inference was why I should get recompense for my services when they didn't?

To cover my backside, Johnny Gibson and Brian Lawrence told me to put it in writing and submit the report to Geoff Price. Utterances were being made that I might be in the service of a foreign organisation. It seemed to the sources of the fabrication, that the car was payment for these services. A few other operatives in CI Division, Hans Sittig and Cliff Perrins, had already been accused of working for our friends south of the border. I was warned that I had better cover my arse!

I built my own darkroom at Daventry House. Special Branch, augmented into CIO with Dan Stannard as Director Internal, felt they needed more independence, possibly because of the 'secret' connotations in the new name. We purchased equipment from a commercial photograph development company that had gone bust, but the CID still provided us with chemicals, paper and film. Later we managed to get our British liaison to bring in a steady supply of these materials and we thought we were rid of CID forever.

That's when John Alsford came onto the scene, fresh from CID where he had been their photographer. John had transferred to the CIO and was given the title of Chief Photographer. He was in the process of building a new darkroom facility at Central Police Station, with the assistance of two helpers, both ex-terrs who had been filtered into the system. Although I would eventually befriend him, John initially pushed his weight around and tried to close down my darkroom at Daventry House. In his opinion, anything to do with photography had to fall under his jurisdiction and he didn't want any independent effort to rain on his parade. This was an order from Dan Stannard, he told me. Geoff Price and Mike Crafter didn't agree and argued my point of view with the director.

CI Division had sensitive 'for your eyes only' material, that needed to remain confidential, and they didn't want the whole of CIO knowing about it. Much to John's chagrin, my darkroom remained and he had to supply me with equipment. The independence I was granted allowed for much-needed discretion when it came to the work I would eventually undertake.

CHAPTER 34:
IMPRISONMENT

Midway through 1981 an amnesty came into effect. Unlicensed weapons in private possession were rampant in the community and the government still feared a coup attempt might take place. To guard themselves against this, all weapons had to be handed in by a certain date. Most of these weapons were in the hands of ex-servicemen and serving reservists in the police and the CIO. Many were issued weapons that were never handed in at war's end and others had been taken off dead guerrillas.

All the CIO reservists brought their contraband to our office in Daventry House for safe keeping. We were the CIO, after all, and it seemed to us there wasn't anywhere safer they could possibly be stored.

As we didn't have a lock-up armoury on site, most of the weapons were kept in an end room which housed the radio equipment. Phil Hartlebury had a heap in his office, ranging from .303 Lee-Enfields to RPD machine guns. Some belonged to him and the rest to friends. When I enquired about them, Phil told me that what I saw was only half of it. His garden shed at home was filled with military weapons that he did not want to get rid of. I told him he was crazy and that he was inviting trouble. Each to their own, I guess, and he did as he pleased.

In my office I kept my Tokarev pistol in a drawer and I stored an SKS rifle, which had been handed in, as well as a brand-new FN rifle I had found at Callsign 24, not on the inventory, in one of the cupboards. I kept the FN as I intended to take up service rifle-shooting on the weekends. Around the place there were a few boxes of ammunition, as one might expect to find in the offices of an intelligence agency, including a box of .303 rounds which was used as a doorstop.

At the end of 1981 I travelled to South Africa with a colleague from the organisation. The shopping facilities were vastly superior across the border and we took the opportunity to go on a spree. Sheila stayed with the boys and handed me an enormous Christmas shopping list before I departed. The currency had already started to lose value at a steady pace and we took advantage of the savings we had before it declined further.

While on holiday, I caught the evening news in my hotel room one night. The ZANU-PF headquarters at 88 Manica Road in Harare had been blown up with a powerful charge. I remember commenting to my friend how fortunate we were to be away at the time, as the incident was certain to trigger a massive investigation.

When I returned to work after Christmas, things just didn't feel right. Everyone in the office was regarding the next person with scepticism and mistrust. I couldn't really blame them and I had my own suspicions about who among us was working for a foreign power.

New Year's Eve was upon us and I let my feelings ride. I hadn't yet got out of the stage of revving it up with a few drinks at the nearest opportunity. Hans Sittig invited me to a party at his house and I gave him some security flares I had acquired, so we could let them off at midnight.

I left the office in a jovial mood at lunchtime, for my habitual meal with Les Milne at the Flagstaff Bar in Meikles Hotel. I would return to work at 15:00 as normal. I was certainly becoming a creature of habit! In the mornings I was meeting John Alsford regularly at the Brazzitta Coffee Shop in town. I vowed to change my ways.

At around 15:30, after chatting with John across the way at Central, I returned to my office. Outside Daventry House, I noticed armed Police Support Unit officers milling about in their blue drab uniforms. These guys meant business and were complete with chest webbing and a full complement of AK magazines. I thought it a bit strange but paid them no further attention. At the main entrance to the top floor, another two Support Unit cops stood at ease with their weapons. Inside there was a hive of activity that was unusual considering everyone was preparing for the festivities that evening. Ambling over to Johnny Gibson, I asked what was going on. There would be a meeting in the main office in five minutes which everyone had to attend. What I could have done with those five minutes! Instead I did as I was told and made my way toward the office where all of CI Division had gathered.

Seated inside there were a few black faces I didn't recognise and an older white gentleman who was also unfamiliar. I quickly learnt he was the Director-

General of CIO, a man I had never met.

After a few minutes, a roll-call was taken and the conspicuous absence of Les Milne, with whom I had just lunched, was noticed. I informed the director that Les was at the Flagstaff and would be in shortly. The director peered at me over the rim of his spectacles, made a quick note on the pad in front of him and called the meeting to order.

In brief, but with an overriding tone of seriousness, he informed us that there was a great deal of trouble in the land over the bombing of 88 Manica Road. It had been ascertained at high levels of government, that certain individuals were in the employ of foreign intelligence agencies and under the Special Powers Act privileges had been invoked to detain these individuals without right to legal council.

I must say that the topic of conversation was intriguing, to say the least. I listened intently to find out who had been fingered. It would certainly prove useful in explaining some of the troubles we had been through. Firstly, I looked around the room to see if anyone was nervous. No-one ran or tried to get out of the building, which set me at ease thinking the meeting was just a formality. I figured that we were being briefed on the government's findings and as Counter-Intelligence Division, we might be expected to have a hand in bringing the culprits to justice.

The privileges of detention, we were told, were a directive from Minister Mnangagwa himself. The accused individuals would be detained on a 30-day detention order, while investigations were being held. The detentions would be immediate.

Concern washed over me and ran down my spine like a million spider legs. Why was he telling us this? The director then told us that no-one must panic, as each of the individuals who were accused would be assigned an officer in charge of a team, who would search their offices and their homes, and then accompany them to Goromonzi police station. The rest of us were to return to our desks, open all drawers, cupboards and briefcases, and leave the office until the following Monday. We were to take nothing with us except the clothes on our backs and under no circumstances were we to leave Harare.

When I heard the mention of Goromonzi I got really worried. In truth, Goromonzi police station was Goromonzi Political Detention Centre. The facility had been built by the Rhodesians and in its time, had imprisoned some important political detainees. Just the thought of it was chilling, particularly in the hands of the new regime.

I had nothing to worry about, but I feared that something might be made of the Peugeot if the matter were investigated. The chill I was feeling quadrupled when I remembered the SKS, the FN and the Tokarev in my office.

Phil Hartlebury was the first name they called out. Looking over at him the apple in his throat bobbed visually and audibly as he gulped. I thought of his stash of weapons at home and figured it all out. That was it. It was about the weapons!

When Colin Evans was called out, I second-guessed my initial assumption. Colin had no illegal weapons, not that I knew of anyway.

When my name was called it didn't sink in. I was still coming up with a plausible excuse for the firearms in my office when I heard my name repeated above the din emanating from my fellow employees. Suddenly all eyes were on me. There was a sudden weight on my shoulders and a sick feeling in my stomach. I imagine the feeling was similar to that which a prisoner on death row feels, when he hears the words 'dead man walking'.

A thousand worries hit me and I wondered what I had done. Would they investigate my past and find out I was one of the dreaded 'Skuz'apo', a Selous Scout? Did they know already? Would the hand of reconciliation become the hand that swings the axe? Bar my small indiscretion of accepting a vehicle from a foreign agent, also a mate of mine, and in supplying a few photographs of a lousy funeral, I couldn't think of any reason why I should be detained.

Brian Lawrence searched my office accompanied by two of the unfamiliar black men. I soon figured out they were former terrs when they set to with great enthusiasm, dishevelling my belongings in their search to find the white man guilty. In the cupboard they found the rifles and two 80 mm mortar bombs I had forgotten about. One of the reservists had handed them in during the amnesty and I had been deemed responsible as I was an ex-mortar man myself. In the drawer they found the Tokarev and some ammunition. At the door they found the doorstop.

Brian leaned over to me and took a chance. With pursed lips he whispered in my ear and asked if there was anything at my home that I shouldn't have. If so, he said he would go there and dispose of it before the house was searched. I told him about a Winchester carbine I had and ammo galore in a box in the spare room cupboard, magazines, camouflage uniforms and other trinkets of war I had kept as souvenirs.

When we eventually got there it was not without Brian's two dedicated helpers. In a tricky situation, he managed to detach himself on the pretext of searching another room and with Sheila's help they scuttled all the damning evidence by scurrying it away outside into the boot of his car while the ex-terrs weren't looking. It was a great risk he took in helping me. Sheila too. I dread to think what might have happened if she was accused as an accomplice.

Brian then took Sheila aside and told her I was going to be locked up for a while. He told her not to worry as there were still whites in the CIO who would look after me. 'Thank God,' he muttered. 'Otherwise he might disappear!'

I still had no clue as to what was going on. I felt that my arrest was a stab in the dark to see if they could come up with anything solid against me. Maybe they thought I would break under interrogation and reveal what they were really after.

Walking outside, Brian asked if I was guilty. Was I a South African agent? I assured him of my innocence and he tried to comfort me by telling me the big boss would clear my name. Geoff Price wouldn't let things sit as they were!

Next, he told me not to do anything stupid. I wasn't sure what he meant by it but I had a feeling he assumed I was guilty. With my guilt I might try and escape or possibly commit suicide.

I was handcuffed, and we got into the police wagon and drove out of town on the Umtali road toward Goromonzi police station. When we arrived the sun was setting and I knew I would be detained for at least one night. Or until the problem was cleared up. I was going to miss out on the News Year's Eve party!

The Goromonzi political cells hadn't been used since the war days. They were dirty and dusty and had no beds. I was given a blanket and my shoes and belt were taken away. When the cell door locked behind me, the worry hit me. I just sat there all night in a corner thinking about the madness of my arrest. It didn't help when I thought of Hans and my mates celebrating in the New Year. I imagined they were enjoying themselves with my security flares.

There were no lights. I was locked in this dark, stench-filled cell. I consoled myself with the knowledge of my captors realising their mistake in the morning and releasing me.

The next morning the door opened to reveal four uniformed policemen sporting a decent breakfast of eggs, bacon and a cup of coffee. I asked the policemen if anyone was coming to see me but they didn't know. They waited around until I polished off the breakfast and closed the door when they left. With a bit of food in my stomach I felt more confident about my release. It couldn't be that bad if they were serving me a quality breakfast.

I didn't see anyone until two days later. A crew of CIO goons pitched up and I was taken to a car outside the prison ground in the police lot. I hadn't seen Hartlebury or Evans since the office meeting, but I knew they were there when I heard other cell doors opening and closing.

I kept on asking the CIO goons what was happening, but they ignored my every utterance. They didn't even confer among themselves. The uncertainty was killing me. I was handcuffed and bundled into the car. The vehicle started and headed away from the prison, turning toward Harare. My heart began to lift and I thought my internment was over. I would be apologised to and I could return to work on Monday with war stories to tell. At the Arcturus junction the car turned right, this time heading towards Chikirubi Prison. After the recent elation my heart sank, as I realised I was just being moved elsewhere.

When we got to Chikirubi I caught a glimpse of Hartlebury and Evans arriving in other vehicles. They were handcuffed but had the addition of shackles around their ankles. That small difference in prisoner treatment gave me a surge of hope. I must be in a different and lesser league of trouble than they were in, I thought. Then I saw my shackles in the back of the car. The locking mechanism appeared to be broken.

In the reception area of the prison, I was forced to strip naked and given a khaki uniform and a bar of soap. While I changed, the black prison guards chuckled among themselves, with frequent reference to my genitals. I was taken upstairs to a maximum security cell. It was small, but at least it had a toilet and a bed. On the door of the cell there was a window of thick glass quite high up, at about eye level. Every 10 minutes I would hear a guard approach who would peer through the aperture to check on me.

The building housing the maximum security cells was round and each cell had a small window. It would take the guard 10 minutes to walk around the complex checking on all the prisoners.

The first few days I was there passed monotonously slowly. I got three lousy meals a day and I was let out into the yard under armed guard for 20 minutes every morning, to walk around. The yard was entirely built from concrete with massive brick walls and barbed wire on top of them. This was the only part of the prison I got to see. From the top floor, which housed prisoners on death row – murderers, thugs and one or two gold and emerald smugglers – nothing else was visible. Despite that, I got to know the prison system quickly. There was nothing else to focus on.

The daily routine for prisoners in maximum security, was that locks were opened at 07:00 and everyone would stand in their doorways. On command, in single file, they would then filter through to the shower point in the yard with towels and soap. There were two showers and each prisoner had one minute to scrub himself down and dry himself. Afterwards they returned to their cells and waited for their 20 minutes of exercise.

With exercise over, they then queued for breakfast in the yard. Breakfast consisted of two slices of bread per prisoner, with jam only and a tin mug of coffee. The coffee was disgustingly weak and sugarless.

I was in solitary confinement, so my breakfast was brought to my cell. I had no contact with the rest of the prisoners and showered alone after my exercise. After the third day, someone began to send me a daily gift consisting of a cup of hot water and a used tea bag. One of the guards tried to stop the practice and I heard him being threatened by another prisoner who was in for five counts of murder. The prisoner told the guard to fuck off and leave Harper Ronald alone. The guard backed off. The tea bag was an 'I look after you, you look after me' gesture. I found out that, being one of few whites in the prison, the black prisoners thought I might eventually get visitors loaded with bags of goodies and trinkets. I could return the favour with chocolate bars and cigarettes. We got a ration of a few cigarettes each day which I handed out when I went into the exercise yard.

Every two hours there would be a guard change. I could hear them marching down the corridors outside doing foot drill, while their keys rattled. It started to drive me mad as it went on for 24 hours a day. You would hear the cell doors open and close constantly and the rattle of keys and chains.

Lunch procedure was similar to breakfast for the other prisoners. The meal would consist of more bread and soup after which the prisoners could mingle in the yard. There were a few weights around and some of the men trained. One or two could be seen bullying the boots of a guard with dirty rags and a few others polished the brass window latches with tins of Brasso. I stayed in the cells.

At 16:00 dinner would be served, and once again the prisoners would line up to receive sadza (maize meal) and stew.

At 16:30 they would again stand in their doorways. They would all bid each other goodnight and be locked up until the next morning.

When night fell the prisoners would talk to each other through the walls. Some nights they would have spelling contests, or would swap stories. This would invariably go on until about 21:00 when all went quiet. The only sound thereafter was the changing of the guards.

One evening, an inmate went berserk, banging and screaming in his cell. The guards bought restraints in and cuffed him to his bed to quieten him down. It seemed to do the trick.

The following day a young white lad was brought into maximum security. He had been in Internal Affairs during the war and had cached a considerable amount of weapons which the authorities found. He was interned while awaiting trial. One night he attempted to commit suicide by stabbing himself in the throat with a ballpoint pen he had managed to smuggle past the guards. From my cell I heard the guards panic, calling for help, while the young man gurgled grotesquely through a hole in his throat. He was taken to the prison hospital. I don't know what became of him.

When I could, I communicated with the other inmates, but as I was in solitary it was frowned upon. Having very little communication with anyone at all, on top of which I still had no idea of the reasons for my arrest, I resorted to the library to maintain an outside link with the world. One of the cells had been converted to a library where prisoners could exchange books. For me it was temporary relief from the monotony. I used to request picture books, gazing at landscapes in distant lands as a form of escapism. One particular *National Geographic* magazine had obviously been in the system for years and seen many inmates come and go. For some of them I'm sure it was one of the last things they saw before meeting the hangman. Its corners were tatty and its pages stuck together, but I gained a lot of solace from its beautiful photos. I longed for the outside world.

I think I had only been in the system for five days when an inspection was called and the director of prisons paid us a visit. I learnt later that he was the last white director and, in his time, had brought a lot of stability and fair play to the system. He was an elderly gentleman. He saw my name on the door and poked his head in to see if I had any complaints. I asked if I could have rice instead of sadza for my main meal and that night it was granted. I even got boiled potato on some occasions.

I was developing pins and needles in my fingers and the small of my back was aching. I asked to see the doctor. Sick parade was downstairs where all the prisoners were lined up, stripped naked and anally searched by a guard before they saw the doc. I think they thought that one of us may take the doctor hostage or stick him with a plastic fork we had hidden up our bum. Whatever the reason it was a thoroughly degrading experience!

After my check-up, the Indian doctor told me I had a pinched nerve in my back and he would give me something for it once he was finished with the rest of the prisoners. I was sent to the back of the queue until the last prisoner was seen and was then subjected to the cavity search again. There was no reason for it – the doctor didn't even give me a painkiller, and I was sent back to my cell. I decided it had been worth it just to get out and about for a few hours.

When I did leave my cell for exercise, there were usually a few prisoners ambling about in small groups chatting to one another. I wasn't allowed to talk to any of them and each time one of them did approach me he was warned off by the guards.

There were no other whites in the section where I was imprisoned, other than the youngster who was taken out on a stretcher with a crater in his throat. I wondered where Hartlebury and Evans were. There was one Indian prisoner and all the others were blacks or coloureds.

One particular coloured guy kept on approaching me and managed to get in a few words before being told off. He then started to write me notes on scrap paper and cigarette boxes and push them under my door, along with a pencil when he was passing. He asked me what crime I was in for and why I was there.

He told me that he was in for murdering someone over an emerald deal that went sour. One day he said he was going to see his lawyer that afternoon and if I wanted to write a letter to my loved ones, he would pass it on to post. He said it was safe as he had done it for other prisoners on many occasions.

I thought about it and decided to write a letter to Sheila to let her know I was OK. In it I asked her to contact Johnny Gibson, Brian Lawrence or Bernie Evans and tell them to clear my name with the authorities. I said she must let them know the ammo and weapons in my office weren't mine and were there because of the amnesty. The Tokarev was mine but I had been cleared to use it by Geoff Price.

I said she must tell them that a terrible mistake had been made and I shouldn't be imprisoned. I had no doubt that my attempts for clemency were as good as pissing against the wind, but I had to do something. I passed the letter on to the inmate and waited for a response.

On the sixth day I was taken downstairs to a big office. Inside Ray Ritson from CI Division and Brian Lawrence sat astride a long bench that was pulled up to a bare desk. With them were a few black guys, obviously ex-guerrillas, who I didn't know and Rogers Mutonga. Rogers was also an ex-guerrilla who had murdered a white farmer in the lowveld when he was seeking amnesty. He was a nasty piece of work and if looks could kill I would have been dead. The black guys stared at me with utter contempt and hatred.

I was fortunate that Ray Ritson was in charge of the investigation, so tempers were kept in check. He did all the talking and I was asked to give a verbal statement of my life history while he wrote it all down. I had to go back as far as Milton Junior School in Bulawayo, right up to the day I was arrested. It took about two hours of questioning and analysing the various moves, motives and changes in my life. I was worried when it came to my service in the Selous Scouts, as I knew how much the former guerrillas hated them. They wanted to know how I had facilitated a transfer from the Scouts to Special Branch. They also asked me about the Peugeot 504 and questioned me about the whereabouts of other ex-Scouts I had worked with. They wanted to know where they were, who they were working for and when I last saw them.

At the end I was sent back to my cell. Before I was marched off I looked at Brian, searching for an answer. He just stared away.

I was in Chikirubi for another week. During that last week my sheets were taken away from me. I was under the impression that they thought I was going to do myself in by rigging a sheet from the ceiling and hanging myself. In so doing I would rob them of the opportunity to prove me guilty. As there was nowhere to tie the damn thing, it must have been just another form of cruelty.

The next time I was taken downstairs I was told to put my civvy clothes on. My heart skipped a beat and I thought I was finally being released from my nightmare. I was handcuffed to a uniformed policeman, taken outside and put into a car. Two plainclothes CIO operatives were sitting in the front of the vehicle. Next to the vehicle was a BRDM armoured personnel carrier with a MAG mounted on the cupola. Loitering outside were eight fully equipped Support Unit cops. When I turned around I saw a Crocodile troop-carrying vehicle loaded to the hilt with more Support Unit guys. They were also armed to the teeth and I suddenly knew that I wasn't going home. Why all this for me? Was I that important a prisoner to warrant 20 armed guards with machine guns? What were they scared of? It must be serious!

Our convoy left Chikirubi and headed out of town on the Arcturus Road. My hopes were dashed when I realised I was being returned to Goromonzi. To have an armed escort of this size and weight in firepower meant that I was in very deep trouble indeed.

On arrival at Goromonzi I noticed there were new additions to the facility. A marquee tent had been erected just outside the political cells in the police yard. Housed inside were my armed guards as well as 20 more. MAG bunkers were being built on every corner and this work was nearing completion. They were already manned and loaded with belts of shiny ammunition from metal boxes. I was really in the shit!

My captors obviously knew something I didn't. Maybe they feared a rescue attempt? If that was to be the case it could only come from one source: South Africa. Did they really think I was a South African agent? Maybe Hartlebury and Evans were agents and I had somehow been caught up in it.

While my mind bubbled away, I was put into a dingy cell. Everything was much the same as it had been before, although the grounds outside had been tidied up and the lawn cut. In the corner of the cell was a single blanket and next to it a hole, sunk into the floor, to use as a toilet. Opposite the toilet was a metal ring pegged into the concrete for shackling ankle chains. The cells had been designed during the war for political detainees. The walls were three metres thick and to gain access, there was a three-metre hallway through one of the walls with dual doors. The idea was to enter the outer door, lock it behind you, then open the inner door, so there was nil chance of escape. Each door had two locks. The cell was soundproofed, so that a prisoner could scream until he was blue in the face with little chance of anyone hearing him.

If you inhabited a political cell, the authorities simply didn't care about you. There were no windows. On one of the walls inside there was a little grill, covering a hole with a small lightbulb hidden inside. It was on for 24 hours a day.

I looked at my new home and wondered how long I'd be there. Just after I arrived, the door opened again and I was presented with a 30-day detention order to sign and hand back. The uniformed officer smirked with his obvious disdain of me, while he wiped the remnants of his snotty nose on a filthy wall. For a moment I thought of not signing the paper. What more could they do to me? They had caught me in a weak moment and I didn't want to invite any repercussions. I signed, and hoped that the two weeks I had already been detained would be deducted from the 30 days.

The door slammed shut and the walls closed in on me. An intense fear filled me. I wanted to be free. I wanted to be out in the open with nothing around me. It was the most intense yearning I had ever experienced, but I knew it was hopeless. The hopelessness surmounted the fear and I was caught in a dizzying quandary of anguish. I wasn't physically crying, but the tears flowed freely down my cheeks. I wanted Sheila. I wanted familiarity. I wanted my mom and my dad.

After what must have been just a couple of hours, I thought a day had passed. When a day passed it seemed like a week. With the light constantly on, the cell was designed to confuse the prisoner, so he would not know whether it was night or day.

Next to twiddling my thumbs, there was nothing else to do except read my toilet paper. A half-sheet from the *Herald* was supplied every couple of days, but even that wasn't necessary with the measly amount of food I was given. If I crapped twice in a week it was a lot. Most of the time I just sat there blowing bubbles.

The next morning, my first back at Goromonzi, the cell door opened and I was taken to an interrogation room next to the guard room. Without a belt, I kept on having to hitch up my trousers as the weight had melted off me. While I walked I made a note of all the cells. There were six in total. There was a small yard with 4½-metre high walls around it, and outside that there was a taller fence with barbed wire. If the fence didn't stop my attempt at escape, a company of Support Unit policeman were permanently stationed outside.

In the interrogation room, I was made to sit on a chair in front of a panel of nine black men, made up of ex-guerrillas and ex-BSAP and SB personnel. Sam Magadze from the BSAP was the team leader and I knew him from the past. It was a familiar face at least. The 2IC was Rogers Mutonga. They all seemed quite polite at first and I figured that they had been briefed to carry out an interrogation in as humane a way as possible. Thank God for Sam! I am sure if Rogers had his own way I would be tortured with every method conceivable.

Not that it was a secret, but I was accused of being recruited into Special Branch from the Selous Scouts. Rogers wanted to know why and by whom. They wanted to know why I was the only Selous Scout in the whole organisation and why I was the only Selous Scout walking around in the whole country. I told them that I wasn't. I told them there were hundreds of Selous Scouts who remained in the country. I asked them if they knew that the Selous Scouts and RAR had been absorbed into 1 Parachute Battalion at Inkomo Barracks. They said that I was lying. I told them there were others who were now farmers and civilians. They didn't believe me because I gave them no names.

Rogers leapt up suddenly and accused me of being an agent, with other ex-members of my unit. He said I was working for the South Africans and I was conducting reconnaissance operations for them. He mentioned some of my former colleague's names like Kriel and Schulenburg, all ex-Recce Troop operators and said that I was one of them.

I told them it was rubbish and they were making it up.

His next comment floored me. He asked me about the 'Beadles'. Who were they? I was totally confused and said I had no idea what they were talking about. After a moment it dawned on me and I asked if they meant the Beatles. They said yes. I professed that the only 'Beatles' I knew of was a rock group. They confirmed that was what they wanted to know about.

Now I was really confused. What the hell did the Beatles have to do with my interrogation?

I asked them if they wanted to know about John, Ringo, Paul and George and they said yes, they wanted to know about them. I was just about to crack my first smile in two weeks when I saw the seriousness on their faces. It could only be a wind up!

Before I had made up my mind, a file was slammed down in front of me followed closely by Rogers fist as he struck the desk.

'We know about you and the Beadles' he screamed. 'Don't play games with me!'

I opened the file and began to read a report which I soon realised had been compiled by the coloured prisoner at Chikirubi. Behind the report was my letter to Sheila. The bottom of the letter was torn off for some reason. There was another letter from the prisoner as well. In it he stated that he had spoken to me and I had admitted that I was indeed working for the South African government with former comrades from the Selous Scouts. The group of agents I was involved with was called the Beatles!

How he got the names I don't know, but he referred to Johnny Gibson as Paul, Brian Lawrence as John, Bernie was George and I was Ringo. We were an elite group of agents, with radios and weapons, sending information to the South Africans.

I don't think it was appropriate, but I burst out laughing. I told Rogers that if I ever got my hands on the prick from Chikirubi I would strangle him. I said that he would sell his grandmother to win favour with the authorities and his possible early release. I added if they believed that, then they would believe anything. They might as well hang me now.

Rogers was fuming and without Sam there, I think he might have shot me on the spot. Dismissing the file with a broad sweeping hand he declared that he had more damning evidence in the form of letters he had found at my house, addressed to me from the Bluff. Why was I in contact with white racist soldiers from the base area of South African Special Forces?

I told him that there were a lot of South African soldiers who were black.

He told me that they were all puppets of the white racist regime.

The letters could have been a stumbling block, but they were quite innocent.

They were from Ian Suttil before he was killed in action. When the Rhodesians had arrived at the Bluff, they were more or less ostracised by their South African Special Forces counterparts. Due to different military systems and religious beliefs, the Rhodesians were considered ungodly Philistines. The Rhodesian Army never enforced religious doctrine upon its soldiers, unlike the South Africans who had prayers every morning on parade. The Rhodesians in general had a more personal view of God and not one which was institutionalised. Because they didn't agree with morning prayers, the South Africans had dubbed them the 'Philistines'.

Ian had also heard that I was unpopular amongst my ex-brothers-in-arms for staying on in Zimbabwe. He made light of it and sent me a cartoon depicting a helicopter flying over me while I ducked for cover, with Suttil and the 'Philistines' hanging out the doors shooting at me.

I was asked to explain the pictures. I used the opportunity to tell them about the 'Philistines' and how I had heard that they wanted to kill me for serving Zimbabwe. I told them that the very people they thought I was mixed up with, had dubbed me a white sell-out. It was little consolation when I discovered that the letters had actually helped me to some degree, because from their own investigations the authorities had discovered I was indeed on a hit list and the South Africans did want to kill me. I still wasn't released though.

Rogers continued to insist I was a spy, but he changed tack. Subduing his manner he leaned over and told me that Minister Mnangagwa was genuinely concerned about my well-being and if I were to admit that I was in the service of the South Africans, they could show some leniency. I think, in his mind, leniency meant a quick bullet to the back of the head rather than a long painful torture and ultimate hanging. He even told me that the minister could understand my reasons for being a spy, what with the changes that had taken place in the country.

My lips were sealed. I had done nothing wrong and I knew nothing. This I told them. When I was put back in the cell I wondered how long it would go on for.

Each day I was dragged out in front of the same team and the whole process would start over again. They began to get nasty and slapped and shoved me around. They asked me about 88 Manica Road and said they had evidence that placed me as the person who had planted the bomb. I defended myself by saying that it would have taken a miracle for me to be in South Africa and Zimbabwe at the same time.

My passport would prove that. They said that I had connections and it wouldn't be hard to organise a fake immigration stamp.

I made a mistake when I asked what all the fuss was about. I had read in the newspapers that only two people were killed in the blast.

They told me that the relevant Press release had been a cover and that many ZANU officials had died as there was a meeting going on when the bomb exploded.

Rogers inferred that resistance was futile and I should just give them the names of the other agents I worked with, or else things were going to get nasty. When I refused, he slapped me around some more and sent me back to the cell.

The next day it all started over again. And the day after that. My interrogators changed tactics time and again and told me that the torture would soon begin because I wasn't co-operating. I told them to go ahead as my answers weren't going to change. Deep down I realised that, even if I did falsely admit to anything under duress, the resultant ends would certainly outweigh what I was going through now. I was saying nothing.

Sam interrupted and said he knew, as I was ex-SAS, that I had undergone resistance to interrogation training. I don't know if he was trying to help me by implying that torture would be futile, or if he was trying to implicate me further. I just told him it was bullshit as underneath we were all human beings and we all have pain thresholds and tolerances. They were quiet for a minute.

They blew hot and then they blew cold. Suddenly they became friendly. They said they had seen my wife the other day and she was well. She had come to see me and was concerned about my well-being. I didn't want to give them anything, so I continued to look at the floor. Inside, the mention of Sheila sent my pulse through the roof. With my indifference the mood swung. They told me Sheila had asked for a message to be passed on. I was a stupid loser and I deserved to be in jail. Rogers' eyes rolled with malicious fervour, when he added that Sheila was fucking my best friend. The interrogators all laughed.

When you are in this sort of situation, your mind plays tricks on you and you are not sure what to believe. The rational side of me said it was all part of their game, but I suddenly started thinking about Sheila being with other men. I knew I couldn't take much more of the uncertainty. I felt like a mushroom – kept in the dark and fed on shit.

Rogers' next move was to hand me a piece of paper. He said I should write everything down concerning my involvement with foreign agencies. He wanted to know who recruited me and when. He said I had better follow his instructions and then sign the document. I finally snapped and told him to fuck off. I told him he was a callous killer and he should go and fuck the minister. Silence.

My interrogators were certainly not masters of original rhetoric. Every day it was the same routine with a slightly different flavour. They wanted to know if I was ever in the military engineers. I told them that I worked for a living and not to insult me. They were just words but my belligerence cloaked me in comfort.

Sam intervened again and said it didn't matter if I had been an engineer or not because I had done a demolitions course in the SAS. He certainly knew a lot about my SAS days! The others asked if it was true and I said it was. Again they said I must admit I was the operative behind the 88 Manica Road bombing. They said I was to write a confession and sign it, or the next day they would subject me to torture with electricity. I remembered from resistance to interrogation training, never to sign any document, as the signature could be copied and used against you. I began to worry about my signature on the detention order.

After one session, when every day had melted into the next, they eased up a bit. I was questioned for 15 minutes and put straight back in my cell. As they left, and the door was locked behind me, they said that it was over. I now had all the time in the world to think about my actions as my lack of co-operation had secured my detention.

In solitary, you start to think about all the things they had said, especially what your wife was doing. It drives you mad because you don't know what's going on at all. Every little thing plays on your mind and you second-guess your decisions. Did I say the right thing here or there? Was it wise to be cocky? I just knew that it was pointless writing anything down, as there was nothing to write.

I managed a glimpse of Evans one day and he was looking haggard and awful. I didn't know what he was going through, but he certainly appeared worse off than I felt. Maybe I looked the same; after all, I hadn't seen a mirror in weeks.

After three weeks in solitary confinement, give or take a few days, the interrogation team paid a visit and told me they were not happy with me.

Hartlebury and Evans were co-operating and had told them everything. They were going home in five days, as it was 30 days since they signed their detention orders. I was to remain locked up until I confessed to what they wanted to hear.

On the bright side, they informed me they weren't going to interrogate me any more. They said I could languish at Goromonzi until I was prepared to call them for a confession. As far as they were concerned I could rot in Hell. Then the door closed behind me for the most helpless period of my life.

At Goromonzi we weren't allowed to exercise. Once in a blue moon I was taken out of the cell to a cold shower and given a few seconds to wet myself and rub down my body. I wasn't afforded the comfort of soap and a towel.

Breakfast consisted of a splodge of maize-meal porridge with no milk, sugar or utensils. I had to slurp the cold porridge over the rim of a well-used enamel bowl. The remnants of other breakfasts a few days prior were always caked up on the edges.

Lunch was a little better and consisted of two meat balls with a leaf of cabbage and gravy. I was allowed three cups of water a day and I was constantly thirsty.

At night I used to bang on the door until I got the guard's attention. He would open a small window in the outer door to see what I wanted. The flushing facilities for the toilets were outside and I would ask him to flush as the smell inside the cell was becoming unbearable. While he headed off to entertain my request I would kneel over the toilet bowl, with my hands cupped, ready to scoop up water when it came. I could always get five handfuls of water from a flush and it managed to alleviate the thirst. Drinking the toilet water was my only means of hydration as the keys for the inner door were kept by the goons in Harare. Although they hadn't seen me for a while, I knew they came out daily to check on me, as my meals were delivered when they brought the keys.

After a few days I started to go mad. My daily reading ritual was negated when they stopped bringing toilet paper and I had to wipe with my hands, scraping the faeces off on the edges of the toilet bowl when I was finished. I'm sure the practice did nothing for my hygiene.

A small reprieve from the boredom came one day, when my cell was privileged to have three new inmates. Monty, Sheila and Mr Berkinstein were wall spiders which I named and had conversations with, depending on my mood.

Monty was inanimate and I could discuss a wide range of topics with him, such as my personal interests and needs. Sheila filled in when I felt hopeless and insecure. She was a wife and a motherly figure rolled into one. I think she saw more tears come out of me than anyone ever has.

Mr Berkinstein was the largest and most sinister of the arachnids and his domain was the top right-hand corner of the wall with the door. More mosquitoes gathered there than anywhere else in the room as it was closer to the light, and he gorged himself on their blood after they'd gorged themselves on mine. Mr Berkinstein was the outlet for my frustration and hate. In those times I screamed at him for subjecting me to the torture I was going through. Why was he doing this to me, I asked, and why was I here? Alternately, Mr Berkinstein took on the various characters of my nemesis. His anthropomorphism changed him into the individuals prevalent in my worst nightmares. Occasionally he represented Rogers Mutonga and at other times, quite strangely, my old headmaster at Guinea Fowl School. In a futile attempt at understanding, I would plead with him to know the circumstances of my detention. 'WHY AM I HERE?' I would scream. 'Why the hell did you cane me when I wasn't even smoking?'

I must say I got a little concerned when Mr Berkinstein revealed that he was actually Mrs Berkinstein. On one of the mornings I noticed thousands of little baby wall spiders crawling all over her. As far as naming them all I was fucked!

I developed a lot of hatred while I was interned at Goromonzi. As I have stated before, it is quite all right to do the time if you've done the crime, but I was completely innocent. If for the sake of leniency I was to admit to anything I wouldn't even know what to admit to anyway.

One day – and I don't know which one – a guard came in and presented me with another 30-day detention order. He said I could sign it or not sign it as it wouldn't make a difference to my well-being. I was going to be held anyway. I signed. At that point I felt that any brownie points I could accrue might work in my favour.

That day I also noticed Hartlebury and Evans were still around. The five days were up and they hadn't gone home. It gave me a little selfish hope to know that I wasn't in this alone.

The next morning, while I was conversing with Monty, the door opened and a familiar face walked in. Finally I was joined by a cellmate with whom I could actually converse and the conversations would be reciprocal.

It was Steven Mpofu, my old mate from Selous Scouts Recce Troop, who had been partnered with John Gartner in those days. My initial reaction was one of suspicion and I wondered what tactics my interrogators were using now. Had they brought in Steven to lull me into a sense of false confidence?

Steven told me that the CIO had just driven into Inkomo Barracks and arrested all ex-Recce Troop personnel who were serving in the Parachute Battalion. He had been brought to Goromonzi along with Aaron Mlambo, Martin Chikondo and a few other black operators I didn't know. They were all being detained at Goromonzi and as there were only six cells, we had to share.

I tried to warn Steven with hand signals not to talk too much as the cell was probably bugged. We guardedly spoke of the situation we were in. I asked Steven about John Gartner and if he had seen him since he had left the army. He told me that he hadn't seen anyone since the days of the Selous Scouts.

On his third morning, Steven started doing press-ups and karate exercises in the confines of the cell. He asked me to get stuck in with him as our only chance for survival was escape. He felt that the new regime would never forgive us for the havoc we had wrought against them during the war. As he saw it, our detention precluded our imminent death and he wanted me to join him in his planned escape. The next morning, when the guard delivered breakfast, we were to jump him and fuck him up. We would then help each other to get over the walls and run for our lives.

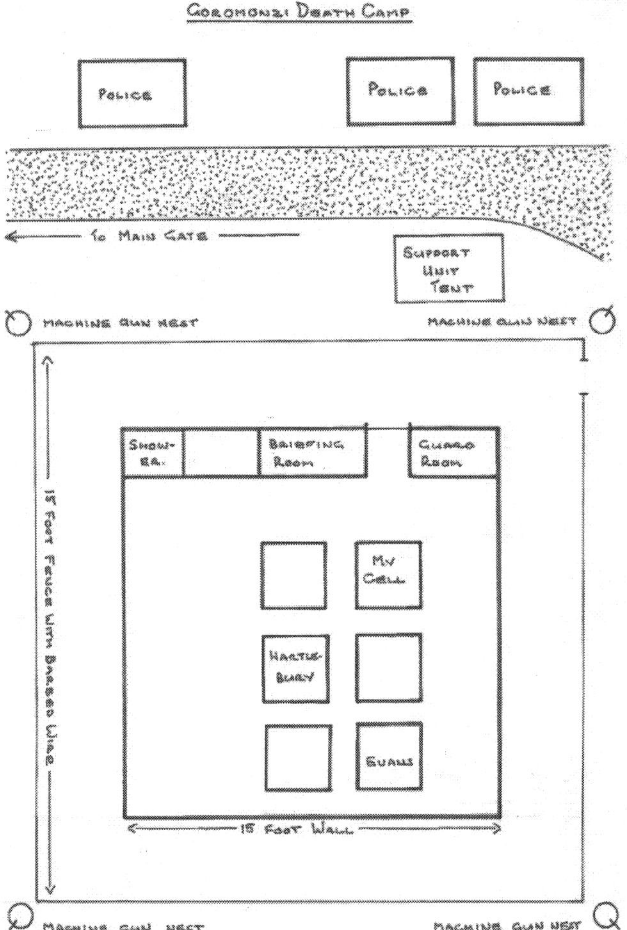

Goromonzi Death Camp – as it became known. The diagram depicts a not-to-scale layout of the camp and the position of Jake's cell.

It was a simple plan and lacked imagination. I told Steven we would never get away with it, as there were machinegun pits on all the corners and an entire company of Support Unit guards. Steven, typical of his courage, stated that it was better to die fighting than to die a coward in the cells. He said we would die together as brothers-in-arms fighting those bastards outside.

With a little more dissuasion I managed to convince him to slow down. I mentioned arbitrary things like human rights and lack of evidence. I argued that the state didn't have a case against any of us. I didn't fully believe that any of these things stood us in good stead, considering the people we were dealing with, but I didn't feel like dying that day. Steven relaxed for a while but then got hot under the collar again.

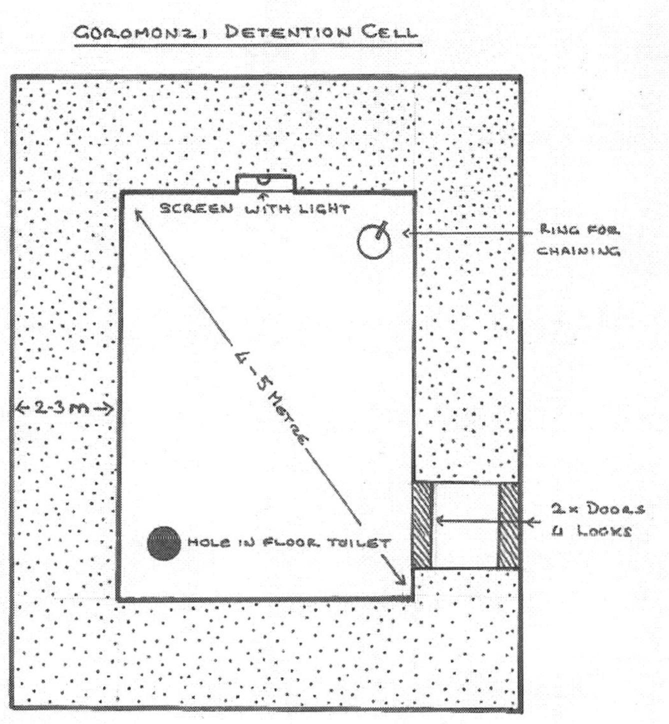

A diagram of Jake's cell at Goromonzi Political Detention Centre. The comforts were sparse!

On my next interrogation I asked to have Steven removed from my cell. I said he was convinced that we were all going to die in prison and that he was fucking with my mind. They moved him that afternoon. I never heard from him again but I learnt some years later that he was released shortly after our meeting. Some time after his release he was murdered on a train from Harare to Bulawayo in mysterious circumstances.

Martin Chikondo became a security officer in a commercial company and was shot by a disgruntled employee in a cash-in-transit operation.

Aaron Mlambo, I last saw being interviewed on the BBC television programme called 'Rebellion' about the Rhodesian days. He was a company commander in 1 Commando Battalion (Zimbabwe) and was being asked about his involvement with the Selous Scouts. What happened to him I don't know.

My interrogators confessed they had done their homework and it was true about the other Selous Scouts who remained in the country. They couldn't believe it as they thought the majority had moved to South Africa to form a new Reconnaissance Commando.

There was also some confusion about the Peugeot 504, its log book and how I came to own it. I was asked where the radios had gone as they said they had found where they were mounted in the boot. I told them I had swapped them for an engine overhaul kit with a South African who worked in Kariba. Rogers told me they knew the car was used as a reconnaissance vehicle and they had gone to Kariba to investigate. I didn't admit to any knowledge of their claims and reiterated that I had been given the vehicle by an ex-Selous Scout friend. There was no hiding that.

The CIO was not happy with what they had found in Kariba in general, and were convinced that a conspiracy against the government was being hatched. The guys who had licensed the car for me in CMED were also under suspicion. On investigating the Peugeot, they had opened up a can of worms and come across other vehicles that were missing from government departments and had been sold by CMED to private people. There was a whole lot of crooked dealing and corruption, and I was asked if I was involved in it. I said I wasn't.

I found out eventually that Brian Lawrence had been sent to Kariba by Danny Stannard to warn the community in general that Rogers Mutonga was travelling there to conduct a witch-hunt. He was convinced that everyone who lived in the town was a spy and he was particularly interested in those who frequented the Bung Club at The Heights. The Bung Club, also known as the C & C Club (Cock and Crutch) was where ex-military members gathered for drinks. They heeded Brian's warning and one night the club mysteriously burnt down. Those people in Kariba, who were involved in dodgy dealings, dispersed and hid in nooks and crannies all over the country.

I was asked questions about my boss in CI Division, Geoff Price. Gradually they leaned on me more regarding my acquaintance with Geoff and how I came to know him. I told them that he had hired me on the pretext of my photography experience in Northern Ireland. When they asked where I had obtained the unlicensed Tokarev, I told them about the dead guerrilla and said Geoff had given me permission to use it.

I wore a beard at the time and I told them that Geoff had told me to keep the beard in case I needed to change my identity by shaving. I confessed to not knowing the reasons for his request.

Fifteen days into my second 30-day detention order, which already exceeded 60 days anyway, I learnt that Sheila was making enquiries about me. She wanted to know why I was under arrest and why she wasn't allowed to see me. She went to Central Police Station and had a meeting with the member-in charge of CIO. She was told it was out of CIO hands and only time would tell what happened as I was incommunicado. I was told later that she got really boisterous with the boss and stormed off to see the British High Commission. They were not interested in my plight and said that although I was a British subject, they could not involve themselves in Zimbabwean politics.

After the High Commission rejected her, she went to Daventry House and insisted on a meeting with Danny Stannard, Director Internal, and asked him what he was hiding. She didn't believe I was alive at the time and told him just that. She said that if something wasn't done she was going to the international press to scream human rights abuse.

Stannard relented and said he would organise a meeting for her to see me. Sheila then contacted Hartlebury and Evan's wives, both of whom had been kept in the dark as to the whereabouts of their husbands, and told them of the meeting. Unfortunately they weren't granted the same privilege and a hornet's nest erupted. There were accusations that I was being shown leniency because I had dropped my two colleagues right in the shit. Danny contacted Sheila and warned her not to see the wives of the other two inmates. She was told that things were a little different between my investigation and theirs. This made Sheila think things were looking OK for me.

One Saturday morning, the door opened and Rogers walked in with a guard. I was told I could go for a shower, after which I was to comb my hair. It seemed a bit odd, but I told Rogers that I didn't have a comb. He sent the guard off to fetch one and I used the reflection in the outer door window to untangle the nest on top of my head. It was the first time I had seen myself properly since my detention. I looked a real mess and noticed how drawn my face was.

When I had finished with the shower, I was taken to one of the guard's rooms that had a bed, a radio and a table in it. There was a bowl of maize meal on the table, with milk and a spoon, and I was told to eat it. While I ate, Rogers informed me that Sheila would be visiting in five minutes. I was not to discuss anything about the conditions I had been kept in or how I had been treated. I was told to say that everything was all right and I was being treated well. I was warned that if I said anything untoward to my wife she would be escorted out and I would not see her again.

I continued to eat and when I looked up Sheila entered the room. I couldn't help the tears that welled up in my eyes as much as I didn't want to give Rogers the satisfaction of seeing them. She was appalled at my appearance and stood with a blank expression on her face. She told me later that she had to look twice to recognise me. After we hugged and greeted, she let out a little guffaw and told me I looked like Ben Gunn from *Treasure Island*. My hair was long and unkempt, and my beard and moustache hadn't been trimmed. To eat I had to lift my moustache and hold it above my upper lip. I must have looked appalling!

While we spoke, Rogers sat on the end of the bed with his back to us. Sheila asked me loads of questions which I tried to answer without compromising the situation. She kept on referring to the comfort of the guard's room and telling me it wasn't too bad. At least I had a bed, sheets, blankets, a radio and decent food, she thought. I tried to use signals and facial expressions to indicate that it wasn't my cell. Rogers kept on turning an ear so I didn't get the message across.

She had brought along a goodie box that contained tinned fruit, biltong and magazines. I asked Rogers if it was all right to keep them and he said it was OK, but he would take them and dish them out to me on a daily basis. Although I never saw much of the food after that, I knew then that things were looking up for me. I began to live in hope that my time served would be up in two weeks. The only question which remained was: would they give me another 30-day detention order?

I had 15 minutes with Sheila under the ever alert ears of Rogers Mutonga and I was returned to my cell. I found out later that it took him two and a half hours to drive her back to Harare as he had to stop and show her off to all his mates, ex-comrades in arms who were easily impressed by his innuendos of dating a white woman. He was apparently very affable and asked if Sheila was 'taken care of' while I was locked up. He even went as far as to offer his services in the form of 'you take care of me and I'll take care of your husband' kind of thing. He wanted to know what she was doing socially while I was away and culminated with a polite invitation to 'socialise' with him one night. Sheila was naturally terrified and I am sure there would have been no end to his gloating if he could have told me that he had shagged my wife. If I saw Rogers Mutonga today, I would kill him!

Sheila lived in fear of Rogers arriving at our house for the remainder of my detention, but he didn't show. I continued to solidify my relationships with the wall spiders, while knowing absolutely nothing about what was going on outside my four walls. A week after Sheila's visit, I developed a chronic toothache. Not brushing your teeth in over six weeks is sure to do that. I harangued the guard at every opportunity to see a dentist and eventually he bought some painkillers with the money I had on me at the time of my arrest. They didn't really help me.

On one occasion, a guard asked me if I knew what day it was. They thought that I had no idea due to the sound and light proofing in the prison. I told him it was Saturday. He was shocked and asked me how I knew that. I said it was because he wasn't wearing a suit, so it must be the weekend. He laughed and told me I was clever. I kept a crude calendar on the wall, using a stone I picked up in the showers to mark each day, and knew roughly how many days had passed and what day it was.

As time dragged on, my toothache got worse. My entire body began to ache within the confines of the cell. My toenails grew so long that I had to sit and rasp them on the walls. At least it alleviated the boredom.

In general, my appearance was beginning to worry me, as my skin had taken on the grey pallor of death and my teeth were loose in my gums. I had read about these signs of malnutrition beforehand during the droughts in various African countries, and in the German concentration camps and British ones during the Boer War. I was sure they weren't healthy signs although I couldn't be sure if they were the signs preceding death. It certainly felt that way.

One morning – during my shower – I managed to pick up a piece of broken glass in between my toes. I hid it in the cell among some loose rubble that had decayed off the walls and vowed to take my life with it. If push came to shove and I could take it no longer, I would slit my wrists. By the time my goons found me 16 hours later, I would be long gone. At least I would have the last say and they'd be in the shit. At best I wouldn't have to put up with the bullshit anymore. I didn't have the guts, really – but who knows what a couple more months would have done.

I began to worry when my second 30-day order was drawing to an end and I had heard nothing. I wanted a piece of the outside world once more and I wanted freedom. When the guard next opened the door early on a Saturday morning I asked to see the dentist again. I told him the painkillers had done nothing at all and besides, they were finished. I was more than surprised when the guard complied and said that I was to go for a shower. After that he said I was to go to cell number 1 and collect my shoes and belt. I was to take my blanket from my cell and hand it in at reception.

I didn't want to experience the anti-climax of futile hope like I had before, so I tried not to think about the reasons for the change of procedure. If I was going to see a dentist, then I would be satisfied with just a glimpse of the outside world.

I was escorted into the briefing room where my breakfast awaited me on a plate, with utensils again! I sat to wolf the food down, when one of the interrogation team came in. He greeted me like a long-lost pal and in a matter-of-fact manner told me I was going home. As pleased as I was to hear the news, it angered me that he could treat it with such triviality. I thought it was a trick and sat back suddenly. It was strange that the thing I had longed for most suddenly terrified me. What if they were pulling my leg and it was a nasty joke? I thought I wouldn't be able to cope with it if it was.

After breakfast he took me to the front entrance, where we were stopped by a Support Unit sergeant who seemed a little unsure of the situation. The sergeant ushered us back inside threateningly with the barrel of his FN rifle. If he was unsure, then I was even more so. After all I had been through it would be a pity to end as simply as this. I wondered if my colleague was trying to free me illegally. There was no signing of papers or show of occasion whatsoever.

It turned out that my release was official, but Support Unit had been briefed that only Rogers Mutonga and Sam Magadze had the authority to release me. The member-in-charge made a call and told us to wait, as Rogers was coming from Harare to pick me up later that morning. The notion of a fix began to worry me again and I resigned myself to languishing there forever. When you are so close to freedom the mere stress of waiting any longer seems unbearable. I had been at Goromonzi for so long that another hour, on this occasion, was going to make a difference! What if they brewed up further charges and kept me detained? I sat for two horrible hours waiting, but Rogers eventually arrived with a huge smile on his face.

When he drove me out of the Goromonzi Police compound, the sense of freedom hit me. I had never noticed how green the grass could get with the summer rains. The air was fresh and its smell was something strange and new. It was as if I was a newborn child fresh to the world. The sky had never been a prettier shade of blue and the sun had never been brighter. For the first few minutes I strained my eyes through narrow slits to become accustomed to the natural light. It was an incredible feeling, but I retained reservations about the circumstances of my release.

Rogers was nonchalant about my experience. He informed me that Minister Mnangagwa was not happy about the situation, but was giving me the benefit of the doubt. As we drove toward Harare I prayed that we wouldn't turn off on the Chikirubi road again. As it drew close I shut my eyes and focused all my attention on the sounds of the engine. The gears didn't shift down and we drove on. I began to believe I was really free.

A few kilometres later I summoned the courage to ask Rogers about Hartlebury and Evans. I wanted to know if they were being released also. Rogers told me that they would remain in detention until the minister was happy with their story. I left it at that as any possible inference of association with them, with whatever they had done, might drag me back into the nightmare.

At my home Rogers made no attempt to leave. He told me he was having a drink when he was ordered to pick me up and the trip to Goromonzi had interrupted his social calendar. He hoped I would offer him one. I obliged. It was a bit odd to be having a drink with the man who had been so rabid to me days previously, but I didn't want to rock the boat.

It was fantastic to see Sheila and the kids again. Sheila had been informed by Toni Reid in the morning that I was to be released and she put on a spread. Toni was the self-imposed spokeswoman from the CIO Russian desk, who represented the three wives of the detainees while we were inside. She was ex-Rhodesian Military Intelligence and was once married to Captain Scotty McCormack of the SAS and Recce Commandos. A fantastic lady was Toni.

Sheila didn't expect to be entertaining my nemesis, but she went with the flow and was a gracious hostess. We had a few beers to celebrate my freedom, but after my enforced abstinence from alcohol I got drunk after only two. Rogers noticed my changing mood and decided to be discreet. Before he departed he informed me not to leave Harare or to talk to anyone other than Danny Stannard or Sam Magadze. They would be around on Monday to see me and I should remain at home until then.

I still had my doubts and I trusted nobody. Deep down I believed that the authorities were up to something and were trying to make me lapse into a false sense of security. With that they could then detain me once more, and after my taste of freedom this time, I might break. Sheila had booked a ticket for me on a flight to South Africa and insisted I leave immediately. I knew how the organisation worked and told her I wouldn't make it past the check-in counter at the airport. I wanted to talk to Stannard first anyway. I wanted to know what the fuck was going on. We were both worried that ulterior motives lurked behind my release.

It absolutely floored me when Sheila asked if the 'South African team' would swoop in and pick me up. That she actually believed I was guilty the whole time came as a bit of a surprise. I don't suppose I could blame her, as communication was not the strong point of our marriage.

Later that afternoon we ignored Rogers' order and went to visit the wives of my fellow detainees. They immediately got the impression that I was a sell-out, because I was free and their husbands were not. I had hoped that the sight of me would strengthen their resolve and invigorate their own faith. I expressed my innocence, but I don't think they believed me.

While I was there I noticed some of my old surveillance footmen walking outside on the main road. When I got home there were footmen there too. Instantly I knew my house was bugged and I warned Sheila, despite having nothing to hide. In the new Zimbabwe the authorities could make something out of anything, so we took the precaution of playing music all the time to interfere with transmitters, or we walked to the middle of the garden when we spoke.

Contrary to what I had dreamed of every single night in prison, my first night at home was one of the most uncomfortable I have ever spent. After months of sleeping on a hard, cold concrete floor, the comforts of a warm, soft mattress were alien to me. I couldn't sleep anyway, so I ended up moving to the lounge floor where the hardness under the carpet was familiar.

The following day, on Sunday afternoon, the telephone rang and I heard a familiar voice. It was John Gartner, ringing from Pretoria, to see how I was. I thought it was uncanny that he knew I was out of prison, but it really stumped me when he asked about the welfare of Hartlebury and Evans. How the hell did he know about the situation?

John asked me what my future intentions were, but I didn't say too much over the phone. He was also careful in choosing his words, being an old salt at clandestine work, but it didn't escape me that the fact that a known South African operative was phoning might just drop me back in the shit. Those were the circumstances of post-independent Zimbabwe.

Danny Stannard and Sam Magadze came to visit me on the Monday. With little remorse for my ordeal, they briefed me and said that I was welcome to come back to work now that it was over. They said the organisation was sorry for what had happened to me, but it was all par for the course and had to be endured while I was under investigation! They said that it was necessary to clear my name.

The feelings of hate I had built up at Goromonzi arose in me again and I nearly went berserk. I couldn't understand the calm normality that these people had placed over what was for me a life-changing event. For them it was as if nothing had ever happened. They didn't have to put up with the appalling conditions and Rogers Mutonga breathing down their necks. Put it down to a bad cxperience, they said!

I subdued my anger, gritted my teeth and didn't react. My hatred was gagging me and I struggled to breathe. Stannard requested that I remain in Zimbabwe. He said that if I made a run for it I might appear to be guilty and Rogers would be on the warpath again. Chances were I would be nabbed at the airport. With a little chuckle, he added that I was the safest white man in Zimbabwe now, because the government knew everything about me. Easy for him to say! My only downfall, in fact, was the possession of an unlicensed weapon which could have landed me with a five-year prison sentence. The minister was prepared to overlook this, I was told, on condition that I didn't take any further action against the State for my wrongful arrest.

I was taking this all in when the facts were presented to me. Stannard told me that the person who was supposed to have been arrested was in fact Geoff Price. Because of my background in Special Forces, they thought I was more likely to be in the service of a foreign intelligence agency. There he was, right under their noses the whole time, he said.

Halfway through my detention, Geoff got cold feet and fled to England. Together with Hartlebury and Evans, the State had accumulated evidence against the three who were working for South African Military Intelligence. Geoff left when he thought the other two might break under interrogation and reveal his part in the treason. They had all been recruited by Project Barnacle, although that wasn't apparent at the time. I would be filled in on the details but in the meantime, I was told to have no further contact or association with anyone either involved with Hartlebury and Evans, or known to be in the service of the South Africans. I mentioned John Gartner's call to cover my arse.

As compensation for my detention, and the subsequent hell I had endured, I was paid 60 Zimbabwe dollars by Sam Magadze and given time off for a holiday in Kariba. The 60 bucks paid for the fuel. Sam went the extra mile and asked if I had any complaints about the treatment I had received in prison. I replied that the only ones I had were why was I put in solitary confinement without having been cautioned first, for over two months with no bed, thirsty and starving. Having been a keen squash player and running five kilometres a day, I had been reduced to a skinny wreck, whose body was feeding off its own flesh! I had chronic tooth problems due to the 'fantastic' oral hygiene I had been provided with, and I couldn't feel my fingers any more because of the cramped confines of my cell and lack of exercise. Other than that I was just dandy!

Stannard frowned, replaced it with a quick smile and added that he had travelled to Goromonzi to inspect my conditions. How was the food, he asked? He was looking for one shiny apple in a pile of rotten ones. He had been shown my breakfast which consisted of eggs and bacon with baked beans on toast. He was quite satisfied with the nourishment I was supposed to be getting. As far as he was concerned, the accommodation and meals were above standard! What a load of horse shit!

CHAPTER 35:
PAYBACK

I just couldn't win. The Zimbabweans thought I worked for the South Africans. The South Africans wanted me dead because I worked for the Zimbabweans and now I was branded a sell-out by my own friends, or associates of friends, for supposedly fingering my fellow detainees who were rotting away in detention cells. I had no idea of what they were up to in the first place!

It took a very long time for people who knew of the arrest of Hartlebury, Evans and me to understand that I was not connected in any way with their dealings, nor with their downfall. In many circles I was ostracised and considered a turncoat and it remains that way to this day.

I gave myself two weeks off before I returned to work. On arrival at Daventry House, the reception I received from most colleagues was warm and welcoming. In some quarters I would draw a suspicious stare here and there, but I tried not to let it bother me. The first thing I noticed about CI Division was the lack of familiar faces. There had been a large exodus of white personnel who had thrown in the towel in case they were next. Bailey, Harries and several of the other guys had left because of the situation.

Brian Lawrence invited me to his office, to fill me in on events during my absence. He told me that the arrest had caused considerable damage to the organisation and to the white community as a whole. Countless staff had left the organisation and 'taken the gap'; a popular euphemism for those who got cold feet and departed to greener pastures. He himself had resigned and was going to Australia. I didn't really blame him because the white community's security was really hanging by a thread. Anyone could be arrested at any time.

Brian informed me that Geoff Price had recruited Hartlebury and Evans when they were on a course with German Intelligence. As a colonel in the South African Defence Force, he gave them both the rank of lieutenant. Their mission was to provide intelligence on anti-South African forces based in Zimbabwe. Brian inferred that they might have had something to do with the assassination of Joe Gqabi, when he was erroneously dispatched while being a source for the NIS. It was Gray Branfield, a former SB operative who worked for Barnacle, who actually shot Gqabi and he was associated with us all.

When Gqabi was taken out, the NIS was so irate that they informed our organisation that there were three operatives working in CI Division who had links with South African Military Intelligence. And so the witch-hunt began.

Hartlebury, Evans and I were the obvious choices because of our backgrounds. Hartlebury had been attached to SB (Selous Scouts) Bindura during the war and Evans to SB (Selous Scouts) SALOPS Braeside. Then there was me, ex-SAS and Selous Scouts. And to top it all off I was Recce Troop – arch enemy No 1!

When Geoff Price realised that Hartlebury and Evans might crack under interrogation and therefore identify him as The Godfather, he staged a letter from the UK stating that his mother was severely ill and on her deathbed. He took compassionate leave and travelled to the United Kingdom, never to be seen in Zimbabwe again. He continued to work for the South Africans.

It turned out that Hartlebury and Evans were indeed to leave Goromonzi when the first detention order lapsed, but I was to remain as the guilty party. Their interrogators had managed to glean between zero and fuck all on their alleged treason and were going to release them. During the processing of their release, one of them had asked to see Geoff Price and was told that he had fled to England. For reasons unknown, possibly because he thought it was a trap and that Geoff had deserted them, he panicked at the last minute and confessed all, effectively sealing their fate. After they had signed confessions, the authorities searched their houses more thoroughly and found weapons and communications equipment.

Brian then told me that they had searched my house a second time, in an effort to corroborate evidence against me. In doing so they went through letters and photo albums in search of visual evidence of my connection to those known to be working for the South Africans. My saving grace came in the form of a particular photo of Recce Troop in the Selous Scouts. The photo is included here and depicts most of the operators from Recce Troop, many of whom became Project Barnacle members.

Selous Scouts Reconnaissance Troop. Dave Scales and Jake sit in front row on the ground. This is the photo which helped save Jake when he was interned at Goromonzi after the war.

At the time, the Zimbabwean authorities had captured a former SB black member, while he was clandestinely trying to cross the border. Under interrogation, he revealed he had been trained on a farm near Pretoria with other ex-Rhodesian SB and Special Forces members. This was the same farm from where Tim Callow, Dave Scales, Chris Schulenburg, Neil Kriel, Butch Atkins, John Gartner and others operated. When he was shown the photo, he pointed out these men and said he had seen all of them except John Gartner before.

When I was indicated he said he had no knowledge of me and I was never there. He fingered one of the men for being the bomber behind 88 Manica Road and told them how the deed was done. The man had climbed a wall at the back of the building and placed a large shaped charge on the roof. Anyone inside the building when the charge went off was toast. I knew nothing of those activities at the time and it is only now I can laugh about it. I must admit the laugh always comes with rough edges in my throat and is a bit hard to swallow.

It appeared that Military Intelligence and the NIS weren't in communication with each other, much like the SAS and Selous Scouts hadn't been during the Kazungula debacle. They were often working against each other in the field, as shown by the Gqabi assassination.

My troubles didn't end there. After batting off most inferences of being a sell-out for many months, another break was in order. With a few friends from the department I organised a Zambezi canoe trip from Kariba to Kanyemba along with a couple of mates who now lived in Durban. The member-in-charge CIO Kariba, Karl Gibbard, managed to get permission from CAFCO, the electricity authority in Kariba, for us to launch from the dam wall. Given the strategic value of the hydro-electric scheme such permission was a rarity, as the wall was well protected. The trip was a welcome break but unfortunately the Durban party couldn't make it.

Shortly after the trip I was summoned to Sam Magadze's office where he asked me about certain ex-members of the Selous Scouts who were known to be working in Phalaborwa. He wanted to know how well I knew them. I shrugged off any connections that could be harmful, but acknowledged the obvious: that I had worked with them in the past. I left it at that, not wanting to stir the hornet's nest further.

As I left Sam's office, he called me back with something more trivial on his mind. Would I mind attending court the following week to stand as a witness in the Hartlebury and Evans case, he asked? It was more of an order than a request. He wanted me to give evidence of our treatment at Goromonzi and handed me a list of answers to probable questions. They included our fair treatment in prison, our daily exercise routine, our three square meals a day, the fact that we were given cold fizzy drinks to drink, our cell doors were never locked but left open for us to roam as we pleased within the prison yard, and we had beds, sheets, blankets and pillows. It was the furthest possible thing from the truth.

Feeling uncomfortable with the situation, I approached Johnny Gibson and asked his advice. I told him that I wasn't willing to lie in court, particularly as we had all suffered the same dismal treatment at the hands of our interrogators. Johnny suggested I go on leave over the period of the court case and ably assisted me with a leave pass. My parents had just moved to Durban and he suggested I visit them. I didn't need any convincing and put the plan into motion.

While I was in Durban I met up with the friends who couldn't make the canoe trip. I rubbed it in that they had missed out on an experience of a lifetime, but promised to send photographs when I returned to Zimbabwe. I had just completed a colour photography course with Johnny Alsford and wanted to show off my prowess.

On my return to Harare, I addressed a letter to this friend and set it aside waiting for the development of the photos. On the same day I received a call from Danny Stannard and was told to report to the Harare morgue, to identify three bodies that had been brought in, photograph them in colour and take Polaroid pictures. I was told that one of them might be the body of a mate of mine, Dave Berry, from SAS days. I was struck with an immediate sense of foreboding if what I heard was true.

I arrived at the morgue and was shown to a room containing several cold stone slabs. Three of them were occupied and covered with white sheets. When the door closed behind me, a tingling chill ran down my spine. Recent memories of Goromonzi flooded back with the sound of the metal door locking into its frame. Despite the drop in temperature in the refrigerated room, a sweat trickled from my brow.

On inspecting the bodies I discovered that they were in such a bad state of decomposition that identification was impossible. The funny thing was their decomposition was in different stages, which meant they had each died at different times. I met up with Stannard and informed him of my findings, passing on the Polaroids at the same time.

A few days later I had a discussion with a white ex-RAR officer who had stayed on in the Zimbabwe military. He had seen the corpses lying alongside an airstrip in Umtali a week before and had enquired of the black ex-RAR officer present why they were rotting in the sun. He was told that the Zimbabwe Army refused to put the bodies of their enemies in the shade.

The white officer told me that the corpses had belonged to a Recce callsign, obviously from South Africa, who were conducting an operation in the lowveld. One of the dead was ex-SAS and the other two ex-RLI. The callsign had been unwittingly compromised by locals, who had reported their presence to a Zimbabwe Army post. They had watched them closely and recorded the whereabouts of their LUP. The particular troops, who responded to the incursion, led by a meticulous black officer, were all seasoned professionals and had learnt their trade in the RAR during the bush war. They tactically approached the LUP and attacked the callsign at dawn. It was believed that Dave Berry was killed in the initial contact and the remainder fled, developing into a running battle in which several others were wounded or killed, the RLI guys among them. Hearsay was rife but rumour had it that one of the bodies, while still identifiable, had a bullet hole between the eyes indicating that he had been captured, tortured and then executed.

That's all I was told about the incident and my involvement extended as far as taking photographs at the morgue. When the story finally reached South Africa, it had been twisted and turned so much that the version they heard had me complicit in the death of Dave Berry. Darryl Watt, another former SAS member I had served with, was infuriated and believed I had contributed to the downfall of the patrol. He queried how it was possible that seasoned SAS operators were taken out by a bunch of terrorists. Someone, it was thought, must have informed the Zimbabweans of SAS protocol in the bush. Who else could it be but me?

I was perturbed by the accusations, which filtered through to me from my contacts in South Africa. They were unfounded and unfair. The story was clearly being used as propaganda against me for staying on in Zimbabwe, but I had no idea how I could clear my name. The bottom line was that the callsign was very unfortunate to be surprised by a highly professional ex-Rhodesian unit.

What made matters worse was the fact that, while out of my office one day, one of my ex-terr colleagues snooped through my drawers and found the letter I had addressed to my mates in Durban. Believing it to be the perfect opportunity to frame me and get me out of the system, he doctored the letter with a recent photo I had taken of the dead bodies in the morgue, and ran off to HQ to tell tales. What it was going to prove I don't know, but he said that my intentions were to pass on the photos to my intelligence contacts in South Africa. I was called into Ritson's office and I explained the circumstances of the new evidence against me. Fortunately he believed me and the matter was dropped, but I have no doubt that the story reached my former colleagues in Phalaborwa who naturally assumed I was boasting about my latest exploits.

Like others, my parents saw no future in the country and wanted to settle into a peaceful retirement by spending the remainder of their years on the coast. Unfortunately, my Dad fell ill with cancer of the throat and underwent surgery. The surgery was not successful and he died a short time later.

I was granted permission by Danny Stannard to travel to South Africa for his funeral. I left for Durban and spent the time consoling my mother and meeting with old Rhodesian acquaintances from the war years.

After being in Durban for about ten days I noticed that I was under constant surveillance. There were Indian footmen tailing me, and young white guys in cars. The white guys in particular stuck out like sore thumbs and were very military in appearance. The Indians were a little harder to spot but gave themselves away with movie-like antics like raising newspapers to conceal their faces every time I passed. On one occasion, while having a drink in a popular bar on the Bluff, I approached two guys and invited them to share my table rather than just sit there watching me. They saw the comical side of it and after getting over their initial embarrassment joined me for a beer and a laugh.

The day before I was to return to Zimbabwe, I visited my brother Ian who lived on the Bluff. While I was there, there was a knock on the door and in walked Ben Pretorius, an old acquaintance from Special Branch and Callsign 24. He sat down for a beer and asked me how things were going in Zimbabwe, offering his sympathies for my imprisonment. He had heard about it through other 'friends' who had remained in SB after the war, he said.

Ben didn't beat around the bush. The reason for his visit was to recruit me. He briefed me on his own employment in the NIS and suggested that I, as a recruiting target, couldn't be riper, considering my bad experience. He wanted a one-word answer: would I be interested in providing intelligence for the South Africans?

The anger in me smouldered away like a fire liberally dosed with oil. I replied that I was interested but it wasn't that simple. I told him that I knew of others who had been recruited, like Hans Sittig and Cliff Perrin, who had been picked up and questioned immediately on their return home. I told Ben that I was not impressed with his security. He assured me that I would be working under a different branch to that which had recruited Hans and Cliff and admitted that they were a bunch of idiots. Could I think about it and meet him at the Malibu Hotel, at 11 a.m. the following morning before my departure?

That night I gave the issue a lot of thought. My time at Goromonzi had changed me as a person and left me disillusioned about the organisation I worked for. I had sat in solitary confinement for over two months, ridiculed, starving, thirsty and going mental – for what? I hadn't done anything wrong and all I got in return was a half-hearted apology and petrol money for a trip to Kariba.

With the mistrust placed in me, I was left in no doubt that it could happen again. If I was going to be accused of something then I had better be doing something wrong in the first place! I had never worked for the CIO with any political conviction anyway, and if anything, their treatment of me had pushed me into a corner. The only thing was that in the corner where I sat there were ropes behind me and I was coming back fighting. I was a fabrication of their lack of trust. I realised I could work against the bastards who had locked me up, but in a discreet manner. They had really screwed my mind up and I have never been the same since. I had become more emotional and prone to worry and I still suffer from claustrophobia! Yes, I would do all in my power to get payback. If there was financial remuneration on the sidelines, then that would be an added bonus. Revenge was sweet!

I met Ben at the Malibu shortly before my return, where he introduced me to another gentleman. I was told that the other man would be my controller and would be 'running me' when I was in Zimbabwe. Contact with the NIS would be only through him and under no circumstances was I to divulge information to anyone else. I was to proceed as normal and sometime in the future I would be contacted. Naturally, a thousand questions beckoned. How would I be contacted and when? What was I supposed to do and what would be asked of me? With a pat on the back my controller winked at me and said to leave it up to him.

Work resumed as normal and it was several months before I was approached. I had begun to think that the NIS would never get hold of me, when a stranger sidled up to me at the urinal of the Flagstaff Bar during a typical weekly lunch outing. When my name was mentioned, I was shaking off the last drops of dew. I looked up to see the gentleman I had met at the Malibu in Durban. Without fanfare, he went about his own business of relieving himself, staring ahead at the bright stainless steel of the toilet facility. When he was done he casually requested a meeting in the car park of the Red Fox Hotel that evening.

When I met Mr Z in the car park we sat in his car and he briefed me on what information he wanted and how I was going to get it. All I was to do was photograph anything and everything in the division that I had access to. If there was any information that I wanted to pass on I would write it down and photograph that also.

On the last Wednesday of every month, at 20:00, I was to meet alternately at the Red Fox, Greendale or at the Howff Restaurant in Chisipite, where we would liaise in the gent's toilet. I was to make my way to the toilet from the bar while my contact came in from the restaurant. If someone was watching it would appear that we were both on our way to relieve ourselves. In the toilet someone would stand next to me, on my right-hand side, at the urinal and would greet me with a predetermined code phrase, so I would know it was the right person. On rebuttal of my password I would reach into the person's left dinner jacket pocket and deposit a roll of film. If someone else was present and using the facility, then we would leave without contact and convene at the same place half an hour later. It was a simple plan and it worked. Mr Z then asked if I had banking facilities in South Africa for purposes of depositing my retainer. I gave him my mother's account number although I wasn't really interested in money at the time.

I was furnished with rolls of high-grade black-and-white film which was available commercially in South Africa, in case suspicion was aroused if they were found.

I was told that I was going to get a phone call from a woman named Janelle in South Africa and I was to pretend that she was my girlfriend. She was to be the link between my controller and me. We were to speak to each other as if we were lovers and in that way I could communicate whether I had any problems, if I was travelling across borders, or needed anything, or wanted to warn them. For instance, if I said something like 'I miss you and I really need you now' it would mean that I was in trouble and I needed to contact my controller urgently. If Janelle said something like 'I've sent you a small package in the mail and it should be there in two days' it meant my controller wanted to see me and I should be at a predetermined place at a certain time in two days. A typical warning would be to the tune of 'Darling, my period was late last month. I think next time we should be cautious' which would translate into 'be careful at the next meeting, possible compromise'. In writing it now it sounds pretty lame, but we never experienced problems with communication. It was a tried and tested method that South African Intelligence had used for many years.

And so commenced a period of espionage that I had never possibly dreamed I would be involved in. The more I did the better I felt. Absolutely everything I had access to inside the CIO was photographed and passed on through my regular monthly meetings.

With each titbit of information I divulged, it was as if I was landing a punch on Rogers Mutonga's nose. I knew that if I was caught I would be history. Everything I had experienced before would come back and haunt me tenfold, as the authorities would believe I had escaped the net previously and was guilty the whole time. I really didn't care and the money was good. Initially I explained to my mother that the large deposits into her account were from bits and pieces I was selling for my retirement, or in case I moved to South Africa. When the deposits became too large to explain, I told her the truth. She took it well and understood my motives but was concerned for my wellbeing.

I must say the NIS and a few of my old mates in Durban, looked after her well and checked in on her at regular intervals after my father's death. It suited me fine. My mother was being well taken care of and so was I.

Janelle came to visit me in Harare midway through the year and met me at the Wine Barrel Bar. We snuggled up close in a corner and looked for all the world like a pair of lustful lovers. She briefed me that Ben Pretorius had moved on and my controller was going to change. She gave me a new name and said that things would continue as they had but with a few minor changes.

For one, how we handled the film was to be revised. I would use colour film now, supplied by the NIS, that was only possible to develop with special chemicals. If standard developing procedure was used the film would appear blank. The film was to be inserted into a black-and-white video cassette and passed on by the same means as before. If at all it were to be picked up, it would appear as an entirely innocent blank cassette.

For purposes of emergency, if I had information that was urgent, I was supplied with a piece of rubber dog shit that contained a secret compartment. For all intents and purposes, the fake turd looked like the real thing, complete with a high-gloss, slimy finish in parts. I have actually seen similar devices since in toy stores, where they are sold as gimmicks for kids, and wondered how many people knew what their real purpose was.

In an emergency, I would put my film inside the dog shit, phone Janelle with a codeword and leave the turd at a certain place in the Red Fox car park for collection. Naturally, nobody would be too interested in picking up the shit, unless the person was a cleaner, so it couldn't be left for too long.

As time passed, my regular drops occurred more frequently. Each time I visited either the Howff Restaurant or the Red Fox Hotel, I would have four or five rolls of film to pass on, some of them photos I had taken, others just loads of information I had written on paper, photographed and then destroyed. All the photography I was doing for the organisation and for liaison, MI6 and CIA, was filtered to my friends in South Africa. If it was something I felt would discredit the Zimbabwe government in any way I passed it on. The NIS started paying a handsome amount of money into my mother's bank account.

John Alsford had got his way. While I was locked up, he had wormed a way into having my darkroom at Daventry House shut down, under the pretext that my belongings needed sifting through. After prison, I had to report to him as my member-in-charge, although I was still the CI Division photographer. Central Police Station studios were to be my new workplace, where it gave John great pleasure delegating tasks to me which I would otherwise have done naturally. It became John's favourite saying, when he left the office, that he was going to be out on a job for Mike Crafter in the Bat Mobile.

Once again, I became a camp lackey and was left to look after the studios when John was out. It really pissed me off, particularly when I saw the quality of work that John was producing. Much of it was amateurish in comparison to what I had been taught professionally. Of course there was always an excuse and it was generally blamed on the darkroom assistants, who weren't developing the films properly.

Sorry John, other than that you were great to work with!

Covert photography is an art set quite aside from standard photography. To illustrate what I mean, a small story is necessary. I was once assigned a reservist photographer with 25 years' experience in the commercial photography field. He had taken pictures for newspapers and magazines as well as doing a stint as a CID photographer.

On a particular job, while he remained in the Bat Mobile, I told him to take photos of a subject whom I would mark by walking up behind him and raising the rolled newspaper in my right hand to my ear on the pretext of scratching. It was a very simple job and the reservist had minutes in which to take pictures of the target.

When we got back to the laboratory to process the film, it was a disaster. The very professional photographer told me that it had been an exceptionally hard task, as through the dark windows of the vehicle there were few chances to take a picture. If you miss your opportunity it has gone. John had the same problem. He was a highly skilled photographer and I never doubted his talent. But as a covert photographer he was left wanting.

On another occasion, I took photos outside the Russian Embassy, for the CIA liaison. They were highly impressed and even asked if they could attach agents to me to learn the art. The request in itself was an honour, to say the least.

The liaison was even more impressed when he saw the conditions under which I had taken the photos. I snuck him into an old building, with several blocks separating ourselves and the embassy, and shot through a hole in a dusty window. This sort of photography requires an eye for the big picture – something not everyone's got – and an ability to envisage a view from a particular place while nowhere near it. That way I could immediately see the best vantage points for achieving my aims.

The lack of trust in the department grew with every day. John Alsford and I noticed that anyone who was ex-BSAP or military, white or black, was being monitored by a shadow agent. The shadow agents were all ex-terrs who weren't particularly good at their craft. They stuck out like sore thumbs, but despite their ineptitude, it did worry us. We began to leave traps just to confirm our suspicions, like a pile of photos left in a particular order. As we suspected, they were always sifted through and replaced without due care. You can't really catch out the master at his own craft!

In time, we found out that there were weekly meetings at Red Bricks CIO HQ that were solely to report on the findings of the ex-Rhodesian servicemen still serving. It was really a debrief, where every shadow agent would submit evidence, good or bad, on his target. The information was sent directly to minister Mnangagwa who would file it for later use. In the event that one of us messed up, and we felt they really wanted us to mess up, the minister could retrieve his file and fabricate all sorts of nonsense. I was always questioned about additional photos of subjects I had kept back in the lab. They were surplus to requirements, or hadn't been developed properly and I was accused of keeping my own dossier for independent purposes, possibly to hand on to foreign intelligence.

It was very hard to work under these circumstances as the mistrust was flagrant. Our terrorist buddies were forever submitting false reports to frame us in innocent situations. It wasn't long before I was called in by Ray Ritson, who had replaced Geoff Price as member-in-charge, E Desk. He began to scrutinise my motives on particular jobs and questioned my loyalty. I explained that many of us were under the impression that the minister wanted us out of the organisation altogether. They were making life very difficult and he agreed. It only took another two months before Ray resigned.

The next member-in-charge of Special Projects Section was Hans Sittig. Hans was incredibly hard to work with, in part due to his German roots. He knew the answers to everything and would never listen. It was always Hans's way or the highway. This turned out to be disastrous on many an occasion.

Hans would often ignore proven procedure, in a bid to save a little time. On one job at the Monomotapa Hotel, instead of sending KK up to identify a subject, he walked straight up to the reception and asked if the target was still in his room. The receptionist noticed the key for the subject's room wasn't in the pigeon hole and offered to call him. Hans declined the offer and took up station in the lounge while we blended in. He told KK to remain in the reception area, until the subject came downstairs to return his key.

When the subject finally appeared, the receptionist told him that a gentleman was enquiring about his whereabouts and pointed out Hans sitting in the lounge. It was embarrassing to say the least when the subject approached a red-faced Hans and asked what he wanted. Hans threw up his arms in typical German disgust, accentuating his accent, and said it was obviously a mistake. The receptionist butted in and was adamant that Hans was indeed the man who was looking for him. In this particular case we got away with the inexplicable lack of protocol, but there were many others when an alert or dangerous subject would have cottoned on immediately and possibly gone covert himself, making our task all the more difficult.

On another job, run hand in hand by Toni Reid of Russian Desk and Hans Sittig, we had to spend a few weeks in Bulawayo, where the Trade Fair was in progress. Our CIA liaison had an interest in the Russian businessmen and dignitaries, who had established a stand which they thought was a front for more sinister dealings. Our own government was worried that the Russians, who had supported ZIPRA throughout the war, were trying to re-establish support with bandits still operating in the region, for an armed insurrection against ZANLA, and wanted to know their every move. It was believed that, after the fair closed each day, they would meet with ZIPRA officials at night and plot whatever they were up to.

The team moved to Bulawayo in advance of the Russian party's arrival and set up an LP in one of the rooms at the Holiday Inn where they were staying. Through our contacts, we acquired keys for their rooms and placed transmitters around the place which would monitor their conversations. It was old school-spy technology and required a little more initiative. Many of us were certain the Russians would sweep their rooms, or employ other tactics to interfere with any eavesdropping equipment.

Hans was of the opinion that nobody would beat him at his own game and the transmitters were sufficient. No phones were tapped or technically advanced equipment sought, which was available to us through liaison, in the form of sound-wave transmitting receivers, which could have been bounced off windows.

My job was to tail certain individuals around Bulawayo in the Bat Mobile and photograph them. This turned into a mundane exercise as after leaving the hotel, they invariably drove straight to the Trade Fair where they remained for the whole day and then drove back to the hotel.

The LP was a disaster and recorded nothing more than inaudible interference. As we suspected, the Russians turned on the televisions in their rooms or had possibly brought along 'squelch' transmitters of their own to render their voices inaudible. The sum total of the two-week exercise was zip, except for a huge expense account and a lot of embarrassment when it came to briefing our American liaison. If we had gone the extra mile, we may have come up with something worthwhile.

Shortly after Bulawayo, Hans was up to no good and started an affair with the Russian transcriber, a petite little woman who worked for CIA liaison. Toni Reid, of Russia desk, took exception to this and filed a report to Mike Crafter. As far as she was concerned, it was unprofessional, unethical and interfered with her work. Hans was summoned by Crafter, confronted by Reid and an argument ensued. It was only rectified when Hans stormed out, after tendering his verbal resignation. Karl Gibbard became member-in-charge J Desk.

CI Division was going to expand and had plans to move from Daventry House to a building on Enterprise Road in Highlands. The building had been revamped with a coat of paint, but it didn't escape my attention that it was the same building that Ian Suttil and Callsign 24 were going to attack just before elections.

Mike Crafter had snuck in as member-in-charge of CI Division and told Danny Stannard that he was not happy with the photographic situation in the division. CI needed its own darkroom facilities and an independent photographer, as much of the work was sensitive and for CI eyes only. He suggested that I once again have autonomy and move from Central in order to establish a facility at Enterprise Road. At the same time, new studios were being built at Red Bricks HQ to facilitate the organisation countrywide. John Alsford moved to Red Bricks with his three ex-terr assistants and I built a darkroom at the new building and was supplied with photographic material from there.

Karl Gibbard looked after me on J Desk and we had two vehicles assigned to us. I was permitted to use one of them as a 'company vehicle', but my old mate KK pulled the race card and filed a complaint that I had been shown preference because of my colour. The matter was provoked when ex-terrs in the division sided with KK and also filed reports. Karl sought Mike Crafter's advice, as I had only been given the vehicle because I was on 24 hour callout.

Karl managed to get KK out of the way by putting him on a key-cutting course at Key Den, a commercial company in Newlands. One of our reservists owned Key Den and it temporarily put the situation on ice.

CI Division bought a second Bat Mobile and rigged it out with battery chargers and surveillance equipment. They gave it to KK and for purposes of keeping the peace, afforded him the unusual title of 'Key Master and anything to do with keys'! As he was already in charge of surveillance, I was instructed to teach him photographic and darkroom techniques in the event that I was unavailable. Despite the race card stunt, KK and I got on extremely well, as we had done since we first met in Callsign 24.

Our American buddies at the CIA gave us another van, completely kitted out for surveillance. Of course, the hierarchy at HQ ensured it underwent careful sweeping, in case it had been bugged by the CIA to eavesdrop on our activities. The new vehicle was parked at the premises where it remained unless in use.

Karl Gibbard, although affable and down to earth, was very much a 'yes' man. He had come from Kariba, where he had helped obtain permission for us to launch from the dam wall on our canoe trip. Mike Crafter and Karl were big buddies and Karl got whatever he asked for. He was given a brand-new VW Golf, which had been passed to CIO as part of an aid package from the Germans.

KK and I assumed dual control in the 2IC role in Special Projects. KK always thought he was senior, as I was a civilian attached and he was a regular. He was being pushed by other elements in the organisation to take over from Karl as member-in-charge E Desk when he left.

Karl decided it was time to make a break, get married and move on. One of the perks that he enjoyed was subsidised rent by American liaison, in return for boarding one of their transcribers. He looked after different people who moved through that particular embassy on three-month cycles.

Karl approached Mike Crafter to tender his resignation and also put in a few good words for me. He believed a power struggle would develop among the black members when he left and wanted to ensure that responsibility was given to the right person. While he knew KK was a seasoned veteran, he believed that I was the ideal candidate for the job, as I had been involved in Special Projects since its inception. The overriding problem with any promotion I was given, was my status as a civilian attached. Karl believed that KK and Olaf Reed, another probable for the post, were both too immature for the task of running Special Projects despite their professionalism.

Crafter called me into his office one morning and asked if I wanted the job. He explained that if I accepted, diplomacy would be in order as there were others in the department who might cry foul. He wanted to be as fair as possible and promote the most experienced individual, but he had received a directive from HQ that it would be preferential if a black man got the posting. To circumvent this, he broke from conformity and promoted both KK and me to head Special Projects, J Desk. I would take ultimate responsibility and KK would have half the desk, which dealt with surveillance and anything to do with locksmiths and keys! The things we do to keep people happy!

Thus I became member-in-charge Special Projects Section, J Desk.

We expanded our operations at the airport terminal. John Alsford erected several cameras at the immigration desks, to photograph people coming in and out of the country. Our staff would load and unload the cameras each day, after immigration officers had snapped away at suspicious or marked individuals. One of my jobs was to keep a library of photos of these individuals, to which was attached any particular information we had on them. We had daily reports from the hotels in which they were staying and these accurately tracked their movement around town.

The Bat Mobile was often used at the airport in a surveillance role, disguised as an ambulance. With large magnetic Red Cross stickers attached, it was rolled out to the apron next to aircraft that had just landed, where we would snap away at arriving suspected subversives. Most of the jobs I did were against opposition parties like ZUM and ZAPU.

CHAPTER 36:
SHENANIGANS

When Samora Machel died in a plane crash on 19 October 1986, on his way home after meeting other African leaders, 'rent a crowd' went on the rampage in the streets of Harare, attacking South African Airlines, Air Malawi, the Malawian High Commission and the South African Trade Mission. The latter was on the top floor of the building in which it was housed, so the rioters weren't too successful. Unsatisfied, they marched on the US Embassy and tried to scale the walls. After stoning the building they managed to steal the American flag and burn it in the street. The riot police arrived and rapidly dispersed the crowd with tear gas and dogs. Most of the rioters fled back to the university from where they had come. Mike Crafter sent us on a mission to apprehend one of the rioters for interrogation purposes.

We set off in two vehicles from Highlands, to intercept 'rent a crowd' as they ran down Second Street. We drove past the shops at Second Street Extension, and managed to separate a small crowd and close in with the vehicles. When the car I was in passed one of the rioters, it slowed and a few of us leapt out upon a startled rioter. His buddies had no idea what was going on as they saw white men abducting their pal and they began hurling stones and other missiles at us. In order to regain control of the situation, I brought out my firearm and waved it in the air at them. They lost their sense for adventure and desisted from stoning us, leaving their screaming friend to his fate.

Back at Highlands, when we questioned the individual, we were informed that members of the university had been approached by the Libyan Embassy to cause disruption at all the places that were attacked. The main aim was to give the Americans a scare and the rioters were to focus their attentions on the US embassy. We couldn't really understand the connection between Samora Machel and all the targets for aggression, but we understood the motivation when we discovered the amounts of cash that had been liberally dished out. Confirmation of the Libyans' involvement came, when undercover operatives in CIO, who had infiltrated the crowd, reported that they had seen the lead elements of the mob enter the Libyan

Embassy as they passed. Inside they conferred with Arab-looking men who seemed to be orchestrating the whole affair.

The next morning the newspaper presented an article on the disturbances and said that widespread damage had occurred. Cars with South African or Malawian registration had been stoned and burnt; fortunately, with little injury to the passengers. There was a great deal of resentment toward the South Africans, as they were accused of sabotaging Samora Machel's aircraft and ultimately having a hand in his death. The Malawians were unpopular for supposedly harbouring RENAMO guerrillas who were fighting the Mozambique government.

The end of the article was the cream on the cake, as it dramatically described one of the student rioters being abducted at gunpoint in broad daylight at Second Street Extension by South African agents! It just goes to show how the news media can misinterpret incidents.

The year 1988 was a terrible one for those of us still serving in the security services. The South Africans were on the prowl again, disabling ANC targets in Zimbabwe, Botswana and Zambia. When elements of 1 Reconnaissance Commando at the Bluff began preparations to kill me, I learnt about it first hand. It seemed ironic that the men I had served with for so long, and with whom I'd sweated blood, were now being trained to assassinate me. In hindsight, given my innocence of whatever allegations they levelled at me, I hold little respect for the powers that believed I might have been a threat. I wonder how many other innocent men, in similar difficult and trying circumstances, were actually neutralised for the greater good of South Africa.

Dave O'Sullivan, with whom I'd worked in the SAS, phoned me one evening to warn me of his latest mission brief. At the Bluff, the ex-Rhodesians in the Recces were formulating a plan to take out those who had stayed on in military positions after the transition of power. I was among them. The orders, I was told, came as a directive from South African Military Intelligence.

Captain Bob Mackenzie, with whom I had also worked on numerous occasions in the past, was tasked as mission commander and commenced a period of intense training. Among the methods of 'taking us out' which they discussed were direct methods, like shooting us while we lounged at popular drinking establishments or at coffee shops, or to gun us down while we drove to or from work. To this end they planned to infiltrate intelligence agents to place us under surveillance. Dave told me they already knew many of my habits and were well versed on my daily routines. When the agents had established a pattern of our movements, the assault teams would be sent in the form of two operatives per target, using motorbikes. The passenger on the bike would wield a silenced Uzi submachine gun and use it to dispatch a target when he pulled up at the traffic lights. The motorbike would allow for greater ease of escape than a car and could be dumped before the operatives got a heliborne uplift to South Africa. I was told to watch my back and stay away from my regular haunts. Dave wasn't sure when the operation would take place, but felt obliged to warn me.

I had enough on my plate as it was, but I heeded the warning. The Beefeater pub became less frequented as did morning coffee at Brazzitta with John Alsford, and lunch at the Flagstaff. When I travelled to work every morning, I carefully checked my rear-view mirror at all times and every day I took a different route to and from work, trying hard not to establish a pattern that was easy to follow. I am a very careful person naturally, but I must admit I had let my guard down.

Before and after the attempted Brickhill assassination, Project Barnacle operatives provided intelligence on, or had a direct hand in hitting various targets inside Zimbabwe. Initially it was the sabotage of Zimbabwe Air Force aircraft at Thornhill Airbase in August 1982 and then the attacks on ANC offices at 16 Angwa Street, Harare and an ANC facility at 29 Eves Crescent in Ashdown Park in May 1986.

In January 1988, they hit the ANC transit facility in Bulawayo, but due to a planning error the culprits were caught and detained by the Zimbabwean police. All of them were elements of South African Intelligence cells, working hand-in-hand and they were all ex-Rhodesian servicemen. Kevin Woods, a NIS agent, was ex-BSAP as was Philip Conjwayo. Then there was Mike Smith and Guy and Barry Bawden, all working for Military Intelligence.

In the ensuing months, the captives were subjected to a highly publicised trial, not to mention torture, of which I had first-hand experience. Like me they were shackled and detained under heavy security in the event of a South African rescue mission.

Shortly after the incident, CI Division received intelligence that I might have been the next target on the list. The capture of the former Rhodesian South

African agents might have been what put paid to the effort, as within a few months, I had received word that the operation to kill me had been called off. By that stage I was a nervous wreck, jumping at every shadow and everything that went bump around me.

Later that year, while I was conducting routine business, a report came in by radio that Olaf had seen a suspicious group of eight young white males, all wearing denim outfits, with short-cropped hair, hanging around outside a service station in the Borrowdale suburb of Harare. Since the cessation of compulsory national service in the country, it was unusual for young men to sport short hair, as most preferred to follow the fashion of long hair. With so many short-haired individuals in one bunch, Olaf was sure something was askew. He reported that they were all athletically built and seemed serious in their manner. Stopping for a cold drink mightn't have been a good idea for them!

Olaf pulled into the garage and managed to get the registration numbers of the two vehicles they were driving and ran them through VID (Vehicle Inspection Depot), only to discover that they were either stolen or false. The youths left the service station and drove down Borrowdale Road towards town and turned right into North Avenue. Olaf followed at a distance and saw them entering a block of flats in the Avenues suburb. Suspecting that the youths were a South African hit squad, or possibly a rescue team for Woods, Conjwayo, Smith and the Bawdens, in which case they were most likely Reconnaissance Commandos, he requested assistance. Inexplicably, Olaf was told to head back to CI Division and file a report, instead of remaining 'eyes on' target. A police Special Tactics team from the Support Unit was summoned and deployed to the block of flats. Between Olaf's departure and their arrival countless minutes were lost.

I was sent to the scene to take photographs when the Support Unit raid went in. Bill Chambers, an addition to the organisation (strangely having just served in the South African Defence Force), warned me to be careful. If the subjects were indeed South African Commandos, he had first-hand knowledge of their prowess. I didn't need warning as I knew of their levels of professionalism and armed myself accordingly. Although I would not take part in the assault, I resolved to be careful. In the event Support Unit proved no match for the youngsters I was next in line.

When I arrived at the block of flats, there was a quandary over identifying which flat the 'commandos' had entered. Olaf had put in a surveillance team across the road but they had had no luck. The footmen who had been milling around the area were in a similar boat and hadn't seen anything out of the ordinary. Support Unit wanted to drag the whole complex for a mass arrest and sift through the chaff once it was done. Bill, who had taken over as on-site commander, suggested that it would be too risky as civilians might get caught in the crossfire if a gun battle erupted, which was likely, given the nature of the people we would be dealing with.

Fortunately, the caretaker appeared and identified one of the vehicles in the car park. He knew the owner and gave us a flat number. Bill and I disappeared upstairs a few flights and settled in to watch the breach from the third floor. With my camera at the ready and Bill with his weapon, we looked on as a group of policemen approached the flat door with a battering ram. On reaching the door, they all stopped and backed off. Behind them a heavily armed detail of Support Unit troops began arguing, unsure of the safety of their actions. We couldn't believe it as we witnessed the raid go dead in the water due to the policemen's lack of certainty. At any minute I expected the commandos to burst out and gun everyone down.

More policemen appeared at the door with heavier weapons in the form of two MAGs. The commotion increased as fear took hold of the entry team. They argued over who would be lead man as none among them wanted the honour of being first killed by the enemy commandos. If anyone was inside, all surprise was lost.

Bill took charge and stormed down the stairs with his five shot .38 Special snubbie. I remained in position, as Bill and the police member-in-charge began a verbal slinging match at one another. Totally exasperated, Bill threw his arms in the air, exhausted by their incompetence and let out a sharp expletive. They were all cowards, he said, and charged the entrance with his revolver. Reaching the door, he grabbed the handle and was surprised to find it open. The door yielded with a push and a squeak and he stepped inside, ready to take on the world. I don't think it crossed his mind that his five rounds were barely sufficient for half the expected commandos!

The police followed Bill in, poised for battle and I cringed in expectation of gunfire. After none came he exited the flat and called me down. Inside the bachelor residence hardly a thing stirred. On a couch in the corner a young white male with long tatty hair bobbed, droopy-eyed from the excessive intake of alcohol and marijuana. The television blared out inaudible rock music, which was quickly turned down by a nervous policeman. The surf rat on the couch was nonplussed by the sudden invasion, but was not really taken aback. It seemed as if the intrusion was a welcome one and heralded new talent at the party. As I approached him, he smiled and offered me a joint. I had to chuckle.

We searched the rooms and it appeared that in two of them people had slept on the floor in sleeping bags. The few bags remaining were of green parachute material and obviously military. It didn't mean anything, as in Zimbabwe a lot of military surplus floated about. However, whoever had been there was gone. The operation had been a balls-up from start to finish and we couldn't believe the incompetence of the Support Unit members, who had been reluctant to carry out their duty. I cringe to say so, but in Rhodesia such a fiasco would never had taken place. Suffice to say it was a sign of the decay that was forever creeping in, to spoil the professionalism of the Security Forces.

There was no solid evidence to support the theory, but speculation had it that the escaped commandos, if indeed that is what they were, were the team that was going to spring the captured South African agents, including Hartlebury and Evans who still languished inside. Of one thing we were certain: had the commandos been in the flat when we entered it, there would have been a lot of dead policeman.

Our CIA liaison was extremely interested in recruiting an insider from the North Korean Embassy. Apparently no North Korean had ever been recruited as a double agent either in Zimbabwe or elsewhere.

It took a few weeks of surveillance, using the Bat Mobile and our ground network of footmen, to target a young man from the embassy who we thought, might be swayed by financial gain. It was a risk approaching him, as the North Korean people, in general, are unmotivated by such issues, in part due to fear of recrimination as well as a fiercely indoctrinated loyalty. We came up with another plan.

It was suspected that the embassy had been involved in the illicit trade of rhino horn and emeralds, so we used that as our 'in'. Utilising our assets, which meant the availability of National Parks' stock rhino horn, as well as emeralds from the Reserve Bank, we had KK approach the young man with an offer he couldn't resist. It turned out that the North Korean could speak English relatively well and he jumped at the chance of procuring our wares once he was shown a small sample. A meeting was arranged in one of the CIO safe houses in the suburbs.

I set up a video camera behind one-way glass and filmed the whole transaction. While the trade was in progress, the house was raided by Mike Crafter and a few uniformed policemen. KK went along with the ruse and put up a sterling struggle before he was overpowered and handcuffed. The Korean was placed under arrest and taken to another safe house for interrogation. There he was questioned by a transcriber from our South Korean Liaison and told if he didn't cooperate, the video I had filmed would be released to his embassy, upon which he would become an embarrassment to his country. The young lad seemed genuinely concerned for his wellbeing and even more worried what his own people might do to him if they found out about his independent indiscretions. We only held on to him for a couple of hours, as we didn't want to raise suspicion at the embassy with his prolonged absence and briefed him on a further meeting. As far as we were concerned the cat was in the bag.

When the next meeting was due to take place, the North Korean didn't arrive. Through immigration records we found out that he had returned to the embassy and was immediately spirited away to Zambia in a vehicle via Chirundu. He had obviously confessed all to his masters, who then decided his fate. What lay in store for him we didn't know. Maybe he was shown leniency because of his honesty, but I somehow doubt it. More than likely he was interned in a political re-education camp in his home country.

Another North Korean agent was brought to our attention when he placed an advert in the personal column of the *Herald*. In return for living with a 'western' family and learning western culture, he was willing to teach martial arts. We managed to get one of our reservists to respond to the advert and take him in with his family. It wasn't a dangerous situation for them, as these sorts of arrangement only require the agent to be prepped in western ways. They then remain as sleeper agents until their services are required, possibly in an entirely different country.

The union turned out to be a happy one and we learnt much about the North Korean while he thought he was learning about us. The family became fluent in many of the languages he spoke, including Japanese, and the reservist's two daughters became proficient at several martial art disciplines over the next few years.

The North Koreans often advertised this way to enable their agents to infiltrate western society and pose as Japanese or South Korean immigrants. You just never know if the Japanese guy living next door to you is all that he claims!

Working with foreign liaison was a pleasure. One of the perks I was entitled to was a free trip once a month to Victoria Falls, Inyanga, or to one of the resorts at Lake Kariba. The transcribers who worked with most foreign embassies, essentially for the intelligence service of that particular country, were on a rotational basis and all of them wanted to see the popular tourist attractions. To this end I was assigned to them as tour guide par excellence. My association with them had other benefits as well, in that we could keep a watchful eye on our counterparts in the guise of having fun. It was one lackey job that I didn't mind at all!

On a few occasions I travelled with the transcribers outside Zimbabwe's borders and arranged to meet friends in South Africa. On one such trip, a few mates from Durban who were serving in the South African Defence Force, met my transcriber and me at the Tshipise resort for a weekend break. It seemed odd that the guys I met up with probably had personal knowledge of the operation to kill me, although they claimed otherwise. They in turn were most likely keeping a watchful eye on me.

These meetings would eventually serve my purposes well. I was first wooed into service by foreign intelligence, other than the NIS, on one such trip. Our American CIA liaison had long been impressed with my photographic skills and offered recompense if I could share a few images with them. In return they would pay me in luxury electrical goods, such as a television, video recorder or appliances which were fast becoming unavailable in Zimbabwe. That way there was no record of financial transactions that could be traced.

After what I had been through at Goromonzi and with the mistrust that was placed in all whites in the security services, I felt obliged to take up the activities of which I was being accused. If you're going to finger me for something and I'm going to pay the dues, then I had better be doing the crime you're accusing me of! The way I felt was that the new regime had had its chance to prove themselves worthy of being in power – and all they had done was give me trouble. If it were treason they were after, then it was treason they were going to get. I decided that if I could contribute in other ways to bringing the government to its knees, I would.

My view was solidified after an incident in which John Alsford and I caught one of the ex-terr assistants up to no good. We had noticed a large amount of photographic paper and developing chemicals missing, and KK informed us that he had evidence that this particular gentleman was stealing it and selling it to a commercial film developer. We put the ex-terr under surveillance and caught him red-handed, selling CIO stocks to a photographic shop. I wondered when he would progress to selling official secrets! A report was filed complete with pictures of the transaction and submitted to Red Bricks HQ.

The following day we learnt that the assistant had received a minor verbal warning when he reported back to work. The powers-that-be almost condoned his actions, feebly proclaiming that temptation was put in his way. It was OK because he had to supplement his meagre income! Arrogantly our ex-terr turned his nose up at us, as if to imply that he was untouchable. John and I were enraged. If *we* had been caught stealing CIO property it would be the excuse they needed to lock us up. I suddenly knew the mentality of the people I was dealing with.

Many of the jobs we undertook in Special Projects often involved the aid of foreign liaison, which lent credibility to my dealings with them. On these jobs I would furnish the liaison with intelligence that I had gleaned while conducting 'wet jobs' for the Division. Often the Division's interests and those of liaison were the same, and it wasn't hard to provide my foreign controller with photographs I had duplicated, or occasionally with recordings.

We managed to place another bug in the Cuban Embassy and set up an LP down the road. We bugged the East German Embassy in Avondale and set up an LP in a block of flats opposite. Some of the time, our entry into embassies was under the guise of a telephone repairman or the like, but many of the embassies had to be covertly breached, as their security staff and own intelligence personnel knew the tricks of the trade. A telephone repairman on the doorstep would immediately arouse suspicion.

Over the course of a year we managed to install transmitters or telephone taps into every embassy, high commission or trade mission in Harare. We would then play each liaison off against the other, trading information here and there. To listen in on the telephone taps, for instance, we would use a transcriber from

Cuban liaison, who could speak the language, to translate on the East German Embassy tap. Meanwhile, down the road, we had an East German listening in on the Cubans! I'm sure we were being played off much of the time as well.

The only place on which we never managed to eavesdrop was the South African Trade Mission, despite continual demands made from HQ to do so. Understandably, our bosses wanted to know why we couldn't access this particular outpost, when we had managed to access everywhere else. I never did find out why, but I suspect we could have – if we had really wanted to.

One of the jobs I carried out for J Desk, was to update the identities of individuals serving at the embassies of several foreign countries. This tied in well with my CIA liaison's demands, as they were also interested in the comings and goings of embassy personnel. For instance, Toni Reid of Russia Desk required continual reference to employees at the Russian Embassy, as they often changed. Surveillance on the Russians was simple and all I had to do was park the Bat Mobile outside Honey Dew farm each Wednesday lunchtime. Honey Dew is a popular fresh produce outlet in the Greendale suburb of Harare. Without fail, the embassy bus would arrive laden with staff members to buy their weekly vegetables, at which time I would snap away merrily as they exited their transport. It sounds like really boring work, and much of the time it was, but over time I developed pet names for certain permanent staff and entertained myself by compiling dossiers on their habits, mannerisms and distinguishing marks. It was thorough work and the CIA was highly impressed.

We also put a photographic observation post into a building near the Russian Embassy and using telephoto lenses, we were able to monitor their every move on CCTV. All the equipment provided for these jobs came courtesy of the liaison department that held the most interest in the particular target at the time. Mostly, it was the Americans who pressed us for constant up-to-date intelligence.

We mounted a job against the ambassador of the PLO. We had heard of the infidelity he was involved in, with the Arab wife of an Austrian Embassy official. To this end we bugged his home and recorded several titillating, and highly revealing, episodes between the two lovers. The tapes were held in case we ever needed leverage on the ambassador. As far as I know, our organisation never used them but naturally, I passed copies on to the Americans so they could achieve the same ends if necessary. Who knows where they ended up or what goals they ultimately achieved.

Undercover intelligence work, I would say, is 99 per cent boredom and one per cent adrenalin rush. In reality, it's nothing like the movies portray. The individuals I came across, spanning every foreign liaison department I worked with, were mostly middle aged ex-military men a little past their prime. Some were certainly capable individuals, with a wealth of experience under their belts, from places like the Falklands or Vietnam. Not all of them represented the side of the West in those wars and it was interesting to meet Cubans, Russians and Vietnamese, who provided me a clear perspective of what it was like to be on the opposing sides of where I would have sat naturally.

The biggest job we did, involving our British liaison, was against the Libyan Embassy in 1988. These operations were high risk and had to be totally deniable. On several occasions we breached the embassy at night, along with two representatives from MI6. I was invited to their residence to discuss plans for the operation over dinner.

The embassy had several armed guards, some supplied by the Zimbabwean police, so we entered the premises covertly dressed in black outfits with balaclavas. We carried an assortment of nondescript weapons, like sawn-off shotguns and revolvers with the serial numbers filed off. That way, if we got into a shootout, we wouldn't leave cartridge cases lying about, as our brief dictated that if we were caught we should fight our way clear.

On the first operation, I was part of the entry team and was designated photographer. My task was to document any paperwork we found. When all the embassy staff retired to their respective homes, we deployed in the Bat Mobile to the service alley behind the embassy. The private security guards, previously infiltrated into a commercial company responsible for the Libyans' security, opened the back gate and let us in. The key man, KK, opened the back door to the staff entrance and the staircase which led upstairs and then opened the glass security doors to the offices. He then went on to open the safes which were in the ambassador's office. Inside the embassy safes we found everything that liaison was interested in, like stores manifests, communications transcripts, communications codes and personnel travel itineraries. In our final breach of the embassy, I read a report in which the CIA was specially interested. It outlined meetings and dates that were to take place between the Libyan government and representatives of a North Korean Weapons Programme. The CIA were particularly interested in the Libyans after things heated up when US aircraft bombed targets in Tripoli in 1986, in response to a terrorist attack on a discotheque in West Berlin. The Americans feared Libya might soon obtain the technology for 'the Bomb' and they kept a close eye on them all around the world.

On most of these operations, I provided security for the breaching team. Once in the premises I would keep watch to make sure there were no intrusions. These tasks represented the one per cent of excitement I spoke of earlier, but even so and most fortunately, we were never caught. We were damn good at our jobs and avoided the repercussions of creating an embarrassing international incident.

My time spent in Belfast, Northern Ireland, came back to haunt me under the strangest of circumstances. I had closed that chapter in my life and viewed it as the moulding period of my military career. When I left Belfast for the last time, I would never have guessed that the IRA would try reach out and touch me in sunny Zimbabwe.

During late 1989, Mike Crafter was summoned by the British High Commission to answer some embarrassing questions. During a raid on an IRA bomb-making factory in a block of flats in London, British police had found terrorists in possession of Mike's CIO identity card and his licence to carry a weapon. Among other things, which included powerful explosives, the police had also acquired several letters to the tenant of the flat from a Harare address. This indicated that the IRA had connections and therefore some interest in Zimbabwe.

Mike told British liaison that he had quite innocently misplaced his wallet one evening, while visiting the Harare Catholic Club. The club was a popular drinking venue for all and sundry on Friday evenings, whether one was Catholic or not. He was genuinely shocked to find that his possessions had turned up in the hands of the IRA and informed the High Commission that he would personally investigate the matter. To this end we were furnished with one of the letters, on which was a Harare address, which had been found during the raid.

The task of following up the address on the envelope was given to St. Claire Roberts and me. I was only to assist him with the task; he was to do all the groundwork. It didn't take long to discover that the individual under investigation was an illegal immigrant in Zimbabwe. He had entered the country several months earlier, posing as a journalist and had overstayed his visa. He was now running an import/export business from offices in Karagimombe Centre in Harare.

Utilising the Bat Mobile and our mobile footmen, the subject was placed under surveillance for a couple of weeks. During that time we recruited his gardener, who worked at his house in Hatfield, just off the airport road. Tailing the suspect one day, we managed to follow him to a car rental firm and discovered that he had hired a vehicle, using the identity on a stolen British driver's licence. That alone was fraud, but we left the subject to his own devices in the event that a larger haul was in the offing. A few weeks into the surveillance, the subject left on holiday to the Victoria Falls, where he met an Australian acquaintance. Mike Crafter, along with liaison agents from the British High Commission and a few Immigration officers, planned to spring a trap when he returned. We weren't sure what he was up to, although it was suspected that his presence in Zimbabwe might have something to do with the upcoming Commonwealth Heads of Government Meeting (CHOGM). We decided to strike while the iron was hot and curtail the embarrassment that would arise in the event that the subject's larger plans escaped our attention.

KK and I were given the task of mounting surveillance on the airport, when the Irishman returned from the Falls. We were to disguise ourselves as Immigration officers and seize the subject under the pretence of his illegal immigrant status. At no time were we to let on that he might have been fingered as an IRA member. Once we had him in custody, he would be arraigned before an interview committee composed of CIO and British High Commission officials and genuine Immigration officers at his residence in Hatfield.

Given the very sparse intelligence on the man, Mike Crafter warned us that he could be armed and dangerous and to take no chances. We knew that the security checks at the airport's domestic terminal were not what they should have been and the subject could well be carrying a weapon.

The intercept at the airport was no big deal. Once we had detained the Irishman, he relaxed in our presence, seemingly unperturbed about our Immigration officer ruse. He furnished us with a letter from the Zimbabwe Immigration Department granting him several more months in the country. I explained to him that certain information had come to our attention regarding the sanction of his stay and we would like to clear things up once we had visited his residence. KK kept a careful watch over him all the time in case he tried something. As Immigration officials we could not legally search him without police or Customs officers present.

I raised Crafter on the radio and informed him that we would meet him at the subject's house as we had him in custody. The journey was without incident until we arrived at his modest home, when the real Immigration officers identified themselves. I think the enormity of the amount of people interested in the Irishman put the wind up his arse and he suddenly changed his tune. In general, I've always known Irishmen to be irrational people, more so than any of the other nationalities and this guy was no exception. He went from being the picture of peace and innocence to a mad raging bull in no time. Why were we contravening his civil liberties? he screamed. Did we not know he had rights? If we were ever in his neighbourhood again he would '*foock us all up*', he said.

Mike Crafter, having briefed Immigration, was having none of it and slapped the subject across the cheek. He informed him that he was in the country illegally and was being deported to the UK immediately. The subject was told to pack a travel bag and he would be escorted to the airport. Suddenly, the Irishman changed his tune again, becoming soft and affable. In his eyes I could see his real intent – burning holes into Mike's forehead. His eye contact, or lack of it, gave it away but he continued to plead his innocence as he played the pity card. Could he at least choose his own destination if he was to be deported, he enquired? That utterance sealed it for him and we knew he was guilty of something more sinister than letting a stamp in his passport lapse, or driver's licence fraud. His aversion to returning to the UK was something in itself.

He asked to see a lawyer. The Immigration officers told him that he had no privileges and would be on the flight to London that night. He floored us when he again turned bitter and stared in my direction. 'I know what this is about' he said. 'I know why you're really deporting me!'

It wasn't an admission of terrorism, but he sealed his fate right then. We knew straight away he was hiding something. I accompanied the subject into his house to pack his bag. While I watched him he got really angry, sizing me up for the fight. If looks could kill I would have been six foot under. 'You foocking fag! What you foocking watching? You wanna piece ah my foocking arse?'

I ignored him. He tried to write a note and I interjected. He wanted to inform his sister of the situation. She was apparently handling his affairs for him. I confiscated the note and the Irishman went crazy. At one point I considered calling in the others as he needed restraining. I kept my cool and told him I was there to make sure he didn't try anything stupid.

I was the only stupid one there, he said. 'A stupid foocking Englishman!'

Now I've been accused of many things in my life, but this was getting absurd. I quite like the 'English' but with my own people, the Rhodesians, calling me a Pommie, the South Africans calling me a Zimbabwean and the Zimbabweans calling me a South African, I was beginning to have an identity crisis. I looked on, smiled and in one of my most unprofessional moments I said 'Mate, you're the only one who's gonna be *foocked* when you get on that plane tonight.' With that I gave him a clip around the ear.

He quietened down. That he wanted me dead was plain to see, but he quietened down.

My Irish friend was escorted to the airport straight from his residence with the Immigration officers. I searched the house with a MI6 operative and we photographed all the documentation we found. The subject was arrested on his arrival at Gatwick International and remanded in custody. From evidence obtained during our investigation he was charged and incarcerated.

A few weeks later I was shown a newspaper cutting from the *Sunday Times* complete with a photograph of our man. Underneath the picture the caption stated that he was indeed on a mission in Zimbabwe – to assassinate Prime Minister Margaret Thatcher when she attended the Commonwealth Heads of Government Meeting.

CHAPTER 37: MISTRUST

Toward the end of 1988, whilst holidaying in Durban, I decided to use some of my earnings to purchase a beach house in Port Shepstone. I used Sheila's name on the lease for security purposes and moved my mother there. She looked after the place in return for lodging and I helped her out financially with living expenses. I had to do something with my money and property investment seemed like the wise thing at the time.

At the end of the year I travelled to London, where I was met by my new NIS controller, who briefed me on future intentions. I was told that I was doing a sterling job and was given a credible increment to the large amount of money I was already receiving. As far as my controller was concerned, I was the most useful inside source they had, if not the highest placed. The advantages my position offered were considered extremely useful and exposed me to the dealings of most departments. As a photographer, although I may not have known exactly what was going on, I did have an inkling of all operational commitments from the films I developed.

I was reassured that I would not be compromised under any circumstances, unless I slipped up, as I was too valuable. To this end I had to swear that I would never tell a soul about my double dealings. It suited me fine at the time, as it slotted in well with my purposes for doing it. A little part of me would have loved to let my ex-colleagues at the Bluff know what I was up to. If they weren't briefed on the situation, I prayed that none of them would take matters into their own hands if the chance arose. I was led to believe that many of my mates still thought I was a sell-out.

While I was in London I began to worry about being away from the organisation for so long. I happened to be travelling at the same time as Johnny Alsford and in fact, we met up for a few drinks on occasion. John was also concerned about what our untrusting cohorts were up to in our absence and said as much.

On my return to Harare, everything was normal except for KK. He was on edge, shifty and jittery about something, but he wasn't letting on. On a few occasions I sensed he wanted to talk to me, but he always backed down or glanced off at another angle after his initial approach.

A week after returning, I cornered him in the darkroom and asked what the story was. KK was worried about the internal politics in the organisation and was under the impression that all ex-BSAP serving members were under close scrutiny, and were to be 'disposed of'. A meeting had been called at HQ, to which KK had erroneously been summoned. For some inexplicable reason, HQ messed up and mistook KK for an ex-terr. He innocently attended and was sworn to secrecy, when information, not for his ears, was revealed. All in attendance were ex-terrs, who threatened his life if he told anyone, or if the information should ever get out to the rest of the organisation. KK stressed that he was taking a huge risk just talking to me. He said that he trusted me one hundred per cent and he was afraid to approach anyone else. If I told anyone, he was sure he'd be killed. He did seem very nervous at the time and his instability lent credit to the story.

I was really getting it from all angles now. It seemed to me that I could please nobody and everyone wanted me dead.

KK continued his story. During the meeting he was instructed to carry out operations for and on behalf of the HQ element, against all those former Rhodesian servicemen and operatives. The instruction came from minister Mnangagwa himself, who told him to target mainly white ex-BSAP members. The minister wanted anything incriminating that could be used, to make a case against these members. To achieve these aims, KK was to help covertly searching the ex-Rhodesians' offices and homes, using his lock-picking skills. As the only qualified locksmith in the organisation, he was to gain entry for the minister's men to search these premises. They were to place taps on phones to glean further information.

Of most concern was what he told me next. While I was away in the UK, KK had breached John Alsford's house in Greendale, on instruction from the minister. They were looking for particular evidence following a tip-off from an undisclosed source. KK thought it was most obviously an ex-terr with a personal vendetta against John. They had also been over everyone else's homes with a fine-toothed comb, although KK informed me that he hadn't personally searched mine. He had managed to slip out of that one, on the pretext of urgent family matters. He did know that my gardener, Simon, had been recruited and was to report on all my activities and write down the vehicle registration numbers of all those people who visited me. He knew that a bug had been installed in the flat and an LP had been set up. He thought it was in No. 5, a few flats down, as one of the minister's brothers lived there. Alternately, he said, they were using Simon's domestic quarters as an LP.

I was very concerned about this revelation, as it affected almost everyone I knew in the organisation. I had to assure KK that it would go no further, but the onus was on me to do something about it. I felt I needed to speak to Mike Crafter, but KK was not happy with that option. I thanked him for his fortitude and resumed my work.

A few hours later, I was as concerned as I had been when I first heard KK's tale. I got hold of Steve Jennings, a close friend, who was member-in-charge: Libyan Desk. Steve was glad I told him and we both agreed to approach Mike Crafter in the strictest of confidence. Mike was enraged at the information and in turn set up a meeting with Danny Stannard. He was sure that Danny knew nothing of the mistrust that had been placed in us all. Primarily we all agreed that the source of the information must be protected.

A week passed and nothing more was heard of KK's confessions. Retrieving some files from the walk-in safe one day, I reached up to a top shelf and exposed a wire that ran through the air vent. Tracing it I followed the wire to the reception area where it eventually led to the PABX box. Taking the PABX box apart I noticed the wire was connected to my telephone line. I immediately went upstairs to Steve Jennings office to lodge an official complaint. It stood to reason that whoever was listening in on my calls had used the walk-in safe as an LP.

The question was whether it was still in use, or the remnants of a bygone LP, before I took over the line. I had to keep my nose clean and so I phoned Janelle in South Africa from a secure line. I told her I wasn't happy with life as I had heard rumours that there was someone else in our relationship. Someone was fucking around and it wasn't me! No longer was our liaison monogamous.

Understandably, I suppose, a certain amount of trepidation had crept in on my complex career. I had grown quite accustomed to burning the candle at both ends, although my time spent at Goromonzi had certainly given me a nervous disposition. I wasn't likely to panic and make mistakes. Far from it. Instead, I became smarter and craftier when it came to my double-dealings. I began to circumvent problems before they arose, by presenting myself as the picture of innocence. I think most people who knew me, except those who held a grudge, would have thought I was the gentlest person in the world.

CI Division expanded and we had a new desk. Crafter, always the diplomat, had come up with Surveillance Desk to appease those who were jockeying for my position. Once again, our American liaison provided finance for the purchase of several vehicles to be used by this desk, under the watchful eye of Olaf Reed. A team was established, incorporating two new members whom we nicknamed Bill and Ben – Mutt and Jeff would have been more appropriate names for the two, since they stuck together like glue when conducting their 'heavy' antics. Both were ex-Rhodesian SAS who had also served in the South African Defence Force from where they were recruited by Danny Stannard. Dangerous men, one was an ex-Para and the other a Royal Marine. They were purely Stannard's boys and I always had the feeling there was more to their job description than met the eye.

I received a phone call from Bill's wife one day, who was separated at the time, warning me that she had overheard a conversation between Bill and Ben that if I 'got in the way' I was to be eliminated. I spoke to Crafter about this. He phoned Stannard and the next thing I knew, the woman was declared a prohibited immigrant and deported from the country. As far as I could see it only meant one thing. There must have been some truth in what Bill's ex-wife told me. Why else would they make her incommunicado?

Despite the warning I got on well with Bill and Ben, as we had much in common. The bond that the British Army formed, was a lasting and international one despite one of them being a former cabbage head. Both men had an aversion to Olaf Reed and at times refused to recognise him as team leader. For some reason they had little respect for him and would often ignore him entirely, preferring to speak to me – thereby, in essence, deviating from the chain of command. There were so many hidden agendas in the Zimbabwean CIO between the 1980s and 1990s, I preferred not to try and understand it all.

Maybe Bill and Ben were also burning the candle at both ends and had information on Olaf that I was unaware of. Olaf was eventually posted to South Africa, as Intelligence Representative at the Zimbabwean High Commission, for a year. Sydney Nyanungu, an ex-guerrilla, took over his position and appeared to be more popular, even among the whites. Truth is stranger than fiction!

I heard that Olaf had a hard time in South Africa, being as he was, a white Zimbabwean in the Intelligence services. My NIS guys asked many questions about him while he was there and told me that they wanted to recruit him before South African Military Intelligence killed him. Whether they did recruit him or not, I never found out, but I would go so far as to say that he must have been recruited, because he is still alive today.

Later, the NIS told me that they had evidence that Olaf was recruited by another organisation, but not one of the ilk they liked. They said that his position, in the Zimbabwean High Commission in Johannesburg, made him a ripe target for ANC recruiters, to which they believed he had offered his loyalties. Having attended, in later life, the Rhodesian SAS reunions, which are held in Durban every year, I learnt that certain people still maintained a grudge against Olaf, even then. One of them was Colin Evans, for what Olaf did to him while he was in custody when we were all interned. Colin told me that while he was travelling to the dentist from Goromonzi one day, Olaf had been part of the security detail in the armoured vehicle where he sat with Evans in the back. Olaf smacked him around the face and implied that he was 'white trash', who would die for his treason against Zimbabwe.

Funny thing is, Olaf visited Durban a few times while I was there and nothing ever happened to him. But I did notice he was being tailed on one occasion, which indicated that he had some form of protection. Were the ANC looking after him or was it South African Intelligence?

I still worried about the stories that rattled around about me and always wondered what my ex-colleagues really thought. I learnt that another two ex-SAS members, both former friends of mine, were 'taken out of the system'; the expression coined in South African Intelligence circles for 'neutralising' no longer needed human assets.

These men had been among the SAS group that travelled to the Bluff with Ian Suttil, to become members of South African Special Forces. It turned out that they were deep-cover agents working for Danny Stannard and filtering information to the Zimbabweans from Phalaborwa, where they were later based. Both of them died in mysterious circumstances: their official deaths were recorded as 'poisoning' and 'parachute accident'. Although I won't mention names, given the amount of publications regarding that era, it's not hard to put two and two together and figure out who they were.

After nine years in Special Branch/CIO, I'd had enough and began to seek employment elsewhere. I began to believe that eventually, my luck really would run out.

I never held any regrets for providing information on the Zimbabwean Government. They had caused my family and me a lot of grief and my marriage problems had become unsolvable. Sheila moved out with the kids and alternated in residence between Harare and the new house in Port Shepstone. It was understandable, considering how maligned their existence in Zimbabwe had become, due to their association with me.

Being ex-SAS and Selous Scouts, working for the enemy regime, I was always considered a sell-out. It got to the stage where working for the CIO became unbearable. I was particularly perturbed when my position caused stress to the family, when my kids were ostracised at school for their Daddy's endeavours. I knew then that it was time to leave, regardless of the 'good wicket' I was on with my South African friends.

A position as security manager for LONRHO assets in Mozambique arose and I was given the option of taking it then, or losing it all together. The remuneration was exceptional and it seemed a good prospect at the time.

Just before I left the CIO, Manyard Mazarere, the up-and-coming kingpin of Counter Intelligence, approached me. Mike Crafter had joined the throngs of people leaving the country and had left the organisation. Manyard replaced him and was saddened at my departure. He pretty much told me that I was the greatest thing ever and was upset that I had resigned without his consent, as he had been away in the UK at the time on an Intelligence course. He offered me my job back and wanted to know if I could resume within six months. He reasoned I wouldn't be content with the Mozambique posting after the excitement of CIO work. Given what I had been through and what he didn't know, his surmise was an understatement, to say the least. He couldn't have guessed that my Mozambique adventure was to expose me to more cruelty and killing than I had ever experienced.

News travelled fast and I was approached by my liaisons at MI6 and the CIA when they heard of my resignation. One offered a fair package for me to remain in the organisation, as they were worried that future jobs, undertaken by others on retainer, would not bear the same mark of professionalism. The British expressed sadness at my loss and bade me farewell and good luck.

When he heard the news, my controller at the NIS was devastated and asked to see me at the first opportunity in South Africa. On the pretence of a holiday, I met him in Durban, where I was summoned to face a board of five senior Intelligence representatives. The South Africans offered me the world and agreed to match my LONRHO offer, which in those days was the equivalent to about R15, 000 a month. Had I stayed on and had my luck held out, I would have been buying properties all over the South African coast within a year.

But I had made up my mind. I could no longer serve under the conditions that prevailed in Zimbabwe. I explained that, as virtually all the others had left, being the only white man would eventually draw attention to my *raison de'être*. I was losing friends and I couldn't mix in my own society without drawing criticism. I couldn't stand in a bar without someone trying to pick a fight with me and I always had people talking behind my back. The CIO, largely because of the actions of minister Mnangagwa's boys, had a very bad reputation at the time. People were being picked up on a whim and beaten senseless, while the ex-terrs jumped at shadows, seeing trickery in the most innocent of actions.

Most of all, I was concerned about my family's welfare. Information was still trickling in about plans to assassinate me and there was no way I could let my friends know who I was actually working for. It was a frustrating necessity, to keep quiet about my activities, but once again I was being accused of something of which I was entirely innocent. I was in danger due to the ignorance of the very regime I was risking my life for.

My NIS controller had to agree with me, when I pointed out the amount of covert security they provided me on my trips down south. They too thought I might be 'taken out' by accident on one of my frequent visits.

To this day, my work for the NIS is a closely guarded secret. A small hope is that some who read this and who have treated my family and me with so much disdain in the past, will realise the error of their ways.

While we all agreed that there was no persuading me to stay on in the organisation, my NIS handlers didn't want me to leave alltogether. For a smaller retainer, they insisted I keep in touch and pass on anything interesting I found in Mozambique.

I continued to work for the NIS until the end of 1997, well after the transition from apartheid to the new ANC government in 1994. In effect, the NIS continued to operate on its own agenda, much as Special Branch had in Zimbabwe after independence. After leaving Mozambique three years later, I was assigned two new controllers, who insisted that I meet them on a month-to-month basis. Their main aims were for the provision of intelligence on ANC activities in Zimbabwe, prior to the 1994 South African elections.

In 1997, I was informed that the NIS were cutting me loose, as, three years into independence, the new government had formed strong bonds with its Zimbabwean counterpart. My controllers were worried I might be compromised, or traded for the sake of political expediency. In a final meeting in Durban, I was informed that all files and information I had provided, or anything pertaining to my services or whereabouts, had been destroyed. As far as my 'double agent' activities went, there was no longer any trace on the payroll of the NIS that I had existed.

It was a sad farewell and we shook hands and said goodbye. A final bonus was paid into my mother's account, for the work I had undertaken for the NIS for over a decade. After the last meeting, I was on my own. As suddenly as it all started, it ended, and I marked the day as the last time I ever saw any of my NIS controllers again.

I put everything behind me down to an interesting experience. The bad far outweighed the good and I needed to move on in life. The weight that was taken off my shoulders, having escaped detection by the Zimbabwean authorities for so long, was immediately apparent, but I felt like I was in limbo for a period. The level of danger to which I had exposed myself caught up with me and I couldn't believe the absurdity of my actions. Goromonzi haunted me during the night and I began to experience anxiety attacks over what might have happened had I been caught. What could still happen!

Comfort came, in the form of knowledge that the authorities would have had to be damned good to catch me. I always felt that if the likes of Darryl Watt and Richard Swan, respected operators in the Rhodesian SAS, couldn't catch me during my escape and evasion exercise, then who could? It did have enormous risks though.

I would go so far as to say that two out of every three operatives in the CIO, working in important positions, were on retainer to a foreign intelligence service, some of them even to several. For instance, Doug, who was on the course in Havana, when the Cuban Embassy bug was found, was almost certainly recruited by Cuban Military Intelligence.

After I left the organisation, I ran into Ian McLaren, an ex-technical department operative. The news he told me was startling – all the black ex-BSAP operatives who had worked as footmen for my desk in later life, including KK – were dead. They had all died in mysterious circumstances, one after the other. I heard later they had been poisoned.

In the time I knew KK, we had our ups and downs, but we had become firm friends and work colleagues. I partly blamed myself for his death and wondered if it had anything to do with the information he had given me after I returned from London.

At the time of his death, KK had left the organisation. Occasionally, I would run into him in town, where he operated an emergency taxi business which he had bought with his pension payout. He always seemed quite happy with the way things had turned out. Some said he died of AIDS, but my sources were more reliable. I have often contemplated KK and the deaths of the other footmen and believe that they eventually paid the price for having fought on the wrong side during the war. I know KK would have laughed at the inference, had I been able to tell him, but he had become a threat to the new regime and he knew too much. It's with great fondness I remember you, my friend!

For me, it was time to change tack.

CHAPTER 38:
OUTWARD BOUND

So began one of the most fulfilling contracts of service in my life, a period that bought me immense satisfaction and a feeling of well being. Aside from the virtual autonomy I was granted to do as I saw fit, I was finally doing what I loved best and receiving fair remuneration at the same time for doing it. Having said that, the period I was to work in Mozambique was not without its frustrations.

It was August 1989 and the Mozambique government, now in its fourteenth year of independence since the Portuguese departed in 1975, was still in the throes of battling banditry across the country. The MNR (Mozambique National Resistance) – or RENAMO as they were called, although once with a legitimate political agenda, had somewhat decayed and among its cadre were many individuals who sought personal gain, power and riches, using the advantage of their armed status. The situation of civil war inside the country had turned to one of attrition, neither side gaining the advantage, while across the land, the peasantry suffered. It was no different really to when FRELIMO had fought the Portuguese. The victims were always the peasants, suffering at the hands of the so-called freedom fighters.

With a constant escalation in civilian casualties, it was to be another long three years before a ceasefire came into effect and the politicians were forced to meet at the conference table in a battle of another kind.

To put things into perspective, in comparison with the Rhodesian war in which it is estimated upwards of 30,000 lives were lost, the fighting in Mozambique after independence, was to result in an estimated 700,000 deaths and more than three million people displaced.

Under the rule of the 'Iron Lady', Margaret Thatcher, Britain in the early 1980s had promised a military assistance package to Mozambique. On the surface, however, she did not like the idea of sending troops to the country, as it might be seen as extending her policies in a region she had been so vocal about and involved in bringing to independence. In conjunction with the obvious, aiding a now Marxist government, this served to highlight the need for a more covert means of assistance to be sought.

Yet having personnel on the ground in the country was a two-edged sword. Firstly, she could gain some kind of influence over a government with which she was friendly and secondly, her people on the ground could act as eyes and ears in an intelligence-gathering capacity.

In order to disguise her government's efforts, personnel from Defence Systems Limited (DSL) were sent to Nkala in Mozambique to train FRELIMO's Forca Especial. With a distinctive red beret, sporting an emblem of a circle encompassing a dagger in hand, the Forca Especial were a mixture of ex-Portuguese Flechas – Pre-75 Special Forces under Portuguese rule, those who were not purged by the new FRELIMO order – and FRELIMO itself. Most of these men were press-ganged into service in the first place and held no hard political convictions. The Forca Especial was equipped with the SA80, the British service rifle, with second-generation night-sight.

To maintain the guise of British troops actively assisting the Mozambican government, all DSL personnel had to be serving, or ex-serving members of 22 SAS Regiment and while in the country, had to wear British military uniform. However, if a situation arose that could be potentially embarrassing to Her Majesty's people, deniability was the name of the game and DSL could absorb the fallout.

As well as a training capacity, DSL personnel fulfilled the role of advising on and assessing security requirements for private agricultural, mining and industrial enterprise, in order to encourage foreign investment.

I met Barry Lundgren in Harare, to discuss the job offer at hand. He sat me down to talk over the situation in Mozambique and what would be expected of me if I were to accept his proposal. DSL were responsible for the security of Barry's employer, LONRHO's (London Rhodesia Company) sister company LOMACO (London Mozambique Company), which had estates, factories and plants in the Chilembene region of Mozambique.

LOMACO, 50% owned by FRELIMO, was, like LONRHO, one of the many assets of the multinational conglomerate, owned and chaired by Tiny Rowland and had its beginnings in Rhodesia and Zambia during the heyday of the federation, when the two countries, along with Malawi (then Nyasaland) formed the Federation of Rhodesia and Nyasaland. Since those formative years, LONRHO had grown in size and wealth to include mining and agricultural assets throughout Africa and elsewhere. Rowland himself became so wealthy that he was listed as one of the richest men in the United Kingdom and boasted statesmen and world leaders from around the globe among his friends. So important were LONRHO's dealings in the region, that Rowland often deliberated between feuding parties and even countries, as was the case when Kenneth Kaunda, Zambia's president, utilised his services as messenger between himself and John Vorster, the South African prime minister, over the Rhodesian crisis.

Barry told me that the Chilembene region, the birthplace of Mozambique's former president Samora Machel, was under siege, while stability there was crucial in setting an example for the entire country. People, such as Barry, were expected to introduce into the region a sense of safety and well being.

DSL suggested to LOMACO that its assets should be protected by teams of former professional soldiers, whose mission it would be to command and train local militia groups. The initial assessment would warrant six personnel for each estate or interest, who would then oversee militia groups, whose numbers would depend on the actual area and threat assessment.

Once Barry had laid out the basics, I was told that LOMACO would be interested in my services to command the militia at Chilembene.

I flew out to Durban from Harare for a few days and caught up with Sheila before flying to Mozambique's capital Maputo. Despite the strain, our marriage had taken over the years, we still tried to keep it together. Sheila now lived in the house at Port Shepstone on the South African coast.

When I arrived at Chilembene from Maputo, in mid-September 1989, I held the formal rank of major. I was not too enamoured with this rank, but I was told it was necessary in order to fit in to the grand scheme of things. I feel, just as strongly as the next man that rank is earned, not apportioned by whim.

My mission statement said I was to train and manage the militia, as well as liaise with the local militia and the FRELIMO Army, who were to provide me with intelligence, situation reports, uniforms and weapons. I was introduced to Jim Shand, who temporarily oversaw security at Chilembene. Jim was normally based at a citrus estate south of Maputo, but was often called in as a temp, when others went on leave. A former Royal Navy officer, he could not have been further from his vocation than in rural Mozambique.

Chilembene lies on the banks of the Rio Limpopo. The river is seasonally dry for a large part of the year, when at most there is a collection of small ponds and stagnant pools along its sandy course. Not far under the sand, is an abundance of water which was pumped into a canal system that serviced the various estates' irrigation needs. The canals were a remarkable feat of engineering ingenuity that had remained from the Portuguese era.

It was only in the monsoon season, between January and March that the river actually flowed with some regularity, flushing the past year's decay out toward the Indian Ocean.

Not far from Chilembene, by road to the west, was Chokwe and it was here that LOMACO's headquarters for the region were based. I met Charles Dean, the manager of the HQ estate and processing plant, and his security manager and militia commander, Jim Young. Charles was responsible for all LOMACO interests in the area, which included farms producing tomatoes or cotton, in and out of season. In addition, a few kilometres east of Chilembene, there was a pig farm at Casa de Porka. The main farms were based within an area of about 1,600 square kilometres around the towns of Hokwe, Chokwe, Malhazene, Muianga and Chalaquane, with Chilembene in the centre. These towns were surrounded by other smaller satellite towns with names such as Chiguidela, Maramajani, Muhamba and Chaimites.

I was to form an immediate bond with Charles and Jim. Jim Young was an affable fellow and a strong man. Older than myself, his wealth of knowledge on all matter's military, had been instilled in him as a Royal Marine.

At Chokwe, Charles gave me the tour of the tomato-processing plant. Here, with the assistance of East German machinery, hundreds of thousands of tons of tomatoes were processed into tomato paste, canned and exported to East Germany each season. Alongside the tomato-canning plant, was the railway station. From this siding, tomatoes and cotton bales were sent to the ports in Beira and Maputo for exporting.

Chokwe also boasted an 'international airport', although I would hazard a guess that this could be ascribed to a rather optimistic view on the part of the town planners, when they drew their maps. The Chokwe airport consisted of no more than a small dirt strip, alongside which were built three corrugated-iron rooms. These included a departure lounge, an office and a highly unusable latrine – so unusable and permeated with the stench of misdirected faeces and urine, that the sole official of the strip preferred to let nature take its course in the surrounding bush, bandits or no bandits. Of course, a complement of FRELIMO troops was stationed near the airstrip, but left unchecked, they were always drunk, asleep or not around when they were most needed.

More often than not, the banditry in the area was very random. Whenever there was a full moon, bandits would cross the Limpopo River in small bands and harass, rob, rape and murder the local people.

Every so often, larger bands would assault and take over one of the smaller towns. They would ransack the entire place and loot everything they could in the way of alcohol, clothes, food and cigarettes. This would call for a rapid response from the militia, who would do what was possible to help the fleeing refugees and then recapture the town. Most of these affairs were high on gung-ho and were fuelled by drunkenness, with a terrific volume of firepower for few kills. As the bandits attacked, townspeople and refugees would flee into the fields, only to return the following day, after the militia had counter-attacked and put the bandits to flight, often after the first shot was fired. Invariably, FRELIMO would only turn up the next day, when the chaos had subsided and normality prevailed once more.

Given the volume of firepower during these attacks, I expected more casualties, but as I was to learn the whole affair had become a choreographed stage play. Shots were fired, civilians would flee, bandits would loot and pillage, the militia would counter-attack, the bandits would flee, the civilians would return home to resume their interrupted lives. All of which would be repeated a few days later. Still, it didn't bode well for those who were injured, maimed, raped or killed, while going about their daily business.

After these attacks, our militia would conduct a follow-up operation, by tracking the bandits as they fled north, but they would return with nothing to report. Even after I became involved and personally carried out follow-ups, little changed, as my trackers lost the spoor (or at least said they did), or the bandits dispersed in different directions.

At times, when we did pick up a distinct spoor, it would gradually blend into civilian or domestic animal tracks on the well-used footpaths in the area. I was to form my own opinions while I was in Chilembene about these discrepancies.

One of the characters I was to meet, who was then a member of the Chokwe militia, was Dickson Sithole, who would later become my interpreter. Dickson, who belonged to the Ndau clan, was a Zimbabwean by birth. He was born and raised in the north-eastern area of the country, on the border with Mozambique.

A former enemy of mine, while still a member of the ZANLA forces fighting for Robert Mugabe, by the time I came to know him, he was affectionately called Sergeant Dick. I was to learn from him that he had gone AWOL from ZANLA while stationed in Mozambique, at some time during the war. The reasons for this were never entirely clear, but as with many of the ZANLA cadre, abducted and forced into service, the onset of disillusionment may have been his basic reason for doing so.

Staying on in Mozambique, Sergeant Dick assumed the life of a rural African, but, shortly after his escape from ZANLA, he was accosted, while riding his bicycle, by a FRELIMO patrol and press-ganged into five years' service with the Mozambican Army. A talented linguist, who could speak four languages – English, Portuguese, Shona and Zulu – he was of great use to both FRELIMO and later to me as a translator. On a more personal note, Sergeant Dick became a man on whom I could rely and trust and a close personal friend.

At Chilembene I had at my disposal 80 personnel, most of whom had at some time received military training. The majority of the men had once served in the ranks of FRELIMO, although some, I'm sure, had been among the MNR cadre, or had themselves been bandits.

It was not without irony that I pondered my own situation. Some nine years previously, I had been part of a system that had been instrumental in creating the MNR.

Under the inspiring leadership of Andre Matangaidze, the MNR had been fostered by the Rhodesian government, with my own SAS, Selous Scouts and Special Branch, having at various times been involved in their founding and development. Once the Portuguese had left Mozambique, opening a new Marxist frontier along Rhodesia's eastern border, the Rhodesians set about creating the MNR as a thorn in the side of the new FRELIMO government. With an internal bandit crisis of their own, FRELIMO could not actively assist Rhodesia's enemy ZANLA, by providing bases, support and rear echelon administration, as much as they had in the past. The atmosphere in Mozambique at the time, was ripe for the creation of such a resistance movement. Not all of Mozambique's largely peasant population were comfortable with FRELIMO's policies. Many didn't even know what Marxism was and saw in it just another domineering power, which had wielded brutality and cruelty in order to sway others to its cause.

I was now expected to fight against a system that I had helped create. Many would be uncomfortable with this, but I have always thought of myself as a professional soldier and although I wouldn't fight for just any cause, as I've said before the MNR had to a large extent lost its political agenda and its members were now ranked as opportunists, out for a quick buck and a cheap thrill.

In addition to my 80 militia, a larger contingent of 100 personnel could be called upon from the Chokwe militia.

The assets I had at my disposal were innumerable. Supplementing my personal Land-Cruiser, were a few lightly armoured Land-Rovers, an 82mm mortar and crew, RPG7 launchers as well as PKM, RPD and RPK machine guns and AK-47 and AKM assault rifles. The icing on the cake came in the form of an obsolete T34 tank, complete with a crew of four, who were always pissed. Diesel, oil and ammunition came courtesy of FRELIMO.

My first test at Chilembene was an inspection of the water tower on the estate. Here was stationed a complement of six militia, whose task it was to guard the tower and act as a permanent observation post, using the commanding view from its crest. On top of the imposing concrete structure, was a forward observation light that had come from a 747 aircraft. It was fixed on a swivelling mount, enabling the crew to remain ever vigilant, providing it was used to its best advantage. The precarious iron rungs that served as steps ascending the tower's concave walls immediately struck me as somewhat unsafe, given that the accompanying steel safety girders, that were supposed to surround them, were now a pile of scrap lying on the ground below.

As I approached the tower, I saw lying around its base, the bodies of four men. My immediate concern was that sometime, during the past few days, the tower had been attacked and the militia wiped out. As I came near, no one stirred, but the sour stench of alcohol soon reached me. The prostrate figures I gazed upon were inebriated, so much so that their breathing was shallow and they appeared to be dead. Even a swift kick in the ribs failed to waken them, so I gathered their weapons and piled them in the back of the vehicle.

I was still missing two men. A short patrol of the area revealed them, passed out in a ditch a short distance away, complete with drained bottles of the locally produced and almost volatile wine drunk by the locals.

Also in the ditch, I discovered covered in branches, the PKM machine gun, that was supposed to be in the nest at the top of the tower and another AKM rifle. I considered myself lucky that no weapons had been stolen and that at least an attempt had been made to hide them. God only knows how the men would have woken up, let alone climbed the tower in the event of an attack by bandits!

The following morning I called my first muster parade. I assembled the men and Sergeant Dick had occasion to humour me. Although he was normally part of Jim's outfit, he had come along to assist in breaching the language barrier.

After calling the men to attention it was soon apparent that communication was to be a stumbling block. Sergeant Dick had informed me that, aside from Thomo, another veteran militiaman, he was the only one fully conversant in English.

This I needed to find out for myself. Standing to my full height and in my most authoritative voice I inquired of the assembled parade if anyone could understand me, or for that matter speak any English at all. Obviously someone did, as one man raised his hand. Signalling him to speak up, I was rewarded with a staccato burst of foul language in the form of 'fuckoffbollocksyoupillack', rattled off in one sentence!

Later I learned the origins of this satire. Some months before my arrival, as part of the DSL initiative, a former member of the Staffordshire Regiment had assumed my command. Peter, as I will call him, had found himself way out of depth in war-torn Mozambique and was frustrated with the ineptitude of his militia. Unable to communicate, he had resorted to virtually those three phrases during his brief stay. It was no surprise that my militia members had gained nothing in the form of language acquisition. If memory serves me correctly, I was told that Peter's stay came to an end after he turned to the bottle for comfort on one occasion. Upon hearing shots fired in the distance, he scrambled into the attic of his residence where he was found cowering, some time later.

It was this and other incidents with foreign soldiers, that gradually led the ex-pat farmers in Mozambique to call upon the services of Rhodesian servicemen, whom they felt were more experienced and adept to the adversities of life in Africa, as well as seasoned veterans of bush warfare.

I had to set an example to my erstwhile tower detail. Not hard to pick out among the men, due to their lack of weapons, I singled out the guilty party. Through translation I enquired as to the whereabouts of their weapons. Naturally, they all had a legitimate excuse, which had been conjured up when they realised that their firearms had been stolen. Emphatically I was told that a FRELIMO patrol had come by the tower and short of arms had borrowed theirs for an impending operation. They would be returned the next day when the operation was over.

What they had planned to do the next day, I don't know. Of course, on producing the weapons from my vehicle, much consternation was made about witchcraft and magical powers, as to how I could have come by them. All six were promptly fired and told to leave the estate by that afternoon. I had to make an immediate impression to avoid being labelled as soft and the opportunity had presented itself.

New methods of effective discipline were to be administered, as time went by. I found the most effective form of punishment to be the dreaded 'long march'. This entailed more than it sounds, given the complexity of the area.

Within the bounds of the LOMACO estates, on a farm that had belonged to the late President Samora Machel, lived his widow Graça Machel. Due to her presence, the entire area was policed with roadblocks.

Not wanting to accept responsibility, in the event of anything happening to the former president's wife, the troops manning these road blocks tended to be a little over-zealous and would treat all passers-by with some scepticism. If found guilty of a charge, and if the man was one of our militia, we would drive the unfortunate miscreant about 40 kilometres out of town, where he would be left, with little more than the clothes on his back. If he was to resume his position with the militia, he would have to find his way back to town, under his own steam, within a certain time-frame. This would mean negotiating the road blocks with caution, where, at the very least he would undergo questioning, as to his reasons for being there; or more likely, he'd cop a severe beating or two. The alternative was to walk through the bush, where he'd almost certainly be shot as a bandit by FRELIMO, or shot by bandits themselves. Few militias who had run this gauntlet, would dare venture out of line again.

I set about identifying areas of need in my militia training schedule and organised for them to give me a demonstration on drill, weapons handling and fire and movement. It was interesting to note the largely Soviet influence, as the Russians had supported FRELIMO throughout their campaign to defeat the Portuguese and continued to provide military advisors thereafter. The predominance of Russian technique was particularly apparent among those who were ex-FRELIMO.

The next few days disappeared in a blur of activity. In between administrative tasks, checking and test-firing weapons and honing basic battle skills, I was tasked with escorting the British and American military attachés from Maputo, around the area. Their respective governments were anxious to see what measures had been taken to eradicate banditry. The visit also enabled me to set up channels of communication for the future, as I was still on a sweetener to both countries' Intelligence services.

Accompanying us in the armoured Land-Cruiser, were three of my more seasoned veterans. To the Land-Cruiser's roll bar, I had fitted a Soviet SG43 7.62mm x 54R Goryunov medium machine gun. The Goryunov, in its original form, comes on a wheeled mount with an armoured deflector plate to give its crew a modicum of protection. By inverting and reversing its mount, the gun can be used in either ground situations or in an anti-aircraft role.

After an uneventful trip around the LOMACO area, we returned to Chokwe HQ in order to receive Graça Machel, who was also on a visit to the estate. An amiable lady, she would often conduct official visits to the LOMACO HQ, during which she showed a genuine interest in touring the estates and seeing that the needs of its people were met. After exchanging pleasantries with the attachés, the former First Lady departed to her farm. Graça was later to marry Nelson Mandela.

As she left, I was radioed by the Chilembene militia, who reported an incident about seven kilometres away at Hokwe, where bandits were attacking. They wanted the 82mm mortar, in order to conduct a follow-up. Barry Lundgren accompanied the two excited attachés and me to retrieve the mortar and join the militia in pursuit of the bandits. It's incredible how time has a way of changing perspectives and I look back on that incident with sheer terror and a cold sweat. I would have had much explaining to do had I managed to lose an attaché or two.

At the time, taking them along seemed like a good idea – after all, they were both military men. Fortunately, our pursuit was uneventful and the incident turned out to be very minor. A few mortars had been fired across the canal at Hokwe, exploding with little harm done. Our reaction time was satisfactory and we had arrived at Hokwe bristling with fire power, the militia in tow and four 'white men' ready to do battle.

Some days later it was confided to me that the entire incident had been set up by the militia, to test the capabilities of their 'new' commander. I was told they were impressed, but the incident left me with more nagging doubts as to why my militia were actually testing me. As time went by, I became convinced that, at least some of them, were militia by day and bandits by night. The fact that they could acquire a mortar and bombs from some secret cache to test my capabilities, was a mystery in itself. Certainly the bombs were of a different size to those we possessed in our armoury.

The same mistrust could be placed in FRELIMO, who gave me more than a few doubts as to where their loyalties lay. On one occasion, Jim Young was involved in a skirmish, when his group accounted for a couple of enemy dead. On searching the pockets of the dead rebels, a FRELIMO leave pass was found, along with the rebels' identity cards, all in the names of the deceased. There was no doubt that these particular bandits had dual identities – an occurrence which created a lot of mistrust.

There had been several reports of attacks, as well as intelligence gathered which signified imminent bandit action, although they rarely amounted to anything. One incident typified the jumpiness of the troops with whom I was to work.

I had heard a rather unsubstantiated report that the tomato-paste factory was to be revved (attacked) by bandits at some time. Although I assisted Jim Young in securing the guard detail at the factory, there was little else we could do. The report had come in from the FRELIMO garrison, who had in turn received it via the 'bush telegraph'.

Whereas, in intelligence circles, all information must be processed, at the end of the day it is only a small percentage that is of any value. What cannot be ignored, is information with regard to any direct action, so we took the necessary steps in the event of an attack. What we were lacking at the time and with hindsight, could never quite get together, was an efficient system of sharing information with FRELIMO.

Given the scanty information, Jim had quite correctly assessed that one of the most vulnerable areas was the rail siding, where cotton was being loaded onto wagons for the haul to the coast. Thus our militia complement was doubled and a messenger was sent to inform FRELIMO of our actions. Whether the message ever arrived I don't know. The resulting friendly-fire incident was nonetheless costly to my employers and a major embarrassment on the part of FRELIMO and the militia.

On the eve of this mishap, Jim and I were at the estate production manager's residence, having a braai. Mark Lucas, untiringly friendly, often held socials where we could get together and let our hair down over a few beers. I remember sitting on the patio of his villa, watching dense grey clouds gather overhead and being entranced by the lightning display a few kilometres distant.

Suddenly, concern washed over me. As the flashes of bright white light took on orange hues, the noise hit us. Simultancously, we all leapt up, realising that what we were witnessing were air-bursting RPG7 rocket propelled grenades. Green tracer followed, lighting the sky with ribbons of burning phosphorescence and it soon became apparent that the vicinity of the rail siding was under attack. After a flurry of activity, trying to raise the militia on radio, a mad dash was made to the Land-Cruiser, as the three of us hastily picked up our gear and sped in the direction of Chokwe.

When we arrived, the firefight had subsided and all that remained of the five-minute madness were the raging flames created by spent tracer and rocket fire. To our shock, we noticed that six fully laden wagons of cotton were ablaze.

The chain of events that led to the fire was revealed to us. FRELIMO had apparently been unnerved about the reports and were a little jumpy. In haste, they had set up an ambush upon noticing a larger number of armed men at the siding than was usual. Skittish at the best of times and wanting to retain the advantage, they prematurely opened fire on the militia with a torrent of RPG7 launchers and small arms. How not one man was injured eludes my understanding to this day.

The militia, certain they were now being engaged by a large group of bandits, responded with small arms, light machine gun and mortar fire, hastily erecting the mortar tube and sending a couple of bombs in the direction of the aggressors.

It was not clear who disengaged from contact first, or realised the error of their ways, but thank God it happened when it did. We were able to get the blaze under control and although the wagons were a great loss, we thankfully escaped with only the six being burnt out and with our egos slightly bruised. We personally resolved to keep FRELIMO informed of our movements at all times.

One evening, during late September, I made my rounds as usual, checking up on the sentries at Chilembene and Chiguidela. As I was about to leave Chilembene, a report came in from the tower of a bandit sighting. I advanced on Chiguidela where tracer and explosions could be seen from about four kilometres distant.

Nearing the village, my crew and I left the Land-Cruiser and moved about 500 metres along the canal on foot toward the access road. Some of the locals had fled into the fields and they informed me that the bandits were raiding the town in strength.

When the crew set up the mortar, I noticed they hadn't brought along its base plate. I asked them about this and was assured that the base plate was not necessary. The method they used was how the Russians had trained them to use the weapon, in a commando mortar-type role. Amused, I watched as one of them began prodding the tube into the ground, looking for a hard spot. Satisfied, he lined up the tube by sight, closing one eye and his compatriot fed in a bomb. The resultant 'whoomp' imbedded the tube a foot into the ground, whereupon the third crew member, hands wrapped in cloth, squatted down and hugged the tube, prying it back and forth to release it from the earth's grasp. It apparently worked for them, but I enforced the carrying of the base plate from then on.

We fired another round in the direction of the tracer, but the bomb impacted harmlessly away from the built-up area. No fire was returned; in fact it ceased altogether, so we advanced further into the village. Ill-disciplined and lacking the gumption for a fight, the rebels had fled, leaving vast swathes of loot in their tracks. This was generally the rule, although there were exceptions, as I was to find out at what I called 'The battle for Casa de Porka' some weeks later.

The one area, for which I could not criticize FRELIMO, concerned their provision of stores and ammunition as and when it was requisitioned. We were certainly never short of training ammo and I managed to get in some good range practice and conducted a live-fire exercise to see how the militia would perform. Of course, this was closely supervised and run with small numbers firing in allotted fire lanes, as accidents would not be acceptable.

At 21:30 on 6 October, Chiguidela was hit by an unknown number of bandits. I could see tracer fire from my position and numerous explosions lit up the distant horizon. Gathering the troops, we advanced from Chilembene on the southern route toward Chiguidela. I called a halt about a kilometre short of the town to assess the situation. The weight of fire we witnessed was distressing. Tracer arced across the sky in every direction, ricochets pinging off obstacles before burning out and fading from view. To our rear, lay the pig farm at Casa de Porka.

As we left the main road, we travelled east along the canal, adjoining a dirt track that entered the outskirts of Chiguidela. Again I called a halt and shortly afterwards, as the battle raged closer, we witnessed a mass of combatants fleeing in our direction. Initially I could not identify them so I formed a defensive perimeter, taking advantage of what little natural cover there was and set up our PKM and RPD machine guns to cover our arcs.

We held our fire and were soon joined by FRELIMO and the militia, who ran straight over our position, many of them continuing to flee in a terrified dash to safety. Despite this unorganised flight I was able to collar the FRELIMO ranking officer, who briefed me and explained that they had expended their ammunition and were withdrawing for re-supply and reinforcements. Apparently the bandits had attacked from the east and had entered the town.

After ascertaining the whereabouts of the town residents, I had the mortar crew fire three bombs. This was answered by a hail of largely inaccurate automatic fire. We replied with three more bombs, which whistled toward their impact point, exploding with a satisfying 'crump' where I expected the enemy to be.

Suddenly, and much to my consternation, shooting started up to our left and behind us in the direction of Casa de Porka. The volume of fire steadily intensified and I assumed that my small guard detail based there were now in the thick of it. Toward Chilembene I noticed tracer coming in our direction from the machine gun based on the tower. The situation was rapidly turning chaotic, as ordnance and small arms fire rained in from our front and rear and from both flanks. The firing in Chiguidela soon ebbed and it seemed that the attack was a diversionary tactic, while a larger force engaged the pig farm. We had been caught unawares, yet I still felt the situation could be reversed and our advantage gained.

Leaving an RPD crew and a few men to cover our rear, we returned toward Casa de Porka on foot in extended line. I was pleased to see my machine-gun crews taking the high ground on the left bank of the canal, without needing me to say so, as we retraced our steps.

Some time had passed since the first shots were fired on Chiguidela, but as suddenly as it had started, the shooting stopped, interrupted only by the occasional volley in our direction. For a moment we were stuck in the low ground on the banks of the canal, as rounds ripped into the mud around us from a position to our west, which was possibly our own. The firing died and we resumed our march, arriving at Casa de Porka weary, solemn and confused.

On investigation I learnt that only a small number of bandits had attacked the farm. The militia, firing at shadows, was responsible for the large weight of fire we had seen and heard. Effectively, the rebels had choked us, again demonstrating a degree of tactical intellect. Their ability to appear rapidly and disappear, as well as the ensuing mayhem they caused, left me with little hope that my men would stand and fight when the need arose.

I wondered what the rebels were trying to achieve. It appeared to me that something greater was on the cards, and that these encounters were designed to cause confusion and instil fear. It worked well and effectively split my forces, as well as those of FRELIMO, as we didn't know when they would hit next, or where we should concentrate our men.

We returned to Chilembene in a sombre mood. After an appraisal of the situation, I redeployed my men where I thought they would be needed most and settled down to a cup of coffee and some much-needed rest. Once again we were lucky, and although FRELIMO had sustained a few casualties, we were more fortunate and had withdrawn unscathed. Next time luck might not be on our side.

Unable to sleep, I ran through the events of the night and decided to take stock of the situation the next morning. A few hours later I was visited by the 8 Brigade commander, who wanted a brief on the night's events. I explained my understanding of the situation and requested a meeting at his convenience in order to prepare for the battle that I knew would come. He promised to be in contact, but more important matters were at hand in the form of a follow-up operation.

After rejecting my offer of assistance, the major left. Not before administering a severe bollocking to those FRELIMO troops, still among my militia, who had deserted their posts at Chiguidela. He also robbed me of five 82mm mortar bombs, promising to replace them the next day. True to his word, the following morning I met the 8 Brigade major. In a jovial mood and glowing over his recent triumph, he presented me with a captured 7.62mm PPSH sub-machine gun and five mortar bombs.

Over a cup of sweet hot tea, we developed a strategy of mutual support to be put into place during the high threat alert. The major too was convinced that the attacks on Casa de Porka and Chiguidela were in preparation for something larger. It was decided that, due to the increased enemy activity and as FRELIMO and the militia always deserted their positions, we would redeploy them where greater control could be kept over them.

I consoled myself with the knowledge that I had Sergeant Dick, Thomo and a few other committed individuals to rely on.

Good news was received from FRELIMO, when I was informed that another battle a few days previously had resulted in four kills for the LOMACO militia. A feather in our cap at last! Jim Young, with Sergeant Dick and three others, had responded to an incident at Maccatuane in the Chokwe area and had become entrenched in a half-hour gun battle with an unknown number of bandits. As usual, the rebels had disengaged, withdrawing into the bush and leaving behind them signs of heavy casualties. Jim told me that he himself had followed blood spoor for a few hundred metres, before FRELIMO took over. While conducting the follow-up, the shallow graves of four rebels had been discovered. From signs on the ground it was believed there were at least two other casualties.

I respected the fact that the rebels took their dead with them – an occurrence which was to become common practice in the months to come and a sure sign of disciplined troops.

N
W
E
S
TANZANIA
ZAMBIA
CABO
DELGADO
NIASSA
Pemba
Montepuez
NAMPULA
Nacala
TETE
Zambezi
River
Tete
ZAMBEZIA
MANICA
Quelimane
ZIMBABWE
SOFALA
Chimoio
Metuchira
Beira
Mozambique
Channel
Limpopo
River
INHAMBANE
GAZA
Inhambane
SOUTH
AFRICA
Chokwe
Xilimbene
MAPUTO
Maputo
INDIAN
OCEAN
Lomaco estates where Jake worked

CHAPTER 39:
THE BATTLE FOR CASA DE PORKA

By 21 October, I was satisfied that all possible measures had been taken to bolster our defences. In addition, I made sure each man was equipped with enough ammo and provisions for a couple of days and I had requisitioned from the stores mortar bombs, RPG7 rockets and .30 calibre ammunition for both small arms and machine gun, if re-supply became necessary.

At 23:30 that night, rebels attacked the pig farm in strength. From my residence, tracer could be seen arcing across the sky. Scrambling into my gear I mustered together 10 militia from the Chilembene guard. We mounted our transport and left for Casa de Porka. On the radio, I alerted Mark Lucas to organise a rear guard at the factory, as I couldn't be sure if the pig farm was another diversionary attack.

For some reason I felt very alone that evening and at the time put it down to Sergeant Dick's absence. To assist Jim with his duties, Sergeant Dick had departed a few days earlier. My grasp of Portuguese was tenuous, to say the least. Not only did this leave me with a huge communications problem, but his absence left me feeling rather naked. In the time I'd been at Chilembene, Sergeant Dick and I had bonded. I am sure this was owing, in part, to the fact that he was one of the few Africans with whom I could converse. There were others I trusted, but my instincts told me to watch my back.

By this stage, I had affectionately bestowed upon the Land-Cruiser the title of 'Gunship'. Bristling with firepower, aside from her Goryunov machine gun, I had made it a habit to carry the 82mm mortar and crew. This boosted my confidence, as we approached what appeared to be a rapidly escalating firefight.

On reaching high ground along the canal, about one kilometre outside Casa de Porka, I drew the Gunship to the side of the road. Thanks to the full moon I could view the battle through binoculars, although I could not see any specific actions. Tracer continued to come from the farm and return fire from the south. At least it appeared that my militia were standing to the fight and not retreating, as had happened so often in the past.

I was mesmerised by the fireworks. Battle at night had always enthralled me with its brilliant display of bright flashes and laser-like fire. Around the main farm complex, the fight seemed intense. In a tit-for-tat display, air bursts of RPG fire flashed in the distance, temporarily lighting the battlefield.

My momentary trance was shattered, as dirt and stone whined through the air to my right and 50 metres in front of me. Next, 60mm mortars impacted against the canal bank but exploded harmlessly; however, they came over with increasing accuracy as the gunners found range.

The bandits, now directly in between the militia to the south and my detail at the canal, fired wildly, as our positions were engaged from two quarters. Machine-gun rounds slammed into the grit around us, as if the angels of hell were seeking to scythe a fresh harvest.

The enemy we faced seemed more determined than on previous occasions. It seemed to me that they were well armed, as I was able to pick up the different sounds of heavy weapons. Over the noise of battle I screamed the advance, ordering my men to take the bridge across the canal in preparation of our counter-attack. Our repetition of training came to play, as in mad spurts, each group devoured the ground before them, diving for sanctuary only as the next gave covering fire. With the bridge so near, I moved forward with the Gunship, taking up a position behind some dense foliage in order to bring the Goryunov to bear. I shouted orders to my mortar crew, who leapt from the vehicle and imbedded the mortar's base plate in the sandy earth.

My forward details had already crossed the bridge and were engaging the enemy from the safety of its northern bank. I couldn't help but feel a surge of pride when with practised efficiency, they poured out accurate return fire.

We then put down very effective mortar and machine-gun fire. The enemy temporarily faltered, as their own fire subsided. I could hear screams from across the bank so I knew we were doing some damage and immediately increased our tempo, to capitalise on our success.

Just to let us know that their backs were not quite broken, the bandits directed a massive amount of fire power toward the bridge and beyond, into my defences. Impressing upon me the difference between 'cover from fire' and 'cover from view', tracer rounds punched through the foliage to my front, missing the vehicle by centimetres. Above the bridge, more RPG7 fire burst in a brilliant display of whining red-hot steel, as shrapnel ricocheted off the bridge's steel girders. The largely inaccurate fire sufficed to make us keep our heads down and kept my men at bay on the northern bank.

I could see that unless I took charge from the front, our advance would peter out. Leaving our heavy weapons to hold the bridge and cover me, I dashed forward to take control. I think all combat is frightening, but on this occasion my terror was tactual. As I ran from cover to cover, the dirt exploded at my feet, metal aglow with luminous reds and greens as it punched into the earth.

Momentarily trapped, the enemy pressed on with their defence. Had I more men, I would have deployed them west and east to assure no avenue of escape remained. After what seemed like minutes, my feet found traction on the gravel road, on the opposite side of the bridge. Diving for cover behind the canal's earthen embankment, I looked around to find my men. I was relieved to see that, apart from a few minor scratches, no-one had been hit although with the voluminous fire that continued, fear had set in among them and panic was about to be our new foe.

Whether I misjudged the situation that night, or was hoping to salvage the unsalvageable, what I did next still makes me cold to this day. With a direct assault in mind, I had a flare fired over the pig farm. Popping at the peak of its trajectory, its light cast eerie shadows as it swung down under its canopy. I was certain that in the face of a determined counter-attack, the bandits' resolve would wane and we would gain the advantage.

The bandits' target appeared to be the farm's store rooms. As far as I was aware, nothing of any value was inside, but the centre of their defence massed around those few brick structures. Moving across shallow ground, I formed the militia into an extended line along the ridge, overlooking a paddock. Drawing on what I'd learnt and from past experience, I rallied the men with shouts of 'Advance!' and pressed on with the task, hoping to unnerve the enemy in the face of aggressive action.

From my position the embankment ran along the canal behind the buildings, thus affording some cover, but it meant a gradual uphill advance. Leaping to my feet I charged the store rooms, firing as I went, reaching the gates to the farm. Ahead of me a small mound loomed behind which I took cover. To my rear I could hear the RPD and RPK gunners' rhythmic fire punctuated by the crack of small arms. Imbued with a sense of victory I again leapt to my feet and charged my adversaries. 'Advance! Advance!' I yelled.

Within a hundred metres of the first building, I could recognise the dark forms of individuals and what appeared to be a hundred muzzle flashes aimed in my direction. I could not falter now as I would let my men down, so I pressed on.

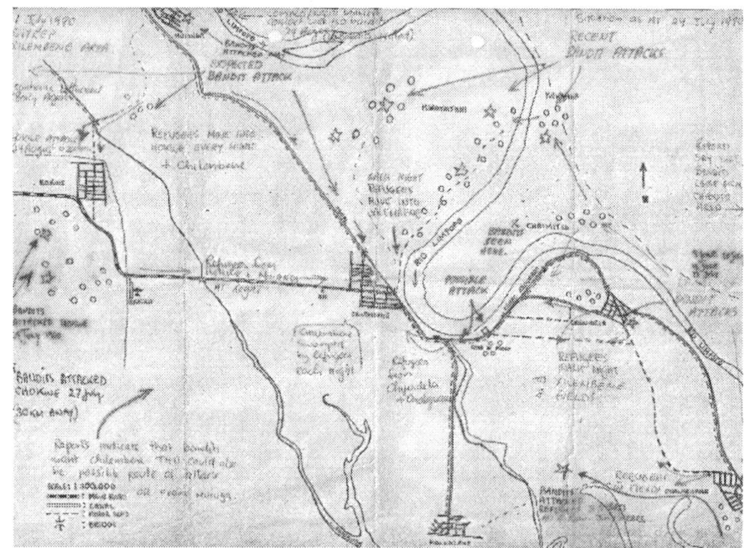

Hand drawn sitrep map that Jake used of Chilimbene and surrounding area.
The red stars indicate bandit attacks over a period of less than three months.

Self-doubt, it seems, is the seed of decay and once it has taken hold the tide can turn to disfavour. Although I was unaware of it at the time, my 'Charge of the Light Brigade' was an individual effort. Some 50 metres away from the enemy I glanced back and realised I was alone. Taking cover I screamed and shouted for my men to join me, but of the 20-plus men I had formed in the assault line, only two had ventured out beyond the safety of the embankment, albeit uncertainly. If I hadn't been so terrified at the time I would have laughed. Here I was 'storming the gates of hell' and my best men had stopped their advance in line with my last cover. I can only assume both my men and the enemy thought I was utterly mad.

With the comedy of errors firmly at hand, I dived to the ground, as bullets stitched the dirt at my feet. More worrisome were the tracer rounds that buzzed past my ears, for I knew that for every one I saw, at least two other rounds passed by unseen. For a second I contemplated continuing alone, but that would have been certain death. The bandits were still trapped and would fight it out as they had nowhere to run. Even if I did get in among them, badly outnumbered, I would surely be injured or killed.

There was only one thing for it. Mustering my internal reserves I pushed myself backwards with my elbows into a small depression. There I fired a short burst, changed magazines and shouted for my men to cover me. As I peered above the high ground to my front, the enemy could be seen ducking under a withering return fire and with a final effort, I screamed the retreat and prepared to retrace my steps over no-man's-land. Finding my balance, I scrambled for the bridge, diving for cover the last few metres, like a rugby player scoring a try. I landed with a thud, the magazines in my chest webbing dug into my ribs, knocking the wind out of me, but at least I was safe. In the face of enemy fire, and in view of friendly fire, my militia were now engaged on three different fronts – the pig farm could not be entered without sustaining heavy casualties. The fact that we had not already come to harm amazed me, as it had been literally raining lead and shrapnel.

The situation being untenable, we withdrew across the bridge for reinforcements.

On entering the outskirts of Chilembene, automatic fire again poured into our midst, peppering one of the Land-Rovers. A stern expletive over the radio put an end to it as I realised our own militia were responsible, thinking we were rebels entering the town.

At Chilembene I noticed that two FRELIMO BTR APCs had returned from their operations north of the Limpopo. I asked the commander why he had not assisted us at the farm. I was lavished with his excuse of not wanting to interfere in 'my' action. Taking stock of our ammunition, we re-equipped and returned to the pig farm with the armoured personnel carriers at our front.

The shooting stopped shortly before we arrived at the bridge. In the distance, across a paddock, I could see my militia emerge from the bush. On recognising the FRELIMO vehicles, they realised it was safe enough to return to their posts. It was evident the enemy had fled after the initial engagement, the recent shooting coming from an increasingly jittery militia.

At the store room I found signs of a break-in, but little other damage. The bandits had fled during our departure, leaving only a bloody trail in their wake. Once again they had taken their casualties with them, if at all there were any, although I was sure of it from the screams I had heard. Around me it was apparent that our mortar and machine-gun fire had been very effective. White plaster from the buildings littered the ground like dandruff on a collar and the buildings' walls were pockmarked with the acne of battle. The mortar craters, pitting the once flat feeding area around the store rooms, indicated a high degree of accuracy.

I learnt from the militia on site that the rebel group had been at least 50 strong and had entered via the main entrance en masse.

I had been extremely lucky. It seemed to me that I had come very close to meeting my Maker!

It came to light that on the previous night, moments before our battle at the pig farm, bandits had attacked four other positions along the Limpopo River. They had hit Maramajani, Mvani, Chilagavu and Chiguidela simultaneously. Eye-witness reports said that each group was about 30 to 40 strong.

I made an inspection of each town to see if I could assist in any way and was chilled at what I found. Worst affected was Maramajani, where five people were killed: four children and one woman. Each had been hacked to death with pangas, the large bush knives that the locals used. The woman appeared to have been executed, as she lay bound hand and foot. Of all the panga blows I could see, only one might have been instantly fatal. By the looks of things her death was obviously a long and agonizing one, with limbs and joints dismembered before the final blow came. Another woman had been shot through the arm and I took her to the Chokwe clinic where she received treatment. I wondered what all the terror was for.

Of the 40 or so bandits who had attacked Maramajani, only three were adults. The remainder were youths between 14 and 16 years old, both male and female. What drove them to this insanity?

Western civilization makes much of Hollywood 'desensitisation' among youths and attributes such things as school shootings and the like to this phenomenon. But these children had not seen any movies, nor had they played computer games. They were largely illiterate and I would be surprised if they had ever read a book.

Personally, I believe that the temperament of youth, along with personal traumatic experience, is the catalyst. Children, in their misunderstanding, are capable of incredible acts of cruelty. They will allocate personal pain to a category and in their naivety cannot differentiate between extremes of pain – 'If you kill my goldfish, I'll kill your dog' sort of a thing. That, along with a need to belong, can be very dangerous. A child who wants to be a part of something might well commit a crime far in excess of what a mature person may be prepared to do. It was the same in our society when I grew up, although instead of killing my neighbours I just stole a chocolate bar in order to belong to the gang.

The futility of the death I witnessed made me angry. It also made me a hypocrite, because right then I might have done exactly the same thing to the culprits had I caught them.

I returned home despondent. FRELIMO had brought in a battalion for mopping-up operations. I was told they had the bandit situation under control.

Still reeling from the atrocities of the day before, I was visited by the liaison officer of the Chilembene police. The news he brought was uplifting.

After follow-up operations were conducted, it was confirmed that the battle of Casa de Porka had resulted in six enemy killed and a number of wounded. Four of them had been killed by machine-gun fire and two as a result of mortar shrapnel. Witnesses had revealed that another bandit had been seen limping, grievously wounded in the leg, while retreating with his comrades from the vicinity of the pig farm. They had seen the rebels carrying their dead in the direction of Maramajani.

In response to this, the police had mounted a search and found the bodies along the banks of the Limpopo between the two towns. The liaison officer asked if I could assist him in retrieving the bodies, so I accompanied him in the Gunship to the site of the graves. Pulling off the main dirt road as we arrived along the Limpopo I reversed the cruiser toward a large gathering of people at the river's edge. Exiting the vehicle the soft sand gave under my boots with the noise of chalk being scraped on a blackboard. Approaching the melee it was evident that the gathered crowd were from Maramajani and had come to exact vengeance on the dead rebels. Their bodies, now half exhumed, the targets of retribution and their souls of vitriolic abuse as boots, sticks and stones laid into them. The villagers couldn't be blamed. Such is war in Africa.

Looking more closely, I could see that the dead had been stripped of all their clothing before they were hurriedly buried. I saw bullet wounds and broken bones in a mess of dried blood and plasma. The corpses, bloated from the tropical heat, looked like boulders protruding from the earth. It was only as I came nearer that I recognised them for what they were. A dust devil whirled across the beach and oscillated for a brief second. Just when it was about to peter out, it picked up speed and pirouetted in a neat ballet off into the distance. The hairs on my neck stood erect. The Grim Reaper had paid his respects in a macabre dance of death.

We loaded the bodies onto the Gunship and were glad to be under way, the wind dragging with it the offensive smell that emanated from the corpses. I was told to drive north for about two kilometres, as a report had come in that more corpses had been found.

On a bend in the river, in amongst a thicket, others had died. We found one body lying in a foetal position under a bush. A few metres off lay another body, ragged, torn and fly-blown. Next to the bodies we found the dead men's weapons – two AKMs with four empty and two fully charged magazines lay on a bag of rice. Tied to the bag were a couple of water bottles. The events which had led these men here were obvious; slowing their comrade's pace, they were left to fend for themselves. Because their wounds were so severe they were unable to travel and they retired into the thicket to escape detection. There they had died, lonely and in pain.

That afternoon we had an influx of refugees. With the intensity of attacks villagers for miles saw Chilembene as the only safe haven. From then on they would arrive each evening to sleep in the streets, in the park and in the nearby fields, until the next morning when they could resume their lives.

This presented further problems. I could hardly begrudge them their safety, but LOMACO property was being stolen in the town and tomatoes were being trampled on or eaten in the fields. As it was my responsibility to avoid such occurrences, I had to deploy guards overnight which left me short staffed.

I had been in the country for a month. My initiation had been stark and although it wasn't always as intense during my stay, it had given me a good idea of what to expect. I was due for a few days' leave and Sheila would be flying from Port Shepstone to Maputo where I would meet her for the weekend.

On 26 October, FRELIMO deployed an additional 400 troops to the Chilembene region. I wasn't certain who was winning the war, but bandit activity had necessitated the extension of FRELIMO forces across a wide front. As guerrilla campaigns go, RENAMO were hugely successful. Whether through sympathy or terror, the way I saw it, they had largely subverted the people to their cause. If the fighters weren't given the food and shelter they badly needed, they simply took it.

The atmosphere around Chilembene was tense. An attack was expected the coming weekend. Unfortunately, I would not be there.

I returned from Maputo fresh and ready to take on all comers. My leave had come and gone, but I was able to strategise over my dilemma and came up with a few sound ideas. For one, I would request a FRELIMO liaison officer to be permanently assigned to me and kept in the net as regards FRELIMO operations. In addition, I insisted that I be able to call on FRELIMO support, in the form of armoured personnel carriers and heavy weapons.

As a force multiplier I reviewed the tank and its crew. Unlike in Rhodesia, I was without the benefit of support in the form of casevac and air support. I had learnt that my militia were very superstitious and believed strongly in witchcraft. For example, they believed their nangas (witchdoctors) when they were told the bandits could not die. As was evident from our recent success, this belief was unfounded and I was assured of the rebels' mortality.

I felt it best that the tank should remain at Chilembene where I could watch over it rather than have it patrol as it had done previously. The saying 'out of sight, out of mind', while holding true to some people, had a different interpretation with the tank crew. While patrolling and 'out of sight', I could guarantee that they would end up in a bar somewhere and proceed to get 'out of mind'!

In the kind of warfare in which I found myself engaged during the vast period of my service life, the players on both sides were guilty of atrocities. There were no 'angels' in these theatres. This holds true for guerrilla armies everywhere, whether they oppose West or East, but does not include the professional armies I had served with in both Rhodesia and the United Kingdom. Of course, there was always a bad apple among the bunch, but that was an exception to the rule and I can state categorically that I was never witness to killing without sanctity or sound military reason.

The Christmas period passed without elaborate fanfare, but New Year's Eve brought with it a fireworks display the likes of which I had never seen. As we celebrated, RENAMO put on a display to match our own. In the distance, at the foothills of Gorongoza, the night sky was lit up as if by the power of a billion candles as the rebels acted out their defiance. Tracer shot heavenward and rocket-propelled grenades popped below the cloud base, highlighting their luminous elegance. Before I was taken in by the spectacle, I had to remind myself that these clouds definitely had no silver lining.

The town of Barragem lies 50 kilometres north-west of Chokwe, on the banks of the Limpopo River. I travelled there for lunch with Sergeant Dick, to meet Charles Dean. For me it was a step back in time.

My former unit, the Rhodesian SAS, along with the RLI and military engineers, had attacked the town on 5 September 1979 to cut road and rail communications and to neutralise a forward admin base at Mapai, which so ably assisted ZANLA and FRELIMO. I was in the Selous Scouts when the daring strike took place and although it did not achieve its entire objective, it was largely successful and created a huge disruption to the enemy. The Barragem bridges, large two-lane road and rail structures, were damaged and the rail link was severed. Another four bridges on the Limpopo River, between Chibuto and Barragem, were totally destroyed and a large number of FRELIMO and ZANLA troops were killed. Conducted 320 kilometres inside Mozambique and over a vast area, Operation Uric was one of the largest raids of the war and was testimony to the efficiency of the Rhodesians' prowess.

Unfortunately, the operation was not without its loss. A South African Puma helicopter, on loan to the Rhodesians, was shot down by RPG7 fire. The aircraft, flying low over a small enemy satellite camp north of Mapai, banked sharply and crashed into the ground, bursting into flames and killing everyone on board. I knew many of the men who died that day and the loss was profound.

The Rhodesians lost a second helicopter during the raid, one of the precious few we had. Early in the operation a Bell helicopter was hit by rocket fire, as it flew over an enemy position on the banks of the Limpopo River. The aircraft's technician, Alexander Wesson, was killed in the crash. The pilot, Dick Paxton, was dragged from the flames by a brave SAS soldier, Sergeant 'Flash' Smythe. Paxton, a personal friend of mine, was lucky to have survived the crash!

Arriving at Barragem's traffic roundabout, I was surprised to see the tail section of the Bell helicopter in the middle of what might have been a lawn. I had heard that this artefact from the war was still in Barragem, but to see it so suddenly was chilling.

Sergeant Dick and I inspected the remains. I learnt from Sergeant Dick that FRELIMO paraded here every Sunday morning as an ode to their small victory. It was here that they also dumped the bodies of those rebels who were killed in action, for the townspeople to see. I took a photograph of the tail section and later sent it to Paxton as a memento. Taking leave of my thoughts I bowed my head and said a small prayer for Alex Wesson.

My interest as a tourist aroused, Sergeant Dick told me of other places he knew of that I might want to see. As our lunch appointment was not due for an hour, I humoured him and together we walked to the outskirts of the town, only a few hundred metres from where we had parked.

Crossing a small drainage ditch running alongside the road, we clambered up a steep verge and were soon standing on top of a sand mound. On the other side were some concrete structures encircled by a high fence. Military in appearance, the fort before us served as a light air defence battery as it had done for many years.

Looking around, I noticed the camp was in a bad state. Bricks had crumbled off corners and paint was hanging off the walls in strips. The structures were scarred and pockmarked by bullets and shrapnel. I asked Sergeant Dick to explain the devastation to me. With a wink in my direction he taunted me. 'You know,' he said. 'You were here before, weren't you?'

My quizzical expression begged his explanation.

The scars remained a testament to the Barragem raid, when Rhodesian troops had revved the camp. The incident was cause for much hilarity in the future, as our visit to the camp would often be recalled whenever we passed by other artefacts and evidence of Rhodesia's war against ZANLA. In Sergeant Dick's view I had apparently been everywhere at the same time!

CHAPTER 40:
SETTING THE COURSE

The Chokwe Club had been built up over the years as a regular little 'Club Med' and was far removed from its mundane surrounds. It serviced the expatriate community and was complete with a large gazebo bar and a swimming pool. Popular at the weekends, it was the venue for many gatherings and impromptu drinking sessions that resulted in innumerable hangovers. Over the period of my contract I met some unusual characters there and it was to the Chokwe Club that I escaped in order to forget my troubles.

One day I drove the few kilometres to the Club to sink back a cold one. A function was in progress and the first person to greet me there was Victor.

Victor was a young, good-looking lieutenant in the Russian Army who hailed from Georgia. On attachment to FRELIMO in an advisory capacity, he was based with 8 Brigade at the Chokwe garrison. He wanted us to believe that his parent unit was an artillery outfit, but as he became better known to us, our suspicions were aroused. An affable fellow and quite likeable and charming, Victor's failure to grasp the fundamentals of Western social culture left him a little out of his league, whenever he joined us at the club.

With every visitation he brought along several bottles of Russian vodka and would proceed to ply us with neat tots while he consumed soft drinks. As time passed and the drunker we became, his conversation would inevitably change from low-key social graces such as 'how do you do?' and 'where do you come from?' to obvious military interrogation-type questions like 'how many British soldiers are there in the area?' and 'why are you assisting the government here and for what purpose?'. Following that, the camera would come out and he would try to snap pictures of us in our British Army uniforms. We were convinced that Victor thought that we were serving British regulars and possibly members of 22 SAS. I can't say that we tried to change his mind, as we would often drop hints to nurture the image he had of us.

As a liaison officer he cut a fine form. Highly intelligent and with a respectable IQ, he could speak eight languages including Portuguese and was learning a ninth, Shona, from Zimbabwean troops on the Beira Corridor.

In time, courtesy aside, we would affectionately refer to him as 'The Spy', as it became crystal clear that his mission was something other than what he professed. Since his common sense was somewhat lacking, Victor became a source of much hilarity to us and his angry insistence that he was not a KGB agent provided us with hours of side-splitting laughter.

As obvious as the character of the British airman masquerading as the French policeman in the hit comedy 'Hello, Hello', the Russian never seemed to figure out that we were on to him. Despite our good-humoured accusations, he did not once tire of questioning us and each time we met he would again enquire about the latest 'strategic' news, after the customary two bottles of vodka were consumed and after he had taken a couple of snapshots. Heaven knows what reports eventually reached the KGB Mozambique Desk, as we filled his head with unfounded garbage and trivia!

The flip side of the coin revealed Victor for who he was, in my reports to the Africa Desk at the Harare based British High Commission and the American Embassy. Although this information was of little real importance, it was the kind of information that would eventually find its way into a file in the headquarters of both MI6 and the CIA. Trivial though my information might have been, with other intelligence the pieces of the jigsaw could ultimately be fitted together.

Victor and I eventually became good friends and he would often visit me during his off-duty hours. Together we would spend much time arguing the pros and cons of Western military doctrine versus Eastern. Victor also provided me with up-to-date intelligence that could be relied on. He gave me the facts, unlike his FRELIMO counterparts, who often embellished the truth in an attempt to gain respect.

Victor later told me that he lived for our weekend meetings. He didn't get on with Africans, he said, as they treated him like a pariah. I imagine it had something to do with Russia giving the country all its hand-me-down weapons in return for 15 years of exploiting Mozambique's coastal fishing grounds.

The light of the moon hung in a haze over Chilembene during April. Acting on reports of rebel movement, this time from Victor, I once again revised my strategy and cushioned my bets.

The full moon was expected at 23:00 and the daylight hours were spent in preparation of the attack to come. A tragic fate had befallen the village of

Chaimites, only four kilometres distant. I accompanied two policemen and drove the short distance over the canal, collecting the bridge detail on the way. I was told that a few civilians had been murdered, but nothing really could have prepared me for the scene that lay in store.

The inhabitants of Chaimites, unlike those of other villages, preferred to stay overnight in their homes instead of trekking into Chilembene for safety. Up until then, they had managed to escape the horrors of a bandit attack.

What confronted me was the worst atrocity I had ever witnessed. Strewn around the village were dismembered corpses, limbs hacked from bodies. Everywhere blood stained the earth and fly-blown pieces of flesh rotted in the morning sun. It was like a bloodied abattoir and I could not give an accurate figure of how many people had died there. After a collection of body parts was undertaken, there were too many limbs for the number of torsos and heads we recovered. Among the dead were old women and children. One militiaman carried a dead toddler by the ankles, as the child's arms dragged lifelessly through the dirt.

It transpired that the 'bandits' had entered the village and not wanting to alert FRELIMO and the militia, had carried out their silent orgy of killing, with machetes and knives. Littered about the place were posters of the RENAMO leader, Alfonso Dlakhama, who had taken over after Andre Matangaidze's demise. It struck me as odd that people would proudly advertise the fact that they were responsible for such heinous slaughter. Definitely no way to win hearts and minds!

I made my views known to the police chief, who had arrived on the scene, momentarily forgetting that I couldn't very well blame his own people for such barbarity. I was certain that this wasn't the work of RENAMO, but was an atrocity carefully orchestrated to look like it was. It seemed to me that the savagery was staged to give RENAMO a bad name. Fortunately, I don't think the police chief heard me, or at least pretended not to for reasons of his own.

On debriefing my militia, I was informed that the survivors of Chaimites had heard vehicles pull up across the canal at about 19:00. Half an hour later the 'bandits' arrived and commenced their killing. I'll put my life on it that Chaimites was the victim of a dirty deeds campaign. RENAMO rarely, if ever, used vehicles, rag-tag as they were.

For a while things didn't get better. The following day Muhamba was hit.

This time it was plain to see that RENAMO had done it. The rebels shot and then killed Acacio Muxanga, force number 055. The loss was sad. On his day off he had been assisting the local militia in fighting off the bandits, when he was injured in the right leg. Captured, he was dragged into the bush where the bandits cut his throat and stole his uniform and weapon. His body was recovered naked a short while later.

Amid the chaos of rapidly escalating violence, Sheila arrived with our son Paul. We spent a casual few days together although I was constantly interrupted by call-outs and the need to tend to my duties. I admired the bravado of my family and wondered how many other families would put their lives at risk to visit their loved ones in a combat zone.

The peace was short-lived. A report filtered through of an abduction that had occurred the previous night. The Muianga militia commander called for a head-count of his men and discovered six missing. At first he thought they had deserted at some time during battle, but his concern was raised when civilians said they had seen the bandits capture and disarm the six men. Being out of ammo, they could hardly have put up a fight.

FRELIMO conducted a follow-up operation the following day, but despite their best efforts, were unable to close with the bandits. When the trail petered out they returned to base a few days later. I caught up with the major a short while afterwards, to see if I could learn of the men's fate. FRELIMO trackers confirmed that the six abductees had been among the bandits, as they fled toward the mountains, their tracks distinguishable from the others from the weight they carried.

It was apparent that the six were used as porters and while they were useful alive, their fate thereafter can only be assumed. Had they been civilians, I guess they would have been released and then found their way home. However, as militia members, something more sinister awaited them. Such is Africa. Despite regular enquiries they were never seen again, at least not while I was there. Their families had to pick up the pieces and carry on with their lives.

On 13 May 1990, I was informed that the Massinga Dam on the Limpopo had been opened, as the river was running high. The news left me in high spirits. With the river in flood it formed a natural boundary from the north and bandits would find it hard to cross.

It became apparent that we couldn't let our guard down when Maramajani was attacked on the night of 20 May. Crossing the river at Muhamba, in a typical raid, bandits overpowered the militia by sheer weight of numbers and firepower and they proceeded to loot the town. In a display of brutality they massacred seven civilians and abducted a further 20 to act as porters. I felt for the souls of Maramajani and wondered why people continued to live there.

For a change, the weeks preceding the full moon, usually quieter anyway, were abnormally so. In the silence that settled one could hear a pin drop. The silence irked me and I thought that something must be afoot. After getting used to the constant gunfire, the lack of it was deafening.

Jim Shand arrived to assist in the defence of Chilembene. The full moon came and went without incident, but the following night Chalacuane was the target of a rebel raid. I was away at the time, but arrived back the next day, to be met at my residence by a gathering of civilians. It transpired that they had come to complain about Jim, who through inexperience had not responded to the attack. I liked Jim, but I felt he was a little out of his depth. I don't think he could have done much anyway, limited as he was to his Royal Navy experience. His usual post was a quiet one so he hadn't gained much experience there.

I could only apologise, as Jim was new to the game and I assured them that it would not happen again.

I investigated the attack immediately and was horrified to learn that 11 people had been killed or wounded for no apparent loss to the bandits. It came to light that they had also sustained casualties, but true to form had retreated with them after the battle. Among our dead were four local militiamen and five civilians. Two other militiamen were wounded. The incident did not bode well for LOMACO as it created bad public relations.

Jim returned to his citrus estate for a couple of weeks, before he was to go on leave to the UK. The dust settled and I prepared to salvage LOMACO's reputation. Had I known Jim's fate then, I am sure our farewell would have been far greater.

CHAPTER 41:
ENTER THE GURKHAS

With the scale of bandit activity on the increase, LOMACO sought additional help in the form of GSG. Gurkha Security Guards Limited, as the name implies, was a private enterprise that had been put together to conduct security operations in troublespots around the world, by using the services of ex-Gurkhas. In Sierra Leone in 1995, the company was to attract prominent media attention when it lost one of its employees (my old compatriot Bob Mackenzie of SAS days) and another went missing.

During my service in the British Army I had come across the Gurkhas and was highly impressed with their standards of professionalism and their soldiering ability. Tales abounded about the aggressiveness they displayed in combat, which enhanced the mystique that surrounded them.

LOMACO hired 13 of these fine men. Of these, 12 were to be posted at various company-owned estates and factories, working hand-in-hand with the LOMACO militia, while one would be on standby in the event of injury, absence or death of another member. I was to get to know some of these men on a very close personal basis and for the most part I can say they never let me down. However, on a few occasions, I questioned their motivation and more than once our differing views of work ethic resulted in a row.

Whether it was company policy or whether it came down to a personal view, it became evident that some GSG personnel preferred to refrain from engaging bandits when other options existed. Often I found myself at the sharp end of contacts while my GSG counterparts lagged behind.

The Gurkhas' introduction to Mozambique was to leave a lasting impression. Responding to a raid on Hokwe, I travelled with them to assess the damage. Our arrival at the town was met with the screams and howls of bereaved townsfolk. In the town's centre, several stores had been looted and burnt down and outside one of them lay the body of a militiaman. The tale I was told sent chills down my spine.

After a short battle the militia contingent had fled, leaving behind a wounded comrade. Shot through both legs, he was unable to move. He was soon captured and was at the mercy of the bandits. After looting and burning the stores the bandits ordered aside a few civilians for use as porters and called for a gathering of the townsfolk. As a lesson to them, the bandits then proceeded to disembowel the militiaman alive – testament to the fate that awaited 'sell-outs' and those aligned with the government. I was well accustomed to the unspeakable horror that beset Mozambique. My newly arrived compatriots were not so fortunate and were visibly shaken by what they saw.

If it was an easy ticket they were after, then the Gurkhas were to be disappointed. Shortly after their arrival, I was radioed by Mark Lucas, who told me that Jim Shand had been killed at the citrus estate.

On returning to his estate after the Chalacuane debacle, Jim had revised his duty roster and toughened up his stance in preparation for his leave. One of the issues that constantly worried Jim, like us, was his militiamen sleeping on duty. On several occasions during his rounds he had caught guards asleep at the citrus processing plant. The plant was a veritable Fort Knox and was surrounded by a perimeter of anti-personnel mines on all sides, demarcated only by danger signs.

On one of the numerous occasions of finding the militiamen sleeping, Jim lost his cool and set to administering disciplinary action, during which the guilty party made their views known. Apparently Jim was told that the processing plant was never likely to be breached, as the rebels wouldn't dare negotiate the minefield. Established as a deterrent to rebel attack and not an excuse to sleep on duty, Jim began dismantling the minefield before his departure to the UK. His reasoning, quite correctly, was that without the benefit of a 'safety blanket' the militiamen would be ever so vigilant.

Some days later, while Jim was reunited with his family in England, the enterprising militiamen, pulling strings with FRELIMO, had the mine cordon reactivated, so that they could resume pushing ZZZs on duty. FRELIMO engineers came one day and planted a whole bunch of nasties around the plant, including various types of anti-personnel and POM-Z 2 mines.

Jim's leave came and went and about two weeks after his return he noticed the grass on the perimeter had grown to dangerous levels, impeding the view of possible rebel advance. He ordered the militiamen to enter the perimeter and cut the grass with slashers. Much to Jim's consternation, when he returned some hours later, the grass had not been cut and the militiamen stood by, idly twiddling their thumbs. Enraged, Jim again ordered them to do as they were told, but there was much hesitancy. The men knew what Jim didn't. They weren't about to tell him either for fear of being reprimanded.

It was never established whether Jim was warned or not. In his righteous anger, he snatched a grass slasher from the nearest militiaman, declaring that if they couldn't do the job themselves, he would do it for them. He didn't get far into the cordon before stepping on an AP mine. The blast blew off his foot, throwing him sideways into the air, landing with his head next to a POM-Z 2 mine, with an instant pull striker mechanism. The second mine detonated next to his head, effectively and messily decapitating him. It was a sad loss. An internal witch-hunt was held to find the culprits. If memory serves me correctly, the perpetrators were never bought to book and Jim's death was put down to an accident.

Most of the militia commanders, like me, had previously been privates or NCOs in the British Army. Jim Shand's replacement was a young, former officer who had graduated from Sandhurst Military College and was commissioned in the Royal Green Jackets. After Jim's death, Mark Lucas excitedly told me that finally someone with officer status was joining us. A Rupert [army slang for a junior officer], if ever there was one, he was an entirely likeable chap, although much to his chagrin he was put in charge of all LOMACO security. While visiting Chilembene on a familiarisation tour, he confided in me his fears. He felt he was imposing and realised that his experience would never add up to the wealth of knowledge inherent in the other militia commanders, whose experience had been gained under the stresses of operational deployment.

I liked our officer friend and tried to encourage him to relax, assuring him that we would assist where his experience fell short. A while later, he managed to get involved in a punch-up with RENAMO, fortunately escaping unscathed. He stayed with us for a short while before returning to England, fully aware he had entered into a very dangerous realm. His departure could be excused, as even I had had no idea that my service in Mozambique would be so intense.

The position the young officer left behind remained vacant for a few weeks and was eventually filled by Lieutenant Colonel Allan Shaw. A former officer of the RLI and subsequently CO of 1 Commando Battalion (Zimbabwe) after the war, Allan was far more suitable for the task. He was later to become firm friends with General Fondo, FRELIMO's commander – something that was of great advantage to LOMACO.

My reunion with Allan was at Chilembene, which he visited to familiarise himself with the organisation. From what he had learnt so far, he was unimpressed with the commanders of many of the estate's militia. As he saw it, these former British soldiers were generally lax and were always pushing for better conditions and pay. The first thing he asked of me was to see my duty and training roster and he was most surprised when I produced it from my drawer. He told me that I was the first to have actually shown him a schedule. The others, while purporting to have them somewhere, had failed to produce anything like it, which set me off on a good footing immediately.

Hokwe and Mapapa were the scenes of many minor skirmishes over the next week. Our defences were in place and the attacks met with little success. The same could be said of our own success in the field, as I had received no confirmation of bandit casualties. Invariably, our follow-ups ended with nothing to report.

A flight was arranged to take our Gurkha team to the far north of Mozambique at the end of July. Deo Kaji and two others, Ram and Padam, would remain with me while the rest were given the responsibility of protecting LOMACO assets in the north of the country. I didn't know it then, but my path would eventually lead there too, when duty called me to LOMACO's estates in Nropa, south-west of Pemba in the Montepuez Province.

I arrived back from leave during August to relative calm. Abductions had been on the increase, but other than that, everything was in a satisfactory order. Within a few days of my return Malhazene, not far distant, was attacked. I was still settling in so I left the reaction to the charge of Deo Kaji. It wasn't long before he returned with little in the way of useful information. He did tell me that bandits had occupied the town for two hours and then fled in the direction of the Limpopo River. This got me to thinking. While on leave I had arrived at the conclusion that with the river now in constant flow, there could only be few places where bandits could cross.

Africans in general are not the best of swimmers and many are absolutely terrified of water. I resolved to conduct a reconnaissance of the river the next day to look for likely crossing points, which I assumed would be relatively few along our front.

The recce was rewarded with the discovery of only two points that in my estimation could be safely crossed along a 20 kilometre course. One was in a shallow gorge, where the river narrowed to 50 or 60 metres wide and the other was at a bend in the river where, in the middle of a wide sandy tract, it snaked from one shallow pool to the next. I entered the vicinity of the two crossing points on my hand-drawn map.

On 24 August, Hokwe was attacked by bandits during the early hours of the morning. Together with members of Jim's militia I responded to the incident with Thomo, my right-hand man. We arrived at the scene at 04:30 as the bandits were fleeing, heading east toward the Limpopo River.

Sergeant Dick was engaged elsewhere at the time and I felt unfortunate not to have his company, although Thomo had proved himself on several occasions and I had confidence in his ability.

Taking the direction of the rebels' flight into account, I opted for a follow-up to be conducted. Together with a section of Zimbabwe National Army (ZNA) soldiers who were on the scene, I ordered my men to advance ahead of the bandits and set up an ambush at the bend in the river which I had mapped a few days earlier. Thomo needed no urging and jumped into the driver's seat of a VW Cougar which I had equipped with the Goryunov machine gun. He was about to leave with several of the militiamen when Deo Kaji arrived. To my surprise and in violation of my authority, the GSG man stepped in and ordered Thomo to stand down. I overruled his order and a brief argument ensued. The incident left me incensed at the time, as every second was critical if our plans were to be successful. I vowed to take it up with him at a later date.

Despite the delay Thomo arrived at the river as the sun rose and cast its light across its huge sandy expanse. In the centre of the river bed, a good 200 metres across at this point, the river snaked in an easterly direction toward the Indian Ocean. Waist deep in water, the bandits and their porters, 150 all told, were caught as they trudged to the opposite bank. Surprise was complete and the Goryunov gunner let rip with two belts of .30-calibre ammunition.

The scene that was described to me later was classic: Unaware of pursuit, as the rounds found range, the bandits dispersed in every direction and many of them fell face first into the water. Abandoned loot floated everywhere and pandemonium reigned, as the porters tore back towards the direction of the fire while the rebels ducked and weaved for safety. Those who chose to fight were raked with effective small arms and machine-gun fire and one rebel, bravely standing his ground, was hit and disappeared, thrashing under water.

Three rounds punched into the Cougar vehicle with little effect before the return fire ceased and the rebels who had survived scrambled up the far river bank. If they thought their problems were over, they were wrong. The rainy season was at an end and the land had become dry as it settled into the winter months ahead. Vast tracts of devil-thorn bushes had shed their cloaks of evil, spear-like thorns that now lay on the ground awaiting unsuspecting hoof and foot. V-like in appearance and razor-tipped, they were Nature's own booby trap and the rebels tore right into them.

The carnage that followed was tragic: Thomo and his fellow militiamen had crossed the river in pursuit and ascended the far bank to find the enemy trapped. It was a turkey shoot and easy to distinguish between rebels and porters. Panicking, some men fled on, despite the thorns which lanced their feet as rounds buzzed between and through them. Others tore off in one direction, then another, as it dawned on them that their flight was useless and they resigned themselves to the bullet. Heaven knows the final tally, but after the short engagement eight rebel bodies were recovered, one being that of their commander, complete with two Makarov pistols. Reports then and from subsequent intelligence revealed that the damage inflicted on the enemy was grievous. The amount of wounded was disproportionate to the number killed.

A follow-up revealed four more bodies, but many of the rebels would have died later of their wounds. The blood spoor, I was told, could be read as clearly as a blind man reads Braille.

News of our success travelled fast and the contact was heralded as a huge victory. The following Saturday the district attorney of the area held a party in celebration of the event, to which we were invited as honoured guests. LOMACO managers mingled with government and FRELIMO officials, as beer flowed, while a goat roasted on the spit. It was a pity the honour was afforded only to us, Deo Kaji included and not its rightful recipients. Thomo certainly gained in my estimation that day and received a gratuity in the form of a bonus.

I looked around me at the time and knew our celebration would be short lived. Already the bush telegraph resounded with the boastful cheers of the militiamen. It could only mean one thing: the bandits would be back for revenge.

As I retired that night, the militia camp at Hokwe was attacked in strength. I went the next morning to have a look. Caught in their revelry, the camp was decimated by mortar fire and several of the militiamen were wounded. To add to my woes, after having out-done himself in the earlier contact, Thomo, drunk and high on the thrills of battle, had stolen a Land-Cruiser and rolled it in Hokwe. He later stated that he was on company business, but the journey was unauthorised and unfortunately it came to the attention of Mark Lucas before I found out about it. Had I known about it sooner I might have requested some leniency, but Mark was resolute in his decision to fire him. It was an unfortunate loss of a man whom I believed was a great asset.

There was another event which solidified my opinion of the GSG men I worked with. On a separate occasion Deo Kaji spent a frightful night alone and under continual fire from rebel positions. Taking it in turns to patrol the area, respond to banditry and look after the factory, I had remained in Chilembene while Deo accompanied the tank to Hokwe. A few kilometres from their destination the tank ran out of diesel and Deo continued on in his Land-Rover with a few militiamen. He hadn't travelled half a kilometre when a roadside ambush was sprung. The men in his vehicle dived for cover, exiting the Land-Rover at speed. Deo continued through the killing ground shrinking his form as close to the pedals as he could get, but in so doing drove the vehicle off the road until it became stuck in a ditch. Diving for cover himself he wedged himself against the Land-Rover's body. He spent the rest of the night pinned to the ground, as he and the tank exchanged fire with the rebels. When dawn approached, the battle subsided and the rebels fled. On his return to Chilembene, Deo swore that he would never go out on patrol again. It took many days of persuasion to get him to resume his duty.

A grievance over pay was first aired by the militiamen, when they went on strike during September 1990. In a bid to disrupt the flow of business, the Chokwe militiamen spread seeds of discord among the farm labourers, who then joined them on the picket line outside the LOMACO HQ. As the situation deteriorated, I was called in to assist Jim Young.

It was thought that my militiamen would remain onsides although, as their terms of service were the same, I doubted that they would. Their arrival only added fuel to the fire when they joined in the strike. Outnumbered and with a sense of foreboding, I put in a call to FRELIMO and requested support. The militiamen needed to disarm and it was beyond our means to do it.

FRELIMO arrived at the scene 30 minutes later, heavily armed, in three GAZ trucks. With short, sharp commands, their ranking officer directed gun groups, armed with PKM machine guns, while infantrymen encircled the crowd. Standing menacingly, weapons at the ready, he shouted commands, as his men cocked their weapons and checked safeties. Behind the machine guns the gunners and their number twos lay prone, cradling ammunition belts. I was suddenly filled with dread. It looked all too similar to an execution squad. For a moment I froze, expecting the silence to be shattered by staccato bursts of fire. In my mind, around me I saw the militiamen and the labourers' fall, bullet ridden.

The sight of the armed soldiers was obviously a bit too much for the militiamen as well. The chorus of discord ceased abruptly. You could see the pleas on their faces and their terror manifest in cold sweat. Instantly, more money was no longer important and Life itself was in the balance.

You could hear a cricket fart as silence fell. The expected gunfire never came. Jim and I gathered the weapons. With only two of us it took some time, but the situation was resolved.

I called a meeting with my senior militiamen and explained that the matter of pay would be addressed. I explained that it would take some time as the LOMACO head office in Maputo would have to process it. This seemed to satisfy the men temporarily and I ordered them to their posts. I thanked FRELIMO for their assistance and left to make a phone call. In my heart of hearts, I knew our troubles were far from over.

My time at Chilembene was drawing to a close and I was due for a change of scenery. I have always been a man who could control his emotions and I had managed to remain indifferent after many of the events I had witnessed. I felt that I had done all I could in Chilembene and I needed something that could offer me a fresh perspective.

I bid my farewells and returned to Harare for a week's leave. It was a sad departure and although I kept in touch with my former co-workers, I was to return to Chilembene only once more in the future. LOMACO had been more than satisfied with my service and improvement had been noted in the general security situation all round. Whereas rebel attacks had been on the increase, LOMACO had recorded a decrease in property theft and they were happy with the much-improved public relations that had been achieved with the government, thanks to our successful contacts with rebels.

My services were needed at Metuchira, further north, where the militia commander was to go on leave. Metuchira is a small town, 120 kilometres from the port of Beira, nestling near the Pungwe River and 14 kilometres off the main Beira-to-Zimbabwe road. As the crow flies, the Gorongoza Mountains – then the heart of rebel territory – lie between Chilembene and this small, dry town. Here too, LOMACO operated a cotton estate in conjunction with its other undertakings. My duties would be much the same as they had been at Chilembene although the militia I was to command was smaller.

With little to worry about in the way of bandit attack, due to a large ZNA base in the area, I set to training the militia at my disposal with constant revision of weapon handling and minor tactics. I acquired another 82mm mortar, which brought into the order of battle an effective means of fire support. To this end I trained a mortar crew from scratch, although in my time at Metuchira they were not once used in a supporting role. The action I did hear of mostly took place outside our area and reached my ears as third-hand news from the transport drivers, or via the bush telegraph. I loathed the inactivity and caught myself wishing for the thrills of battle again.

To ease the boredom, during December I went grenade-fishing at the Pungwe River. Taking along with me six militiamen, in hope of an attack, we spent a lovely day in the sun and even managed to concuss a fish or two. Our journey to the river was pleasant and passed without incident, although I must say it was quite hairy being exposed on the river bank while around us, geysers of water burst up from exploding grenades.

I've never been much of a fisherman, but the size of the bream we caught was impressive. After an hour or two we had our fill and gathered the fish for the return journey.

Back at Metuchira I grabbed a basketful of fish and headed off to do some public relations with the Zimbabwe Army. Meeting the B Company commander at his tent I handed over my gift of fresh fish.

He expressed his gratitude with much surprise, so I told him of our grenade-fishing expedition.

'But Mr Jake! What about *mutsanga* (bandits). That is the heart of *mutsanga* territory.'

I waved off the commander's concern, telling him that we'd seen no sign of activity. We'd been in and out before they even knew we were there.

The next morning, a Crocodile armoured vehicle arrived at Metuchira from the ZNA camp. A few minutes later, after my refusal to join the B Company commander and his men, they left on their journey to the river. I sat down to a cup of coffee and some 15 minutes later in the distance I heard a muffled crump. I realised at once what had happened and raced to the scene. The ZNA Crocodile had detonated a landmine that had been laid the previous night after bandits had witnessed, or heard of, our journey. I drove towards the river expecting to find carnage. The commander was infuriated, but other than a few cuts and perforated ear drums, his men had escaped unharmed. I resolved to be more careful in the future.

Early the following morning my militiamen reported that a woman working the fields a kilometre north of the shooting range had discovered another mine. I drove to the ZNA base again and collected the army engineers. Two men accompanied me and arriving at the scene we confirmed the presence of an AP mine on a footpath. The engineers cleared the area and with use of cortex and a fuse they detonated the exposed mine, only to unearth another one a small distance away. How we had not trodden on it I don't know, but I had ignored an elementary rule of soldiering and I cursed myself, even though I was lucky to have escaped injury. The second engineer, a little more carefully this time, probed forward with his bayonet to reach the second mine. He had only crawled about 20 paces when there was a terrific thump as another AP mine detonated under his blade. Tracing his steps, I rushed to retrieve him with the aid of his team-mate. A little concussed, he was extremely lucky to escape with only nasty shrapnel wounds to his hand. He had been well kitted out with gloves and a safety visor and by all accounts he would soon regain the use of his hand.

We left to seek medical assistance after leaving a few militiamen to cordon off the area. The engineers said they would return the next day and conduct an intensive search for more mines. The following day, within a few hours of their arrival, the engineers had unearthed a veritable Aladdin's cave of unexploded ordnance. No more AP mines were discovered, but in the days to come they were hard pressed unearthing and detonating unexploded 60mm mortar rounds and RPG7 rockets. There had obviously been a lot of action here at some time, but it wasn't during my stay. By late December I was given the all clear for work to resume in the fields.

Lieutenant Colonel Shaw, overall commander of LOMACO security for Mozambique, arrived in Metuchira to assess the security situation. Further north, bandit activity had been on the increase and LOMACO were losing two vehicles a week on average to enemy ambushes. GSG had been of little use in the grand scheme of things, and their reluctance to commit themselves to what was a potentially hazardous pastime – the very thing for which they were hired – left company management somewhat aggrieved.

Although GSG personnel were much cheaper on the books than I was (one third of the price per man) it was thought that the Gurkhas were not accustomed to the ways of Africa and a communications gap existed between them and the militia, something of fundamental importance if greater control was to be exerted on the latter. I was told that once my spell in Metuchira came to an end, I was to be moved to Nropa, where I would assume overall command of the militia as well as of the GSG personnel. Of even greater importance was a new assignment: to keep the expatriate farmers happy who had raised a vote of no confidence in the Gurkhas.

Sheila and Paul visited again and returned home via Maputo. In the northern hemisphere my son Richard was preparing to move out with his unit to Iraq. He had joined the British Army in 1986. I was more than relieved about his choice of pursuing a career path in REME (Royal Electrical Mechanical Engineers) rather than become cannon fodder like his Dad had done. In his service he had travelled to Germany attached to the Tank Corp, where he was a recovery mechanic and trained to retrieve damaged tanks on the battlefield. He also did a tour of Northern Ireland during his seven years' service, although Ireland had become a more peaceful place since I had been there. During the Gulf War, Richard ended up as his Squadron commander's driver in a scout car, as the Desert Rats rumbled into battle with the main armoured advance into Iraq on *Operation Desert Storm*. It was valuable experience and his service did me proud.

CHAPTER 42:
Moving north

The ZNA always appeared to be far more professional than their FRELIMO brothers they were assisting. It was largely owing to their presence in the area that bandit activity was less frequent than it had been around Chilembene. In February 1991, a ZNA patrol shot some bandits at the fence of the estate in a sharp contact. I ordered the militia to stand to in the event of further activity, but was disappointed when nothing came of it.

On 4 March I received news that the Metuchira militia commander had been dismissed. Lieutenant Colonel Shaw was to arrive with Jej Gurung, a Gurkha, who was to take over at Metuchira while I moved north. After handing over command to Jej, I left for Maputo on 8 March.

My first few days at Nropa were spent familiarising myself with my new co-workers and my surroundings. I was thrilled to learn I had at my disposal air support in the form of a Turbo Thrush crop-spraying aircraft, flown by a young, debonair South African pilot by the name of Juan von Ginkle. Juan was to become a close friend in the next few months and he always amused me with his eccentricities and his 'devil may care' attitude.

Although the aircraft was unarmed it did serve as the ideal aerial reconnaissance platform and was even used on occasion to 'buzz' RENAMO, and keep them busy in future contacts, while we pressed home our attack. I must say that this was done with incredible bravery on Juan's part, as inevitably he came under heavy enemy small-arms fire. On several occasions I was almost certain I heard a cowboy-like 'Whoopee' above the noise of the engine, as the aircraft dipped to 'attack' the enemy before climbing in altitude in preparation for its next dive. Juan always boasted that he had been born too early and should have been a Battle of Britain fighter pilot. Had he been, I believe he would have terrified the Germans, or any adversary for that matter.

His flying skill was supreme and he, with his dare-devil antics, would have been more at home in the cockpit of a Spitfire or a Pitts Special. I even gave him a callsign and he was always eager for action when a request for 'Yellow Section' support came over the radio. Some time later I decorated his aircraft with stickers of the US 101st Airborne Division, the 'Screaming Eagles'.

When I arrived at the LOMACO head office in Nropa, I learnt that all security personnel had been convened to meet with Colonel Shaw. Inside, in what served as the company boardroom, sat all nine GSG personnel as well as Charles Dean, with whom I was happy to be reacquainted. Colonel Shaw addressed the gathering and told the GSG men that in view of their poor performance, they would now fall under my command. I was to retain the rank of major, but despite being outranked, it was to me that they were answerable.

The GSG officer in charge was a highly respected man in the British Army. HS, as I will call him, was most indignant at this move and I sensed the tension in the room. I had never compared my military experiences to others', or viewed any man's experience as lesser than mine, but I had learnt that HS was a decorated veteran and I felt somewhat humbled, as he sat there without a sound, erect in his chair and stern-faced. He almost looked as if he was pushing a stool as his yellow skin flushed and contorted. I wondered if I would have accepted the demotion had the tables been turned.

The thought hadn't left my mind when he stood up, faced the colonel and calmly submitted his verbal resignation. I suppose he didn't really know me and I couldn't blame him. To him I was nothing more than a junior NCO from the British Paras. He knew nothing of the years I had served in the SAS, the Selous Scouts and the CIO and while I had never attained the rank he held, my service did add up to a wealth of experience and much time under fire. A dignified man, he most likely saw me as a young upstart out to prove a thing or two.

HS was not alone in his thoughts. Ram, who I had met before at Chilembene, was also put out by the move, as were the other Gurkhas who had once been officers. None of them resigned, but I could sense they were quite resentful of my new post and their disgust in me was obvious. The rest, mostly former NCOs, seemed a little more receptive to change, although they too were put out and nattered among themselves in their native tongue.

Charles Dean stood up and called the meeting to order. In no uncertain terms he informed GSG that if they did not like the situation, they could pack up and ship out. This had the effect of temporarily quelling the unrest, but like the little boy with his thumb in the dyke, the torrent was yet to come. I had upset the balance and it would be many months before I won the acceptance of the younger Gurkhas. As for the rest it would be never.

I was a little displeased with the way things had panned out, but I accepted my new responsibility with relish. Colonel Shaw outlined my duties and I was thrilled to learn that I was to form a quick reaction force (QRF) team, manned with personnel selected from my own 'Special Forces'. At the top of the list was an order to select and train about 40 men, who were to be the cream of the militia. It was my prerogative how to go about this and it was entirely up to me to set the standards of acceptance, just as long as they were high.

To assist me, I would have direct access to a FRELIMO colonel, who was already prepped and was to ease my path through the red tape of equipment requisition. I was given autonomy to do as I pleased and I was told that if I needed anything, I was to ask. The first problem I would run into would be communications. To alleviate this I requested that Sergeant Dick be transferred to Nropa, where he would become training officer as well as interpreter. Sergeant Dick duly arrived on 19 March to take up his post. Although he did not fit in immediately, I was not too concerned at the time and put it down to cultural differences, which I assumed would ease over a few weeks.

The enormity of the task at hand hit me when I learnt exactly how large an area I was responsible for. Montepuez lies 200 kilometres inland of Pemba in the far north of Mozambique, towards the Tanzanian border. LOMACO's cotton estates in the region stretch across a massive 150 kilometer radius with an area of about 90,000 square kilometres – half the size of the United Kingdom! Its headquarters and a cotton ginnery were based at Montepuez and Nropa, and serviced five farms in the area. Security for these assets was a militia force numbering 700. My duties would be exactly as they had been at Chilembene: to protect the farmers, LOMACO property and the labour force, as well as raising a Special Forces unit to act as a QRF (quick reaction force).

LOMACO's main concern at the time of my arrival, was the loss of vehicles in ambushes. As there was no railway in the region, LOMACO relied on road transport to haul its cotton to the port at Pemba. The 200-kilometre journey was fraught with danger, with the 10-kilometre stretch of road between Montepuez and Nropa by far the worst. One could expect to be ambushed just about every time it was travelled.

With my work cut out for me, I got stuck into preparing a programme to be implemented over the next few months. Firstly, with the assistance of Juan and the Turbo Thrush, I visited the farms at Nampula and Namara to check on the situation there. As I suspected, the security arrangements at most farms were inadequate. Namara alone could boast an effective security system and a militia, which was the brainchild of one of the junior GSG men. The Namara militia shone above the rest and were immaculate in their attire as well as appearing to be highly disciplined.

I spread the word at each stop that I was looking for volunteers to form a Special Forces unit and selection would commence in April. As I did not want a disaster on my hands, with a mass desertion of posts, I instructed all aspiring candidates to report through the chain of command to their superiors. I then requested the GSG militia commanders not to discourage anyone wishing to join and asked them first for their recommendations regarding any potential candidates. After our initial shaky start, the GSG men were quite compliant and over the next few days I received a steady stream of volunteers. One man in particular was quite a ferocious individual. He was from a warrior tribe in the north with cannibalistic tendencies and sported teeth filed to sharp points, while his face was dotted with tribal tattoos.

I took down their details and they were told to report to the LOMACO office at Nropa when selection started.

I decided that the selection process should focus more on a man's mental attributes than his physical ones. In rural Africa, owing to vast distances on poor roads with little transport, most people are already of above-average fitness and are used to carrying heavy loads. I designed a programme that would not only test a man physically but mentally as well while under pressure. To this end I modelled my programme on the lines of British Para 'P' Company and the old Rhodesian SAS selection.

The course started on time and over a six-week period I put the men through a rigorous regimen of physical training, intermixed with tactical training in the form of field craft and minor tactics. To gain confidence the men were put through live fire advance-to-contact exercises.

At all times, potential recruits would be required to carry one telephone pole per 10 men. I wanted to inspire a high degree of team play among them and I let them know that if anyone dropped out of selection, then that group would be disadvantaged with fewer men to carry the load. I hoped this would encourage the men to push one another and also place a degree of guilt on the shoulders of a potential 'dropout', who would know he was letting down his team. Guilt can be a great motivator when the chips are down.

The poles were to be used not only to exhaust the men but to serve as their seating arrangement during meals and lectures. At any time, impromptu tests were thrown in which included orienteering and weapon skills. I would expect my men to look after their weapons at all times. If a weapon was found in a shit state, then everyone would be punished.

At the end of a 10-kilometre march, they might be expected to strip and assemble their weapons, complete an obstacle course and then conduct a live fire exercise. Whatever the test or lesson, I wanted them to be always 'knackered', at which time they would be expected to think on their feet and act as if they were as fresh as when they started.

The key to any unit's effectiveness, once the basics have been covered, is repetition of training. To hone their combat skills, at least once a day, a couple of hours would be spent on the range. I would start by making the men run to the range first and then spend an hour practicing patrol formations with dry weapons. After that a simulated contact would be initiated and the men would repeat what they'd just learnt, advancing towards the 'enemy' (army style figure 11 targets) firing live rounds. I wanted to instil in the men a level of training that would make their contact drills second nature.

The course went extremely well and I was pleased with the competence of my recruits. Of course, they were not quite on par with the other regular units in which I had served, but compared to the standards I had seen among FRELIMO and the other militia members, the LOMACO Special Forces' members were regular little James Bonds.

Sergeant Dick had been of great assistance and had filled the role of training officer quite admirably. There were even times when he appeared to have gained acceptance, his strict but jovial manner going down well with the men.

A passing-out ceremony was held on the parade square at LOMACO headquarters in Nropa. It was an elaborate affair, to which the entire expatriate community was invited, along with the family members of those who had passed selection. Sheila was present and had arrived to see me on 19 May. I was in a jovial mood and happy to have her by my side.

I had found the general standard of fitness among the men was of an extremely high calibre, but, through the selection process, we had weeded out those who were not up to scratch mentally. Thus we were left with a satisfactory 40 men who made the grade. I had put in a formal request to FRELIMO, that the LOMACO Special Forces be accorded the honour of wearing the Forca Especial cap badge, as testament to their status.

The request was made via the correct channels, but at the time of the parade, bureaucracy had proved a hurdle and nothing had come of it. I knew that the men revered and respected the Parachute Regiment badge I wore on my beret and they would have been quite happy wearing one themselves had I not turned them down. Interestingly, they misinterpreted the badge: they thought it symbolised an owl with outstretched wings, while the crown on top of the parachute represented to them the bird's head with large eyes. When one looks at the badge closely, it can be seen that their reasoning was not all that fanciful. The owl is greatly revered by Africans as a sinister and dark force, associated with the intricacies of witchcraft. No matter how much I tried to point out that the badge depicted parachute wings, a parachute and a crown, they preferred their own interpretation of the owl – hunter, predator swooping in from the dark to catch its prey. As misconstrued as they were, I thought the description was quite apt.

As a substitute, until such time as our request was met, I obtained 40 maroon berets to be worn by the men. Charles Dean, as LOMACO representative, was guest of honour at the ceremony and sensed a real sense of achievement among the men, who appeared to be genuinely proud of their accomplishment. After the ceremony, a small demonstration of their skills was conducted. We then inspected the parade, congratulating each man as he was awarded his maroon beret before retiring to well-earned drinks from an impromptu bar. The real test of the men would come when they deployed the following Monday.

While the selection course was underway, GSG had overseen the militia and were responsible for day-to-day activities. Patrols had been posted on the Nropa-to-Montepuez road, but the ambushes continued. Subsequent follow-up operations invariably resulted in spoor being lost and nothing to report. It was almost as if the bandits just melted into the surrounding hills. It did cross my mind that perhaps the patrols and the bandits were the same people, as that was the only way one could explain the apparent 'ghost-like' ability of the ambushers.

At this time LOMACO was in the throes of extending its interests by establishing estates further north of Montepuez. John Hewlett, LOMACO's director, implemented Operation Pink Panther, which was the name for the land preparation of cotton fields at Namara, a small town 50 kilometres north of Nropa. I was to ensure security for the labour force that travelled there every day and so I provided an escort of Special Forces personnel, and an armoured Land-Rover with a mounted PKM machine gun. Aside from convoy duties, my men were to guard the labourers during the day and return with them to Nropa before sunset.

Intelligence came in that a group of bandits had set up base about 15 kilometres from Nropa, at Namara by a bend in a stream north-east of Tatonga, a small village. The reports came in via the locals, who told me that the bandits seemed firmly established and were casual about their comings and goings. I sent a patrol of Special Forces to carry out a reconnaissance of the area and to set up an observation post. I equipped the men for a week's patrol and sent Sergeant Dick as their commander. We had covered the basics of close target reconnaissance in training and I was confident the men could handle the task under his supervision. I approached John Hewlett and let him know about the operation. He was thrilled with the prospect of action and gave the green light for the reconnaissance. Easing into the mood he dubbed it Operation Pink Panther II.

Just before Sheila was to return to South Africa, my presence was requested at a meeting with the farmers, who were concerned by the amount of rebel activity in the area. I liaised with Chris, the Nropa manager and together we travelled the 10 kilometres to Montepuez, where I was to allay their fears.

I had insisted that Sheila travel with Chris and his wife in the armoured Land-Rover, along with four militiamen, while I travelled behind in another vehicle with eight of the men. About four kilometres outside Nropa, lies a small rustic village, inhabited mostly by workers and their families from the estates. The air at that time of the year was very dry, with little rain or moisture to keep the dust down. As the lead vehicle passed through the village I slowed down, increasing the gap between us, as I could barely see the road. I was still negotiating the haze two kilometres after the village, when I heard a terrific volume of automatic fire up ahead. I knew immediately that we had run into an ambush and I accelerated through the dust. My progress was fraught with anxiety, as I could only go so fast. I could not see the road ahead and did not know what I was running into. I knew that I could not have been more than 200 metres behind the lead vehicle and therefore at risk of entering the killing ground. Chris screamed over the radio to warn me, but incoming rounds were already hitting the soft aluminium skin of the Land-Rover. The dust was thicker now and I was driving blind. Not even the verge of the road was clear and it was unsafe to return fire. Most of the militiamen debussed in panic from the moving vehicle. Those who stayed kept their cool and pressed themselves into the vehicle, the aluminium skin affording little protection against the bullets. I accelerated a short distance before skidding to a halt. The engine cut of its own accord, when I didn't gear down for the stop. I was worried I would run off the road, or worse still, into the other Land-Rover – but the shooting died and around us the dust settled.

About 30 metres to my front, the shape of Chris's vehicle emerged through the haze. Reckoning that it was now safe to exit the vehicle, I got out and assessed the situation. I saw that one of the militiamen in the back of my vehicle had taken a round through the arm. The rest had already deployed in a defensive perimeter. I ran the short distance to Chris and was relieved to learn there were no casualties in his vehicle. Everyone was visibly shaken, but otherwise unscathed.

Chris said that without warning, about 20 bandits had stood up from hiding on the side of the road and emptied their magazines into the Land-Rover at point-blank range. Considering the closeness, I was surprised to find that only 14 rounds had found their mark. Neatly stitched into the door where Sheila had been sitting, were four holes that had punched through the aluminium at a 90-degree angle. Their forward momentum was brought to an abrupt stop by the armoured plates inside the door. The two right-side tyres had been shot out as well.

Returning to my vehicle I found that it had taken eleven hits. The gear lever had been shot off – which was the reason why I had been unable to change gears earlier. After checking out the ambush position, we found close to 180 empty shell casings. We had been extremely lucky and God had smiled on me once again.

I left eight militiamen to conduct a follow-up and instructed them to return to Nropa afterwards. With our nerves frayed, we continued to the meeting, where I hoped to allay the farmers' fears of ambush.

Sergeant Dick returned from Namara with good news. They had established an OP overlooking a stream, from a knoll of slightly raised ground. The topography of the area was not ideal, with gently rolling scrubland, but all things considered, they'd done well and remained undetected for the duration of the patrol.

I briefed the men and learned from them that the group of about 10 rebels, with porters in tow, had established a temporary base in the thick papyrus alongside the stream. From there it appeared they made daily forays into the rural lands, to conduct ambushes and raids and returned every evening to stash their day's haul. My men confirmed that the bandits appeared to be lax and over-confident and the last thing they would expect would be an attack. The patrol left two members behind to keep an eye on things and establish a pattern of activity.

I sent Sergeant Dick back to the OP with a radio and ordered him to keep me informed at all times. I was keen to capitalise on our good fortune, and told him to notify me as soon as the whole group was present at the base camp. It was an opportunity not to be missed and if we could take them by surprise and kill or capture them, we would gain the community's confidence.

Several days passed uneventfully. Then, in the early hours one morning I was shaken from my sleep by a very excited militiaman. He hurried me to the radio in the control room, insisting that Sergeant Dick had made contact. I radioed Sergeant Dick and was told that there was a lot of activity in the camp, and that a larger group of bandits had appeared a few hours earlier, arriving with more porters. At the time of the call the camp was silent and he told me that it would be ideal to put in a raid just before dawn. I instructed him to meet me on the main road at a given time and left to seek approval.

After explaining the situation to Phil Tonks, he phoned John Hewlett at LOMACO head office in Chimoio, who gave express permission to carry out the attack. The remaining members of my Special Forces were engaged elsewhere at the time, so I called on the GSG personnel and their militia to assist me. Arriving at the residence of the GSG men, I was met by Major Ram, who awoke to my hoots at the gate. With our timing crucial, as we still had a 15 kilometre journey ahead of us, I insisted he grab his gear and rally the militia.

It wasn't long before it became obvious that Ram and his fellow ex-Gurkhas were still a little sore about my promotion. It was evident that they were not going to listen to me and asked if I was not breaking company protocol by carrying out the attack. I told them that the orders had come from John Hewlett directly and they had better get their act together. Just short of an outright refusal to heed my demands they procrastinated and insisted on phoning John themselves. I let them know what I thought of them in no uncertain terms and told them that raising John on the telephone, the only one being in the control room, would delay our timing and compromise the entire operation. Dilly-dallying about, Ram and his cohort casually donned their uniforms, muttering excuses all the time, while questioning the validity of my intelligence reports. I told them that I had had an OP in place for some weeks and the intelligence was sound.

I was powerless to do anything. My face flushed with rage and I considered forcing them out at gunpoint. Aware that it would only create further problems, I left to consult John Hewlett.

It took some time to raise him after the journey back to the control room. When I eventually raised him, he was enraged by the GSG men's insubordination and demanded that they contact him immediately. About 15 minutes later, Ram arrived with further excuses that he couldn't raise John on the radio and wanted to use the phone. I left the control room and waited outside. A short time later, after many 'yes sirs' and 'no sirs' emanating from the room, Ram emerged with a sheepish grin on his face. I was furious at the delay, but we managed to leave for Namara a couple of hours after the first call had come in. Arriving at the scene, we were met on the road a few kilometres from the camp, by an impatient Sergeant Dick. The sun had risen 15 minutes earlier and he guided us to the OP, arriving there half an hour later. When we got there I was disappointed in the extreme. My men informed me that the bandits had vacated the camp just before sunrise. One of the men had snuck in close and had seen the bandits and their porters carting off their loot. He was sure they had left for good.

I approached the camp carefully, with Ram and the militia behind me, reaching the banks of the stream where a huge cluster of papyrus grew. The papyrus stems were trodden down into a path which led to an enclosure. I feared the worst when I saw that the camp was totally deserted, with signs of a hurried departure. The pattern the bandits had established, indicated that they would normally leave their loot hidden in the grass if they were to return. I was sure they could not have been warned. If anything, our arrival was just ill-timed. I was infuriated at the opportunity we had lost, but I asked Sergeant Dick if he wouldn't mind remaining in the OP for one more night. Our efforts were fruitless and the camp remained vacant.

The fall-out from the incident was ongoing. I never really saw eye to eye with GSG thereafter and many people wanted to get rid of them altogether. It was decided to review their contract when it next expired, with the possibility of terminating it; but that was still six months away at the end of the year. I didn't know it at the time, but many things were to change before then, not all of which were in my favour.

CHAPTER 43:
Sergeant Dick

On the evening of Sunday 1 August 1992 at about 20:00, I was approached by some militiamen while attending a braai in Nropa. They told me that some Africans travelling on bicycles had been ambushed about one-and-a-half kilometres away. One of the survivors had fled back to Nropa to report the incident. It was said that the bandits were still in the vicinity and had been seen entering a wooded area just off the main Nropa road. I made my excuses and left the braai to organise a follow-up, stopping only to collect my kit, while raising GSG on the radio. They were to meet me at the crossroads on the north side of town within 15 minutes.

I collected my AKM, got into my vehicle and drove toward the rendezvous. On the way I pulled in at the LOMACO office, to collect Sergeant Dick and about 15 Special Forces militiamen who were permanently stationed there as the QRF. Together we left, and arrived at the crossroads where the Gurkhas were awaiting us.

Men shifted nervously, while I organised the mortar crew to set up well within range of the supposed bandits' position. I instructed the Gurkhas to remain with the mortar and wait for my orders on the radio if supporting fire was needed. I felt that they could not be relied on at the sharp end of a contact and left them in the rear. I am sure that they were a lot happier with my decision than I was.

The wooded area harbouring our foe could be seen in the light of the half moon, about 800 metres further down the road. I formed the men into an extended line and whispered the order to advance. I carefully placed my feet on the loose stone and gravel as I stepped forward. As was usual and second nature as a result of training, Sergeant Dick took up position on my right flank about two metres away and passed on the order to move. The rest of the men extended to the left evenly spaced at two or three-metre intervals. With the utmost stealth we crept forward, ears perked for the slightest sound. Our advance was painfully slow. On the road there was the crunch of gravel underfoot to contend with, while for those men at the extremities of the formation, there was the dryness of the bush and its leafy coverage. From where I was I could hear the men furthest from me, as leaves and twigs crackled under their weight. We slowly moved on with our hearts in our throats.

About 200 metres from the thicket, Sergeant Dick gave the signal to halt. Half bent, he doubled over to my side and raised his hand to his ear. Not far off the faintest sound of raised voices could be heard. The chirp of bush insects ceased and the night took on an eerie silence. With even more care, we resumed our advance until we were in position, about 100 metres from the woods. Ahead, the noise of voices steadily grew until it was obvious that they belonged to the rebels. Listening closely it became apparent they were arguing over the loot from the cyclists. Signalling the men with a raised hand I called a halt and in unison everyone shrank to the ground.

Ahead of us loomed a culvert which crossed a dry river bed. The road was somewhat raised at this point, as it ascended the crest of the bridge. Over to the left front of the bridge, the argument among the rebels continued unabated. I could not see them through the gloom, but the ground was open between us and the thicket and the lanes of fire clear. Taking cover in the shallow ground, just off to the left of the road, I raised the Gurkhas on the radio and requested them to fire three bombs on the signal of a flare. Looking to my right I whispered to Sergeant Dick, slightly higher than me on the verge of the road, to ready the men, and in turn he passed on the order to open fire and advance on signal. Reaching into one of my pouches I retrieved a flare and unscrewed its base. The cord firing mechanism dropped from the bottom of the tubular barrel and I took it up in my right hand with my AKM resting across my knee. Taking up the slack I pulled the cord and with a loud 'fizz' the flare arced skyward.

Nothing could have prepared me for what happened next. As if they had been waiting, as the flare 'popped', the rebels opened up with a withering hail of small-arms fire. With the proverbial 'everything they had' coming my way, I dived headlong into the earth to my front, burying my rifle barrel as I did so. For those who have not been in combat, a bullet doesn't whizz past when it comes close; it makes a tiny cracking sound, almost like a miniature jet aircraft breaking the sound barrier. Neon green 'light sabres' buzzed and cracked around me, shredding branches of leaves, as tracer buried itself deep inside the wood. Every time I came under fire, I was sure it was worse than the last, but this time it was. I pressed myself into the earth, terrified, digging a shell scrape with my chin and every other part of my body that I could. Adding to the racket of gunfire, RPG7 rockets 'whooshed' on deadly track and hit the ground to my left. Red-hot shrapnel whined and pinged over my head, cutting more leaves from branches, before tearing into soft wood and soil.

It dawned on me that there was no return fire. In the confusion I barely knew which way I was facing and I thought I heard a burst from behind me. I could swear that all the enemy fire was concentrated on my position and also on Sergeant Dicks' position, although I couldn't be sure. Looking around I realised I was in the river bed and what had seemed like minutes were only seconds. Above me the flare burned out, thank God and with it the intensity of fire.

I jumped to my feet and ran up the bank and onto the road, screaming at the top of my lungs 'ADVANCE, ADVANCE'. I could not see Sergeant Dick, but as I crossed the road I saw another of my sergeants and I bellowed my orders at him.

The men got to their feet, each looking to the other for direction. I could still not see Sergeant Dick, but then something caught my eye on the verge of the road, unrecognisable and lifeless, crumpled in a heap. My heart raced and then ached when I feared the worst, but the enemy didn't know that and they continued to probe fire in our direction.

'ADVANCE, ADVANCE', I yelled.

While the militiamen pressed forward, I stayed in the rear. I turned around and raced to the lifeless form and skidded to a halt beside it, like a baseball player hitting home plate. What lay before me was an 'it', no longer a 'he' as he should have been, but an inanimate object spilling its life blood into the red, dusty soil. Rolling his body, I felt for Sergeant Dick's pulse, but there wasn't one. I didn't know which way he had been facing when he took the round, but there was a small entry hole in his back just below the left shoulder blade. The bullet had punched through his chest, traversing his heart in its path.

Sorrow and anger swept over me in waves. Toward the woods, I could see my men entering the thicket but the fire by now had largely subsided and it appeared the rebels had fled. There was no disorganised chaos when they went. No disarray. Instead, they just melted away into the darkness as if they had been ghosts.

My suspicions came to a head that night, but I felt powerless to act. With my friend dead, who else could I trust? The enemy had been waiting for us and it became clear to me that we had been ambushed. Not everything had gone their way, though, and I was still alive. The whole contact seemed orchestrated. When it was initiated, they knew where Sergeant Dick and I would be placed in the formation. How did they know? Were they familiar with our training methods? Had Sergeant Dick spun to take cover and then taken a bullet in the back? Had the bullet come from the enemy? Was the enemy among us in the form of my own men? If so, they couldn't finish me off, as the Gurkhas were so near. Either that or they lacked the fortitude to finish the job.

I called the Gurkhas forward in the Land-Cruiser and we wrapped Sergeant Dick's body in a poncho. Gently I placed him on the back seat of the vehicle and we slowly made our way back to town. I hadn't had time to look at myself, with the constant barrage of thoughts that bombarded me. I hadn't noticed that the pistol grip on my AKM was shattered from a round passing through it. It had been a close call!

Later I discovered that another round had passed through the heel of my right boot. The angle at which it penetrated was evidence that I had been hit when I dived for cover, the round entering at the top lip, where the leather meets the sole and exiting through the bottom rubber. God had been watching over me that night.

Sergeant Dick's death was to mark the beginning of the end of my time in Mozambique. With the hassles I had already experienced with GSG, the blame was put squarely on my shoulders for his demise. It was almost as if I had pulled the trigger.

Inwardly I did feel responsible for his death, in some way, since I had called for him and it was at my insistence he had moved from Chokwe. Nonetheless, I could not allow myself to sit in the doldrums because we had lost a man. I couldn't break up emotionally because I had lost a friend.

The events of that night haunted me for some time to come. Sergeant Dick was ostensibly an outsider. Not only was he not of the same tribal affiliation as those in Montepuez, but he was not even from Mozambique in the first place. Africa is uniquely cliquey in that way. Outsiders generally are not trusted and in some cases are even despised.

I began to form my own opinions about what had transpired that night. As I had long suspected, I believed that certain elements of the militia were involved in bandit activity, although in the north, I think that it was a lot more deeply rooted than in the south. Around Montepuez it seemed to me that the militia and the bandits were one and the same, carrying out attacks with impunity to justify their presence and therefore their income. As a bonus they could take what loot they liked and could therefore make a good living out of their dual identities, until we came along that is! I believe that Sergeant Dick had stumbled upon this and knew a little bit more about it than I did. I think he had not yet decided how to convey this information to me, as he thought he would be in the greatest danger if he told anyone.

I let my views be known to the relevant authorities, but they were cast aside as the machinations of grief. I was told that I had probably spent a little too much time under fire and that I needed a break. Bollocks! Sure enough, I had been under fire, but I would have to watch my back from then on.

It took many months for me to accept Sergeant Dick's death. Of course, I was no stranger to losing friends in combat, but this was different. Every time I came across the militia I felt the anger well up inside me. The nagging feeling of betrayal never left me, and I knew in my heart of hearts that mine weren't the best of feelings to be harbouring, given the circumstances. I would still have to work with the men I thought were responsible and I knew that I would find myself in other situations alone with them. I don't think they ever learnt of my suspicions, so I never felt as if I was next in line for 'termination', so to speak. I was not frightened as such, but I wanted some answers which unfortunately, I would never get. They had had their go and were now scared because they had failed. They were scared because I had survived.

I kept up an intense regimen of training for the Special Forces and all the militia, interspersed with follow-ups and investigations into incidents. Although I searched continuously for evidence of Sergeant Dick's murder, it was not forthcoming. The ambushes had slowed, but continued to harangue the LOMACO hierarchy well into the remaining months of the year. Charles Dean left LOMACO for good and returned to Nelspruit in South Africa to tend to family business. With him went my biggest supporter, a man who had always stood by me and had high regard for my experience. Phil Tonks took over as general manager and while in Phil I had a good friend, he was a different kind of thinker to Charles and saw things in another light.

Phil was a practical businessman and knew a good deal when he saw one. At that time my pay was US$3,600 a month. For that amount, Phil knew he could retain three GSG personnel, possibly four. He never stopped to think about what I had achieved and with his new post he recommended my retrenchment. It was nothing personal, I was told, but a matter of mathematics. To this end he convinced John Hewlett to side with him, although John did not want me to leave. From what I picked up around town, it sounded as if many other people also did not want to see the back of me.

At the end of August I prepared to leave Montepuez. I was on my rounds to say farewell when I was made another offer. According to Phil, the entire community of expatriate farmers had convened and again put in a vote of no confidence in GSG. The farmers told LOMACO that if I were to leave, they would leave also. They were not prepared to carry on farming if their safety could not be guaranteed.

As a result, John approached GSG and told them that if they wanted to keep their contract, they would have to employ me. He assured them that I would be kept well out of the way of their men and that my new post would be a demotion to Special Forces commander. The package would mean a reduced salary, the same as a GSG man of the same rank, as well as a reduction in annual leave. It was an offer they could not refuse. It would certainly cost them nothing as LOMACO would be covering my expenses. If anything, they could only gain, if not in keeping the contract, then at least by charging my services at GSG rates.

I am sure that GSG accepted the offer begrudgingly, but I cared little for what they thought. The drop in salary was a drastic change for me, but I had nothing else to do at the time and a thousand US dollars in the pocket was better than none at all. I accepted the offer and stowed my kit back in my quarters. I would work on a three-month contract, at the end of which I would seek my fortune elsewhere. Phone calls were made to friends and family who were expecting me and I set about revising my daily duties.

CHAPTER 44:
MUTINY

The months of October and November passed in a blur of relentless training and retraining. I bolstered the ranks of Special Forces with new recruits and initiated a programme to raise the levels of the men's fitness to a peak. There was little in the way of bandit activity and lots of time to do nothing. The very least I could do was give LOMACO something to remember me by.

In view of the chaos that reigned around the country, the FRELIMO government finally met with RENAMO at the conference table and a tentative cease-fire was declared. Incidents continued to occur on a smaller scale, committed mainly by those who had no political conviction.

With peace in sight, LOMACO and other private organisations were pressed to cease employing foreign security personnel. Testament to the effectiveness of these contract soldiers, RENAMO insisted that all foreign security personnel must leave Mozambique, if FRELIMO wanted to continue with the peace talks.

Although on the surface, LOMACO made cutbacks, the reality was different. Personnel were simply moved about, job titles were changed and an effort was made to disguise a foreigner's employment. Nobody could be certain that peace was a tangible reality and certainly, LOMACO wanted to hedge its bets in the event of a crumbling peace process.

At the end of December I flew to Chimoio at the request of John Hewlett, with Tulsie, one of the GSG men. John was having problems with former employees over pay issues and the situation at his headquarters had decayed into one of near-mutiny. We arrived at Chimoio just in time to prevent the enraged workers from overrunning the offices. The GSG man was a little the worse for wear, having just survived an ambush with Phil Tonks up north. Wide-eyed and lucky to be alive, he escaped with only shrapnel wounds above his left eye and two bullet holes through his bush hat.

I took the situation in hand and with guarantees from John of forthcoming pay, we managed to quell the disturbance. John was so impressed with my performance that he offered me yet another contract, this time to work for LONRHO at the ALMA (Alluvial Manica) gold mines in Manica Province. I was thrilled with the prospect of extending my useful employment and I could not resist the offer. With immediate effect my pay was put up to US$3,600 a month and I was to report to ALMA as head of security.

I returned to Nropa and said my farewells, happy to serve out the remainder of my contract. The Special Forces were in full swing now but had very little to do other than patrol. They were working closely with FRELIMO Special Forces and overtures had been made that they would be welcomed into the ranks of the national army, when stability was no longer just a dream. I'd had a gutful of GSG and was eager to leave. I was sure they would not complain when they saw the back of me.

My work at ALMA was in stark contrast to what I had been doing at LOMACO. It was really like chalk and cheese, working for a commercial security company, setting guard rosters and maintaining a vigilant check on theft levels. After the constant and often nerve-racking activities at Chilembene and then Nropa, Manica was a total anticlimax. I was mostly engaged in rectifying pay disputes, the monotony of which drove me to the verge of insanity on more than one occasion.

I fail to grasp how some men think, having often been witness to demonstrations of greed over the smallest amounts of wealth. Allan Shaw, as head of LOMACO security, was also responsible for the security of LONRHO and thus in charge of organising pay packets. The financial sector in Mozambique was in deep trouble at the time and banks were regularly short of cash. On occasions such as pay days, when large amounts of money were needed, a requisition had to be submitted to the bank well in advance. Allan failed to do so on one occasion and a riotous pay dispute erupted. I was left to sort out the mess and nearly paid for it with my life.

It had all started with the initial dispute that Tulsie and I had resolved in December, when we were flown from Nropa at the request of John Hewlett. Although it was not known at the time, the dispute had been resolved with ease, because the LONRHO number-crunchers had made an error and had overpaid the retrenched workers by a large margin. Three months later, news of the error had reached as far as Beira and the ears of former LONRHO contract labourers who mostly hailed from that region.

En masse, they arrived at the Vila Manica head office, with demands for the same recompense that their brothers had been given. Forever opportunists, they no doubt believed their efforts would result in riches.

LONRHO rarely committed serious mistakes in matters of pay. If anything, pay was sometimes a little late, but this time the financial manager calmed the situation by agreeing to review the issue and verify if the labourers were indeed underpaid. Told to return in a month's time, the gang left and returned to Beira.

A month later they were back and the matter had still not been attended to. It had been discovered that their grievance was legitimate, but the error in pay was hardly enough to break the bank. Each of the 30 or so former employees were in fact owed money, but the sum they were each due amounted to no more than 25,000 meticals (about US$ 2.50).

Inundated with more pressing matters, Allan had not put in the order to the bank and the money was not available when they arrived.

Whether it was this that enraged the men, or the realisation that they were no longer to be instant millionaires, I will never know. But the first I knew of their anger, was when I was called from the mine to respond to an emergency developing at the head office. It was reported to me that the disgruntled workers had stormed the pay office and beaten up the financial manager, a white man and two black pay clerks. A hostage situation had developed and the erstwhile hijackers were making demands for money or else they would kill their captives.

I raced to the office armed with my AKM assault rifle to assist where I could and had brought with me a mace gun that I had acquired privately from a friend. The Smith and Wesson GEOC mace dispenser was standard issue to various US police departments and had proved effective on numerous occasions. I always had it with me, as most of the issues I dealt with required a non-lethal means of control.

Arriving at the scene I was immediately aware of how tense the situation had become. The guard detail had fled the compound and was nowhere to be seen. Some 30 metres away, in front of the reception area, the three LONRHO staff members lay motionless on the ground. Even from where I was I could see they had been beaten to within an inch of their lives. Before I could exit my vehicle, two of the gang were upon me, dragging me from the Land-Cruiser with kicks and shouts. The smell of sweat, fear and rage was overpowering and its rank odour hung in the air around me. It was a familiar odour and one I had smelled before. When adrenalin surges through fear, on man and beast alike, it gives off a dour, sweet and sickly stench that manifests through the pores. I had smelled it in Northern Ireland during the riots, when people had been caught up in mass hysteria. I had smelled it on captured terrs, fearful of their fate during the bush war and I had smelled it on terrified dogs which I had witnessed being beaten.

I managed to grab the mace gun and I let go a burst at the heads of my attackers. The effect was immediate and they both dropped to the ground, hands tearing at their eyes. The others, no longer so brave, backed off for the time being, but behind me I did not notice one of them as he sneaked around my periphery and headed toward the guard post at the gate. I was alerted in time by SNASP (Mozambique Secret Police) officers who had arrived on the scene and I spun to see him pick up an AK that had been left by the guards. I dropped to my knees, raising my rifle in one motion and brought it up to bear on the man's chest. I took up the pressure on the trigger and was about to drop him when a SNASP officer ran between us, screaming for me to stop. SNASP, I was informed, had the situation under control and there was no need for a shooting.

Momentarily shaken, I was taken by surprise from behind by the rest of the rioters. My rifle was ripped from my hands and a boot jarred into the side of my head. I was cursing myself for not opening fire but managed to get to my feet under a torrent of fists and abuse. Turning, I was just in time to see an AK butt swing toward my face and I buried my head in my chest. The butt slammed into my forehead and blood streamed into my eyes. I was aware of more men jostling to administer my punishment, as the SNASP officers lost control. I was certain, after everything I had survived, that I was to die at the hands of my own former co-workers, a victim of man's propensity for rage. And over such a minor issue. All for enough money to buy a few cold drinks!

I didn't feel the next blow or the one after that. The fists, boots and butts continued to rain into me as I desperately tried to parry the blows. I knew if I fell the game was over. Once I was on the ground I was at their mercy and their anger grew with each passing second. Just then another butt slammed into the small of my back. The wind was knocked out of me as the first of my attackers who I had maced joined the fracas.

Above the screams and shouts, I heard their indignant complaint as they fought to convince their comrades that I had used 'chemical warfare' on them. I heard them chant for my death, 'kill him', they screamed and my heart raced when the others believed them.

My knees buckled. I could no longer hold my own weight and had the weight of the men on top of me. I wrapped my head in my arms and cocooned myself, dropping to the ground ready to accept the final blows. And there was that smell of fear again, but this time it was from me. With the smell came visions of the beaten dog I'd once seen and I prayed that someone would rescue me like I had rescued it.

I drew my knees into my chest and made myself as small as possible. When would it come? Surely my skull was going to cave in at any moment. I couldn't take much more of this.

But it didn't come. Initially the only thing I knew was that I was no longer being beaten. The commotion was still around me so I gingerly peeped over my forearms to meet my saviour. Was there someone else they had turned their attention to? My attackers were still there, right next to me, but they were focused on something else, gathered like vultures at a kill. I wasn't going to wait for them and I started to get up when I was dragged backwards by helping hands. Once on my feet I withdrew, still uncertain as to what fortuitous event had saved my life. Then I saw it. Some 30 men groping for money lying on the ground. Not a lot of money, but in small notes. No more than 30,000 meticals (about US$3) in fact.

I felt like I had a bad hangover and in my groggy state it dawned on me. I looked down at my blood-soaked and torn shirt and its pockets were ripped off. The money I was carrying had fallen out and this was the reason I was still alive.

I had seen this sort of madness before. It was a reincarnation of Golding's *Lord of the Flies*, a level of rapacity that cannot be fathomed, as each man turned on the other to win the miniscule prize.

I left them to it. More SNASP officials arrived and struggled to gain control of the situation. I got into my Land-Cruiser and drove back to my residence. As I left, I saw my attackers see me. Like hounds on a fox they turned their attention to me once again, high on adrenalin and the smell of blood. They raced after me but I rammed down the accelerator and left them chewing my mud.

The rain came down in buckets as I reached my cottage. Once inside, I grabbed my spare AK and limped back to the porch. I waited for them and this time I was going to kill them, but they never came.

The drive to Mutare through the Forbes border post is a hazy memory. When I arrived at the Mutare hospital, the pain had only just begun to hit me. As I walked into the reception, I jumped at the apparition that faced me. The mirror I stood in front of told a grisly tale. I was no longer recognisable as myself through the swelling and the caked blood. My vision was blurred, as I peeked through tiny slots that had once been eyes. I remember collapsing, but I don't remember much after that. When I left the hospital, the next day, I was a shadow of my former agile self. Every muscle in my body ached as I shuffled out the door, willing one foot in front of the other. If I hadn't gone 10 rounds with Mike Tyson I would not have known it, but at least I had something to show for it and it was not just my black eyes. The 43 stitches that bound my split skin would be hard to beat.

I survived the ALMA mauling with little more than a bruised ego. The times were changing in Mozambique and for the first time in more than 30 years, peace was a tangible prospect. RENAMO was still tender over the existence of foreign security personnel and they batted hard at the conference table to have them expelled from the country. LONRHO was also going through changes. In a swiftly brokered deal, the ALMA mine was sold to a South African company called Benicon.

I retained my post for a while at Manica, but the writing was on the wall and although I saw a prospect of financial gain in the future, I couldn't see the wood for the trees, as the excitement of action had long since fled me. Shortly after Benicon's takeover, the company shuffled the office staff and the employees and brought in from South Africa their own representatives. I was little more than a glorified taxi driver, running the mine's gold to the Forbes border post in heavily armed convoys.

A month before leaving, I was offered a post as stores controller with a reduction in pay, which was tantamount to winning the booby prize at a Grade three sack race. My response, in hindsight, was inevitable, given the drastic change of environment. I felt like an unwelcome war veteran returning home and struggling to adjust to the suddenly imposed peace.

Elsewhere in the country the war ground to an abrupt halt, but there were occasional instances of savage banditry. Everyone was tired of war and people looked forward with fervour to the upcoming elections, and the promise from the political parties of change that would bring prosperity.

It is easy to make money out of other peoples' misery and I wanted no part of it any more. My zest for action had dulled somewhat, after nearly 25 years spent in war-ravaged areas. The future seemed uncertain at the time, but I had a home in Zimbabwe to return to as well as a house on the coast of South Africa. My marriage would require more adhesive to glue it together than Bostik could brew up in a year, but I thought it was well overdue for remedy.

In my heart I knew that what I had been fighting for while in Mozambique, what I had been helping to contain, was only partly a civil war. There were far too many discrepancies for me to believe that RENAMO was behind all the incidents I had witnessed. For instance, there was the FRELIMO leave pass found on the dead bandit, with his name on it and what about the posters that had been left at the scene of a despicable atrocity, pointing blame at the supposed perpetrators? Nowhere in the world is wholesale massacre the kind of thing to do when trying to win hearts and minds. A brutal act of savagery here and there, where the victims already know who their tormentors are, may encourage support by intimidation, but to actually leave your calling card? Who the hell were they trying to kid?

I packed my things and bade farewell to my former comrades. The tides of war had turned and the winds of change swept in keenly from all directions.

With one last look, I turned and saluted the men of LOMACO. The breeze caught my hair as I saluted Sergeant Dick.

CHAPTER 45:
Battle on the Home Front

Many things changed after my stint with Benicon. For one thing, after a difficult transition to civilian life, my marriage to Sheila hit rock bottom. Our partnership had undergone tremendous strain over the years, during which we hardly saw each other.

And that was how it was to remain.

My absence from Sheila had created a rift and not surprisingly, after nearly four years apart, she found her freedom. I didn't last a month in Port Shepstone, before we agreed that separation was the best option. Sheila wanted me to return to Zimbabwe while she remained in South Africa pursuing her independence.

I returned home to Harare. While I was there, I met Maggie through friends. Maggie was adorable at first sight with her long strawberry-blonde hair. She was a strong woman who had raised a child on her own and was establishing herself in her own business importing high-class lingerie from the UK. I came into the picture when she asked me to help her with designing a logo for her company and producing office stationery. Given my artistic flair and the attraction I felt towards Maggie, I jumped at the opportunity and we became good friends.

Sheila remained in South Africa. One day our son Paul arrived, having left his mom in Port Shepstone. I'm sure he felt the same affliction most young men feel at his age, when living with their parents. He was keen to extend his horizons and seek his fortune in the world.

It upset me that my marriage had turned out the way it did. I filed for divorce, which didn't go down well with Sheila, or her lawyer, as she wanted her old life back. It all ended in tears when I was forced to make one hell of a decision. I chose Maggie.

After months of soul-searching, Maggie and I started going out and I really began to enjoy life. At the beginning of 1994 I was offered a job with an old friend, John Lester, who owned two gold mine dumps in the rural lands of

Chiweshe, just past Concession. Chifefe Mine was in production, but Rosa Mine was stagnant. John had rented a huge old farmhouse at the Makore Hills Range, where I took up residence. Maggie continued to run the lingerie business, but she and her son Dayne came out every weekend. It was turning into a charmed and comfortable existence.

Eventually Maggie and I decided to open a general dealer's store, a farm store and a tuck shop servicing the mine labour. We put what money we had left into the idea. It worked out well, paying the bills and kept us very busy.

Running the mines was simple enough. It entailed clean-ups every month and taking the alluvial dust from the clean-ups for smelting in Harare. Security had to be tight, as many of the labourers would lace their overalls with alluvial dust and tread carefully home, where they would shake off every night. Surprisingly, after a few shakes, a credible amount of gold could be stolen and smelted into small pennies which were then sold on the black market.

One of the mines was right next to the Bell Rock Police Keep, from war days. Investigating an old mine shaft one day we stumbled across human remains. Further investigation revealed that all the disused shafts in the area had been used as makeshift graves, when terrorist bodies were dumped into them during the war. After Fire Force contacts, the bodies of all the dead terrs were flown to the police keep by helicopter, in large nets slung under their bellies. Once identified, the corpses were discarded in the shafts. It created an eerie atmosphere around the mine and I often thought of the souls that wandered around in limbo, unable to find peace.

I travelled seven kilometres each day, to and from the mine and just loved working in the bush. I visited Glendale Club often, where the social life was convivial and relaxed. Maggie continued to visit every weekend and before we knew it, our home had become the venue for all our friends to gather at weekends for braais and socials. It wasn't long before I put the past behind me and looked forward to a new beginning.

When the drought of 1997 came, things started to go wrong at Chifefe Mine. There was no water to run production and with the slackening trade, John Lester acquired some new investors. Suddenly there wasn't a place for me in the business any more and the bills were accruing. I began to concentrate on supplying information to my controllers in the NIS again, for a small increase on my retainer. It was mediocre intelligence gathering, but the ends justified the means and kept the wolf from the door. I had to tell Maggie where the bread and butter was coming from, which was an incredibly hard task, seeing as I had kept her in the dark out of necessity and for her own well being. Finding out that her man was a spy left her a little bit shaken!

When Sheila died, it came as a shock and left me with many unresolved questions. She was far too young for a heart attack, although I suppose it could have been built up by the roller-coaster existence we had lived for so many years. The news reached me on the telephone early one morning, when a friend of hers phoned. Sheila had suffered a heart attack while getting ready for work. She couldn't be revived and died en route to the hospital.

I shouldered some of the responsibility for her death, as I had for Sergeant Dick and others close to me who had died. The weight of it hung heavy, dragging my legs into the ground, as if they were made of lead. Maggie was there for me, as she had been beforehand, when I had a hernia operation which had resulted from one of the ambushes I lived through in Mozambique.

Life has a way of correcting wrongs and although it might be little atonement for my part in Sheila's passing and quite immaterial at that, I lost the house in Port Shepstone through various skulduggeries of estate agents and brokers. My dreams of retiring there one day were shattered. The house wasn't in my name and with Sheila's passing, it too passed on to another tenant owner. I didn't chase it up. Doing so would, I felt, have been quite mercenary and although it may sound silly, I thought it would dishonour the life my wife had lived. We win some, we lose some, I guess! Someone ended up with a free house.

While the drama unfolded my older son, Richard, was engaged in driving backpackers from London to Cape Town across Africa, for a company called Truck Africa. He had started this job a few years after he left the British Army in 1994. We managed to get hold of him in Togo, to break the news of his mom's death. Paul was in the UK at the time, having only just arrived there and was aware of Richards's itinerary. They both felt terrible, but I excused them the necessity of attending the funeral, as logistically and financially it would have been a nightmare. Instead, we cremated Sheila's remains and I separated her ashes into two urns. The contents of one I cast into the Indian Ocean, from a sandy knoll on one of the Port Shepstone beaches. The remaining urn Richard collected on his way through Harare and took with him to the Victoria Falls. Standing opposite Devil's Cataract, on behalf of Paul and himself, he cast his mother's remains to the wind and watched as they settled into the Zambezi Gorge. I hoped that mighty river might grant her the peace that I was never able to. Richard returned to Truck Africa, as a driver on the Nairobi-Cape Town backpacker route. He loved the job and would pass through Harare every three months or so. It was always good to see him.

Later that year I proposed to Maggie and we were married in a small ceremony. I adopted her son Dayne as my own and we were very happy together.

Unfortunately, my dealings with the NIS lapsed as the bonds between our respective governments grew stronger. I needed to find an outlet for my free time.

In mid-1999, Richard decided to leave his employers in order to set up a campsite for backpackers on the Zambian shore of Lake Kariba. A friend, Jerry, joined him in the venture. During their travels, they had noticed there were no overnight facilities on the long haul between Malawi and Victoria Falls, the very road on which I had conducted reconnaissances with the Rhodesian SAS and the Selous Scouts so many years before. I knew the route well, so I accompanied Richard and Jerry to seek out a site to establish a backpacker stop.

We found an idyllic spot not far from the lake, about halfway between Lusaka and the Falls. Through careful planning, we arranged licences from the Zambian government to build the campsite and run boats on the lake. With the increasing backpacker trade, we had stumbled onto an idea that was sure to rake in the dollars. We even set to planning the construction of several houseboats for those travellers, who wanted to break their journey and perhaps do a spot of fishing or game viewing.

The whole concept was going from strength to strength, when we were screwed by a conman, who swindled us out of the licences and kept them for himself. I think he realised he was hanging onto a goldmine. As it turned out, after the invasion of white-owned farms in Zimbabwe in 2000 and the subsequent death of the tourist trade in the country, the site became a popular rest stop for the entire backpacker trade between Malawi and the Victoria Falls. There are even houseboats there today and the proprietor, whoever he is, must be coining it.

For Zimbabwe's tourist trade, the writing was on the wall for those who had been established in it. To us newcomers, it still seemed like a viable prospect, despite the economic collapse that was occasioned by our president's promise of correcting past wrongs to the war veterans.

Richard found another campsite called The Rocks, on the outskirts of Harare. The owner had obviously done his homework and he knew a sucker when he saw one. It transpired that he sold the campsite to us, knowing full well that the backpacker companies which had been supporting him were about to pull out of Zimbabwe. Although on our first visits, the campsite and bar had been a hive of tourist activity, within a few short weeks of us taking over nary a truck was seen pulling into The Rocks driveway. The previous owner took the gap to New Zealand and left us high and dry.

It took Maggie, Richard and me six months to get The Rocks up and running again. Fortunately, Richard called on the contacts he had made in the backpacking business. It was a lot of hard work, but with those contacts, we were encouraged to start improving the place and built onto the existing facilities a large gazebo bar and entertainment area. The backpackers, who frequented our lodge, were notorious drinkers, so the bar was always full and running it was a full-time job.

I once again settled into the position of camp lackey. I was responsible for the booze run and had to make sure we always had enough food and alcohol.

Maggie ran the kitchen and oversaw the bookkeeping side of things. It was a stressful position, as she had to look after the staff as well and make sure they received their wages on time.

Richard became our public relations officer and given his experience, he fitted into the position well. Unfortunately, he began to drink far in excess of what he was earning, as he was always mixing with the backpackers and providing them with entertainment. We suffered a little through his antics, which was made worse by the fact that he never seemed to realise he was no longer a driver. Like all overland drivers, he treated the tourists with disdain, something which raised hackles on occasion.

For a while at least we had our work cut out for us and the sky was the limit. By 2002, the situation in the country was so bad that the steady stream of trucks that visited us was reduced to a trickle. Across Zimbabwe, the fourth Chimurenga (liberation war) was being fought over property, farms and ranches. It didn't end there either, as it turned into the wholesale theft of assets such as cars, boats, farm implements and homesteads. After the first few farmers were murdered by war veterans, the tourist trade died completely. The Rocks could no longer sustain our three salaries, cover overheads and pay the wages. We just couldn't continue.

While the farmers suffered, the economic collapse of industry, partly reliant on revenue earned from waning tobacco sales, became more and more evident. The cost of living skyrocketed from an already high 55 per cent to 100 per cent and before we knew it, it was in the thousands. The Zimbabwe dollar plummeted to an all-time low. As the number-crunchers in the Ministry of Finance struggled to keep Zimbabwe afloat, by producing more money in the form of bearer cheques, daily commodities like bread and milk became sought-after items. The standing joke at the time, with reference to the largest-denomination bearer cheque which was red in colour, was that they were called Red Ferraris. They disappeared as fast as they came!

With the economic collapse, came a booming illegal foreign-currency trade. The Rocks was well positioned to take advantage of it and we survived on dealing hard currency with the few tourists who risked travelling in Zimbabwe. It was no walk in the park, but we got by. The new beginning I had dreamed of suddenly seemed unattainable and we all felt the strain. I sensed a distraction in my relationship with Maggie and I began to feel surplus to requirements, which I think stemmed in part from my own feelings of inadequacy. With nothing to do, I lounged about all day drinking coffee or having a beer with mates. My lack of direction began to erode my sense of well-being. Maggie felt it. I felt it. We all felt it. Maybe it was payback. Maybe I didn't need to punish myself when my turn was coming anyway.

By 2003 I wasn't feeling well. What started as common constipation gradually got worse. After careful scrutiny by a specialist, I was diagnosed with cancer of the colon. Further tests revealed a 30 centimetre tumour on my large intestine which had to be removed. The news hit me like a cushioned club. With the strain between Maggie and myself, I had too much on my mind to really care. The doctor's advice was to sit back with the least stress possible. Dream on!

I had an emergency operation on my colon. The medical bills for the operation and the chemotherapy afterwards were not covered by medical aid and The Rocks footed the bills. We just couldn't survive.

Our marriage breakdown came when Maggie told me there was no future. Some months after surgery, I started looking for work outside Zimbabwe, in an effort to give our marriage a break and hopefully earn some revenue to bail out The Rocks. Maggie saw no hope in the tourist industry and suggested any further investment would be like flogging a dead horse. No trucks were coming.

The Rocks was finished. She was right.

In Iraq, friends of mine, men with whom I had served in the Rhodesian SAS and the Selous Scouts were earning incredible money in the security profession. My old mate John Gartner, having returned to Australia after his South African Defence Force stint, had established a security company with other ex-Australian SAS members. They employed former Special Forces personnel, with the intention of conducting security and close-protection work internationally. With the call for private security in the Middle East, John naturally vied for a contract there. Although his company employed primarily ex-Australian SAS men, he retained the Selous Scout cap badge, depicting an osprey, as his company logo.

I heard from John regularly and he told me about his plans of seeking useful employment in Iraq.

Despite my condition, I resolved to get back into what I did best. If others my age could be given the responsibility for the safety of others in a hostile environment, then why couldn't I? I might not be all that I used to be, but I started to get fit again and cut down on my vices. Smoking I still abhorred but I had been drinking with some regularity.

In 2004, I applied to numerous security companies in Iraq, forwarding my curriculum vitae on CDs. I heard from some of the bigger companies like Global and Olive, but they were not interested in employing me. The feeling I got from their responses was that they felt I might have been looking for a top-tier position when really I was willing to get down in the grit and the mud with the boys. Global told me that I was over the hill and their cut-off age for employment was 50 years, as insurance wouldn't cover anyone above that age in the event of being wounded or killed.

As far as they were concerned, at 56, I was a bit long in the tooth.

I learnt then that it was very much an old boy's club conducting work in Iraq. It was a matter of who you knew, rather than who you were.

Other companies also replied, although they said that they were fully booked up. Countless thousands of ex-servicemen were seeking employment in Iraq and my application was too late. They said they would file my details and would contact me should something arise. I wasn't having too much luck and I hadn't yet mentioned that I had recently recovered from cancer.

Some months later I contacted John Gartner, whose company had just landed a new contract in Iraq. John asked me if I would be interested in a position working with him in the Green Zone of Baghdad. Even John thought I might be a bit old to be a shooter with the grunts, but he did think I would be useful as the intelligence clerk for his outfit. He said I was to make my way immediately to Amman, in Jordan, where I would be picked up and shipped to Baghdad with the necessary documentation. I would be reimbursed for the airfares and any associated costs as he needed me there 'yesterday'. His main entourage of 20 ex-Australian Army men, would be arriving within a few days to start the contract and there was a lot of administration to be taken care of.

Anything was better than nothing and I appreciated the opportunity to prove myself once more. I must confess that a trickle of self-doubt lingered when I thought about the age of the men I would be serving with. Maybe I *was* over the hill. Maybe it *was* time to hang up my guns.

As I had done throughout my whole life, I threw myself in at the deep end.

CHAPTER 46:
On to Iraq

When I caught the flight from Harare International Airport bound for Iraq, I was in two minds. Behind me I left my second dissolving marriage and Maggie, part of me that I really had no will to lose. I had never been the type of man to dwell on distraction, something I noticed I was more prone to, and I thought that a step forward was a step on the path to healing. Certainly, remaining in Zimbabwe was no option, as the strain and heartbreak I felt over possibly losing Maggie, was overwhelming. We were in a rut. Our state of union was non-productive. The political and economic situation in the country left a lot to be desired and I was floating in limbo.

At an altitude of 29,000 feet on a long-haul flight, one has a lot of time to think. I worried about my fitness as I had done as a young Para recruit at Aldershot and for the first time since then I questioned the sanity of my actions. It didn't worry me that I might be getting in over my head, but my concern was with those I would be letting down if my health failed, if I were to experience a relapse with my illness, or if the worms and bees in my head interfered with my work. It worried me for a bit, but then I put it behind me.

In Amman I was met by a company liaison officer, and the staff furnished me with an entry visa and a ticket for a ride out of Jordan. The aircraft I would be travelling on was a Royal Jordanian Airlines Fokker with no markings. On boarding, I knew this was no normal flight. The few men who boarded with me were mostly military in appearance, wearing civilian clothes, travelling to take up posts with other security contractors in Iraq. Most would be conducting close protection work, running VIPs between Baghdad International Airport and Baghdad itself. One or two were past their use-by date, swollen around the midriff from too many years of good living. I must say it gave me relief that I wasn't the only one who might be biting off more than I could chew. I consoled myself that I wasn't alone.

On board the aircraft was one female attendant and the rest were male, all of them South Africans. It was a strictly no-food-and-drinks flight and seatbelts had to be fastened throughout. We flew at high altitude for about an hour. When we were directly above Baghdad the intercom emitted a crackle and the pilot warned us to hold on. The aircraft throttled back as the ailerons stalled its forward speed and suddenly the plane dived to spiral down towards the airport.

The drill was a practised one and there was a good reason for it. If someone was waiting with a SAM 7 to blow the plane out of the sky, the rapid descent should give the operator zero chance of locking on. When the aircraft touched down, I breathed a sigh of relief. From the windows it was clear that the entire airport was surrounded by a giant military base, stretching as far as the eye could see.

Baghdad was no place for the faint-hearted in 2004. The nature of the terrorist war that was being fought around the city, was reminiscent of Belfast, Northern Ireland, in the late sixties and early seventies. If anything, it was worse. I was no fool and had done my homework before arriving. In Iraq our enemy was mostly a faceless one. It was booby-trapped cars and improvised explosive devices. Rarely, unless you were part of the military, would you get to face a mortal enemy, an enemy you could actually shoot back at. Despite this there was no shortage of weapons.

Exiting the aircraft, I was met by the sight of hundreds of soldiers and private-security personnel armed with a range of Western and Eastern-bloc weapons. Some milled around cars waiting to collect their human cargo and others walked about with purpose. When I reached the undercover parking it was like stepping into the OK Corral. More men, bristling with firepower, ambled about the place. Most were dressed in civilian clothes and wore body armour or load-bearing gear. From the conversations I heard as I passed through, it was apparent that many nationalities were represented. There were mostly Americans, but I did hear some Australians and a bunch of guys sounded as if they could have been South Africans. It was all guns and lots of cowboys. I must admit it looked good. It did not take me long to find my employer's representative at the airport. MB was the ops manager running the scene and was getting the place in order for the arrival of the main team from Australia. An advance party was in place, consisting of four South Africans and three ex-military guys from the Czech Republic. The Czechs really looked at home with their dark skins and full beards, and were very Arab-looking. One was a giant of a man carrying an AKM with a drum magazine. He seemed cheerful enough, with a warming smile and a hearty laugh, but I must say I was relieved that he was on our side. MB checked me in without much formality. I would be living at Camp

Bristol, which formed part of the enormous base surrounding the airport. Camp Bristol housed an American company called Custer Battle and was shared with another security company from the UK called HART Security. It was pretty crowded and we felt like sardines in a can.

The enormousness of the airport was a sight to behold. The base pretty much cordoned off the airport, which was brilliant for security, but did little to stop the endless bombardment of mortars and rockets. The Yanks had a large barrage balloon aloft, carrying direction-finding equipment which could record any incoming fire by tracking its path and pinpointing its origin or base-plate positions. I was told that most ordnance fired was unaccounted for, as the enemy used many crafty methods of delivering it, in order to evade the QRF team's reaction. Of course, the accuracy they achieved was questionable, but their aim was only to harass the airport, with the bonus of a possible direct hit. One thing they did and as a mortar man myself I imagine it would take some doing, was to freeze mortar bombs in home-made tubes, erect them and wait for the ice to melt. On melting, the bomb would slip down the tube to engage the firing pin at the bottom. Other methods included firing from the back of vehicles, or drive-by detonations of explosive devices that had been planted previously. Crude tactics perhaps, but they were very effective.

I met pilots who told me stories about landing aircraft, while mortars and rockets exploded around them. One of them told me that every time he landed he shat himself. Certainly, every time I visited the airport, explosions could be heard erupting all around it. While I was there, I got so used to the ordnance going off day and night that eventually I no longer heard it.

After stowing my gear we drove to the Green Zone in Baghdad, where John Gartner was based. The drive took us through the main checkpoint at the airport which was well covered by US troops with assorted machine-gun and weapon positions. The activity at the checkpoint was chaotic, with cars coming and going and the constant piercing racket of impatient drivers pressing their horns. Most people just wanted to get through in a hurry because, as I was told, there were daily incidents of car bombings and booby traps in the area. After the checkpoint you're on the main road into Baghdad. You have to pass through the Red Zone, where the terrorists built tunnels laden with explosives, or laid ambush and sniper positions. After clearing the checkpoints, all the security teams would cock their weapons and ready themselves to run the gauntlet at 120 kilometres an hour, until they reached the Green Zone. Slow traffic on the way would be pushed aside in the hustle to reach safety. I'm not entirely sure of the reason, but the route we took had become known as 'Route Irish' and I was informed that it was the most dangerous stretch of road in the world. Hundreds of teams of security operatives and convoys of military equipment and personnel ran the gauntlet to Baghdad every day. I had never seen military hardware amassed like this in my life. The Americans took the cake with their Humvees and Bradley fighting vehicles which appeared almost everywhere. Among this lot one could also pick out the odd British and Australian military vehicles.

It was quite a sight. The road was littered with wreckage and was reminiscent of pictures I had seen of Beirut during the troubles there. There were also goats all over the place. When I pointed out a dead goat on the side of the road the ops manager told me to watch out for them. Apparently dead goats had been stuffed with explosives which could be remotely detonated when a target drove by. Now exploding goats were really something else!

I was told the Yanks had plans to erect a four-and-a-half-metre high wall, on both sides of the road for the entire length of 'Route Irish'. At the time I thought it might stop the goats, but it would do little to deter fanatical terrorists.

The Green Zone was not a much safer place than the Red Zone, what with ordnance landing all over the show and car bombs going off daily. In the Green Zone, I met up with John Gartner. There wasn't much time for trivia, so John briefed me on the details of my job. An intelligence clerk was no longer needed, as the post had been filled by an ex-Australian SAS man. What they needed was a quartermaster and John thought I would slot into the position well. He remembered my time as B Troop storeman in the SAS and 'camp commandant' in the Selous Scout's Recce Troop and believed my experience would lend itself to the position. I was happy with the change, as it offered me a rear echelon post which would not expose me to anything I couldn't handle.

When I commenced work there was one container load of equipment, consisting of the normal stores one would expect to find in war-torn Iraq. This sufficed well enough until the following day, when the first batch of men arrived as the forward party. While I was issuing weapons and uniforms, all sorts of shortfalls became apparent. Within a week, we had six container loads of gear, having 'borrowed' it from a sister security company and the equipment kept coming in. There was bedding, clothing, load-bearing gear, boots, good body armour and inferior body armour. There were AKMs, M4 carbines, Sig Saur pistols, Browning pistols, cleaning kits and tons of ammo.

My downfall came when I had to drive the computer to keep everything in check. Other than the odd e-mail or typing the occasional document, computer technology was alien to me. What happened to the good old days of the counter book and ball-point pen? When they put a PC in front of me it might as well have been the control panel for the space shuttle Challenger. I didn't know one knob from the other. As far as some people were concerned, within a few days, the only knob around the place was me.

Small respite came when larger problems loomed. Management soon realised that the first batch of contractors from Australia were a little out of their depth in Baghdad. They were certainly all ex-Australian Army members, but they lacked practical experience in soldiering in a hostile environment. Most were young, in their mid-20s and had only recently left the army. One or two had East Timor experience behind them, but even they needed the guidance of seasoned veterans. I suppose I must have had the same attitude at that age, but it was great fun to watch the huge amount of gung-ho and testosterone being thrown about the place. Through their lack of experience, these guys were itching to get into a punch-up. It struck a familiar chord when I thought about my youth.

The second lot to arrive were much older men in their mid- to late thirties. They were much more mature and took things in their stride. Meanwhile, I handled the stress in the old-fashioned way, with a ton of paperwork interspersed with loads of signing in and out. The volume of work soon drowned me and I realised how seriously I was in the shit. I had a huge problem on my hands, which was only exacerbated when I was put in charge of the vehicle fleet, in addition to what was already on my plate. With 60-plus vehicles I was expected to keep tabs on fuel, wear and tear and maintenance. When the security teams grew in strength, I was expected to keep a tally on daily camp strength and provide a report to Custer Battle administration, in order for our meals and expenses to be provided. I was a sinking ship surrounded by a sea of sand. When the elections were a week away I was put in charge of the distribution of ballot papers, which had to be delivered all over Iraq. This was the first stage of Iraq's first free and fair elections. After the elections, the ballot papers had to be collected and flown to Dubai for security reasons. It was a huge responsibility. Tight control had to be implemented so they didn't get into the wrong hands.

I noticed there were a few individuals lobbying for my position. Given the necessary computer skills to take care of the stores, it was a cushy number where one could expect to remain intact. Other than a mortar or rocket landing square on your head, there was little chance of coming to harm. Like me, others also realised they were past rubbing shoulders with the grunts and wanted the relative safe haven of the Green Zone.

One of these individuals tried to muscle in on my job while I was away on a chopper trip to Kirkuk collecting weapons. When I returned, I found out he had been interfering with the containers, doing his own inventory checks with my paperwork, trying to find fault. Fortunately he came up with zip, as my old-fashioned ways proved effective. I could account for every bit of kit that had come and gone through my stores.

If my problems had ended there, I might have been OK. The worms and bees that I feared, began burrowing away in my mind and building hives the size of anthills. I constantly had to check myself, as I drifted back to personal issues that were brewing at home. I had been in contact with Maggie via the telephone and e-mail and she didn't seem at all happy. Maggie had decided to close up shop on The Rocks and sell all fixed and movable assets. When she filed for a divorce, it was like a grenade had gone off next to my head while I was tanked up on morphine. The pain wasn't there, but I was tattered and bruised, all masked with a feeling of disbelief. All manner of things raced through my brain and it started becoming apparent to John and the other managers, that I wasn't a full box of chocolates. I didn't do anything stupid, but I just could not focus a hundred per cent on the job at hand. My peers were aware that I was drifting on another plane and I was issued a warning to get my life back on track. I began to think I was a no-hoper, with the weight of my recent health problems, my domestic circumstances and my lack of computer knowledge.

The youngsters who had arrived with the initial lot, whinged constantly about the state of their gear. John, true to form, got a handle on it and ran the company like a professional. It wasn't much different to being in the army again. Through the correct channels, he organised superior equipment and what he couldn't buy, the youngsters organised over the Internet, purchasing all the latest kit and mod cons for their AKM rifles. We called it 'magic gear' because we often thought the guys gained a sense of false bravado wearing it. There was an air of invulnerability, if you had the best gear available on the market. The body armour we were supplied with was top-rate gear anyway. We did get issued inferior gear, khaki sets of body armour, but that was dispersed to the non-combatants or rear echelon people, who weren't likely to get caught in a scrape. However, the guys actually running in hot areas, often appropriated a set of the inferior body armour in addition to that which they wore. What they would do was place it over the door windows in the vehicles to add some additional bullet-proofing.

I had many an argument with these guys, when I told them that it was far safer to soldier without the armour. At least, when the shit hit the fan you could move it up under fire and not get weighed down by the heavy flak vests. What did I know? I was an old soldier and I learnt quickly that everyone else knows better. Once in a while, to really rub salt into their wounds, I would tell stories of soldiering in soft-skinned open Land-Rovers during the bush war. They loved the one about Suttil, the boys and I, getting blown to buggery by the TMH46 mine. Some of the Aussie boys didn't believe that we had all survived the mine blast, as their own regiment had experienced loss in Afghanistan from the same sort of ordnance. I teased them by telling them that we Africans were just tougher. It was a good laugh and the older guys knew what I was up to. They looked on as the youngsters became flustered and got hot under the collar.

Things started looking up when a new ops manager arrived, a Kiwi from the New Zealand SAS. Bill Bisset took an immediate liking to me and seemed to have a good idea of what was going down. He had done a spell in the Aussie SAS and wasn't too impressed with his overall findings. In his opinion, they had softened over the years and weren't all they used to be.

Bill was training to be a doctor and had plans to finish his qualification after Iraq. He showed an amazing amount of concern for my condition, having just beaten the cancer and gave me a medical examination. I was still experiencing pain in my abdomen and had developed a nagging cough. Not one to take chances, Bill took me to see a US Army doctor, who he thought might be better equipped to examine me. His concern was that the cancer might not be in remission. However, the US doctor showed little interest in me and dismissed me without as much as a bodily probe. The least he could have done, I imagined, was prod me in the abdomen or stick a finger up my bum. I felt like a kid in the doctor's waiting room, only there was no sweetie bowl when I left.

Bill told me that he needed me on the chopper protection teams and approached the ops room to inform them of the change. I was over the moon with the posting, as I would be joining the Czechs and South Africans with whom I had a little more in common. I got on well with most of the Aussies, some of them brilliant soldiers, but I felt I was moving a little closer to home. In a world dominated by Americans, Australians and British, all us Third-World boys felt a bit alone. It was nothing personal and certainly it wasn't a feeling born from airs of superiority, but there was a definite difference in values, if not in cultural backgrounds. The Aussies were a step closer than the rest of them, but I suddenly knew how all the foreign soldiers must have felt in Rhodesian days.

The chopper teams commenced with the second phase of elections, which entailed two weeks of uplifting ballot papers from various warehouses, where they were stored after collection from the polling stations. I was given a few days to get my house in order, before taking up my new post. I acquired some kit and an AKM rifle in good working order and got in some range practice. The range we used was an American one, on the base surrounding Baghdad airport. All the guys who VIP couriered or ran chopper protection, had to undergo a weapons proficiency test before they could start operations. For me it was like riding a bike. Shooting was the one thing I was always good at and over the years my prowess hadn't diminished.

When I got onto the choppers, I felt like I was back in the real world. I must say I had more faith in the equipment and pilots we had back in the old days, than those in Iraq. The aircraft were aged Russian Mi8 troop-carrying helicopters, flown by ex-Eastern-bloc pilots. Inside the cargo bay where we sat, was strapped a huge drum of aviation fuel which was painted bright yellow. As you can imagine, it worried most of the protection crew as it would only take one stray tracer round, or an RPG7, to ignite the entire helicopter. It was little consolation, when we were informed that the helicopters were target number one on the insurgents' hit list, as they did not want the elections to take place. If they could destroy the ballot papers in the air before they got to Baghdad airport, it would be first prize.

Accordingly we tooled ourselves up with some serious gear and weapons. One of the guys would always carry a PKM machine gun and would sit with the thing pointed out the door the whole time. At sparrows' fart every morning, we would board the chopper at Baghdad airport and then fly around for the whole day, to collection points where we would meet the other teams. The other guys were vehicle mobile and it was their responsibility to carry the ballot papers from the polling stations to the collection points.

Our main tasks on each landing were to count and sign for all the papers, and escort them to the fixed-wing Air Link aircraft at Baghdad airport for transit to

Dubai. The Australians had another security team that would accompany Air Link out of Iraq, until the cargo was delivered into safe hands. The helicopter crew's safety was also our responsibility, in the event that the aircraft was forced down in inhospitable terrain. We had the pilot and two technicians to look after and they didn't carry weapons. Although we never had to call on them, we were told the Americans had very good search-and-rescue teams on standby, in the event of being shot down. We all got a fantastic aerial view of Iraq because we flew at high altitudes, so as to be out of range of small arms and surface-to-air missiles. Arriving back at Baghdad in the evenings was a terrific thrill. The pilot would fly the chopper at a high altitude until directly over the airport and then descend like a brick, much like the fixed-wing aircraft did. It took a bit of getting used to, as my heart always ended up in my mouth and I felt like I was being gagged.

I began to settle in and apply myself to my work, although in the back of my mind, Maggie still ate at me. The first phase of the elections ended with hardly an incident, except when we were mortared on landing one day, but the bombs landed harmlessly a kilometre away. With the end of elections, came the end of uplifting ballot papers, so we sat on our backsides for a few days.

Typically, the international community made utterances of unfair rigging and the Yanks were accused of having too great a hand in organising the elections. They ranted about America installing a puppet government in Iraq and wanted the elections coordinated by a multinational nonmilitary body.

Private security was the ideal vehicle to carry it on. It was a dangerous mission, in view of the increasing insurgent activity, but behind the scenes, the Yanks always lurked with their quick reaction teams using Bradley armoured fighting vehicles and Apache helicopter gunships.

The company ops room moved into offices at Sky Link, closer to the airport, as communications from Camp Bristol were unsatisfactory. For a few days, many of us were in limbo as our contracts were coming to an end. The guys who had eased me out of the quartermaster's job, were all vying for the post on phase two, if and when it came along. The company management really applied their business acumen, proving they were more than just good soldiers and secured a second contract for phase two of the elections, this time with minimal American participation. They hired a genuine quartermaster to run the stores, an Australian who had once served with the Rhodesian Light Infantry, and a few Iraqi militia members as storemen. Another Aussie, also an ex-RLI member, became admin officer for the company. I used to drink with him during bush war days.

I managed to secure myself a position on the chopper protection crews, for phase two of the contract, and left for Zimbabwe for a few weeks rest and recreation. In my absence, Zimbabwe had changed considerably. A mate picked me up at the airport and I was going to surprise Maggie. I had only been gone for six weeks, but the Zimbabwean money I had in my pocket, enough for a good night out when I left, was barely enough to cover an hour's parking at the airport. I learnt, on the trip into town, that the cost of living was still escalating. Every time it climbed and we felt sure that it could go no higher, the next day would reveal further increases on daily commodities. The availability of fuel was almost non-existent. The commodity black market boomed and pick-up trucks with fuel drums and containers strapped to them were a common sight around the city. The new word for 'naughty' was 'hoarding' and the government banned black-market sales of everything. You couldn't buy it in the shops, but heaven forbid you bought it anywhere else.

The bakers, some of whom had accumulated flour for making bread, were suddenly viewed like cocaine distributors and were arrested, beaten and thrown in jail. If you were caught carrying fuel, maize, fertilizer, literally anything in bulk, you were charged, fined and had the goods confiscated. Some of the senior police officers around town started looking flush and prosperous. Rackets developed when, through a few fronts, you could go into town the next day and purchase your confiscated goods at triple the price. For a country on the verge of bankruptcy, boasting unemployment in excess of 80 per cent, the amount of new luxury cars on the roads was amazing. Someone was making money but it wasn't the layman, either black or white.

The only thing that had not changed on my return, was Maggie. When I walked into my flat, the expression on her face was as if I had returned from the dead. I think that's when I knew how serious our problem was and it left me gutted. In my heart I knew it was over for the time being, but I didn't give up hope. I still loved her. It was one of those things. You second-guess your intuition and experience the pain anyway, but you know it's not permanent. I knew she would be back one day.

I returned to Baghdad thinking I was still part of the chopper team. What had started off as a troop of ex-servicemen, expanded into a company, as new men arrived to take up positions at polling stations around the country.

My employer combined for the particular operation with HART Security and this created a formidable private army of seasoned Iraq veterans. Some of the new boys who joined us, had served in Iraq during the last offensive, when Saddam Hussein had been ousted. I must say that with that experience behind them, the Aussies appeared in a new light, more dedicated and professional.

I met Matt J. He was among the Aussie SAS lot who were first across the border when the allied offensive against Saddam began. In subsequent actions against Saddam's troops, he was decorated for bravery. Matt was in charge of the team I was to join to help guard the ballot boxes for phase two of the elections. We attended a briefing, which was to be the norm for the next few days, on the forthcoming operation.

Teams would be sent nationwide, living it rough in camps with Iraqi militiamen guarding the ballot papers. My team's destination was Tikrit, Saddam's birthplace, in the northern part of the country. We would amalgamate there with another callsign at Camp Danger, 25 kilometres from an American Air Force base which would be storing the ballot papers. When we arrived, it was to a tent city which had been used to receive arriving troops during the war. The Yanks, trying to remain scarce, were using the camp as a transit facility, as they handed over the reins to private security. There were twelve large, holey tents with bunk beds all over the place. It was raining and the rain pissed through the tents which made the extreme winter cold worse. I hadn't experienced cold like this since British Army days in the Brecon Beacons and Ireland. It took some getting used to before we were supplied with the right kit.

After arriving, we commenced a few days of range practice, which was extremely enjoyable. I put into practice firing a few weapons, which I hadn't touched in 10 years, since Mozambique days. We were split into teams, mine consisting of two South Africans and the Czechs, with Matt J as team leader. We were all confident in our ability as a team under Matt's guidance, as he was an extremely capable soldier. Our team was given a warehouse to protect. It was in the middle of nowhere, but was surrounded by a huge wall, outside of which were US/Iraqi Army gun emplacements and tanks. The ballot papers would be stored in the warehouse, after they had been collected from the polling stations. The warehouse was considered a soft target for insurgents. Matt drew up a roster, which entailed dividing into two teams of three who would do three daily shifts. While the one team worked, the other would rest up at Camp Danger and get in some shuteye. Each sub-team was in charge of 12 or so Iraqi militiamen, who we hoped would deter any attack. The Iraqis were poorly trained and we all believed they would run at the first shot being fired. In the event we jokingly considered handcuffing them to a railing to keep them in the fray.

In the field we lived on meals ready-to-eat or MREs, provided by the Americans. Back at camp there were always fresh rations and the chance of a hot shower. Our modus operandi was to collect the ballot boxes from the air force base, where they had been brought in from around the country in night convoys and return them to the warehouse. Travelling to the base, we were on our own, but on the return trip we were provided with an escort of a few Humvees and two Apache gunships lurking close at hand. The Americans were not supposed to be involved at all, but also provided assistance in the form of unmanned aerial vehicles to monitor us the whole time. If we were hit, a rescue squad would descend on our position to deliver us from evil.

The operation went as smooth as clockwork, although we did have a few scares. On one occasion Mac, who was driving and I, headed off like bats out of hell by taking the main road through Tikrit and turning right towards the warehouse, on what stood for a highway. Along the route it was the passenger's task to monitor traffic, in case we were being followed. We would drive a short distance, do a U-turn and back-track, taking another route to throw off any pursuit. In Tikrit there were usually a lot of vehicles milling around, but we noticed one which seemed to be tailing us. It was an old seven series BMW and was closing on us at a rate of knots. I watched as the car came closer and Mac put his foot down to increase the gap between us. The BMW was powerful and caught up with us easily, despite our speed of 160 kilometres an hour. I expected to see a RPG7 launcher come out of the passenger window at any moment and told Mac to open the sun roof. I stood up, leapt through the open top and waved my AKM in the BMW's direction. It had the desired effect and the bods in the car all shat themselves and careened all over the road, lagging behind as we left the highway. We never did find out if the car was full of insurgents, but we got on the comms and sent a description to the Yank QRF team.

The last we saw of the BMW was when it headed south down the highway with a couple of Apaches following it.

At the end of the operation the company threw a huge party, for which they organised a ton of beer. It went down well with the lads and left me feeling pretty happy with myself. I was no spring chicken and I had managed to get through without raising an eyebrow. In fact, there were a few good reports in relation to what our team had achieved. It was good to know that an old soldier could hot-bed it with the grunts and get his hands dirty. For the weeks the operation had lasted I had hardly worried about my condition, nor had cause to. From my previous position of financial insecurity, my bank accounts were looking rosy, with what I had earned in Iraq over a few short months. The nest egg that had previously come and gone and come and gone again, was back in place.

After handing in my gear, I headed back home, having achieved what I had set out to do. I said my farewells to John Gartner, highly impressed with the overall professionalism that he and the two other directors had displayed. Every operation the company had conducted was carried out with military precision. There were a few occasions when the directors wanted to shove their boots up people's arses, but given the fact that the company was commercially orientated, that was understandable. Well done John and thank you for the years of friendship!

I never did get back to Iraq. I should have stayed with Mac and Matt J who were offered jobs with another company. There was an offer for me, but after stepping out of uniform again I had too much on my mind. The dilemma of divorce flooded back and everything I said to Maggie had fallen on deaf ears. When I signed the divorce papers I felt as if I was letting go of the last tangible evidence of my life. The Rocks had gone and so too would Maggie, to a distant corner of the globe.

The cough, when it came back, was dry and hoarse as if there was an insect tickling the back of my throat. I assumed, as my doctor did, that my depressed state of mind had lowered my immunity to influenza. As good doctors do, he prescribed antibiotics when the cough developed into a chesty infection. After that it continued to hound me, on and off for the best part of a year, despite repeated doses of medication. There were times when it wasn't there, but most of the time I wheezed and rattled myself to sleep. After midnight, during the wee hours of the morning, I would shoot bolt upright in bed hacking out the previous day's phlegm. I should have known better.

By the time they found the cancer it was nearly too late. I was told it was not a common occurrence, but the disease had somehow crept its way into my lungs. Initially I couldn't believe it. Lung cancer was for smokers, I thought! The evidence was in front of me, when I was shown proof in the form of scans and X-rays and there it was, a huge blot on my lower left lung looking like the negative of an ink stain marring a piece of blotting paper.

Chemotherapy isn't a pleasant experience and proved to be as taxing on my state of wellbeing as it had been the first time round. Then there were the bills, which in Zimbabwean terms were ludicrous. I still wasn't on medical aid cover and I realised that the treatment might be ongoing. If I were to save any part of the nest egg I had worked so hard for, I would have to find another means of paying the bills. There was only one thing for it: to return to the UK. As a British citizen, I felt sure that the National Health Service would cover any shortfalls. It was an anxious period, to say the least! All the worry seemed worth it in the end, when I beat the disease for a second time. By all accounts the cancer was in remission. Naturally, I was elated, but in the back of my mind something still chewed away, bringing me down into the pits of despair. Canada was where my thoughts drifted to most of the time. That was where Maggie was. We kept in touch via e-mail, although I can't say she wrote anything that I could build my hopes on. I tried to keep the blame and accusations to a minimum, but there were occasions when I let go, when I needed an outlet for my hurt. I was more emotionally distraught than I was concerned about my condition and there was no way I could bottle it up.

On 14 April 2006, the night my son Richard died, I was having drinks with friends. The next morning, when I heard of his death, I had a mild hangover. The cushioned club came out once again and was swinging wildly, but I think I had taken too many blows for it to really have effect. I was numbed to the core. I mourned his passing inside, but outside I was a wall. Everything seemed to be happening at once and my world was falling apart. Richard had found his niche, running a bird sanctuary outside Pietersburg (now Polokwane) in South Africa, where I had been fortunate to visit him a year earlier. The cause of death, in a car accident, was trauma to the head and my poor boy didn't stand a chance. The car in which he drove, was sandwiched between two others as he returned home to the sanctuary. The other drivers were drunk and had attended a wedding reception. I loved Richard dearly as I do Paul in Australia and Dayne my adopted son.

Watching Zimbabwe die around me, was like sitting beside the bed of a dying mother. She hadn't birthed me, but like a mother she had nurtured me and watched me grow. I had watched her grow, nurtured her through the tyranny of terrorism and as I would have done for a family member, I had killed for her. In my time on the Dark Continent I had seen the best and the worst of her. I had watched her first manic throes as she discovered herself, when I discovered myself during the Federation and Southern Rhodesia days. I had seen her struggle to find her feet after declaring independence from Britain and I had stood by her against bullies and braggarts while she found her identity, who would otherwise have seen her sink into obscurity.

You can only watch suffering for so long. I wanted to retain the good memories, somewhere where they couldn't be touched, where they couldn't be stolen. Most of all I wanted peace as all that I loved had already been taken from me. And then the cough came back again. Zimbabwe, for the time being at least, had seen the best part of me.

EPILOGUE

The four walls I stare at are not resplendent with reminders and memorabilia of my former life. Instead, the trinkets that make up my memories are stored in crates and boxes, crammed into the confines of the council house in which I live. Among those trinkets are my military badge collection and my bayonet collection, half of which was stolen by the freighters during the move. It doesn't matter anyway. There is simply no space to put them up.

The move back to the United Kingdom heralded a new chapter in my life and I find myself praying daily that it isn't the last. I suppose it would be a fit ending if my life's ebb were to tie in with the finale of this book.

The treatment for cancer, the insidious disease I was told I had beaten, several times, is ongoing and I have my ups and downs. My lung capacity is almost zero and I am finding the most mundane tasks, a simple walk to the corner store, almost impossible to achieve. Almost, but not insurmountable. One thing I can say for sure is every little step I take, while a victory in itself, is comparable to the hardest selection courses I have been through, in some of the finest airborne units in the world. If you laid the choice in front of me, to either undergo SAS selection once more or walk to the grocer with lung cancer, I would choose the former.

I do have to thank God for small mercies. Maggie, the love of my life, has returned to me and we are battling the odds together. It's been almost a year since I left Zimbabwe and without her, I really don't know where I would be. Government bureaucracy keeps us honed to a sharp knife edge, struggling to achieve things that might afford me some comfort. Despite the best years I gave the British government, her health service sees no reason to afford me any help. Every pound spent on my treatment we have worked hard for.

I still enjoy a beer, on the odd occasion with mates who were with me then. Some are successful, but most are adrift in different places around the world, doing various things without resolve. On these occasions the memories flood back and I always find myself alone later, pondering the value of my life. Pondering the value of all our lives! The country I once called home grows more anaemic by the day. Was my lot a contribution to the decay? I don't think so; but what was it then?

At night, my bedroom walls become the walls of my cell at Goromonzi Political Detention Centre. They close in on me and despite the cold and my condition, I find I have to go for a walk outside to convince myself of freedom. I experience pins and needles in my toes and fingers, although I am sure that has something to do with the chemotherapy. When I do get to sleep, I have strange dreams about people cutting the air supply pipes to my house. I think that is due to the level of difficulty I have with my breathing, but the roots are in the confinement I experienced when I was detained in solitary. The claustrophobia I experience is unbearable!

Once in a while 'Monty', 'Sheila' or 'Mr Berkinstein' pay me a visit. The wall spiders in the United Kingdom are different from those in Africa, but they represent the same thing to me. It might be a sign of insanity, but I do profess to having caught myself conversing with them once in a while.

It's not all bad. I do have Paul, Maggie and Dayne. They and my friends make it all worthwhile. I hope I have lived a full life and one complete with a broad range of emotions. That makes it worthwhile, doesn't it? Without the 'downs' there would never be the 'ups'!

On a clear evening when the moon is full, I am transported back to a hundred other nights when it could have ended for me then. As I've always said, thank God for small mercies!

I am a simple man, yet one plagued with complexities. I find myself purged by the trappings of sentiment.

To those whose lives I have taken, I say this: I make no apology – but that doesn't mean I don't mourn your death. Aren't we all pawns in this ruptured world? Was I the design for your end? When I came forth in birth all those years ago, did that single action seal your fate, while you basked in a lavish African sun on the shores of a great river, or frittered away your youthful years in the fields surrounding your village with the girl who was to become your wife? Even then the countdown was on for the day I would finally meet you.

If I may ask, have you returned to haunt me? Is this the battle you wage against me? If you remember, I hoped my end would be quick. I suppose you had no choice in your dying, so why should I have in mine?

Endai nerugare harahwa dzeZambezi neMozambique. Kurwa kwenyu kwave kwenguva refu uye kwakashinga uye kwave kusvika kumangumo. Nokupfuura kwanga uchaona kukunda kwako! Nokukurumidza ndichabatana nemi mune imwe nzvimbo yatinogona kuseka uye kuseka pamwe chete uye kana Mwari achibvumira kudaro, ndinogona kukupa rukudzo rwakakufanira.

(Go in peace, old men of the Zambezi and Mozambique. Your fight has been a long and brave one and it is nearing its end. With my passing, you will see your victory. Soon I will join you in that other realm where we can joke and laugh together and if God so permits, I can accord you the honour that you deserve.)

AUTHOR'S POSTSCRIPT

It started with the cancer and it ended there also. Within two weeks of completing the epilogue to this book, on 5 August 2007, Jake Harper Ronald, aged 59, succumbed to his disease. Two days before, on 3 August, his son Paul was blessed with his first child, Mae, Jake's first grandchild. With his passing comes a fresh beginning. Jake always saw things through.

Jake, in the flesh, will never get to see his life's story in print. Among his final requests, and those of his family shortly after he left to pay homage to that great General in the heavens, was that I see this through. That his life's story is told to remain as a legacy to him and to those men with whom he served. If the request had not been made, I would have done so anyway, as it is the least I can do for a very special friend.

On 5 November 2007, a plaque bearing the inscription of Jake's name was laid at the Rhodesian SAS memorial in Durban. As testimony to the impression he left, on those whose paths he crossed during his life, are the condolences his family have received from the four corners of the world, some from men with whom he had had no contact since the mid-seventies. At his memorial service in the UK (there were two, one in Zimbabwe), men with whom he served, former SAS members and Selous Scouts, broke down and cried. Among the songs which were dedicated to him were *Hero of the Day* by Metallica and *I'll be Missing You* by P Diddy.

Jake, I offer you my two cents' worth and a coin for the boatman. I see you at peace now and with that, I pay homage to you and I accord you the honour you deserve. Rest in peace my friend. You dared, you won.

Thank you for reading 'Sunday, Bloody Sunday – A Soldier's War in Northern Ireland, Rhodesia, Mozambique and Iraq'.

If you have enjoyed the book, please take the time to leave a review on Amazon or Goodreads, as this really helps a great deal with exposure!

As per Jake's wishes, I am currently producing a pictorial account of his life from the hundreds of photographs he took during his military career. As much as I wanted to include photographs in this narrative, the cost of printing made it an unviable option and so I decided that getting Jake's story told was far more important. Presenting it in a more cost effective format, without photographs, was the temporary answer.

If you are interested in seeing Jake's life in pictures please follow my author page for notifications of when the book will be available. Rarely will you see a histirical biography presented with such a complete personal, photographic record, one which will transport you back in time to experience the events told in (his) story.

Sincerely – Greg Budd (Author)

ABBREVIATIONS AND TERMS USED

25 – Mercedes 2.5 ton 4x4 Unimog truck

45 – Mercedes 4.5 ton 1113 truck called a RhoDef 45 in Rhodesia

AD – accidental discharge (of firearm)

AK – Avtomat Kalashnikova. 7.62mm x 39 intermediate assault rifle of Soviet design

Alpha bomb – Rhodesian designed bouncing anti-personnel bomb

ANC/SAANC African National Congress (South African political party)

AOD – automatic opening device

APC – armoured personnel carrier

A63 – VHF communications set

Boerewors – Afrikaans term for a traditional meat sausage

Braai – **b**arbeque

BSAP – British South Africa Police (Rhodesian Police Force)

BTR – Soviet armoured personnel carrier

Casevac – casualty evacuation (usually by helicopter)

CCB – Civil Cooperation Bureau (South African)

CCTV – closed-circuit television

CIA – US Central Intelligence Agency

CIO – Central Intelligence Organisation (Rhodesia/Zimbabwe)

CO – Commanding Officer

ComOps – Combined Operations (Rhodesia)

Coloured – Southern African term for a person of mixed race, usually of black and white parentage

Crocodile MPV – Rhodesian-designed and built mine-protected vehicle

CSM – company sergeant-major

CTR – close target reconnaissance

Cyclone – helicopter callsign

DZ – drop zone (for parachutists)

Ek sê – Afrikaans for 'I say'

ETA – estimated time of arrival

FAF – Forward air field

FN – Fabrique National 7.62mm x 51 NATO, FAL rifle of Belgian design

Fragging – term coined by US troops in Vietnam for 'killing' an own forces officer

Frantan – Rhodesian version of napalm

Freds/Freddie – FRELIMO troops (Rhodesian Army slang)

FRELIMO – Front for the Liberation of Mozambique

G-car – Alouette troop-carrying helicopter armed with twin .303 Brownings

Goffels – a coloured person (Rhodesian slang)

Golf bomb – Rhodesian-designed antipersonnel bomb with nose proboscis to detonate above ground

GPMG – General purpose machine man. See MAG.

GSG – Gurkha Security Guards

H hour – hour appointed for a military operation to begin

Ishe – Respectful African term for 'father'

IO – Intelligence Officer

JOC – Joint Operational Command

Kap 3 (AOD) – automatic opening device for parachute

K-car – Alouette gunship with door-mounted 20mm cannon

Klepper – wood-framed canvas canoe for military operations

Kraal – African country village

LP – listening post

LUP – lying-up position

Lynx – Rhodesian name for Cessna 337 aircraft armed with machine guns and rockets

LZ – landing zone

MAG – Fabrique National 7.62mm x 51 NATO belt-fed machine gun of Belgian design. Also known as the GPMG (general purpose machine gun).

Matabele – indigenous people of western areas of Rhodesia/Zimbabwe (originated in S.Africa)

MI6 – British intelligence agency

MNR – Mozambique National Resistance (RENAMO)

MT – motor transport

MRE – meals ready to eat

MPV – mine-protected vehicle

Mujibas – civilian youths aiding terrorists

Nanga – African witch doctor or spirit medium

NCO – non-commissioned officer

ND – negligent discharge (of firearm)

NIS – National Intelligence Service (South African)

OC – Officer Commanding

OP – observation post

OpSec – Operational Security

Ouen/s – mate, boy, lad, fellows (Afrikaans)

PE4 – plastic explosive

PJI – parachute jump instructor

QM – quartermaster

QRF – quick reaction force

R & R – rest and recreation/rest and recuperation

RAR – Rhodesian African Rifles

RENAMO – see under MNR

Rev/revved – slang term for shooting or opening fire, or being shot at

RLI – Rhodesian Light Infantry

RPD – Soviet 7.62mm x 39 intermediate belt-fed squad/light machine gun

RPK – Soviet 7.62mm x 39 intermediate magazine-fed light machine gun

RR – Rhodesia Regiment (formerly Royal Rhodesia Regiment - RRR)

RSM – regimental sergeant major

RTU – return to unit

SAM 7 – surface-to-air missile of Soviet design. Also called *Strela*

SAP – South African Police

SAS – Special Air Service

SB – Special Branch (of the BSAP)

Shake shake – home brew alcoholic concoction made by coloured people

skuz'apo – nickname given to Selous Scouts by terrorists

SNEB – 37mm rocket fired from pod on aircraft wing

SSM – squadron sergeant major

Stalin's Organ – BM-21 122mm multiple-rocket launcher

Tab/tabbing – walk/walking long distances carrying heavy weight

Terr – short for terrorist (Rhodesian slang)

TF – Territorial Force

TR28/TR48 – HF communications set

TTL – Tribal Trust Land

Umkhonto we Sizwe – ANC military wing

Unimog – see entry under '25'

ZANU – Zimbabwe African National Union – (now ZANU [PF] led by Robert Mugabe)

ZANLA – Zimbabwe African National Liberation Army (ZANU's military wing)

ZAPU – Zimbabwe African People's Union – (led by Joshua Nkomo)

ZIPRA – Zimbabwe People's Revolutionary Army (ZAPU's military wing)

ZNA – Zimbabwe National Army

Made in the USA
Columbia, SC
12 January 2024

5042c57e-021b-4691-8c4f-d8fdbee2cf67R01